PRACTICAL QUANTITATIVE INVESTMENT MANAGEMENT WITH DERIVATIVES

Practical Quantitative Investment Management with Derivatives

FRANCES COWELL

palgrave

First published 2002 by
PALGRAVE
Houndmills, Basingstoke, Hampshire RG21 6XS and
175 Fifth Avenue, New York, N.Y. 10010
Companies and representatives throughout the world

PALGRAVE is the new global academic imprint of St. Martin's Press LLC Scholarly and Reference Division and Palgrave Publishers Ltd (formerly Macmillan Press Ltd).

ISBN 0–333–92621–8 hardback

This book is printed on paper suitable for recycling and made from fully managed and sustained forest sources.

A catalogue record for this book is available from the British Library.

Editing and origination by
Aardvark Editorial, Mendham, Suffolk

10 9 8 7 6 5 4 3 2 1
11 10 09 08 07 06 05 04 03 02

Printed and bound in Great Britain by
Antony Rowe Ltd, Chippenham, Wiltshire

To my mother, who helped me worry about the deadline.
To Cait and Ophelia, who read the book for me.
To Jean-Pierre, who stoically tried to impose order on incorrigible chaos.
To Dibbs, who never doubted me.
To Vanderbilt and Villeneuve, who sat on the keyboard.

Contents

List of Tables and Examples

Tables

Examples

Preface

ORIGINS OF THE BOOK

With the increasing importance of individual savings accounts and the growth of defined contributions pension schemes, people are required to make decisions about long-term investments that previously could be left to governments or actuaries.

Concurrently, advances in information processing capabilities enable the application of breakthroughs in investment theory to be applied in day-to-day investment management. This has in turn spurred the use of ever-more sophisticated investment instruments, such as derivatives and customized benchmarks. The result is an explosion of information that challenges the powers of assimilation of most ordinary folk, and even many investment professionals; and jargon that can make any real comprehension of the issues all but unachievable.

Most users of investment management services work in professions that are at least as complex as investment management, yet find understanding the investment management process and the techniques applied difficult and the jargon hard to interpret. This gives rise to the need for a comprehensive plain-language description of the basic processes of investment management, an explanation of the underlying principles and a translation of the jargon.

OBJECTIVES

This book seeks to help the reader by translating the jargon and explaining, in plain words, the investment instruments and techniques used in investment management, and putting them in the context in which they frequently occur, together with a discussion of the benefits and potential pitfalls of each.

In doing so, it explains the practical aspects of some of the more sophisticated investment management techniques currently in use by investment managers, so that readers can pose specific questions to investment professionals about investment strategies, portfolio construction and expected outcomes. By explaining the principles underlying investments technology and the jargon frequently used by investment managers, it is hoped that this book will enable the reader to understand and evaluate the responses given.

SCOPE

The purpose is not to offer advice on investments, products or even investment strategies, but to equip the reader with sufficient understanding to evaluate them him- or herself. To this end, the book begins with a discussion of the investment management process, from fund structure, through investment strategy definition to investment manager selection and evaluation of investment results. This is followed by a discussion of the traditional approach and a primer on the basic theory underpinning quantitative investment techniques. Part II addresses, in turn, each stage of the investment process, beginning with asset allocation and followed by portfolio construction for each asset class. In each case the process is placed in its context and the basic underlying theory is described. This leads to a discussion of the peculiarities, including important strengths and weaknesses, of the technique and its applications, and concludes with a description of the implementation process and administrative, valuation and return evaluation issues as well as addressing what can go wrong. Case studies further illustrate some of the important issues.

Part III discusses some of the issues common to most parts of the investment management process and those that pertain to the industry overall, concluding with a discussion of how traditional and quantitative techniques can fit together.

Spreadsheets are included in the accompanying compact disc. They are designed to enhance the reader's understanding by giving him or her the opportunity to conduct live experiments on the examples: to change inputs to see what the effect is on the relevant computations.

THE CAST

The titles and roles applied to the various participants in investment management sound very similar to anyone not engaged full time in the investments industry. Often roles and titles overlap. In an attempt to avoid the confusion this can cause, the various participants are referred to in this book by the following titles:

Consultant	Person or company providing independent advice to investors on investment type, structure and management.
Fund Manager	A person or company charged with overseeing the investments of a pension fund, mutual fund or other jointly owned investment.
Investment Manager	The company engaged by the fund manager to conduct day-to-day management of the investments.
Investor	The owner of the money invested.
Portfolio Manager	The person employed by the investment manager to manage specific components or aspects of the investment portfolio.

OVERLAP OF TRADITIONAL AND QUANTITATIVE

The use of the term 'quantitative' in the context of investment management can be misleading, implying as it does, that traditional investment management involves little or no sums. In fact, a traditional 'non-quantitative' investment manager will find much of the contents of this book familiar, since many techniques for investment analysis are claimed by both groups as their own. In fact, many quantitative techniques, particularly for return forecasting, merely formalize and apply precision, in effect 'quantifying' the intuitive analytic processes that have for a long time been used by traditional investment managers. Surprisingly few 'quantitative' investment techniques are genuinely new.

CASE STUDIES

Most chapters devoted to a particular investment process are accompanied by a case study. The purpose of the case studies is to illustrate the principles discussed in that chapter. While based on actual events, some details have been altered to simplify the illustration and enhance the scope of the illustrations. Therefore, they are not faithful sequences of events.

SPREADSHEETS

Each of the examples presented in the book is represented as a spreadsheet on the accompanying compact disc, with the examples for each chapter collected in a workbook, the name of which corresponds to the chapter. The objective of the spreadsheets is to enhance the reader's understanding of the examples presented in the book by allowing experimentation with the inputs to each analysis to show their impact on the outcome. They are designed to work in Excel 95 and subsequent versions.

To use the spreadsheets, insert the compact disc into the CD drive. It will launch automatically, presenting a menu showing the name of each chapter and appendix for which there are examples.

The workbook will open at the first example in that chapter or appendix. To view other examples, click on the appropriate tab at the bottom of the spreadsheet. The names of the tabs correspond to the names of the examples in the book.

Not all examples are editable. Those that are display the editable cells in blue text. The cells with black text are either fixed values or formulae, and so are not editable. Change the blue values to see how a change in interest rates affects the price of a bond; or how a change in share price affects the value of an option. Spreadsheet cells containing formulae have a comment explaining the calculations. When the curser is moved near a cell with a comment, the comment becomes readable. Alternatively, select the required cell, then View → Comments to read the contents of the comment box.

GLOSSARY

Glossary entries are indicated by a **different bold font** in the text the first time they appear. This is to help readers become familiar with the more specialised terms used in investment management. **Bold** is used in the text font for emphasis.

Acknowledgements

This book could not have been completed without the practical help and encouragement of my employer, Vestek-Quantec, a subsidiary of Thomson Financial. They helped me in every respect, from pure encouragement to allowing the use of their investment analysis software and data, ensuring that I was provided with the best resources possible and of course being patient with me when demands on my time conflicted. In particular, I am thankful to my colleagues Tim Matthews and Claire Robinson for a thousand small favours that made such a difference at every stage of the book, including helping me manage the demands of my day job while preparing the manuscript for delivery. Thank you also to Toks Osokoya for getting hold of data that would have taken ages without him, and to Scott Douglas, for enthusiasm and encouragement, and who, with Alex Senicki, re-equipped me at full speed when my laptop was stolen five days before the promised delivery date of the manuscript.

My colleague, David Vernest, applied his programming talent to transform the compact disc into something intelligible, thereby contributing an invaluable enhancement to the overall result.

I would also like to thank Jason MacQueen, founder of QUANTEC Limited, for his oft-repeated phrase, which provided the opening sentence to the book

James Bevan, at Inscape, provided invaluable help and support, especially in providing everyday language explanations of some of the more esoteric ideas in investment management.

I want also to thank old friends and former colleagues. I am indebted to Satyajit Das, whose idea it was to write the book, and who helped get it started and contributed welcome suggestions for both content and format. Paul Seager helped by sending data at short notice. I am thankful also to the dozens of colleagues and friends, past and present, who provided the inspiration and material for the case studies.

I am also grateful to those at Aardvark Editorial, who were patient beyond the call, when normal people would have thrown their hands up in dismay, and for the encouraging words and helpful comments that made such a difference to the readability of the book. Also, Andrea Hartill at Palgrave, who was full of encouragement and reassurance.

Data came from Thomson Financial Datastream, FTSE, MSCI, Salomon Smith Barney and STOXX, with analysis using QUANTEC risk management and portfolio analysis systems. All the errors came from me.

It would have been more difficult and less enjoyable without Jean-Pierre to keep in order all the non-book-related aspects of life, including settling in to a new apartment in a new city.

PART I

Introduction

CHAPTER 1

Introduction

WHAT HAS CHANGED?

Investment management is one of the few highly paid professions for which no formal qualification is required. Yet few people would dismiss the responsibilities of investment managers as simple or trivial. Even evaluating the quality of their work can be a complex affair requiring considerable analytic skills.

To most of us, the way in which investments are managed seems to have undergone an astonishing metamorphosis in the last decade or so. Gone are the sage men who guarded with prudence and integrity the savings of widows and orphans by purchasing stocks and bonds in only the most sound of enterprises, thus ensuring a steady and reliable income for their trusting clientele. These paragons seem to have been replaced by a generation of red-braces-wearing thirty-somethings sitting in front of banks of computer screens, shifting unimaginable quantities of other people's money to the far reaches in transactions of complexity beyond the ken of ordinary folk.

But has it really changed all that much? It could be that some changes are more apparent than real.

Markets appear more volatile now than they used to be, but there has never been a time when investments did not sometimes go wrong, simply because there was never a time when people were infallible. Soundness of judgement has always been subject to compromise, for example alchemy was once regarded as a trusted mainstream science. Before the invention of the telegraph, markets would swing violently upon rumoured events during wars. Investors from time to time seemed to behave irrationally, giving rise to investment 'bubbles', which burst, 'inevitably', it was commonly reflected after the event.

One need only be reminded of tulipmania to realize that irrationality and investment bubbles are by no means a modern phenomenon. Many people today know somebody who became rich or poor, or both, as a result of the Poseidon boom in 1966.[1]

Many people associate the complexity of modern markets with the widespread use of derivatives. Yet similar instruments were used in the Middle East in ancient times, in the markets in Rotterdam in the sixteenth and seventeenth centuries, and in the USA during the 1930s. With inferior information and nonexistent supervision and regulation, many of these early investments carried risks that would be unthinkable today.

Large capital flows to and from emerging markets such as South America and South East Asia give the impression that investment has become a much more international business in recent decades. In this trading environment, currencies can appear to be growing ever more volatile. Certainly international capital flows are greater nowadays than they were earlier this century, when most countries were subject to controls on international capital movements and very high transaction costs, but currencies were not necessarily less volatile. Rather than stabilizing currencies, controls tended to delay inevitable fluctuations so that exchange rate adjustments were more severe when they did occur. Before the introduction of controls, international investment was a major source of wealth to the economies of the Old World. The South Sea Bubble, the Dutch East India Company and the British venture that followed it are some examples. The very purpose of Columbus's voyage was to seek new markets and investment opportunities in East Asia. The Romans accumulated vast investments outside their home country, transacting in places as far away as Africa and South East Asia. It is true that money moves about the globe much faster now than it used to, but so do goods and people.

However, two major changes have occurred. The most important is that investments are held much more widely than even a few decades ago. In most western countries, investors come from all backgrounds. People who grew up in developed countries after World War II, rich and poor, have collectively accumulated vast sums of personal savings, either privately or in company or government sponsored pension funds, mutual and trust funds and elsewhere. Investments are no longer the preserve of the gentry, nobility and other privileged folk. Since these investments will, for the majority of investors, one day be their primary source of income, risk control and accountability are more important than ever before. The average investor has a fairly low tolerance to losing money, and because there is now a very large number of investors who vote, even governments have an interest in seeing that things do not go too horribly wrong. This 'democratization' of investment management is driving the imperative for greater accountability and risk control.

The other very important difference between the present and earlier decades is the way in which advances in technology have increased the amount of available information and transformed the way it is used. The ability to analyse data in bulk encouraged the development of new ways of applying it to gain insights into the behaviour of investments. Thus we see an increasing number of investment modelling techniques, based on advanced mathematics, which are not immediately comprehensible to many investors. Most of these techniques do in fact have a common-sense explanation, and in essence are often not very different from traditional investment techniques. In many cases their main function is to impose discipline onto the notoriously unruly process of investment management. This trend is in part a response to the need for greater accountability and risk control, and in part stems from the availability of some powerful analytic tools. Investment structures and processes have thus become more formalized in recent decades, often replacing the traditional reliance on intuition, or the abilities of gifted individuals for investment selection. 'Science' is beginning to pin down some of the 'art' in investment management.

A typical investment management process might look something like Table 1.1.

Table 1.1 A typical investment management process

Define Fund Structure	Defined benefit or defined contribution? Open or closed pooled funds? Domicile and tax status
Select Consultant	Research database Fee structure Preferred approaches
Define Investment Strategy	Risk tolerance Benchmark How many investment managers? Specialist or balanced? Investment universe Permitted investments Currency management
Design Mandates	Define benchmarks Define risk tolerance Active or passive? Traditional or quantitative? Define the return objective
Select Investment Managers	Qualifications and experience Service level Sensible processes Fees
Evaluate Investment Managers	Scrutinize both good and bad performance

DEFINING THE INVESTMENT FUND STRUCTURE

Individual investors may choose to do their own investing, by purchasing stocks and bonds on their own behalf, or they may follow the advice of their stockbroker. If, however, tax or other legal considerations complicate their situation, they may choose to engage a financial planner or tax expert. At the other end of the spectrum are investors entrusting their savings to professional investors. These are usually large institutional investors, such as mutual funds, pension funds or insurance companies, who typically conduct their own research, design their own investment strategies, employ their own tax and legal experts, and so seek little outside advice.

Many investors choose neither, but invest in small and medium-sized pension funds and other **pooled (comingled)** funds. These funds make use of a mixture of external and in-house advice for tax and economic analysis. Because different kinds of investment funds can be subject to different fiduciary and tax requirements and constraints, the investor is usually faced with enough choice of investment funds to ensure a reasonable fit with his or her investment requirements.

For pension funds, mutual funds, trust funds and other pooled funds, how investments are structured in the fund depends on the objectives and constraints of the majority of investors. Issues that are usually taken into account when devising the investment structure for a fund are:

- The expected length of the investment horizon.
- Cash flow and other liquidity requirements.
- Domicile and tax status.
- Minimum investment required.
- Special ethical or legal constraints.

The investment horizon should reflect that of the majority of investors in the fund, with consideration for any income requirements. For example, the fund structure should accommodate those investors requiring a steady income stream. On the other hand, investors with no immediate need for income nearly always strongly prefer capital growth. Usually the question of income versus capital growth is closely aligned with the tax status of the fund, and this in turn affects the choice of domicile.

Many funds stipulate minimum investment amounts, both for initial investment in the fund, and for subsequent investment and withdrawal. The purpose of these limitations is usually to contain administration costs: the cost of administering a $1000 investment is the same as a $1 000 000 investment, but because administration is usually charged to the investor as a percentage of the sum invested, the former is more costly to the fund than the latter.

Ethical funds have enjoyed increasing popularity in recent decades. Investors have the choice of avoiding financing arms manufacturers, tobacco companies and companies engaging in environmentally questionable businesses. Sometimes legal limitations are imposed on the fund; for example, many corporate pension funds are prohibited from owning large interests in the company itself.

Funds can be structured as:

- Defined benefit or defined contribution
- Open or closed.

Defined benefit funds assure the investor a fixed payment at the end of the investment period. This is can be paid either as a lump sum or as an annuity. The investor's contribution to the fund may vary over time as the fund's total value fluctuates according to varying returns on its investments. Managers of defined benefit funds usually maintain a **reserve** as part of the fund to smooth the impact of withdrawals from the fund. The amount held in the reserve must itself be carefully managed. If reserves fall too low, some members may receive less than they had a right to expect, while reserves that grow too much deprive some members of assets to which they may be morally and legally entitled.

When reserves do get too high, the fund manager may declare a '**contribution holiday**', a period during which investors pay lower contributions than normal, or none at all, until the reserves again reach an acceptable level. This practice runs the obvious risk of being unfair to some investors while providing a windfall to others. It can also give the impression that the fund is subject to unacceptable volatility, and reduce fund members' confidence in the soundness of the operation and credibility of the fund's manager and administration. To avoid this complication, some defined benefit funds build guarantees into the investment strategy, either of capital or minimum returns.

The other main category of pension fund is called defined contribution. **Defined contribution funds** require the investor to pay in a fixed sum each week, month or year. Upon withdrawal from the fund, he or she receives both the principal paid in and the investment returns to the fund, less fees and costs.

Defined contribution funds do not need to maintain reserves, so the task is a bit easier: each member's account grows according to his or her contributions plus or minus investment returns. Of course, it is not really that simple, because each member's differing appetite for risk depends on such factors as his or her age and whether or not there are other assets and liabilities. When designing the investment strategy for a defined contribution fund, the fund's managers try to accommodate the majority of members' risk preferences, so members whose risk tolerance is very different from the majority may suffer from an inappropriate balance of risk and return. For the fund managers, the defined contribution fund can pose difficulties that arise rarely if ever for defined benefits schemes. Because each member's account is in effect an individual account, similar to a holding in a mutual fund, investors tend to compare the returns of their fund with those of other funds, and can hold the management accountable for any disappointing results. This comparison is often unfair since apparently comparable funds may be managed to different specifications, perhaps because they are subject to different constraints, or it may be that their average membership is older or younger, and so have a correspondingly different balance of risk and return.

An **open fund** allows the investor to put money in and take it out at any time, simply by applying to the fund manager for new units or advising the manager of the intention to redeem units. Units are thus issued or redeemed at the fund's current market valuation, which is the sum of the market values of the fund's holdings.

A **closed fund** does not allow new units to be issued and redeemed on demand. All its units are created at the inception of the fund, after which investors buy and sell them at prices determined by supply and demand. Closed funds are often listed on stock exchanges and traded in the same way as any other equity. Theoretically, their market values should be always very close to the sum of the market value of their holdings, but closed funds can exhibit surprising divergences between their theoretical unit price and their market price. This divergence could be driven by perceived scarcity of units in the fund, or anticipation of a sharp downturn in the market for the assets held by the fund. The observed price divergence can also reflect the cost of transacting the fund's underlying assets.

THE ROLE OF THE INVESTMENT CONSULTANT

Usually the first decision for any kind of pooled investment fund is whether to appoint an independent advisor, or consultant. Consultants provide investment advice and a number of other services. For individual investors, they can help to coordinate decisions regarding retirement savings, insurance and tax. For pension funds and other pooled funds, the consultant can provide the expertise necessary to administer and manage asset and liability structures, and navigate the complex legal terrain surrounding the management and administration of investment funds. An important function is to provide estimates of the likely timing of contributions and withdrawals, thus forecasting the overall growth of the fund, and ensuring a prudent balance of assets and liabilities and, for defined benefit funds, the most appropriate reserving policy. Many investment consultants also help to choose the broad mix of assets for the fund, draw up investment management mandates, help to select investment managers and monitor their ongoing performance.

By providing a source of independent analysis and specialist advice, investment consultants can help pension plan managers and trustees to manage the risks and responsibilities inherent in pooled funds. By following the advice of experts in the field of pension fund liabilities and assets, sponsors and trustees can demonstrate that they have sought the best solutions to these potentially difficult problems, and that they have taken all reasonable steps to ensure the success of the fund.

Most investment consultants are trained either in actuarial studies or financial economics. Many have a strong academic background, are highly numerate and usually extremely well equipped to analyse and interpret the complexity of modern investment management technology. Most consulting firms also have considerable expertise in structuring contribution and payout scales for defined benefit funds, and in estimating the likely reserve requirements for funds based on the plan's membership profile, current assets and likely investment returns. They are often well versed in the relevant sections of the prevailing tax code too, putting them in an excellent position to coordinate asset and liability management to give the most advantageous overall outcome.

The consultant's strong analytic capabilities are combined with often impressive research databases spanning extensive economic data and information about individual investment managers and funds, including past performance data, favoured investment processes and the strengths and weaknesses of each.

The limitations of investment consultants are that they often have little experience of hands-on investment management, so while being experts in the theory, they sometimes misestimate the divergence between theory and practice. Often this is less of a shortcoming than it may at first seem, as the vast majority of funds apply time-honoured strategies, where the relationship between theory and practice is reasonably well understood. However, it can be a limitation if an investment manager is applying an innovative strategy with which the consultant is not familiar. In such situations, the lack of direct investing experience may hinder the consultant's ability to understand quickly the wider implications of the strategy, for example in terms of transaction costs and liquidity management, but perhaps also in terms of risk analysis.

Many consultants also are limited by an inadequate exposure to the most advanced tools and services available to investment managers, such as online price and security analyses, models for risk management, analysis of transaction costs and performance evaluation. In the most extreme cases, consultants may prescribe tools that are to the best of their knowledge the most appropriate, but which, in fact, may not provide the best available solution.

Many of the benefits conferred by investment consultants stem from their independence, which they go to great lengths to preserve. For example, while many firms of consultants are also owners of investment management firms, the relationship between the two entities is generally kept quite distant. It is hard to imagine a consultant recommending, with any degree of credibility, that a pension plan favour the consultant's own investment manager over competent rivals. True independence, however, can be extremely difficult to maintain. It is understandable, for example, for a consultant to favour a particular investment technique over others, perhaps because he or she is more familiar with it. If this leads to one strategy being recommended over another that is more suitable, then some independence has been forfeited, whether or not there is common ownership between the consultant and the investment manager. Some consultants favour quantitative approaches, while others prefer traditional methods of portfolio construction and management. For the trustee or fund manager, this means that the type of investment strategy the plan adopts can depend in part on which consultant is employed, rather than which is going to produce the best results.

Investment consultant fee bases vary of course, but many consultants are paid, as are lawyers and management consultants, by the hour; whereas some have fixed fees for services, rather like a doctor. Both have their advantages and disadvantages. Fixed fees for services may encourage the consultant to recommend services that are only marginally required. The benefit is that the consultant has the incentive to enhance his or her earnings capacity by continuously upgrading the range and quality of services on offer, so some measure of innovation is encouraged. Consultants who are paid strictly by the hour generally perform services according to the investor's requirements, but this leaves the consultant little time and incentive to explore and research new ideas and approaches, which would be of ultimate benefit to the investor. Sometimes the result is that the investor is directed towards investment options with which the consultant is familiar while other, perhaps more appropriate, investments may be ignored.

Once the investor has appointed an investment consultant, he or she is usually very reluctant to change. This is understandable given the gravity of the job to be done. The relationship between the investment consultant and the fund manager is based on a great deal of confidence and trust. But although both confidence and trust are necessary to the success of the relationship between investor and consultant, they may not be by themselves sufficient. In view of the increasing importance of accountability and risk control in all aspects of investment management, ideally the investor would pose three questions:

1. Does the consultant give the most suitable advice in view of the specific objectives and requirements of the investment fund?
2. To what extent is the consultant adding value in terms of investment returns and risk control?
3. To what extent is the consultant accountable for disappointing results?

The first two questions can be fiendishly difficult to answer because it is impossible to say what the outcome would have been if another course of action had been followed. One solution is to examine the performance of other funds that use the same consultant. This is without doubt a good idea, but there are limitations to the insights it can deliver:

- Compared funds may not share the same investment objectives and limitations, and therefore provide little or no valid basis for comparison.
- The other funds may be reluctant to divulge what they consider to be confidential information.
- The results obtained by compared funds may have been due to luck rather than management. It is almost impossible to distinguish between the two.

Given the importance of the consultant's role in the management of the fund, many fund managers would like some means of holding the consultant in some way accountable for the success of the fund.

To this end, some funds have tried to evaluate the performance of consultants by hiring further independent advice: consultants to evaluate the consultants. This might highlight some particular strengths and weaknesses on the part of the consultant, but achieving unambiguous quantification of the consultant's contribution is rarely possible. Because it is so difficult to evaluate fairly the input of the consultant, it is hard to hold him or her accountable.

THE INVESTMENT STRATEGY

Having estimated the current and future contributions and liabilities of the fund, the consultant can help specify the investment objective, which is combined with economic projections to define the investment strategy.

Setting the investment strategy is a formidable task, the complexity of which is difficult to overstate. Arguably the most important element is to set the level of risk appropriate to the fund, also known as its **risk preference**.

Risk is probably the most misunderstood aspect of investment. Although tempting to think of risk as failure, it is more helpful to think of it as uncertainty, or the likelihood of failing to meet investment objectives. The mix of risky and **risk-free assets** determines the risk of the fund. As one would expect, the higher the ratio of risky to risk-free assets in the fund, the riskier the fund will be. **Risky assets** are typically equities, long-term bonds and property, while short-term interest rate securities backed by a government or a major bank are usually thought of as risk-free assets.

The fund's risk level should take account of the expected liabilities of the fund. In practice this means setting the fund's risk at a level that is consistent with the timing of projected demands. Investors with short investment horizons are generally more averse to risk than those able to weather periods of poor returns in order to achieve superior long-term gains. For example, a couple nearing retirement seeking a safe return for their life savings have clearly different requirements to, say, a single person in his or her late twenties investing a large sum from an unexpected inheritance.

The output of the investment strategy is some long-term mix of assets to be used as a **benchmark** for the purpose of constructing portfolios and evaluating the fund's performance. The **long-term benchmark** forms the backbone of the fund's structure. If it is not well specified, the fund will be in danger of earning insufficient returns to meet its liabilities or objectives, or of undertaking too much risk for the welfare of its members. For defined benefits schemes, the long-term benchmark is crucial to maintain the appropriate level of reserves.

It is important that the benchmark reflects the important objectives and obligations of the fund. Ideally it should have six characteristics:

1. **Efficiency:** the benchmark should have an attractive balance of risk and return.
2. **Investability:** the benchmark should only include assets that are available for purchase by the fund.
3. **Measurability:** the total return of the benchmark should be readily available.
4. **Low cost:** turnover and liquidity characteristics should be such that the cost of management is reasonable.
5. **Adequate breadth:** the benchmark should have broad exposure to industries, sectors and countries.
6. **Representation:** the benchmark should represent the universe of assets relevant to the investor.

For defined contribution funds, reality often introduces another consideration. Investors regularly scrutinize the returns to the fund and are wont to compare these returns with other funds. Defined contribution funds are thus nearly always subject to another benchmark, over which they have no control at all. Other funds become the benchmark. The fund will nearly always be compared to the best performing fund and the median fund. The problem has no simple solution save to communicate to the fund's membership the soundness of the reasoning behind the fund's long-term investment strategy.

Some funds choose peer group funds as formal benchmarks. This has obvious appeal, in that it formalizes what is anyway a de facto arrangement. If pension fund asset allocation, as opposed to model or hypothetical asset allocation, is applied as the peer group benchmark, it also ensures that the benchmark return is both investable and achievable.

The main apparent benefit of using peer groups as benchmarks is that it minimizes the risk to the fund managers of delivering poor performance relative to competitors. This does not necessarily help the investor, because it also minimizes the chances of superior returns by building in popular investment biases. It can also build in a performance bias by adopting the consensus asset allocation from the last period.

Closely related to the question of risk tolerance and benchmark asset mix is that of the choice of short-term, **tactical asset allocation**. The **short-term asset allocation** is usually designed to exploit short-term return expectations that are different from the long-term expected outcome.

Probably the most important aspect of the short-term asset allocation is how far it is allowed to differ from the long-term benchmark. The permitted difference deserves careful consideration because it can have a strong impact on the fund's performance. If the fund asset allocation is allowed to differ greatly from the long-term benchmark, then the fund risks delivering returns that vary considerably from the benchmark, possibly affecting its ability to meet its objectives. On the other hand, too tight a constraint prevents the fund from benefiting from short-term asset return forecasts that potentially deliver superior returns.

In addition to enhancing returns, short-term asset allocation can be effective in controlling risk. One way of doing this is by guaranteeing a minimum return. This may be achieved using derivative instruments to deliver the desired result or it may be achieved with cleverly designed sequences of decision rules. Both approaches can allow theoretically unlimited gains, with the minimum return set below prevailing interest rates on short-term bank deposits. Guaranteed minimum return portfolios always earn less than similar portfolios without the guarantee, with the difference reflecting the cost of the guarantee.

For investors who cannot tolerate any capital depletion, a **capital guarantee** may be called for. In effect this is simply a special case of a guaranteed minimum return strategy, where the minimum return is set to zero either in nominal or real (inflation adjusted) terms.

How many investment managers will be employed mostly depends on how big the fund is in terms of assets. The advantage of having several investment managers is that it diversifies **manager risk**. Manager risk is the risk that a manager will fail to perform to specification, breach a mandate, or in some other way seriously fail to meet the expectations of the investor. For example, if the fund has employed ten managers and one disappoints, the overall damage is limited. If the fund has invested with only one manager, and something untoward happens, the situation can be beyond retrieval. Many large pension funds employ dozens, even hundreds, of investment managers, which can introduce the equally serious risk that the fund becomes unmanageable. Too many managers can also have the effect that the fund's carefully thought out strategy is diluted, resulting in a bland, costly mix of investments that fails to meet its objectives.

Even relatively small funds often divide investment management between at least two or three managers, who may have common mandates. This method adds the benefit of a meaningful comparison of performance, by which the fund managers can pose uniform questions to each manager, thus learning as much about why the funds perform as they do by observing the differences between responses as from the responses themselves. For example, two portfolio managers sharing the same mandate may consistently miss their target by a similar amount. This might indicate that the target return cannot be obtained without assuming unacceptable risk or breaching mandate restrictions. Another useful comparison is the level of transaction costs incurred by different portfolio managers for similar portfolios. By this method the investor has a valuable way of judging whether the level of service he or she is getting is reasonable for the fees paid.

Small to medium funds often specify **balanced portfolios** as opposed to specialist ones. A balanced mandate is where the same investment manager decides both short-term asset allocation and manages individual asset class portfolios. Specialist managers, by contrast, manage individual asset classes, such as equities, domestic bonds, domestic property, international bonds and international equities.

The balanced investment management mandate is in some ways the simplest, because there is but one result to evaluate: either the portfolio is doing better than the benchmark or not. Cash flow management is a relatively simple affair: advice of the funds flow is remitted to the investment manager who then invests the sum according to the current asset allocation of the fund. The fund's managers need only ensure that the terms of the investment management mandate are respected.

However, this simplicity can sometimes be a bit illusory because it is often very hard to determine exactly where the investment manager is doing well, and where he or she may be underperforming. The process of scrutinizing investment returns to determine where the investment manager has done well and where he or she has not done well is known as **attribution analysis.**

A major advantage of balanced mandates is that they often attract lower management fees than a series of specialist mandates for a fund of the same size. For small to medium funds, the fee differential can be significant. Even greater economies are achievable if the investor is willing to pool the fund's investment with others. This will only work if the benchmark asset allocation and risk profile of the pooled vehicle is the same or very similar to that of the fund. Thorough checking is of course required to ascertain that this really is the case. If the asset allocation does not precisely match the fund's requirements, the 'gap' often can be filled using derivative instruments.

Most medium to large funds engage separate investment managers for asset allocation and the management of individual asset classes. The advantages of this are that:

- The fund manager can choose investment managers who have particular expertise in asset allocation, and management of individual asset classes such as equities, bonds and so on, thus increasing the likelihood of superior overall returns.
- The level of manager risk is much reduced, as no single manager exerts a dominant effect on the outcome of the fund.
- Because each mandate is different, the value added by each manger is unlikely to cancel out that of any other manager.
- Attribution analysis is made simpler by separating asset allocation and each specialist asset class manager.
- The fund can fine-tune the mixture of active and passive management, and quantitative and traditional management of physical assets.

For funds engaging specialist asset class managers, the choice for the fund managers becomes whether to conduct their own short-term asset allocation, probably with the help of their consultant, or to define an asset allocation mandate, and hire a specialist manager with particular expertise in asset allocation.

The asset allocation manager usually does not manage physical assets for the fund, but simply determines the amount to be invested in each asset class. Typically, asset allocations are reviewed quarterly, with interim reviews on an ad hoc basis following major economic or political events. The decisions thus taken usually incorporate forecasts of returns for each asset class over the next quarter, year and two- or three-year periods. Once the best mix of asset classes has been identified, individual asset class managers are informed of the amount they need to invest or divest in order to implement the short-term asset allocation.

Another way of doing this is to leave the sum invested with each asset class manager unchanged, typically at the level of the long-term benchmark asset allocation, and use derivative instruments to implement short-term, tactical asset allocation decisions. This approach has the benefit of drastically reducing the amount of physical assets being bought and sold, noticeably reducing the regular transaction costs of the fund and automatically improving the fund's performance. The advantages and disadvantages of single and multiple investment managers, and balanced and specialist investment mandates are summarized in Table 1.2.

The investment strategy should also specify what investments are permitted. The range of allowable investments is sometimes referred to as the **investment universe**. At its simplest, this could comprise a simple list of assets by name. The limitation of this approach is that new assets come into existence all the time, and the list would soon become out of date, with the consequence of imposing unintentional constraints on the portfolios.

The investment universe is usually defined as some asset criteria, such as listing on a recognized exchange, or membership of a defined index. It may also impose constraints such as minimum size.

Table 1.2 How many investment managers?

Investment Mandate	Advantages	Disadvantages
Balanced – one investment manager	Can minimize management fees Simplifies administration	Maximizes manager risk Evaluation and attribution of return are difficult Limited choice of asset classes
Balanced – multiple investment managers	Controls manager risk Allows comparison of manager performance	Potential that manager styles will cancel each other out Evaluation and attribution of return are difficult
Specialist investment mandates	Allows separation of asset allocation and security selection Asset allocation can be conducted by fund managers or specialist asset allocation manager Facilitates performance evaluation and attribution Investment manager styles less likely to cancel each other out Maximum choice and flexibility of asset classes	High cost, especially for small amounts under management More administrative complexity

Closely associated with the investment universe is the specification of **permitted investment instruments**. This usually details what kind of derivative instruments can be included in the fund, and for what purpose, such as risk control or liquidity management.

If the fund is investing outside its home country, then the investment strategy should address how **currency** is to be treated. The main choices are:

- to manage foreign currency exposures as part of the asset classes in which they occur
- to hedge all foreign currency exposure back to base currency
- to manage foreign currency as a separate asset class.

THE INVESTMENT MANAGEMENT MANDATE

Having set the broad strategy of the fund so that asset appreciation and yield will meet likely calls on the fund and the level of risk is acceptable, the fund managers, usually with the help of the consultant, design the investment management mandate or mandates.

The investment management mandate is a document describing the tasks of the investment manager. It specifies the investment universe, the benchmark, risk limits and return objectives, preferred investment processes and fees. It forms the basis of the contract between the fund and the investment manager.

It is important to set the investment mandates so that they are consistent with the fund's strategy and will endure the rigours of implementation. Whether the investment mandate is for a balanced portfolio or a specialist asset class, most fund managers usually begin by stipulating the benchmark.

For balanced mandates and pure asset allocation mandates, the benchmark is usually the fund's long-term benchmark. For specialist asset class mandates, it is some representation of the asset class in question, such as a recognized share price index, such as the S&P500, although in theory the benchmark can be anything that delivers a rate of return. In practice, the importance of which benchmark is chosen for specialist asset class mandates dictates that it should, as far as possible, have the following characteristics:

- It should meet the investment objectives of the fund. Usually this means that it must give a broad coverage of the market in which it will invest. In some instances this may necessitate designing a customized benchmark.

- It should be investable. In other words, the securities that make up the benchmark should be freely traded on a recognized exchange.
- Derivatives are a big help. For the purposes of liquidity management and periodic asset class reweighting, there is an enormous advantage in selecting a benchmark on which futures contracts are traded. This is not always possible even for domestic equities portfolios, but remains a desirable characteristic.
- Public quotation reduces ambiguity. While it is preferable to identify a benchmark that is quoted publicly, customized or less widely recognized benchmarks can work well provided their components are publicly quoted. This allows independent computation of benchmark performance by investor, investment manager and custodian; so avoiding confusion about the relative performance of the portfolio.

The next step is to specify some return target and a preferred risk level. Both return and risk are usually described in relative terms, that is, the target return is x% above the return to the benchmark; or the target risk is y% relative to the benchmark. The mandate may also set maximum acceptable levels of relative risk and minimum acceptable returns over a given period. For example, the maximum relative risk may be 3% per annum, with a minimum allowed performance of 3% per annum below benchmark for any rolling three-year period.

Investment managers always compare their own performance with that of their rivals. This is a natural reaction when one considers how investment managers are rewarded. To illustrate, suppose a manager has a strong view regarding the prospects for a particular asset or group of assets. To exploit this view he or she needs to implement a portfolio that is quite different from both the benchmark position and those of other funds. Should his or her view prove to be correct, the happy investor lauds him or her, and if the performance continues, the investment manager will doubtless be rewarded with new clients. But first it is necessary to convince the client and the market that this was good judgement, not just good luck, and that the high returns were not achieved at the cost of unacceptably high risk. A confident manager will not have too much trouble achieving this, but if the portfolio is too unconventional, success can depend on very good communication skills. On the other hand, if this unconventional looking portfolio suffers underperformance, even for a relatively short while, the costs to the investment manager can be enormous because he or she is alone in delivering poor returns. The prudent manager therefore shuns such portfolios and sticks to portfolio allocations that, although different from the benchmark, are not radically different from other managers. That way, everybody either gets it right together, or they get it wrong together; and the consequences for the investment manager of being wrong are much reduced.

Alternatively, if the investment manager is not confident of delivering superior returns, he or she will '**benchmark-hug**', that is to say, keep the portfolio holdings close to those of the benchmark in order to avoid delivering disappointing returns. For this reason, many fund managers stipulate both minimum and maximum risk tolerances in the investment mandate.

Having arrived at this point, the fund's managers must choose between active and passive, or indexed management both for asset allocation and asset class management. Active management incorporates asset return forecasts to select assets that will deliver above average returns and investment management mandates are usually characterized by fairly aggressive relative return objectives and wide tolerance of relative risk. Passive, or indexed management, on the other hand, seeks to give purely benchmark returns, but at a much reduced cost to the investor. It does not therefore have return objectives, but usually has very limited tolerance of relative risk.

Should risk-taking investment managers use quantitative techniques or traditional approaches? There are no generally accepted principles for deciding when one approach should be favoured over the other. It may be that this decision rests on what type of management skills are available among the pool of candidate investment managers, and which of these the fund managers feel most comfortable with.

When specifying specialist asset class mandates, it is a good idea to ensure that each mandate differs significantly from each of the others. The best way to ensure this is by engaging only one manager per asset class, although this can present other problems. Where the fund has a number of managers devoted to the same asset class, it should take care to ensure that the mandates are distinct and do not overlap. Similar mandates run the risk that the sources of superior returns being exploited by one manager are diluted or even cancelled out by the portfolio compositions of the others.

At some point during the formulation of the investment strategy, the fund's managers and their consultants will have formed a policy on how and when guaranteed return and portfolio protection strategies should be employed. If it is decided that some kind of protection against negative returns may be required, then the fund managers must think very carefully about which kind of protection will suit them best. The gritty details are dealt with in Chapter 5, but the very first thing to think about is whether a pooled, balanced approach, whereby the same manager is responsible for protection as well as management of individual asset classes, will suffice, or whether a specialist mandate needs to be designed to complement the rest of the fund. Basically, the yardsticks that apply for balanced versus specialist also apply here, for example do the pooled vehicles suit the objectives of the fund? Do the economies of specialist mandates suit those of the fund? Does the issue of manager risk warrant having separate mandates? How long is the portfolio protection required?

Each investment management mandate will nearly always allow for a part of the portfolio to be held in liquid assets, as new cash is allocated to the fund, dividends are earned by it and so on. This limit should be kept very low to ensure that the fund's asset allocation strategy is not compromised by unintended levels of low-yielding money market instruments.

MANAGER SELECTION

The next step is to select and engage investment managers. Most consultants will have done quite a lot of the work required to prepare for this, such as researching the pool of available investment managers. Thus the fund managers are presented with a list of investment managers that have already been screened for suitability for the job.

The questions that are usually posed during this process are:

- How many other, similar mandates the investment manager currently is managing?
- What has been the performance of these portfolios?
- What service can the investment manager provide?
- What are the investment manager's fees?

The fund manager is usually also interested to know something about the people employed by the investment manager, such as their general level of qualifications and experience, how long they have worked for that investment manager, and what back-up is provided in the event that they leave or become ill.

The temptation of the fund manager is to focus on the investment manager's previous performance. This contains much less information than many people realize because past performance by investment managers rarely provides any indication of future performance.

The performance of investment managers changes from time to time for several reasons:

- As skilled personnel leave and are replaced by people with different strengths and weaknesses, the relative strengths and weaknesses of the company change. This happens very frequently and, when it does, the investment manager's approach changes to accommodate the new range of skills available.

- When senior investment staff leave the company, their replacement nearly always instigates some modification of the investment management process. Even if this is only a change of emphasis, it will impact on investment returns.
- Investment managers also change their approaches to asset selection, either in response to changed market or economic conditions, or because the old strategy was no longer working.
- The investment manager may simply decide that the existing approach, although delivering acceptable results, is ready for modernization or improvement.
- Even without changing the approach to portfolio construction and investment selection, very few portfolios deliver consistent performance in all economic environments either in absolute terms or relative to a benchmark.

When interviewing investment managers, the question the investor would most like to pose is: 'To what extent is the investment manager's performance due to luck, and how much to management?' There is no way to guarantee a reliable answer to this question. Bearing in mind that, in such an uncertain science, it is as easy to be wrong for the right reasons as right for the wrong reasons, it is important that the investment manager's description of his or her approach to asset selection makes sense. Possibly one of the best ways to judge the likely competence of an investment manager is to look for evidence of clarity, consistency and common sense in their explanation of how they select and manage investments, and why they do it that way.

PORTFOLIO EVALUATION

The investor needs to know not only whether the investment managers are providing the required service, but also whether the investment strategy is actually delivering the risk and return profile it was designed to. This means that the investor needs to think ahead to the problem of return evaluation and attribution analysis. Attribution analysis is conducted at the end of the investment period to see if the results were mainly due to luck or management, and in particular to identify which decisions contributed to or subtracted from the overall returns.

Many investors choose not to scrutinize good performance, focusing only on periods when the fund is underperforming. This is a mistake. Close scrutiny of returns, although sometimes difficult, usually rewards the effort. Superior overall returns very often camouflage serious shortcomings in an investment manager's performance. For example, the investment returns may be due to

EXAMPLE 1.1 *Assessing the value of short-term asset allocation*

Asset Class	Return Achieved %	Long-term Allocation %	Short-term Allocation %
Domestic Equities	13.00	30.00	50.00
Domestic Bonds	6.00	25.00	15.00
International Equities	18.00	20.00	25.00
International Bonds	3.50	20.00	5.00
Domestic Cash	5.50	5.00	5.00
		100.00	100.00
Total Return Achieved		9.98	12.35

exceptional results in one asset class, while all the other asset classes and possibly the asset allocation are suffering. If, as often can be the case, the wins are due to luck, when the luck runs out, as it must, the performance of the overall fund goes from highly satisfactory to utterly dismal. Therefore asking the question 'why has the fund done well?' is as important as 'why has it not done well?'

A simple example of portfolio evaluation is given in Example 1.1, where the contribution of short-term (tactical) asset allocation is quantified. This is achieved by comparing the return given by the short-term mix of asset classes to that which would have been given by the long-term asset allocation. One way to do this is to take the returns to each asset class for the period in question and then weight them by the long-term strategic benchmark weights. If the total return thus calculated is less than the one actually achieved, then the tactical asset allocation has been of benefit to the fund, as illustrated in Example 1.1.

In this instance, the manager has successfully foreseen strong performance in the domestic and international equities markets, and has exploited this view to add 2.37% (12.35 – 9.98) to the fund's return.

THE ROLE OF THE CUSTODIAN

The other important participant in the investment management process is the custodian. Custodians are usually subsidiaries of very large banks. If the fund intends to invest outside its home country (which most do, for very good reasons), the fund's managers will seek the services of a global custodian. This organization will have invested in elaborate computer systems to deal with international administration and fund flows. Custodians perform a number of very important functions. They:

- Authorize payments and receipts for purchases and sales of assets, and the subsequent transfer of funds from and to the right bank accounts.
- Provide monthly, quarterly and annual statements of portfolio holdings, transactions reports, currency exposures, derivatives exposures and tax reports as required by the fund's managers.
- Provide portfolio valuations as required by the fund's managers.
- Retain custody of all documentation supporting ownership of the assets held by the fund, for example by taking physical possession of share certificates.
- Provide return reporting for each portfolio as required. Some custodians also provide return attribution analysis, but often this is fairly rudimentary.
- Provide these services electronically, some, but not all, in a form that can be tabulated according to the information requirements of all parties requiring access to the information.

When selecting the custodian, it is important to ensure that the fund's requirements are going to be met both in terms of global coverage and services available. The question of what format is used for periodical reports may sound trivial, but monthly portfolio reports can weigh in the tens of kilograms, so a custodian who is capable of delivering reports in electronic format, which can be easily analysed and edited to meet individual requirements, will save the investor, consultant and investment managers many hours per month in management time.

Changing custodians is extremely messy, and potentially expensive. Most funds do so very reluctantly, so it is worth investing in a thorough evaluation before making the choice. The custodian business has very high barriers to entry because it relies on elaborate and costly computer-based accounting and fund transfer systems to deliver comprehensive global services. This means that there are relatively few global custodians to choose from, another reason to take great care in making the selection.

Custodian fee schedules often are based on the number and type of transactions, with some transactions commanding much higher fees than others. Custodian fees can significantly affect the return to an investment portfolio, by favouring particular investment strategies, instruments and investment destinations.

Most large custodians also provide **stock lending** services. Stock lending is carried out by funds expecting to hold core assets for a long period, and who seek to augment their investment returns by renting out their share certificates or other evidence of ownership of and entitlement to physical assets. Share certificates can come into heavy demand by investors or brokers. Sometimes investors need to borrow share certificates to provide collateral for derivatives positions, or they may borrow on behalf of clients who have sold those securities and lack the necessary documents to fulfil their legal obligations to deliver the assets within a specified time period. Investors who have sold assets that they do not own, perhaps because they think the price will go down and they can buy them back later at a lower price, often need to borrow share certificates.

The returns earned by lending share certificates vary according to supply and demand as well as the prevailing short-term interest rates. In return for accepting the 'rent', the lender accepts the risk that the borrower may not be able to return the stock when required, so the rent usually takes this into account as well. An intermediary, who brings together lenders and borrowers and extracts a small fee for this service, usually sets up the loan contract.

The custodian as stock lending intermediary has the distinct advantage of knowing exactly where to find large quantities of long-term holdings of stocks, and so is a natural first call for would-be borrowers. Stock lending is potentially very lucrative for long-term investors, and is dealt with in more detail in Chapter 17. Importantly, it can be used in conjunction with nearly all investment strategies to add relatively low-risk returns to the overall portfolio.

Note

1. A fairly comprehensive account is given in Mackay, Charles *Extraordinary Popular Delusions and the Madness of Crowds* NY, Wiley, 1996. Also see Braudel, Fernand *Capitalism and Material Life 1400–1800* London, Collins, 1981.

CHAPTER 2

The Traditional Approach

There are many dimensions of investment management philosophy along which traditional investment managers seek to define and differentiate themselves. Investment managers may specialize in managing specific asset classes, such as bonds or domestic equities, or they may have a perceived advantage in selecting asset classes for balanced portfolios. For example, an equities manager may seek to specialize in particular sectors of the economy such as information technology and communications, whose attraction is the promise of very high future profitability. Other investment managers prefer less glamorous sectors such as minerals and energy, or counter-cyclical securities, which give their best relative performance when the general economy is in a period of slowdown. Other investment managers specialize in small capitalization stocks in an attempt to pick future star performers. Such distinctions between investment managers come and go according to investor preferences. A more general distinction is between 'bottom-up' and 'top-down' management, both of which can be combined with most other investment styles.

Bottom-up investment management is based on the premise that investments can be made only in assets with which the investment manager is very familiar, and which he or she believes will do better than most other investments during the forecast investment period. This is, in a sense, the purest form of stock picking, with a great deal of intuitive appeal. It builds on the fundamental characteristics driving the profitability of each investment. The investment manager has accumulated detailed knowledge of all the firm's business activities and presumably those of its competitors and the market or sector in which they operate. He or she will also be familiar with the firm's overall financial position, including projected cash flows, dividends and any other impending corporate actions such as rights issues, bonus issues and so on.

The manager's deep familiarity is relied on to ensure that the investment is held only while superior returns are very likely. Should the firm be subject to some event that could reduce future returns, the bottom-up manager with such close ties will be among the first to know and will reduce the fund's investment correspondingly.

Bottom-up stock-picking portfolios have been known to deliver spectacular results, even over extended periods. They usually specialize in one asset class, such as domestic equities, small capitalization sectors, emerging markets, or venture capital funds. Because of this, pension fund managers often combine them in portfolios with other sector managers.

Stock picking via bottom-up selection does not usually take into account macroeconomic variables. The investment manager takes into consideration only those factors that are directly pertinent to the securities in question. For example, research for a company designing and manufacturing medical equipment takes into account the likely market for the equipment in question, which might be heart disease patients. Along with demographic data, which largely determines demand, this research would take a keen interest in the regulatory environment for such equipment. It is much less likely to interest itself in forecast interest rates, inflation and exchange rates, even though these may be of indirect importance.

Strictly speaking, industry and sector weightings are not an important consideration in compiling a portfolio using the bottom-up approach. However, some managers do check before implementing a portfolio to see what sector weights result from the security selection. Thus the manager may ask questions such as, 'what percentage of the portfolio is held in interest rate sensitive securities?', 'how sensitive is the portfolio to changes in the oil price?', and so on.

There can be problems, of course. This style of management relies on a highly effective research capability, combined with an uncommon level of intuition on the part of individual investment managers and analysts. Even when both these qualities are combined, the bottom-up stock picker faces a number of potential shortcomings:

- Being limited to a small range of stocks, many investment opportunities can be missed.
- If the portfolio is benchmarked to an equity index, then it is implicitly underweight, relative to the benchmark, in those stocks in which it is not invested. It follows that since those stocks are not known, or covered by the manager, they can be underweight for no good reason.

- The investment manager can be dangerously dependent on a few good analysts or investment managers, who might leave the firm and even set up in competition.
- The manager's expertise can be very concentrated in a few industries or regions, so the fund can lack a safe amount of diversification.

The bottom-up approach offers a number of advantages. An important one is that it encourages very active stock selection. A bottom-up manager is much less prone to the danger of benchmark-hugging, that is, allowing the portfolio to resemble so closely the benchmark that it is very unlikely to deliver any significant outperformance.

Some very large investment managers rely on bottom-up stock picking. Their size and consequent research capability allow them to cover a relatively large number of asset classes and sectors at a time, so they are in much less danger of missing out on attractive investment opportunities and can achieve adequate diversification. These managers require high revenue income to defray the high fixed costs of their research. The required fee income is derived either from high fee scales or very large sums under management or both. Since investors are really only interested in after-fee returns, investment managers charging higher than average fees put themselves at an obvious disadvantage. Very large sums under management can pose problems too. Bottom-up investment managers with large sums under management are quite likely to find that even small changes in portfolio composition can be large relative to regular market turnover in the securities in which they invest. This can make the required changes difficult to implement, as the market has difficulty accommodating the volume traded. Having very large sums under management can also present the problem of being the major investor in some of the securities held, and the responsibility that comes with large shareholder status.

Top-down investment managers, like bottom-up stock pickers, typically rely heavily on fundamental security information-based research. These investment managers also know their target investments very well, supporting their investment decisions with well-funded, usually comprehensive research capabilities. Their analysts also continuously revise the returns they expect from each company within their research domain, resulting in recommendations either to buy, sell, hold, overweight or underweight various securities.

The difference between the two methods is that the top-down manager takes into account macroeconomic conditions and the overall composition of the portfolio. The investment manager is as much concerned with the portfolio's holdings relative to a particular benchmark, as with the likely return to each security.

Top-down investment managers usually employ specialist economists, who study national and international econometric statistics issued by central banks and finance ministries worldwide. These economists often attend briefings by central bankers, and seek, wherever possible, individual interviews with the relevant officials. From the work of the economist flows forecast returns for all major economic sectors, including currencies, interest rates, commodity prices, producer and consumer inflation rates and so on. Generally, therefore, the manager is equipped with a forecast of the likely behaviour of currency markets, interest rates, inflation, oil and other commodity prices over various investment horizons, usually up to three years. The results of this research indicate which sectors and regions of the economy will do comparatively well and not so well over the forecast period.

Security selection is a multi-stage, hierarchical process for the top-down investment manager. The top level of the hierarchy is, for a balanced mandate, allocation to asset classes, followed by allocation to country, region, industry group and finally individual securities. For a specialist asset class manager, it typically begins with allocation to countries or industry groups and works down to the level of individual securities.

ALLOCATION TO ASSET CLASSES

Armed with this insight, the investment manager of a balanced portfolio invokes the asset allocation decision process. It is not always necessary that the same composition be applied to all portfolios under management. For example, portfolios with low-risk tolerances, often known as conservative portfolios, hold fewer of their assets in risky investments than portfolios intended to achieve higher returns. The latter are often referred to as aggressive portfolios, and typically hold a relatively large proportion of their assets in risky investments. Often the risk preferences of the investor are incorporated into the asset allocation process as a set of constraints, for example the maximum exposure to equities must not exceed 50% of the portfolio, or exposure to international assets must be less than 30%.

Many investment managers employ the concept of **scenario analysis**, whereby the investment manager identifies a number of 'scenarios' and then assigns a probability to each, with the sum of the probabilities equal to 100% or 1.00. Each scenario represents a set of events that could occur together, such as high returns to equities, low interest rates and a depreciating currency. There might, for example, be five scenarios, ranging from very high growth to economic meltdown. A simplified example set of scenarios is set out in Example 2.1.

EXAMPLE 2.1 *Scenario analysis*

Asset	Current Portfolio Weight %	Scenario 1 Probability: 10%	Scenario 2 15%	Scenario 3 50%	Scenario 4 20%	Scenario 5 5%	Average 100%
Domestic Equities	35	45.00	22.00	13.00	5.00	−20.00	14.30
Domestic Bonds	20	4.00	8.00	6.00	−2.00	−12.00	3.60
International Equities	25	12.00	20.00	18.00	25.00	−10.00	17.70
International Bonds	15	−3.00	4.00	3.50	4.50	−4.00	2.75
Domestic Cash	5	3.00	5.00	5.50	6.50	12.00	5.70
Total	100	19.25	15.15	11.05	8.60	−11.90	10.85

This analysis shows that the most likely outcome is Scenario 3, with a 50% probability of occurring and an expected return for this portfolio weight of 11.05%, while the scenario weighted outcome is a 10.85% return. In this case, the most likely outcome can be significantly improved by increasing the weighting to international equities at the expense of domestic equities, but this would in turn reduce the returns to be gained if scenarios one or two turn out to be more accurate predictions.

In practice, most scenario analyses have many more rows than this one, because portfolios usually comprise more asset classes and the scenario analysis usually allows assumptions for several currency pairs, inflation, commodity prices, short- and long-term interest rates. Usually, there will be more than one table, too, to accommodate short-, medium- and long-term forecasts, and to accommodate holding constraints, if any.

Scenario analyses can be very error prone because they require a large number of estimations and guesses. Defining each scenario is quite difficult to achieve in practice because it requires not only forecasts of returns for each asset class, but also the combination of forecast asset returns such as the likely behaviour of equities in the event of a sharp rise in long-term interest rates. Accurately forecasting these relationships from intuition or even econometric analysis is extremely difficult to do. A typical scenario analysis can include dozens, if not hundreds, of such relationships. The other important input is the probability assigned to each scenario. Usually this is quite subjective, and is difficult to test for reasonableness.

If the investment mandate includes asset allocation, it is nearly always the responsibility of a committee. Usually this is chaired by the **CIO** (chief investment officer), and comprises at least one economist as well as a representative of the management team for each asset class.

Committees tend to be favoured because most managers of balanced investment mandates agree that the asset allocation decision, being the one impacting the overall portfolio performance the most, is too important to be left to one individual. A committee draws on a wider range of expertise and points of view to produce, arguably, a more considered outcome than would be possible if left to one person. It also diffuses responsibility for this important decision.

The committee generally meets regularly, usually once a month, to review the performance of each portfolio over the period and to decide if changes to the current asset allocation are warranted. Comprehensive reviews of portfolio allocations are normally carried out at these meetings, although portfolio rebalancing generally occurs less frequently, say quarterly, or after some significant political or economic event, such as changes in interest rates, a currency realignment or an unexpected election result.

Forecast asset class returns are the most important influence on the committee's deliberations. Economists applying a global perspective are best equipped to provide forecasts for asset class returns, but in practice this decision can frequently be influenced by the views of the investment managers responsible for individual asset classes. The reasoning here is that those people working in the asset class are the best informed, and so are best placed to give an accurate prognosis.

The input of individual asset class managers can no doubt be very valuable, and most CIOs find it difficult, if not impossible, to ignore an investment manager who has delivered outstanding performance relative to a benchmark or has been in charge of an asset class which itself has recently performed very strongly. Moreover, most CIOs do not wish to appear autocratic, as this could challenge the very purpose of the committee.

Another approach is to establish a dedicated asset allocation team to conduct detailed analyses of scenarios and risk tolerances from which to formulate and recommend portfolio allocations for committee approval. This gives the other members of the investment team a say in the outcome, but contains the influence of individual asset class managers. The CIO usually has a right of veto, and ample scope to ensure a disciplined approach, possibly with some risk control. Ultimately, success depends on the analytic abilities of the specialist asset allocation team.

The asset allocation team generally takes economic forecasts and analyses from the economists as primary input. These are scrutinized for their coherence and plausibility. Various portfolio allocations can then be subjected to scenario analyses to identify one which promises the best return under various economic conditions. From this, the viability of the portfolio composition can be evaluated, ensuring that implementing the new portfolio allocation does not incur excessive transactions costs.

SECURITY SELECTION WITHIN ASSET CLASSES

How securities are selected within asset classes depends on the asset class in question.

For **domestic equities**, the universe of securities from which the portfolio is to be selected is categorized, usually by industry group, but may also be defined by asset size, or on whatever basis the investment manager is perceived to hold a forecasting advantage. For example, an investment manager who is good at predicting when small capitalization stocks will do better than large stocks may prefer to define securities by size, and manage the portfolio on that basis.

The investment manager uses the results of economic research to determine which categories of securities are going to do well, and which are not, often explicitly forecasting returns for each category. The next step is to determine how much of the portfolio will be allocated to each category, relative to the benchmark. By contrast, absolute allocations are rarely scrutinized, except that the minimum allocation is usually zero (in most, but not all, cases the portfolio cannot sell assets it does not own). Thus the investment manager might believe that the financial sector is going to do well, perhaps because long-term interest rates are likely to rise more than short-term interest rates. The portfolio would therefore hold more financial assets than its benchmark. He or she might, at the same time, be predicting a rise in the price of oil, so indicating an underweight position in transport stocks.

Having decided the allocation of security categories, the next step is to determine individual security allocations relative to the benchmark. This is where research into individual assets comes in. For bottom-up investment managers, this research sits at the core of its competence. Top-down investment managers, although less dependent on research into individual securities, nevertheless usually devote considerable resources to it. The investment manager's own research is normally supplemented by research carried out by stockbrokers, who usually also have impressive research capabilities. The investment manager therefore has ample information on which to rely to base selection of individual securities. So, for example, having decided on a fairly high allocation to the financial sector, the investment manager might then choose to invest heavily in Lloyds TSB, while choosing a lower weight for Barclays, or vice versa.

For **international equities**, the primary category is usually the country of domicile of the security, so that the international portfolio is effectively a simple sum of other-country domestic portfolios. The investment manager may then choose to subcategorize each country into industry groups, size or some other category, and proceed to select individual securities in the same way as for the domestic equities portfolio. The essential difference between international and domestic equities management rests with the question of currency management and different tax considerations. Currency management can present the biggest challenges. To illustrate, an investment manager may have correctly forecast the equity return for a given country, but still underperform if the currency effects were misgauged. Complicating matters further, movements in domestic equity markets and their currency of denomination can sometimes be strongly related. Thus it is essential to distinguish between expected asset returns and currency returns.

For **domestic fixed interest**, the process of individual security selection is driven by different inputs. In most countries outside the USA, government and semi-government bonds dominate the offerings of fixed interest securities. In such cases, the main distinction between securities is their maturity and income pattern. The economics team usually provides forecasts of pure interest rates, which are first used to decide how to allocate investment between asset classes. This forecast usually also gives some indication of how big the difference will be between interest rates for long-term bonds and short-term bonds, so can help to determine the composition of the fixed interest portfolio.

Forecasting interest rates is not a trivial exercise. Input from the economist usually dominates this process because it needs to take into account a wide range of macroeconomic and political factors. It can be even trickier in countries where financial markets or currencies are regulated, as the investment manager needs to take into account the likely actions of the central bank and the finance ministry.

The fixed interest manager uses this information to decide what mix of short and long maturity bonds is most propitious. In general, if interest rates are likely to rise, then smaller holdings of bonds will be called for, while a large exposure to bonds boosts portfolio returns when interest rates are falling. Other things being equal, long-term bonds are more sensitive to changes in interest rates than are short-term bonds. So if long-term interest rates are forecast to rise more than short-term interest rates, the portfolio will increase its holding of short maturity bonds at the expense of long maturity bonds.

If the portfolio is to hold corporate bonds, which are bonds issued by companies, then the fixed interest manager must also consider credit risk. **Credit risk**, otherwise known as credit quality, is the likelihood of the borrower, or the company issuing the bond, defaulting on the loan. The higher the perceived credit risk, the higher will be the interest rate for a bond of a given maturity. Credit risk can be very difficult to estimate. Bond ratings, given by specialist bond rating agencies such as **Moody**'s and **Standard & Poor**'s, can help to differentiate between borrowers, but these services are by no means foolproof.

The fixed interest manager therefore needs to consider the likely behaviour of interest rates and the likely behaviour of credit spreads. The **credit spread** is the difference between the interest rate on a corporate bond and a government bond of the same maturity. These are usually related to each other. For example, the change in spread between AA and AAA can depend on whether interest rates move from 5% to 6% or 12% to 13%. Higher interest rates usually indicate more volatile spreads between credit categories.

The manager of **international fixed interest** needs to take into account all the same factors of the domestic fixed interest manager, as well as currency movements and tax regimes. The latter are even more important, as fixed interest markets are even more strongly related to currency movements than equity markets. Credit spreads become extremely interesting when extended to emerging markets, all the more so because they are very closely related to currency movements, and not just those of the currency of denomination, but also of other emerging countries.

LIMITATIONS OF TRADITIONAL APPROACHES

Traditional management relies on a lot of research, ranging from macroeconomic research to detailed knowledge of individual securities. This research is combined with the experience, judgement and skill of the investment manager to give a portfolio structure to deliver the best expected returns.

This combination of judgement and analysis is often referred to as art and science. Because of the imprecise nature of judgement, the boundary between art and science often can become blurred, sometimes so much so that valuable analytic input to the investment management process can be misallocated or lost altogether.

Judgement and discipline are very difficult to coordinate, and if their roles become confused, investment processes and strategies that were originally very well thought out can also become confused, with unintended results for the investor.

Decisions based on judgement often defy scrutiny and objective evaluation. When assumptions are not articulated, it can be very difficult to decide at what point they no longer apply, and a good idea becomes a bad idea. Reasoning that is not open to scrutiny can harbour unintended risks.

Traditional investment techniques can tend to focus almost exclusively on security returns and portfolio returns, with little attention to risk analysis and management. This is understandable because risk is very difficult to forecast, especially using traditional forecasting techniques. Some traditional investment managers have been known to be quite hostile to the idea of imposing risk analysis on a traditionally composed portfolio, arguing that the exercise is irrelevant.

Controlling for this and the other risks in the portfolio is possibly the hardest part of traditional investment management. Effective risk control is possible only if risks can be quantified. This means quantifying the likelihood that the portfolio composition will deliver what is expected, and knowing exactly how likely it is that it will disappoint. It also means applying numbers to the chances that the asset return forecasts are feasible and internally consistent, a process that is outside the scope of most traditional investment management techniques.

One way to ensure consistency and discipline is to prescribe the investment management process as closely as possible, imposing a timetable on the overall decision procedure and the individual decisions that make it up. But a process-oriented approach can introduce the problem for analysts that they are 'pigeon-holed' by rigid limitations. Many people find it extremely difficult to work effectively in such circumstances, especially if their job has a high creative, judgemental element. Such individuals may try and change the limitation of their particular part in the process or they might simply leave for a less restrictive work environment. Either way, their focus can be diverted from the principal task of investment management. This problem can affect both traditional and quantitative investment managers, but the clash of 'art' and 'science' is probably more acute for traditional managers because of the higher quotient of creative input.

Portfolio construction techniques that rely heavily on the judgement of individual investment managers are always exposed to the risk that management norms are applied inconsistently. For personal and professional reasons outside the fund, personal management styles fluctuate. People suffer occasional ill health, lose concentration, and leave the firm to go and work elsewhere, or not work. Any process that relied on that person will therefore no longer perform to specification.

TRENDS IN TRADITIONAL INVESTMENT MANAGEMENT

Driven by the search for ever more attractive returns, investment managers experiment constantly with different approaches to investment management. This search can go in one of two directions: the first is to venture into new markets, which may be less mature and therefore offer high returns. The second is to look for new techniques to apply to existing markets.

Investors seeking high returns in new markets inevitably find opportunities in **alternative investments**. As the name suggests, these are investments that do not fit into any mainstream categories. They may include listed investments in exotic locations, such as emerging markets; although many investors would agree that emerging market shares and bonds have migrated into the mainstream. Other alternative investments include seed capital, venture capital, emerging country infrastructure projects and hedge funds.

Many of these investments have kept their promise and yielded impressive returns. Quite often, however, periods of spectacular returns have been followed by severe volatility and negative returns, suggesting that, far from representing excellent investment value, those high expected returns merely compensated for the very high risk that came with them.

For an investment manager or an investor with scope for diversification, high volatility of returns need not be a deterrent, as this volatility can be smoothed substantially with clever diversification. If this diversification is well executed, the investor can indeed profit from venturing away from the mainstream.

The other way investors sometimes seek to improve on the returns to conventional investing is to seek new approaches to mainstream investments. An important example is the **core–satellite portfolio** approach. This is a method of managing a risky asset class, such as equities, in such a way that the investments are divided into a low-risk core and one or more high-risk satellites. In other words, the portfolio is split into a low-risk or **passive investment** component combined with a smaller, very high-risk **satellite portfolio**. The latter can comprise one or several investment management mandates, and may well include some alternative investments.

The argument favouring this approach is that the low-risk, passively managed, **core portfolio** provides a buffer against the volatility of the satellites. Thus the overall portfolio gains access to potentially high return investments while being shielded from the worst of the uncertainty associated with such investments. This approach can yield a number of benefits, including low costs.

Core–satellite portfolio combinations can reduce transaction costs for very large investors because the portfolio being actively managed and traded is much smaller than a conventional portfolio, reducing total portfolio turnover.

The core–satellite approach to asset class management is also popular with quantitative investment managers, and provides an excellent means of accommodating both traditional and quantitative investment management within the same fund.

CHAPTER 3

Investment Management Theory

THE EFFICIENT MARKETS HYPOTHESIS (EMH)

Probably the most basic tenet of quantitative investments is the efficient markets hypothesis, or EMH, which says that the price of an asset incorporates all information currently known about it. The fact that different assets have different expected returns reflects only the fact that some are riskier than others, as investors demand a higher expected return for risky assets than for safe ones. If the price of an asset is too low, implying a high return for its level of risk, then investors will bid the price up until it reaches its 'efficient' return. If the price is too high, then it will be bid down, until the relationship between its risk and return is consistent with other assets. Thus, efficient market theory says that assets will always trade at their equilibrium or 'fair price'.

If markets are efficient, then the relationship between the risk and return of all assets is quantifiable. As risk increases so should return, in a roughly predictable if not linear fashion, as described in Example 3.1.

The curved line is called the **efficient frontier** and shows the relationship between risk and return for efficiently priced assets. The y-axis shows return and the x-axis shows risk. The efficient frontier is always positively sloped, meaning that it goes up from left to right as increased return is associated with increased risk, but the actual shape depends on the market in which the assets are analysed. The line is nearly always quite steep at the low-return, low-risk end. This says that, for very low-risk assets, even a small increase in risk yields quite large increases in return. As one moves into the high-risk, high-return zone, the marginal increase of return to risk diminishes.

EXAMPLE 3.1 *The efficient frontier*

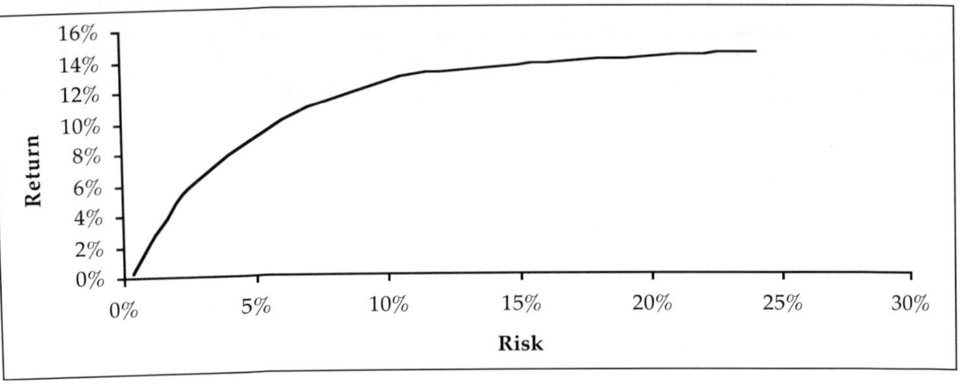

If an asset is overpriced, it will be found below the efficient frontier because its return is too low for its level of risk. If an asset appears above the line, it is in theory underpriced. Before rushing out and betting the rent money on such assets though, it is usually worth the time to review the numbers. Quite possibly it is the risk that has been underestimated, so that the asset should simply appear further to the right, on or below the efficient frontier.

The fierce debate over efficient market theory has given rise to some compromise interpretations, most famously the three versions of possible market efficiency, which are strong, semi-strong and weak.

The **strong** version says that current security prices reflect all information relevant to the firm, including information available only to insiders. This says that even using insider information, investors cannot gain risk-free profits from trading in a security because other people privy to the information will already have traded on it and the price will have adjusted accordingly.

The **semi-strong** version says that all publicly available information about a security is reflected in its current price. Fundamental analysis using company accounts and statements have already been analysed by professional investors and prices adjusted accordingly. According to this version, risk-free returns can be generated only using insider information.

The **weak** version says that security prices reflect all information that can be derived from examining market trading data such as the history of prices, trading volume or the amount sold short (by investors having sold more than they own). This says that trend analysis is fruitless, because these data are freely available and virtually costless to obtain and analyse, but that fundamental analysis and insider trading can yield risk-free rewards.

Are markets efficient? There is evidence supporting most points of view. One source of inefficiency often cited is the fact that different investors have different

EXAMPLE 3.2 *Value of dividend tax credits for domestic and international investors*

Share Price	$50.00	
Dividend per Share	$1.75	
Dividend Yield	3.5%	
Corporate Tax Rate for Domestic Investor	35%	
Withholding Tax for International Investor	15%	
Rate of Tax Credit	100%	
	Domestic	International
Value of Dividend Tax Credit	$0.61	$0.26
Value of Cum-dividend Share	$52.36	$52.01

tax profiles and are subject to different regulatory regimes, and so even if they happen to agree about the prospects for a particular asset, they will place different values on it according to their own perspective.

Example 3.2 shows how differential tax treatment of domestic and international investors affects the value they will place on an individual security. The domestic investor is entitled to a tax credit equal to the domestic corporate rate of taxation, while the international investor is entitled to a rebate equal to the rate of withholding tax payable. Both are adjusted by the percentage of the dividend to which the tax credit applies. In some jurisdictions this is less than 100%, depending on the amount of tax paid by the company issuing the dividends. The value of the dividend tax credit and therefore the security is higher for the domestic investor, who is entitled to the tax rebate at 35%, than for the international investor with a tax rebate entitlement of only 15%.

When first proposed, EMH was quite controversial because it says that examining past asset returns provides no clue about future returns. Financial economists now seem to have agreed to leave it to a conscience vote, as there is evidence for and against all three versions of EMH.

THE CAPITAL ASSET PRICING MODEL (CAPM)

EMH sets the framework for the other principle on which quantitative investment management is largely based: the capital asset pricing model. One of the most persistent misunderstandings in investment management is the assumption that, because CAPM does not provide a precise description of the behaviour of financial assets, it is worthless and should be discarded. Imperfect it certainly is, especially in explaining such phenomena as market bubbles and crashes. But for those of us with imperfect foresight, EMH and CAPM do provide a useful framework in which to think about the risk and return of assets and portfolios. In the absence of a more flawless model therefore, investment managers must make do with CAPM.

CAPM was developed in the 1950s and has since endured extensive efforts to highlight its limitations and even to prove it wrong. The fact that it is still widely used suggests it has some merits, and most of its shortcomings are by now reasonably well understood.

It has long been understood that, in general, investments earning high returns usually also have high risks. 'Safe' investments are those that earn modest but steady rewards. The important insight added by CAPM is that these extra returns materialize only if the extra risk cannot be diversified away. Taking on unnecessary (diversifiable) risk does not lead to an improvement in investment returns.

CAPM is used for analysis of relative risk and returns, thus it can be applied either to a single asset relative to another, a group of assets within a portfolio, or a portfolio of assets relative to a nominated benchmark. The benchmark is fundamental to CAPM: it can in theory be any asset or group of assets, including an asset with a return of zero and zero risk, but it cannot be nothing.

Although CAPM can be applied to any asset or group of assets, it is most often applied to domestic equities portfolios. The selected benchmark can be the local stock market, some measure of global markets, or even a separate portfolio of assets: an alternative portfolio. CAPM divides return and risk into three components called alpha, beta and residual. The return to asset or portfolio i (r_i) is expressed as follows:

$$r_i = a_i + b_i \times (r_m - r_f) + e_i \qquad (3.1)$$

Where:

a_i = alpha: intentional or active risk to the asset or portfolio
b_i = beta: the relationship of the asset or portfolio to the market
r_m = the return to the market
r_f = the risk-free rate of return
e_i = residual or error: incidental risk of the asset or portfolio

Past returns are not taken into account. CAPM agrees with efficient market theory that the future returns to an asset do not depend on its returns in the past. Because CAPM assumes that current prices are efficient, it will give misleading results if they happen not to be. CAPM does not take into account transactions costs and other market frictions.

Alpha is the amount by which the market has underpriced asset or portfolio i. This is what active managers seek in order to gain their return advantage. An asset with a positive alpha is underpriced (above the efficient frontier) and can be expected to deliver high returns relative to its risk. Increasing the expected alpha of a portfolio by adding high alpha assets increases its expected return. If the asset or portfolio is priced efficiently, alpha is zero.

Beta is the sensitivity, also known as the **covariance**, of asset or portfolio i to moves in the benchmark or the market. An asset or portfolio that moves exactly in line with the market has a beta of 1.0. An asset or portfolio with a beta of 1.2, for example, overshoots market rises and falls by 20%, while an asset or portfolio with a beta of 0.9 matches only 90% of moves in both directions. A portfolio consisting entirely of short-term liquid instruments has a beta of zero relative to the equity market. The beta of a portfolio to a market is the weighted sum of the betas to that market of the portfolio's component assets.

Because beta is related to the market return, it cannot be eliminated by diversification without also eliminating the portfolio's market return. Increasing the beta of a portfolio will increase both risk and return.

The **market return** is the return to the market in which the portfolio is invested, such as the domestic equity market. The objective of the portfolio is usually to earn the market return plus some alpha. In practice, the 'market' is some proxy for the overall market, such as the S&P500 for US equities or the FT Allshare for UK equities.

The **interest rate** is the 'risk-free' interest rate, a theoretical rate, since truly risk-free rates rarely, if ever, occur in practice. For applications such as this, the interest rate for a very short-term government or bank-backed bond is substituted.

The **residual variance** is that part of an asset's return that is not explained by either alpha or beta and is a random variable. It is diversifiable, so the residual values of a group of assets within a period will average zero, as will the residual returns to a single asset over time. Adding **residual risk** to a portfolio will do nothing to increase its expected return, so investment managers have every incentive to eliminate this risk through diversification.

Alpha and residual risk are unique to that asset or portfolio, while market risk and its coefficient, the beta, are known as systemic risk because they share this risk with other assets in the market, or system.

The active manager seeks a positive alpha, while a passive or indexed portfolio seeks to achieve a portfolio with an alpha of zero. Both seek a residual as close as possible to zero.

Example 3.3 shows the difference in performance between a portfolio and its benchmark over a 15-month period. The area under the market line is the market return. The distance between the portfolio's performance and that of the market is specific return.

EXAMPLE 3.3 *Active portfolio and market returns*

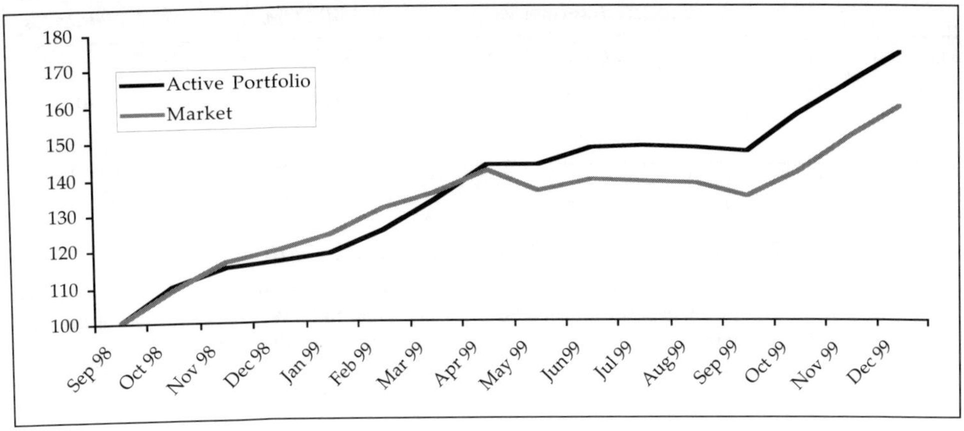

OPTIMAL PORTFOLIOS AND PORTFOLIO OPTIMIZATION

The idea of market efficiency is much more powerful at the level of the portfolio than at the level of individual stocks because portfolios allow diversification, which can reduce the irksome residuals that add to risk but not to return.

Increasing overall portfolio returns by spreading risk is hardly new, but CAPM allows the notion to be quantified by computing relationships between each asset in the portfolio and using this information to carry out a **portfolio optimization**. The result is a portfolio that lies on or near the efficient frontier, in other words, a portfolio with the highest expected return for a given level of risk, or the lowest risk for a given expected return – an **efficient portfolio**. This means that the investor can choose the precise amount of diversification to match his or her risk appetite and return objectives.

Although the theory was developed in the 1950s, the technique only became popular among investment managers in the late 1970s and early 1980s. Finding optimal portfolios using this technology requires large quantities of data and considerable computer processing power. These resources only became available at reasonable cost with the widespread use of desktop computers and electronic provision of data.

Example 3.4.1 shows how the diversification in a simple portfolio can be quantified. The investor forecasts expected returns, while risk is measured by the volatility of the asset. A volatility of 30% indicates that the asset has returned between plus and minus 30% about two-thirds of the time.

This two-stock portfolio shows that, while the return to the portfolio is the simple weighted sum of the return to its components, the risk is not. By adding

EXAMPLE 3.4.1 *Quantifying diversification: a 2-stock portfolio*

	Expected Return %	Volatility %	Weight %
Microsoft	26.00	33.27	50.00
Intel	24.00	37.96	50.00
Portfolio	25.00	32.16	100.00

EXAMPLE 3.4.2 *Quantifying diversification: a 3-stock portfolio*

	Expected Return %	Volatility %	Weight %
Microsoft	26.00	33.27	30.00
Intel	24.00	37.96	30.00
Sainsbury	17.50	24.80	40.00
Portfolio	22.00	22.90	100.00

Intel to Microsoft, the portfolio has reduced its expected return from 26% to 25%, but its risk is now down from 33.27% to 32.16% – even though the stock being added had a higher risk. Now add a third stock, as shown in Example 3.4.2.

Again, the return is slightly different, but this time there has been a more dramatic reduction in the portfolio's risk. To see why, look at the correlations between the individual stocks, shown in Example 3.4.3. **Correlation** is a value between minus one and plus one describing the relationship between two things. A correlation of one indicates that they are perfectly related; zero indicates no relationship at all, while a correlation of minus one says that the two things are perfectly inversely related. Correlation is closely related to covariance; in fact knowing one almost allows the other to be directly deduced.

The relatively modest diversifying effect of Intel to Microsoft is due to the fact that they have a positive correlation of 0.63, not surprising, since they are in related industries. Adding Sainsbury reduces the risk of the portfolio much

EXAMPLE 3.4.3 *Quantifying diversification: asset correlations*

	Sainsbury	Intel	Microsoft
Sainsbury	1.00		
Intel	0.09	1.00	
Microsoft	0.17	0.63	1.00

Source: IDC

more, because it has a very low correlation with both Microsoft and Intel (0.09 and 0.17 respectively).

Portfolio optimization uses the expected returns of individual assets and the correlations between each to find the various mixes of these assets that would lie on or close to the efficient frontier, meaning that it finds portfolios that give the highest expected return for various levels of risk relative to the nominated benchmark. It is an iterative process, in other words, it follows steps very similar to those in Examples 3.4.1 and 3.4.2, each time adding or subtracting a very small holding to or from the portfolio and selecting the portfolio with the best risk and return. At each iteration, the risk and expected return of the portfolio are measured. When the marginal impact on the portfolio's risk and return becomes very small, the optimizer concludes that the mix is optimal and the process terminates. It is important to note that there is no unique solution to the optimization. Because the optimizer works by increments, the outcome depends on the starting portfolio composition, which may be cash, an existing portfolio or a benchmark portfolio.

Optimization is sometimes called **mean-variance optimization**. The **mean** refers to the mean return of an asset or portfolio. This is the expected return, called the mean because it is the average likely return for the asset or portfolio. The variance is another word for the risk of the portfolio or asset, and refers to the likely divergence of actual returns from the mean, or expected return.

The optimization program needs to be told in advance what the expected returns are for each asset in its investment universe. Investment managers usually devote enormous resources to forecasting asset class returns and returns to individual securities, and most regard this part of the investment management process as its core. Because of the diversity of approaches to generating return forecasts, this subject is discussed at length in Chapters 4, 8, 9, 12 and 13 which are devoted to asset allocation and stock selection.

The optimization also needs to be told what the correlations or covariances are between each of the assets. Covariances, and correlations, are similar measures, whereby the covariance takes into account the correlation of the assets as well as their volatilities. Values can range from minus infinity to infinity, with one representing a perfect relationship. Just as it is impossible to predict asset returns with certainty, so it is impossible to predict precise values for correlations and covariances. The investment manager is therefore obliged to make some guesses when applying them to the portfolio optimization process. Normally the manager's team of analysts provides the expected returns. The covariance matrix can also come from the analysts, but it is usually computed from the past returns of the assets in question.

Of course, using past returns to estimate future correlations implies that the future relationships between the assets will be as they were in the past. Most of the time this turns out to be a reasonable approximation but sometimes it does not. There are two main reasons for using historical data to estimate future correlations. The first is that correlation matrices are often stable enough to make this a reasonable thing to do. The second is that actually composing a correlation matrix from scratch is very difficult, so the chances of predicting a correlation matrix that is even less accurate than the one derived from historical data are quite high. The correlation or covariance matrix sits at the heart of the optimization process, so the question is not trivial.

Example 3.5 illustrates how a correlation matrix can change from one ten-year period to the next. Individual values change noticeably, although their rankings remain fairly stable. For example, the correlations between UK fixed interest and the pound, although different, are higher in both periods than those for other pairs.

Unfortunately, deciding to use historical correlation matrices does not simplify things very much. The investor must choose which historical data to use. Using too short a time period might give a misleading picture by ignoring long-term relationships between the assets. Using too long a period might cloud over important, but recent, structural changes in the assets' relationships.

So choosing the period from which to find the best set of correlations deserves some attention. Many investment managers throw their hands up and

EXAMPLE 3.5 *Correlation matrix changes over time*

	UK Fixed Interest	US Fixed Interest	UK Equities	US Equities	UK Pound
January 1984–December 1993					
UK Fixed Interest	1.000				
US Fixed Interest	0.289	1.000			
UK Equities	0.569	0.191	1.000		
US Equities	−0.012	0.274	0.612	1.000	
UK Pound	0.875	0.151	0.474	−0.105	1.000
January 1985–December 1994					
UK Fixed Interest	1.000				
US Fixed Interest	0.327	1.000			
UK Equities	0.545	0.213	1.000		
US Equities	0.030	0.278	0.672	1.000	
UK Pound	0.838	0.105	0.410	−0.099	1.000

Source: Thomson Financial Datastream, Salomon Smith Barney, QUANTEC, FTSE

say the most recent data is probably the best guide to the future. Some take this argument further and say that this being so, the correlation matrix can be improved by giving heaviest weight to most recent data, so that earlier return data become decreasingly important, tapering off altogether.

There is no unambiguously right answer to this problem. The best solution is usually to evaluate each case on its peculiarities, taking account of the overall objective of the exercise. Considerations that are pertinent to choosing what history to use for the covariance matrix are:

- The length of time during which the portfolio is to be held. For example, a fairly short history is probably best for a portfolio that is to be held only for a short time, say one to two years.
- If the investor believes that current economic and market conditions resemble some identifiable time in the past, then the covariance estimation could use data from that period.
- The number of assets in the portfolio is very important. Other things being equal, the more numerous the assets, the longer the time needed to give a meaningful covariance matrix.

The optimization computes allocations for a number of portfolios, each of which is on or close to the efficient frontier. For each efficient portfolio, the optimizer calculates:

- **Expected return in absolute terms**. This is the weighted sum of the forecast returns to the assets in the portfolio.
- **Expected return relative to the benchmark**. This is simply the expected absolute return to the portfolio minus the expected absolute return to the benchmark.
- **Expected risk in absolute terms**. This is also known as the **standard deviation** of portfolio return or the **volatility** of the portfolio. It indicates the range of returns that the portfolio will deliver 68% of the time. For example, a volatility of 15% indicates that the portfolio will return between minus 15% and plus 15%, 68% of the time. It is based on the covariance matrix and the volatilities of the individual assets in the portfolio and the benchmark.
- **Expected risk relative to the benchmark**. This is the standard deviation of portfolio return variation from benchmark, or the **tracking error**. It indicates the range of return variation from benchmark that the portfolio will deliver 68% of the time. For example, a tracking error of 3% indicates that the portfolio will return benchmark return plus or minus 3%, 68% of the time. It is also based on the covariance matrix and asset volatilities.

- **The Sharpe Ratio**. This is the expected relative return divided by the tracking error, indicating the portfolio's relative return for risk.
- **Lambda**. This is the slope of the efficient frontier at the point where the efficient portfolio lies. This is a measure of the incremental return for risk of the portfolio.
- **Downside risk**. This can be expressed as the likelihood of a given outcome, such as a negative return, or it can be the return that is 95% likely to occur.

EXPECTED AND OBSERVED RETURN AND RISK

The comparison of forecast and achieved portfolio return is a fairly straightforward one, both being the weighted sum of the returns to their component assets. The calculation for expected risk is based on the covariance matrix, while the calculation of observed risk, or tracking error, is less complicated. Usually it is based on monthly returns. For each month the **return variation** between the portfolio and the benchmark is recorded. This number is squared to eliminate the negative signs. The squared differences are added up and divided by the number of months being measured, giving the **variance** of the portfolio. The monthly standard deviation, or tracking error, is simply the square root of the variance, reversing the earlier squaring of monthly return differences. The monthly standard deviation is then multiplied by the square root of twelve to give the annualized tracking error. If the observations were taken quarterly, then the number would be multiplied by two (the square root of four).

Example 3.6 gives the following tracking error calculations:

- The sum of squared variations is 0.1270%.
- 0.1270% divided by 12 observations is 0.0106%.
- The square root of 0.0106% is 1.03%. This is the monthly tracking error.
- The annualized tracking error is 1.03% times the square root of 12, which gives 3.56%.

It is important to note that this measure of tracking error counts all portfolio variation from benchmark, including active return, or alpha. This leads to considerable confusion between expected return and tracking error. In fact, it is not easy to unambiguously distinguish between the two, even in hindsight.

For optimization to be useful, the investor needs to know where on the efficient frontier he or she wants the portfolio to be. This effectively means deciding

EXAMPLE 3.6 *Observed tracking error*

Date	Portfolio Value	Benchmark Value	Portfolio Return %	Benchmark Return %	Variation %	Variation Squared %
31 12 1998	100.00	100.00				
31 01 1999	101.87	101.59	1.87	1.59	0.28	0.0008
28 02 1999	98.93	99.37	−2.89	−2.19	−0.70	0.0049
31 03 1999	101.81	103.21	2.90	3.86	−0.96	0.0092
30 04 1999	105.85	106.12	3.98	2.82	1.15	0.0133
31 05 1999	101.82	103.12	−3.81	−2.83	−0.99	0.0097
30 06 1999	106.02	106.74	4.13	3.51	0.62	0.0038
31 07 1999	105.23	107.47	−0.75	0.68	−1.42	0.0203
31 08 1999	105.39	107.83	0.15	0.34	−0.18	0.0003
30 09 1999	104.13	107.77	−1.19	−0.05	−1.14	0.0130
31 10 1999	108.93	111.70	4.60	3.64	0.96	0.0092
30 11 1999	111.20	114.32	2.08	2.35	−0.27	0.0007
31 12 1999	118.19	119.17	6.29	4.24	2.05	0.0418
Total			18.19	19.17		0.1270

either what expected return is required for the portfolio, or how much risk can be tolerated. There are a variety of ways of achieving this.

The simplest way is to nominate a target return, either in absolute terms, say 8% per year, or as a margin over short-term liquid instruments, say, cash plus 5%. Alternatively the target return can be expressed as some return relative to a nominated benchmark, such as the S&P500 plus, say 3%. Using this method, the investor implicitly accepts whatever risk this return might require. As some markets are inherently more risky than others, and the relationship between risk and the return can change over time with the economic cycle, this approach leaves quite a bit of uncertainty. There is the risk that the required return exposes the portfolio to unacceptable losses.

Another approach is to focus principally on risk, allowing the portfolio optimization process to identify the best return possible for that risk. For all but the most aggressive investors, this is probably the most suitable approach. The problem, of course, is how to measure and evaluate risk. The standard measure is the tracking error, or standard deviation of return variation from benchmark over a given period. This is probably the most commonly used measure of investment risk, but it is not uncontroversial. A standard deviation is a statistical measure that describes events that are 68% likely to occur. A portfolio with an expected return of 10% and an expected tracking error of 3% is said to have a 68% chance of delivering returns between 7% and 13% within a 12-month period. Two standard deviations conveniently cover 95% of likely outcomes.

One problem with this definition of risk is that it sets positive and negative outcomes as equally likely. In other words, 7% is as likely as 13%, even though this may well not be the case, as asset prices tend to fall much more quickly than they rise. Nevertheless many investors have become comfortable with tracking error as a measure of risk. For example, if the investor is most vulnerable to a fall in asset prices, he or she will be interested to know that the portfolio has only a 16% ((100 – 68)/2) chance of earning less than 7% in the coming year and a further 16% chance of earning more than 13%. Perhaps more usefully, he or she can contemplate the idea that the portfolio has only a 2.5% ((100 – 95)/2) chance of earning less than 4% (10 – 2 × 3). This is useful because 2.5% equates to one chance in 40.

Another potential limitation is that, because forecast tracking error is generated using the covariance matrix in the mean-variance optimizer, it is sensitive to how the covariances have been calculated. Inaccurate covariances give misspecified risk, which makes effective portfolio risk management all but impossible.

VALUE-AT-RISK (VAR)

VAR was developed originally to quantify and help manage overnight risk for the treasury operations of a global bank. VAR can also be a useful alternative approach to risk analysis for investment managers. There are a number of approaches to VAR, most of which identify some 'worst-case' scenario and compute the loss to the overall portfolio should it occur. VAR is thus similar to a traditional scenario analysis. To conduct a VAR, the investment manager provides return forecasts for each asset in a portfolio that reflect an estimated 'worst case'. This pessimistic scenario is applied to current portfolio allocations to determine the maximum loss to the portfolio under that scenario. The main benefit of VAR is that it can be applied across the whole portfolio, accommodating fixed interest and options, which mean-variance optimization cannot do. Being conceptually very simple, it can be easily communicated to investors and other interested parties.

The limitations of VAR are that it is a short-term measure, covering only the period for which asset returns can accurately be generated. Thus it is suitable for analysis of the portfolio's immediate sensitivity to risk, but less relevant to

EXAMPLE 3.7 *Value-at-risk*

Asset	Current Portfolio Weight %	Scenario 1 Probability: 10%	Scenario 2 15%	Scenario 3 50%	Scenario 4 20%	Scenario 5 4%	Scenario 6 1%
Domestic Equities	35	45.00	22.00	13.00	5.00	−20.00	−25.00
Domestic Bonds	20	4.00	8.00	6.00	−2.00	−12.00	−20.00
International Equities	25	12.00	20.00	18.00	25.00	−10.00	−35.00
International Bonds	15	−3.00	4.00	3.50	4.50	−4.00	−15.00
Domestic Cash	5	3.00	5.00	5.50	6.50	12.00	−20.00
Total	100	19.25	15.15	11.05	8.60	−11.90	−24.75

long-term investment objectives. VAR cannot distinguish between intentional risk, associated with extra return, and unintentional, diversifiable risk that is not. Another shortcoming is that the worst-case scenario is entirely subjective. A poorly constructed scenario or inaccurate return forecasts can easily give a very misleading impression of the risk of the portfolio, as illustrated in Example 3.7.

Bearing this in mind, VAR analysis is more useful when the worst case is assigned a probability for a specified time interval, such as 1% chance of occurring over a horizon of one day. This recognizes the arbitrariness of the worst case and the fact that it can be exceeded.

RISK BUDGETING

One of the benefits of focusing on risk when carrying out optimizations is that it facilitates risk budgeting. Risk budgeting, as the name implies, is the practice of defining a level of risk for the fund in aggregate, and allocating this risk to investments where it is best 'spent', such as investments with high incremental expected return per extra unit of risk, or where the investment manager is most confident of achieving extra returns. Thus the investment manager may implement an aggressive asset allocation while maintaining low-risk asset class portfolios, reflecting that he or she is more certain of the potential rewards to asset allocation risk. Alternatively, more risk may be taken in one period than another if the investment manager believes that more opportunities are available at a particular point in time than another. The aggregate risk for a fund can be defined as the probability of a specified adverse outcome, such as a zero return. One of the benefits of risk budgeting is that it can incorporate options, including portfolio protection; another is that it has intuitive appeal. The limitation is that it can lead to the misunderstanding that risk is additive, in other words, that the risk of the portfolio is the sum of the risk of its components. Applied in isolation, risk budgeting could allocate the whole portfolio to the asset or portfolio with the perceived highest risk for return. This potentially ignores the importance of covariances, such as those between Microsoft, Intel and Sainsbury, and so can lead to misunderstanding and consequent misallocation of the risks in the portfolio.

REVERSE OPTIMIZATION

Optimization is prone to a major limitation, which is that the portfolio allocations given by an optimization can change dramatically with quite small changes in the assumptions put into the model. This problem arises partly from the fact that the assumptions themselves are imprecise. Both expected returns and estimates of covariance matrices are but estimates. Most investors do not think of expected returns in terms of precise numbers, but as ranges. For example, an expected return of 10% probably comes from a range of expected returns of between 8% and 12%. For some asset classes, the range can be enormous: 5% to 40% is not uncommon. But the optimizer cannot cope with ranges; it needs a single number, so the investor enters the central estimate and hopes for the best. The optimizer then uses these numbers in conjunction with covariance estimates, which are also guesses, and produces portfolio allocations correct to two decimal places. It is unsurprising that the results sometimes look odd or are unstable.

One way of dealing with this problem is to discard the optimizer altogether as the incoherent ravings of ivory-tower academics. The risk of throwing the baby out with the bathwater may seem preferable to slavishly following the 'expert' rulings of a black box.

Another way is to invert the process. Of the guesses put into the optimizer, the forecast returns are nearly always the haziest, so why not make these the output, starting with the current portfolio allocations and asking the optimizer what rate of return they imply for each asset, if the portfolio is efficient? If the asset return thus implied seems reasonable, then the current allocation is probably worth keeping. By contrast, an implied return that is higher than the range forecast by the investor indicates that the current allocation could be reduced.

The benefit of this approach is that the investor can start with the portfolio allocations with which he or she is comfortable, and then see if they are consistent with reasonable-looking expected returns. It can also facilitate independent scrutiny of the portfolio because an outsider can see immediately if the portfolio allocation reflects the expectations of the investment manager.

INTEREST RATES

The interest rate is the price of money. It reflects people's preferences for having things now rather than later. For example, $100 today is worth more than $100 in a year's time. In a year's time the real value of $100 will have been affected by inflation. In addition, waiting for the money means that some consumption must be delayed, and this bears a cost. So even if it is absolutely certain that the $100 will be received in a year, it will be worth less than it would be if it were received immediately. The difference is the interest rate. If there is some uncertainty about whether the money will be received, then the interest rate demanded by the investor is higher.

In 'normal' macroeconomic environments, long-term interest rates are higher than short-term ones, usually because investors require a higher reward for leaving their money tied up for longer periods, but other factors are also important. For example, the inflation rate may change over the long term even though it is quite stable in the short term. This pattern of interest rates is often described as a 'normal' or 'positively sloped' **yield curve**.

Example 3.8 shows a normal yield curve before and after a change in the **general level of interest rates**. This is the simplest of all movements in a fixed interest market. But much more complicated things can also happen. For example, long-term rates can go up more than short-term rates, or they can even go down while short-term rates go up. If this effect is severe enough, it can result in a 'negative yield curve'. Often a negative yield curve presages a recession, as the expected future demand for capital is less than current demand. Other factors that can give rise to a negative yield curve are stringent capital controls that restrict some short-term borrowing.

Interest rates and interest rate investments are discussed in more detail in Chapter 12. Pricing of interest rate investment is addressed in Appendix 1.

EXAMPLE 3.8 *The yield curve*

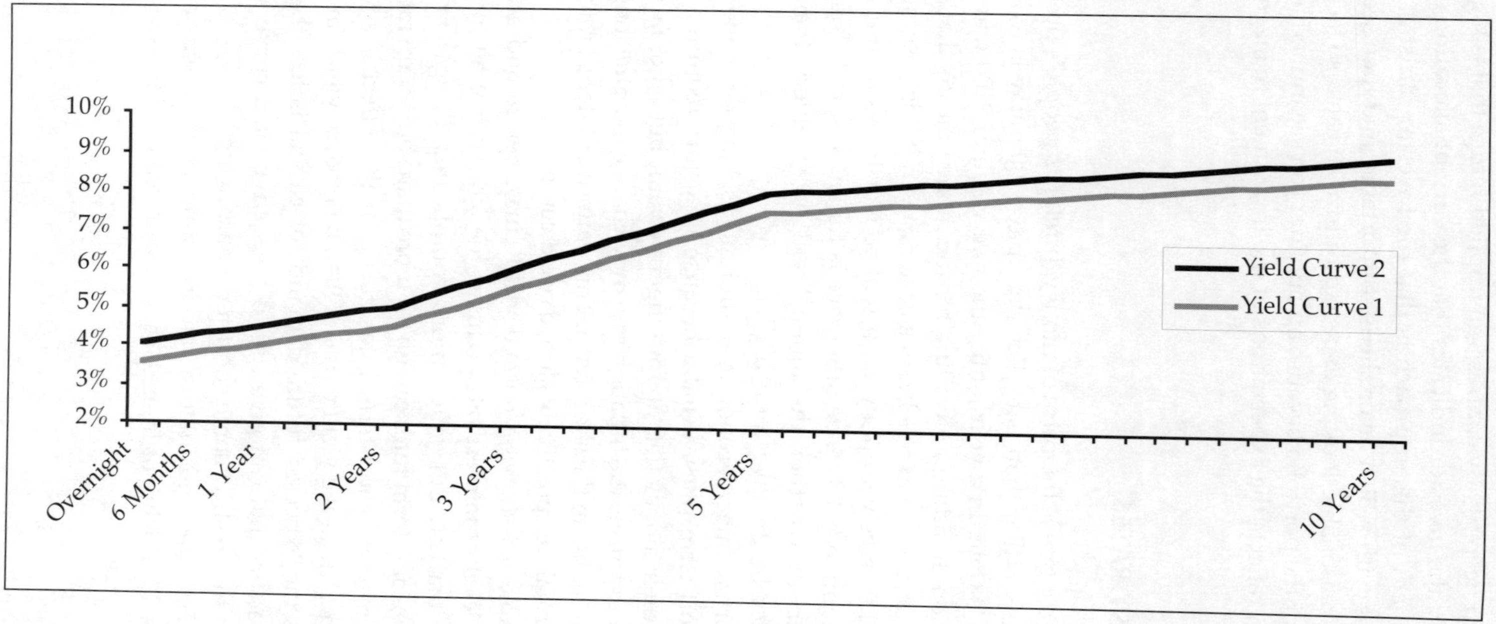

PART II

Portfolio Construction

CHAPTER 4

Quantitative Asset Allocation Models

APPLICATIONS

Asset allocation is deciding how much of a portfolio's value should be invested in various asset classes, such as domestic and international equities, domestic and international **fixed interest**, property, commodities, **liquid assets** and any other asset classes.

There are two stages to the asset allocation process:

- defining the long-term, strategic asset allocation, which is usually the same as the benchmark allocation, designed to meet the overall return objectives of the fund with acceptable risks
- short-term, tactical asset allocation, designed to exploit short-term return forecasts for individual asset classes when these differ from long-term return forecasts.

Long-term asset allocation is usually agreed by the fund's manager, with advice from expert consultants, taking account of the structure of the fund, for example, whether it is defined benefit or defined contribution. If defined benefit, what are the reserve requirements? If defined contribution, what is the investment horizon of the members? The resulting investment structure is most important in determining whether or not the fund will meet its objectives.

The fund manager or an investment manager can determine short-term tactical asset allocation, with many funds employing a specialist asset allocation manager for the purpose. Alternatively, it can be combined with asset class management in a balanced mandate.

Quantitative asset allocation processes differ from traditional asset allocation techniques in that they place a greater emphasis on return and risk modelling for portfolio construction, and apply predefined decision criteria in lieu of judgement to construct and maintain portfolio allocations.

Asset allocation is typically carried out before security selection within asset classes. Having this in common with traditional investment processes allows the two to be combined within a fund, so that any mix of quantitative and traditional asset class management can complement either quantitative or traditional asset allocation.

Asset allocation can focus primarily on forecast returns or on controlling risk. There are two ways of approaching risk control. The first uses option-based techniques to limit the worst outcome of the fund. The second relies on precise measures of diversification to control the likelihood of very disappointing outcomes. This diversification is achieved by portfolio optimization.

If the fund is obliged to deliver some minimum investment return over a given investment period, for example to meet reserve requirements, then an option-based strategy may be indicated. These strategies give up some expected return in exchange for the certainty that, regardless of market conditions, the fund will always deliver a return above the prespecified minimum. They tend to be applied for limited periods of time only; rarely being incorporated into the long-term asset allocation. Option-based strategies are known as portfolio insurance or portfolio protection, and are dealt with in Chapter 5.

Most investors prefer to control risk by diversifying their portfolios. Under most circumstances, this is a more efficient approach than using options because a diversified portfolio always delivers superior returns in the long term than a similar portfolio with protection added.

THEORY

The most effective way of achieving controlled portfolio diversification is by means of optimization. All optimizer-based asset allocation models rely on CAPM. The objective of the optimization is to maximize expected portfolio return with acceptable risk, subject to the investor's constraints if there are any. Optimization takes forecast asset class returns and the relationships between them to find portfolios that give the best expected return for any given level of overall risk. Optimization can be used to define either or both the long- and short-term asset allocations for a fund.

Mean-variance optimization is one of two main methods of defining the benchmark. The other is to use peer-group benchmarks. Peer-group benchmarks comprise actual asset allocations applied by similar funds or they can comprise hypothetical or model allocations. The main benefit of peer-group benchmarks is that they facilitate comparisons between funds, and if actual allocations form the benchmark, then it can be assumed that the benchmark is actually investable. They can also avoid excessive volatility by adopting average peer-group asset allocation. The shortcoming of peer-group benchmarks is that the benchmark by its nature delivers only average returns, and, because they are always based on past period asset allocation, they can simply work to 'rubber stamp' last period's performance.

Optimized asset allocation presents a more rigorous solution, whereby the investor takes full control of the assumptions on which it is based, selecting a long-term asset allocation that is expected to deliver the required long-term return at acceptable risk.

LONG-TERM ASSET ALLOCATION

There are two objectives:

1. To deliver long-term returns that meet the requirements of the fund.
2. To serve as a benchmark against which short-term allocation and actual fund returns are evaluated.

To identify the optimized long-term asset allocation, the following inputs are required:

- **The investment universe**. This is a list of the asset classes that the fund is allowed to invest in. It is important to define the investment universe in general terms rather than simply list specific assets. The universe could, for example, include all securities included in a nominated index, or listed on recognized exchanges. This avoids the necessity of continuously updating the list to take account of newly created assets.
- **Return forecasts for each asset class in the investment universe**. There are many different approaches to generating long-term asset class forecast returns, ranging from simple extrapolation of historical returns to much more sophisticated techniques incorporating econometric models and data. Some of these techniques are described later in this chapter.
- **Treatment of foreign currencies**. The approach can be either passive, fully hedged to base currency or currency exposure can be actively managed.

- **Risk forecasts**. These are the forecast relationships, or correlations between pairs of asset classes in the investment universe. Risk forecasts are usually computed from historical asset class returns.
- **Constraints**. These describe any statutory or fiduciary requirements to which the investor may be subject, such as a maximum exposure to foreign assets, or a maximum exposure to equities. Most funds have a clear policy regarding foreign currency management, and this can be articulated as a **constraint** on the optimization.
- **Required return or acceptable risk**. This reflects the fund's investment objectives and preferences, such as the required long-term return and maximum tolerance for loss.

The investment universe

Investments come in two broad forms: debt and equity. Debt is an investment that pays a predetermined income in the form of interest. Equity instruments deliver a fixed share of the profits and losses of an enterprise. Both debt and equity have many different subcategories, which most investors treat as separate asset classes altogether. For example, property is usually thought of as a separate asset class from equities, although it really is another form of equity investment.

As a rule, investors benefit from including as many asset classes as possible in their investment universes. This allows the maximum chance of participating in asset classes that deliver very high returns, and also to achieve effective diversification. For most investors, asset classes include things such as:

- domestic equities
- international equities
- domestic fixed interest
- international fixed interest
- real property
- alternative investments
- **cash**
- foreign currency.

How many asset classes, and which ones to include depend on:

- the size of the fund
- transaction costs in each asset class
- the investor's tax regime
- any legal limitations.

Large funds tend to invest in a wider range of asset classes than do smaller funds. Mainly this is because the absolute size of the smallest allocation needs to justify the costs of buying into that asset class. For example, a fund may allocate to 25 asset classes, with the smallest allocation set at 1%. For a \$1 000 000 000 fund, this implies an investment of \$10 000 000, enough to achieve a well-constructed portfolio in most asset classes, but for a \$50 000 000 fund, it is \$500 000, which is often not practical.

Asset classes with high transaction costs, such as real property, often deter small and medium-sized funds, although the costs can be mitigated by a long investment time horizon. For example, an asset class with transaction costs of 3% needs to be held for a much longer period to justify such costs than asset classes with transaction costs below 1%. Different investors can be subject to different costs for different asset classes, for example some public pension plans are exempt from government duties on domestic asset purchases and sales. Some stock exchanges impose differential charges and even trading rules on investors from different domiciles.

The tax regime of the investor can affect the choice of asset class, for example by his or her entitlement to dividend tax credits, normally the full benefit of which are reserved for domestic investors who are entitled to full tax credits. Most investors therefore tend to favour domestic assets, even when offshore investments offer superior return for risk.

Legal limitations can apply from time to time, for example until quite recently investors in many rich countries were subject to controls on transfers of foreign exchange. Governments have been known to impose directives requiring certain investors to place a nominated minimum percentage of their portfolios in government bonds.

Things that are not pertinent to the investment universe are:

- The expected return from each asset class
- The historical return to each asset class
- The perceived riskiness of each asset class.

The expected return affects the allocation to the asset class, but not its inclusion in the investment universe. The historical return is of no importance at all. The perceived riskiness of each asset class is not, by itself, important, although the correlations between asset classes is important in determining asset allocation.

Forecasting returns

There are three main quantitative techniques for forecasting asset class returns, which are typically applied in some combination. They are:

- extrapolate from historical returns
- calculate the aggregate value of future income from the asset class
- macroeconomic or fundamental analysis.

A fourth technique is to apply consensus forecasts, simply aggregating the forecasts of other investors.

Given the importance of the long-term asset allocation to the success of the fund, and the impact of forecast returns on optimization results, it is important that the return forecasts that are used to optimize the portfolio are of the highest possible quality.

Extrapolate from historical data

This could be as simple as saying that US bonds returned 5% last year, and so will probably return 5% again this year. A more sophisticated approach might be to separate **real returns** from inflation. For example, if inflation had been 2%, then the real return to bonds was 3%. If inflation is expected to be 1.5% this year, then extrapolating the real return will give an expected return of 4.5%. Quite different results can be obtained by extrapolating from different lengths of history, so selecting the period is critical.

Using this method in isolation to forecast returns has some fairly obvious limitations, not the least of which is that it violates even the weak version of the efficient markets hypothesis (which says that there can be no gains from analysing the price histories of securities). One only needs to inspect a chart of the history of an asset class to see that return histories rarely repeat themselves in consecutive periods.

The S&P500 share price index provides a good example. Example 4.1 shows the history of the index in **nominal returns** as well as inflation and its real returns. It shows that simple extrapolation can be very dangerous indeed.

EXAMPLE 4.1 *Extrapolating from past returns*

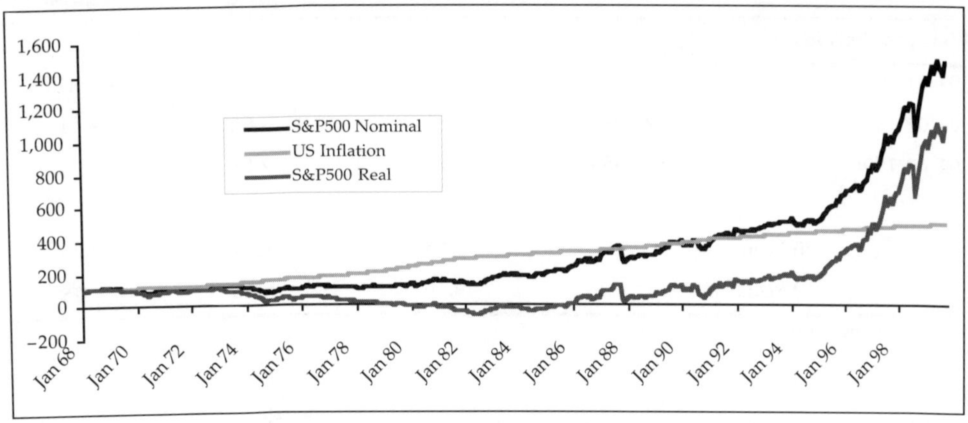

From	To	S&P500 Nominal %	US Inflation %	S&P500 Real %
01 01 1987	31 12 1987	2.03	4.40	−2.37
01 01 1988	31 12 1988	12.40	4.48	7.92
01 01 1989	31 12 1989	27.25	4.54	22.71
01 01 1990	31 12 1990	−6.56	6.27	−12.83
01 01 1991	31 12 1991	26.31	3.06	23.24
01 01 1992	31 12 1992	4.46	2.86	1.60
01 01 1993	31 12 1993	7.06	2.89	4.16
01 01 1994	31 12 1994	−1.54	2.60	−4.14
01 01 1995	31 12 1995	34.11	2.54	31.58
01 01 1996	31 12 1996	20.26	3.26	17.00
01 01 1997	31 12 1997	31.01	1.72	29.28
01 01 1998	31 12 1998	26.67	1.60	25.07
01 01 1999	31 12 1999	31.34	1.82	29.52
Five-year Periods				
01 01 1970	31 12 1974	−5.72	6.66	−12.39
01 01 1975	31 12 1979	9.50	8.17	1.33
01 01 1980	31 12 1984	9.48	6.73	2.75
01 01 1985	31 12 1989	16.14	3.68	12.46
01 01 1990	31 12 1994	5.38	3.53	1.85
01 01 1995	31 12 1999	25.24	2.37	22.87

continued on next page

From	To	S&P500 Nominal %	US Inflation %	S&P500 Real %
Ten-year Periods				
01 01 1970	31 12 1979	1.60	7.41	−5.81
01 01 1980	31 12 1989	12.58	5.08	7.51
01 01 1990	31 12 1999	14.71	2.96	11.75
20 Years		13.85	4.11	9.74
30 Years		9.20	5.15	4.05

Source: Thomson Financial Datastream

Simple projection from one period to the next rarely if ever gives a reliable return forecast. For example, the two ten-year periods ending 1989 and 1999 appear similar in nominal terms, but are very different in real terms. The one-year returns to 1997, 1998 and 1999 are similar in both nominal and real terms, but bear no resemblance to the period before that. Used in conjunction with other forms of analysis, historical data can nevertheless provide useful insights.

Of course there are much more sophisticated ways of projecting from past returns to the future. In practice most quantitative models seek to use history to examine durable relationships between asset prices and the things that drive them. For example, history can be used to examine the impact of currency movements, interest rate changes or commodity prices on equity indices. These kinds of analyses are often incorporated in macroeconomic and other forecasting models.

Dividend discounting

Dividend discounting is based on the premise that the return to an asset is a function of the sum of all future income earned by that asset. Income received in the future is worth less than income received today, the difference being the interest rate. The procedure for calculating the present equivalent of a sum received in the future is known as **discounted cash flow,** and delivers the present value of that sum. The value now of an asset is the sum of all future payments, discounted to reflect their present value. To discount a future payment to reflect its present value, the following formula is applied:

$$\text{Present value} = FP/((1 + r)^{(d-t)/365}) \quad (4.1)$$

Where:

FP = future payment
r = interest rate
d = date of receipt of future income
t = today

The discount rate is an interest rate, sometimes also called a discount factor, that reflects the time value of money and the risk that the future payment will not be as promised.

If the calculated present value of all future payments to the asset is equal to its current market price, then it is said to be fairly priced, and can be expected to deliver a return equal to the discount rate. If the market price is less than the calculated value, the asset will earn higher returns.

Example 4.2 illustrates the principle. The present value of future dividends is the result of dividing the nominal value of each dividend by one plus the discount rate, compounded to reflect how far in the future the dividend occurs.

EXAMPLE 4.2 *Calculating the present value of dividends*

Date Now	01 01 2002		
Current Asset Price	$29.70		
Interest Rate	3.5%		
Current Dividend	$0.50		
Dividends per Year	2		
Annual Dividend Growth Rate	0.5%		
Present Value of Dividends	$31.56	Implied return	9.76%

Date of Dividend	Amount of Dividend $	Compounded Discount Factor %	Present Value of Dividend $
01 07 2002	0.50	1.73	0.49
01 01 2003	0.50	3.50	0.48
01 07 2003	0.50	5.30	0.48
01 01 2004	0.50	7.12	0.47
01 07 2004	0.50	8.98	0.46
01 01 2005	0.50	10.87	0.45
01 07 2005	0.50	12.80	0.45
01 01 2006	0.51	14.75	0.44
01 07 2006	0.51	16.74	0.43

The further into the future the dividend occurs, the less its present value. Eventually the present values converge to zero. Dividend discounting adds all non-zero present values together to get a total value for the asset or asset class. If the asset is sold at any time in the future, its fair price will be the discounted value of its future dividends at that time, so this method theoretically accommodates future disposals as well as long-term holdings. In this example the present value of all future dividends for this asset is $31.56. If the market price of the asset were also $31.56, then the expected return to the asset would be equal to the discount rate. In this case, the market price is lower, so the implied return is higher.

The return to an asset class is theoretically the sum of the returns to all the assets in the asset class. For equities, an aggregate result can be obtained by taking the forecast aggregate dividend yield for all equities in a market, such as the S&P500, and applying growth rates and discount factors to achieve an estimate of the current fair price for that index.

The limitation of this method is that forecasting the income to assets is very difficult, especially over long horizons. Similarly, forecasting the discount factor, or interest rate, is prone to error.

Macroeconomic, fundamental and econometric models

Macroeconomic, fundamental and econometric models combine forecasts of macroeconomic variables, such as currencies, inflation and commodity prices with estimates of how these variables impact security returns to generate asset class return forecasts. This often incorporates a forecast of the **equity risk premium**, which is a measure of the theoretical return differential between equities and bonds.

Currency forecasts

There are two widely used models of exchange rates, both of which have a good deal of intuitive appeal. The first, **interest rate parity** says that the difference between two currencies is a function of the difference between the interest rates in those currencies. The second, **purchasing power parity (PPP)** says that the exchange rate should equate the price of identical goods in different currencies, after adjusting for transport costs and taxes.

Interest rate parity is most often employed when estimating fair prices for forward exchange rates, but can also be useful in forecasting short-term currency movements, as illustrated in Example 4.3.

EXAMPLE 4.3 *Interest rate parity*

Calculating the Forward Price	
Spot Exchange Rate USD/GBP	£0.6500
GBP 90-day Interest	6.50%
USD 90-day Interest	5.00%
Time to Expiry in Days	90
90-day **Forward** Rate GBP/USD	£0.6524

In this example, the exchange rate in three months' time for UK pounds to US dollars is calculated using three-month interest rates for the two countries. The formula applied is:

$$FX = SX \times (1 + rUK \times d/365)/(1 + rUS \times d/365) \quad (4.2)$$

Where:

FX = forward exchange rate
SX = current or spot exchange rate
rUK = UK interest rate
rUS = US interest rate
d = number of days between now and forward settlement

$$= £0.6500 \times (1 + .065 \times 90/365)/(1 + .050 \times 90/365)$$
$$= £0.6524$$

The main limitations of this theory as a forecasting tool are that interest rates may change during the forecast period, and currencies are affected by many factors other than interest rate differentials.

Purchasing power parity says that goods ought to cost the same just about everywhere, after taking account of differences in taxes and transport costs. Probably the best-known application of purchasing power parity is the Big Mac Index, cited regularly in *The Economist* since 1986. This index compares the cost in different countries of a Big Mac hamburger, the premise being that there is almost no difference in the quality of a Big Mac from Moscow to Melbourne to Manhattan, so any price differences reflect under- or overpriced currencies. This index is presented in a mildly tongue-in-cheek manner, but is an excellent illustration of the concept of purchasing power parity, and sometimes gives some interesting insights into currency relative valuations.

Example 4.4 shows the theoretical price of an hypothetical widget as a function of its cost in its place of manufacture (in this case the USA), transport costs, tax and the exchange rate. According to this example, the US dollar is overpriced against nearly all currencies except the Canadian dollar, where the theoretical and actual cost of the widget is $1.45, and France, where its actual price is less than the theoretical.

EXAMPLE 4.4 *Purchasing power parity*

Currency	Exchange Rate	Original Cost of Widget in Local Currency	Transport Costs %	Tax Differential %	Final Value of Widget in Local Currency
US Dollars	1.0000	$1.00	0.00	0.00	$1.00
Australian Dollar	0.6378	1.57	15.00	0.00	1.80
Austrian Schilling	0.0711	14.06	5.00	2.50	15.12
Belgian Franc	0.0243	41.23	5.00	2.50	44.32
Canadian Dollar	0.6902	1.45	0.00	0.00	1.45
Danish Krone	0.1315	7.61	5.00	2.50	8.18
Deutschmark	0.5002	2.00	5.00	2.50	2.15
Dutch Guilder	0.4440	2.25	5.00	2.50	2.42
Euro	0.9784	1.02	5.00	2.50	1.10
Finnish Markka	0.1646	6.08	5.00	2.50	6.53
French Franc	0.1492	6.70	5.00	2.50	7.21
Hong Kong Dollar	0.1285	7.78	7.50	2.50	8.56
Irish Punt	1.2423	0.80	5.00	2.50	0.87
Italian Lira	0.0005	1979.02	5.00	2.50	2127.45
Japanese Yen	0.0093	107.04	7.50	2.50	117.75
Luxembourg Franc	0.0243	41.23	5.00	2.50	44.32
New Zealand Dollar	0.4952	2.02	15.00	0.00	2.32
Norwegian Krone	0.1209	8.27	5.00	2.50	8.89
Singaporean Dollar	0.5881	1.70	7.50	2.50	1.87
Spanish Peseta	0.0059	170.06	5.00	2.50	182.82
Swedish Krona	0.1137	8.79	5.00	2.50	9.45
Swiss Franc	0.6084	1.64	5.00	2.50	1.77
UK Pound	1.6209	0.62	5.00	2.50	0.66

The limitations of both models are that exchange rates are not that simple, being subject to a wide range of influences, such as expected inflation, economic growth and productivity in each country.

In practice, most forecasters apply some combination of the two models, together with forecasts of economic growth, inflation, international trading and investment activity and so on.

Inflation forecasts

Inflation forecasts usually take account of expected currency movements, central bank monetary policy, expected economic growth, productivity growth and capacity utilization and commodity prices. Many central banks issue official inflation forecasts and targets, which can be helpful. In addition, many business associations and economic consultants issue independent estimates of future inflation for their home market.

Commodity prices

Commodity prices and other 'producer price' forecasts can help to estimate inflation, and therefore interest rate and currency forecasts. Because they help to forecast changes in the cost structure for the corporate sector, they can indicate trends in the profitability of companies and help to forecast equity returns.

The equity risk premium

The equity risk premium is the difference in return demanded by investors for the additional risk associated with equities compared with bonds. The basic premise is that if equities become too expensive, the implied return drops to the point where investors decide that there is not enough extra return to compensate for the extra risk, and so shift their investment to less risky bonds. For example, if long-term bonds are promising a yield of 10% per annum, with little likelihood of return volatility or losses, investors will probably choose to place a significant percentage of their portfolios there, particularly if the expected return to equities is in the region of only 11 or 12%, with a strong possibility of much less than that.

The equity risk premium is contentious because it implies accurate estimates of future profitability of equities, which are rarely available in practice. Some economists even assert that the equity risk premium is illusory, pointing out that equities do not always produce higher returns than bonds, and that bonds are not always less risky than equities.

Consensus forecasts

Consensus forecasts incorporate the return forecasts of other investors and analysts. Their main advantage is that they exploit a large stock of wisdom and benefit from a variety of forecasting techniques. Consensus forecasts can be compiled from the research of a variety of stockbrokers, much of which is freely available, or it can be purchased from specialist research organizations. The weakness of this approach is that it incorporates all forecasts, including those based on research of uncertain quality. Often it will simply aggregate information, giving a result equal to the current asset price, which is after all simply the sum of that information. Forecasts generated by stockbrokers can incorporate considerable bias for two reasons. The first is that stockbrokers nearly always produce over-optimistic earnings forecasts. The second is that, if the corporate finance arm of the stockbroker is providing advice to the company in question, it is very unlikely to reveal negative news about the company's prospects, lest it jeopardize the lucrative advisory role.

Currency management

The fund's managers normally formulate policy regarding currency management with help from the consultant, and this policy is usually applied to both long- and short-term asset allocation. There are three broad strategies for dealing with currency:

- neutral or passive
- fully hedged
- actively managed, treating the currency as if it were an asset class by itself.

Many investors opt for taking a **neutral currency position**, meaning that the portfolio holds just enough foreign currency to buy the assets that are denominated in that currency. For example, if the portfolio has $100 million in Swiss equities and another $50 million in Swiss bonds, the fund should have $150 million worth of Swiss francs.

Many investors deliberately choose the neutral or passive approach to currencies on the premise that currency movements correct over time. Well, they don't! Remember 1985, when one US dollar bought 250 Japanese yen? Ask any UK investor who held foreign currency assets during the second half of the 1980s. Example 4.5 illustrates the return to the **MSCI** world equity index from

EXAMPLE 4.5 *Currency fluctuations*

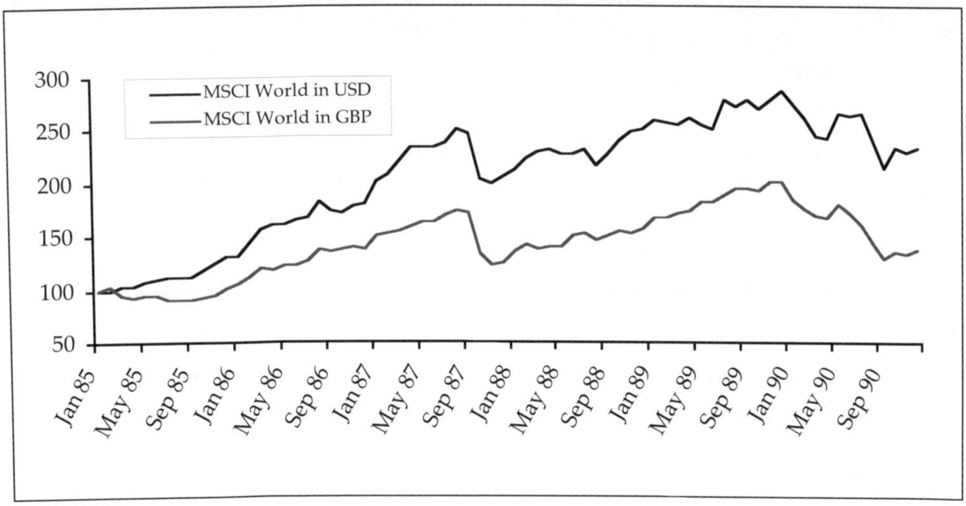

Source: MSCI

Period: 31.01.85 to 31.12.90	MSCI World USD %	GBP %	Difference %
Return for Period	134.21	37.30	−96.91
Annualized	15.47	5.50	−9.96

Source: MSCI

the point of view of both a USD and a GBP investor. This shows that currency neutrality cost the GBP investor nearly 10% per annum over this period. Almost any active strategy would have yielded some value. Of course, it is still possible that $1 could again cost £0.88 as it did at the start of 1985, but only the most patient investors are prepared to wait and see.

The next most popular alternative is to **hedge to base currency**. The idea is to gain exposure to foreign assets without any of the risk of holding foreign currency. Of course it is necessary to buy, say, Swiss francs in order to buy Swiss equities and bonds, but when these purchases are effected, the investment manager sells forward Swiss francs and buys base currency. In Example 4.6, the manager has bought $150 million worth of Swiss francs spot (for immediate settlement), and sold the same face value of Swiss francs forward for settlement in 12 months' time, thereby fixing the rate at which Swiss francs are sold in 12 months' time and removing return volatility due to fluctuations in this exchange rate.

EXAMPLE 4.6 *A simple hedge to base currency*

Spot CHF/USD	1.1000	
USD Interest Rate	7.50%	
CHF Interest Rate	4.50%	
Amount to be Hedged	−150 000	
Forward CHF/USD	1.1316	
Today	USD	CHF
Sell Spot USD & Buy Spot Swiss Francs	−150 000	165 000
Buy Swiss Equities		−165 000
Sell 12 Month Forward Swiss Francs	145 814	−165 000
Appreciation of Swiss Equities	15.00%	
In 12 Months' Time		
Sell Swiss Equities		189 750
Balance	−4 186	24 750

As it happens, the cost of hedging is USD4186, reflecting the difference in interest rates in the two countries. At the end of the 12-month period the investor sells the equities at market valuation. The profit or loss on Swiss equities, in this case CHF16 500, is then converted to USD.

Another approach is to **actively manage currency exposures**, effectively treating currencies as a separate asset class. This approach requires forecasts of currency returns and correlations, but can greatly enhance the opportunities to earn extra returns. An important benefit of actively managing currencies is that it allows the possibility of extra returns from currency exposures, thus replacing unintentional risk with intentional risk.

Forecasting risk

While the expected return to the portfolio is simply the weighted sum of the returns to the assets classes in it, the portfolio's risk takes into account the relationship between the asset class returns, expressed as correlations or covariances.

Unsurprisingly, forecasting correlation matrices is even more difficult than forecasting returns, so investment managers tend to use some sample of historical returns to derive their expected covariance matrices. Using historical correlation matrices has its limitations, the most obvious of which is that the past may not be a very good guide to what will happen in the future. But because attempts at forecasting correlation matrices tend to enjoy much less practical success than forecast returns, and because correlations tend to change much more slowly over time than do asset returns, using the past to estimate the future provides a reasonable, practical, if imperfect, solution.

The next question to pose is 'what history?' Because correlations do change over time, the investment manager needs to select a period for correlation estimation that will best represent the forecast period. Too short a period risks underestimating some important and enduring relationships between asset classes, while choosing too much history risks including relationships that were important, but are now obsolete. Apart from choosing a length of time that will highlight important relationships while excluding irrelevant or obsolete ones, the mathematical imperatives of optimization are that the more asset classes that are included in the investment universe, the longer the history required to generate a meaningful correlation matrix.

Example 4.7 illustrates how correlations can change over time. While most asset classes exhibit stable relationships with each other, occasionally large changes occur. The relationships between domestic government bonds and sovereign bonds has changed significantly, as has the correlation of developed market equities to domestic bonds, and developed market equities to emerging market equities.

The investment manager can also decide to modify the impact of older return data that might introduce unwanted relationships, corrupting the result. Placing more importance on recent observations, and less on older data can easily do this. There are a number of ways of applying differential weights to

EXAMPLE 4.7 *Comparing correlation matrices*

5-year Correlation Matrix	Volatility %	1	2	3	4	5	6	7	8	9
1 US Fixed Interest	4.06	1.00								
2 International Sovereign Debt	20.31	0.01	1.00							
3 US Corporate Debt	4.59	0.93	0.27	1.00						
4 US Equities	14.43	0.15	0.68	0.38	1.00					
5 Developed Markets Equities	13.34	−0.01	0.67	0.21	0.92	1.00				
6 Emerging Markets Equities	26.49	−0.23	0.79	0.01	0.70	0.75	1.00			
7 Real Property	16.53	0.05	0.47	0.22	0.56	0.48	0.48	1.00		
8 UK Pound	6.92	0.11	−0.27	0.03	−0.15	−0.08	−0.25	−0.01	1.00	
9 Euro	8.36	0.06	−0.24	−0.03	−0.21	−0.11	−0.26	−0.17	0.57	1.00
10 Japanese Yen	14.58	−0.02	−0.08	−0.10	0.10	0.26	0.05	−0.14	0.25	0.47

continued on next page

10-year Correlation Matrix	Volatility %	1	2	3	4	5	6	7	8	9
1 US Fixed Interest	4.16	1.00								
2 International Sovereign Debt	17.67	0.14	1.00							
3 US Corporate Debt	4.54	0.95	0.32	1.00						
4 US Equities	12.87	0.27	0.60	0.41	1.00					
5 Developed Markets Equities	12.75	0.17	0.56	0.30	0.84	1.00				
6 Emerging Markets Equities	23.94	−0.12	0.72	0.06	0.62	0.62	1.00			
7 Real Property	17.13	0.17	0.43	0.28	0.59	0.52	0.50	1.00		
8 UK Pound	10.11	0.18	−0.11	0.10	0.00	0.19	−0.18	−0.06	1.00	
9 Euro	10.16	0.17	−0.20	0.08	−0.08	0.11	−0.23	−0.12	0.77	1.00
10 Japanese Yen	12.25	0.04	−0.13	−0.03	0.04	0.25	−0.02	−0.11	0.27	0.44

Source: Thomson Financial Datastream, Salomon Smith Barney, QUANTEC, MSCI

return, the simplest being to reduce by an equal amount the importance of each consecutive observation, known as 'linear weights'. Alternatively, a more aggressive 'exponential' decay function can be applied. Thus recent data are much more heavily weighted than early observations.

Example 4.8 compares the correlation matrices over ten years using **linear weightings** and **exponential weightings** to asset class returns, as opposed to equal weighting as in Example 4.7.

EXAMPLE 4.8 *Linear and exponentially weighted correlations*

Linear Weighting	Volatility %	1	2	3	4	5	6	7	8	9
1 US Fixed Interest	4.30	1.00								
2 International Sovereign Debt	21.83	0.00	1.00							
3 US Corporate Debt	4.79	0.92	0.27	1.00						
4 US Equities	15.71	0.15	0.68	0.37	1.00					
5 Developed Markets Equities	14.84	0.02	0.67	0.24	0.91	1.00				
6 Emerging Markets Equities	29.48	−0.23	0.79	0.01	0.67	0.71	1.00			
7 Real Property	18.58	0.09	0.49	0.25	0.54	0.47	0.49	1.00		
8 UK Pound	8.30	0.16	−0.19	0.07	−0.11	−0.01	−0.23	−0.06	1.00	
9 Euro	9.28	0.12	−0.20	0.02	−0.16	−0.06	−0.24	−0.17	0.62	1.00
10 Japanese Yen	14.74	−0.01	−0.07	−0.10	0.09	0.24	0.03	−0.16	0.21	0.43

continued on next page

Exponential Weighting	Volatility %	1	2	3	4	5	6	7	8	9
1 US Fixed Interest	4.98	1.00								
2 International Sovereign Debt	28.38	−0.14	1.00							
3 US Corporate Debt	5.50	0.88	0.21	1.00						
4 US Equities	21.69	0.00	0.71	0.29	1.00					
5 Developed Markets Equities	20.69	−0.13	0.72	0.16	0.94	1.00				
6 Emerging Markets Equities	39.73	−0.38	0.80	−0.08	0.69	0.73	1.00			
7 Real Property	25.28	0.05	0.46	0.23	0.47	0.38	0.45	1.00		
8 UK Pound	8.56	0.26	−0.21	0.12	−0.20	−0.14	−0.29	−0.09	1.00	
9 Euro	10.81	0.28	−0.12	0.15	−0.12	−0.07	−0.27	−0.16	0.57	1.00
10 Japanese Yen	19.27	0.00	0.01	−0.11	0.15	0.27	0.04	−0.24	0.17	0.41

Source: Thomson Financial Datastream, Salomon Smith Barney, QUANTEC, MSCI

Constraints

Most funds are subject to some constraints, which can be as simple as the requirement to hold no more than 5% and no less than 10% in short-term liquid instruments. Alternatively, it can be the necessity to hold a certain proportion of the fund in domestic assets, or to avoid certain other assets altogether. Most optimizer programs can accommodate such constraints, although each constraint imposes a cost on the optimization, so that the resulting portfolios have inferior risk for return profiles to those generated by unconstrained optimizations. If too many, or contradictory, constraints are imposed, the optimizer may fail to generate any sensible portfolios.

Optimizing the long-term asset allocation

Armed with long-term return forecasts, and a reasonable estimate of likely long-term correlations between each asset class, the investor is in a good position to try to construct the long-term asset allocation. Although this is usually only a hypothetical portfolio, it is very important because it forms the benchmark against which the actual portfolio is evaluated. The long-term asset allocation must generate sufficient returns to meet the obligations of the fund. Therefore it seeks the best absolute return for risk or volatility.

Example 4.9 shows how introducing constraints limits the range of available efficient portfolios. The important output from the optimization is a range of

EXAMPLE 4.9 *Optimization of long-term allocation: constrained and unconstrained*

	Expected Return %	Minimum Holding %	Maximum Holding %
US Fixed Interest	8.00	0	30
US Equities	2.00	10	50
UK Equities	17.60	0	20
European Equities	21.00	0	20
Japanese Equities	22.40	0	15
US Dollar	0.00	5	5
UK Pound	5.00	2	2
Euro	10.00	2	2
Japanese Yen	2.00	1	1

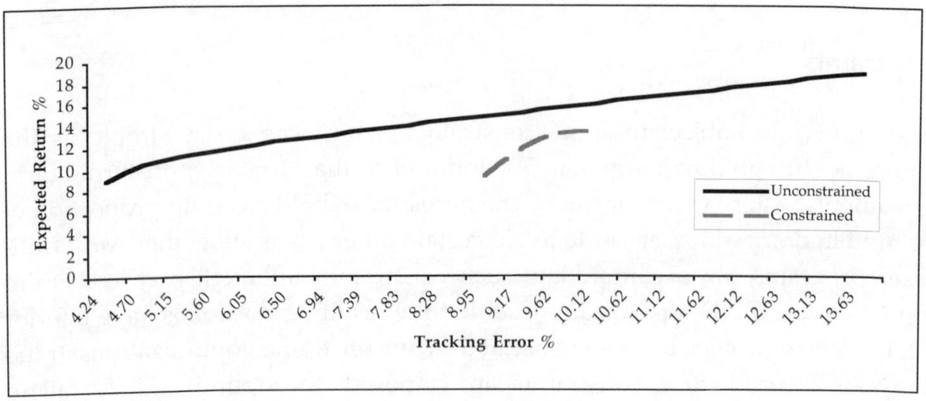

Optimization Summary	Efficient Portfolios				
	Minimum Risk %				Maximum Return %
Unconstrained Optimization					
Absolute Return	8.80	12.20	15.60	19.00	22.40
Tracking Error	4.24	6.05	9.62	13.63	24.94
95% Probable Minimum Return	1.82	2.25	−0.22	−3.42	−18.63
Probability of Negative Return	1.91	2.19	5.24	8.16	18.45
Constrained Optimization					
Absolute Return	9.29	10.37	11.44	12.52	13.60
Tracking Error	8.95	8.98	9.08	9.26	10.18
95% Probable Minimum Return	−5.43	−4.40	−3.49	−2.72	−3.15
Probability of Negative Return	14.96	12.41	10.37	8.82	9.08

Source: Thomson Financial Datastream, Salomon Smith Barney, QUANTEC

efficient portfolios, each with the highest forecast return for a given level of risk expressed as volatility. The ranges for constrained and unconstrained optimizations are shown as lines on the graph in Example 4.9. Constraining the portfolio limits the range of possible outcomes, and is usually only applied as a risk control measure. In this case, however, rather than limiting the risk of the portfolio, the constraints have increased it by limiting possible diversification. For example, for low-risk, low-return portfolios, not only is the volatility significantly increased, but also there is a greater probability of a negative return.

Reverse optimization

Given the uncertain nature of the inputs on which the portfolio optimization is based, and its importance to the long-term asset allocation, it is useful to carry out some kind of verification of the robustness of the portfolio allocations thus obtained. Most investment managers carry out some kind of sensitivity analysis to see how portfolio expected returns are altered by changing assumptions about expected asset class returns and covariances. A complementary procedure is to reverse the optimization, whereby the preferred portfolio allocations are input to the optimizer to see what long-term returns are implied. Comparing implied with forecast asset class returns gives a measure of the consistency of return forecasts and portfolio construction. Reverse optimization is dealt with in more detail later in this chapter and in Chapters 3 and 10.

SHORT-TERM ASSET ALLOCATION

The purpose of short-term asset allocation is to take advantage of insights into short-term market movements. If the investor believes that short-term returns for one or more asset classes will be significantly different from the long-term outcome, it makes sense to adjust the portfolio allocation accordingly. Alternatively, the fund may be running low on reserves, with the consequence that it has a particularly low tolerance for negative outcomes in the immediate future. In this case, a defensive short-term asset allocation may be adopted, selecting a portfolio allocation that will protect it against adverse outcomes over a specified investment horizon. Defensive asset allocation strategies can be effected simply by employing optimization to select a low-risk–low-return portfolio or it can incorporate **protection strategies** to deliver guaranteed minimum outcomes. Guaranteed minimum outcomes are discussed in detail in Chapter 5.

To generate an optimized short-term asset allocation, the following inputs are required:

- **The benchmark asset allocation**. This is normally the long-term asset allocation, but can be an alternative asset allocation. It comprises a list of the asset classes in the benchmark and the percentage held by the benchmark in each asset class.
- **The investment universe**. This is a list of the asset classes that the fund is allowed to invest in. Usually it is the same as the universe used to select the long-term asset allocation, but it need not be limited to the assets in the benchmark.
- **Return forecasts for each asset class in the investment universe**. Each investment manager has his or her preferred method of generating return forecasts for asset allocation, ranging from simple extrapolation of historical returns to much more sophisticated techniques incorporating econometric and fundamental return modelling. Return forecasts for short-term asset allocation should include the time frame, normally about three to six months, for the return to materialize, and some target return and maximum allowable loss.
- **Risk forecasts**. These are the forecast covariance or correlation matrices for each pair of assets in the investment universe.
- **Constraints**. These describe any statutory or fiduciary requirements to which the investor may be subject, such as a maximum exposure to foreign assets, or a maximum exposure to equities or foreign currencies. Usually these are the same as applied in optimizing the long-term asset allocation, but also may include a maximum departure from long-term allocations.
- **Required return or acceptable risk.** The required return is usually expressed as a margin over the forecast long-term return to the fund, a fixed return above inflation or an absolute return. The acceptable risk can be expressed in terms of tracking error against the long-term asset allocation, the probability of a disappointing outcome or some minimum acceptable return, either absolute or relative to the long-term asset allocation. It is important to remember that portfolio-wide risk is not simply the sum of the risk of asset classes and asset allocation. The expected risk associated with asset allocation combines with asset class risk according to asset class covariances to contribute to portfolio-wide risk.
- **The current portfolio allocation.** If the portfolio is already established, the portfolio optimizer will use this portfolio as its starting point, if not the starting portfolio can be either cash or the long-term asset allocation. This is

important since the optimizer works by increments. The starting portfolio composition therefore affects the cost of implementing the optimal portfolio.

Optimizing the short-term asset allocation

Once the inputs to the optimization have been determined, the optimizer can be left to do its job, beginning with an analysis of the return and risk of the existing portfolio and incrementally improving on it until the optimal portfolio is reached.

Reverse optimization

Reverse optimization can be applied to both long-term and short-term asset allocation, providing a check on the consistency between asset class return forecasts and portfolio construction.

In Example 4.10, the investor has a 15% allocation to domestic fixed interest. If this portfolio is efficient, this allocation implies a forecast return of 5.3% to that asset class. Since the investor has indicated an expected return of just less than zero, either the holding needs to be reduced or the forecast return revised.

EXAMPLE 4.10 *Reverse optimization*

	Portfolio Holding %	Implied Return in Base %	Expected Return in Base %
US Government Bonds	15	5.341	−0.050
Emerging Markets Bonds	5	8.120	1.500
US Corporate Bonds	10	5.550	−2.500
US Equities	30	8.035	15.000
Global Equities	10	7.773	12.000
Emerging Markets Equities	5	9.315	18.000
US Listed Property	15	8.347	5.000
UK Pound	2	5.090	−5.636
Euro	2	4.889	−11.584
Japanese Yen	1	5.115	9.536
Portfolio Values	100	7.168	7.168

Source: Thomson Financial Datastream, Salomon Smith Barney, QUANTEC, MSCI

RISK MANAGEMENT

The main purpose of risk analysis and management is to quantify risk and understand what is contributing to it. Because unnecessary risk does not contribute to portfolio return, it is important that all **unintentional risk** be eliminated. In order to achieve this, its sources must be identified.

Example 4.11 is a typical analysis of portfolio variance, showing, for each asset, the short and long-term allocation and how each position contributes to the risk of the portfolio. The major contributor is US equities because the portfolio is heavily overweight in this volatile asset class. If this position is associated with a strong forecast return, then the risk is justified, if US equities are not forecast to perform strongly, then the position could be reduced.

The amount of risk that the fund can tolerate is influenced by its reserves and the investment horizon, with a longer horizon usually indicating a higher risk profile. The risk of the portfolio can be expressed in a number of ways, such as the tracking error against the long-term asset allocation, the likelihood of a negative return, or the return that the fund is 95% sure of beating. For example, the managers of a fund with low reserves may choose a risk profile that gives a 95% chance of delivering a return above the inflation rate.

How the investor combines return management and risk control is determined largely by how the tasks of managing investment returns are allocated between investment managers, for example by means of balanced or specialist mandates, and whether currency management is delegated to a specialist manager or integrated into the portfolio itself. For a balanced mandate, the investment manager simply prepares a forecast of portfolio-wide tracking error, based on the output of

EXAMPLE 4.11 *Contribution to portfolio variance*

	Short-term Asset Allocation %	Long-term Asset Allocation %	Contribution to Portoflio Variance %	Percentage Contribution to Portfolio Variance %
US Fixed Interest	10.00	25.00	0.80	0.55
US Equities	45.00	35.00	80.81	55.63
UK Equities	15.00	10.00	24.86	17.12
European Equities	15.00	10.00	24.00	16.52
Japanes Equities	10.00	15.00	14.78	10.18
Cash	5.00	5.00	0.00	0.00
Total	100.00	100.00	145.25	100.00

Source: Thomson Financial Datastream, Salomon Smith Barney, QUANTEC

an optimizer. Asset allocation overlay managers can also provide tracking error estimates, provided they have the components of individual asset class portfolios and any currency overlay portfolios. Although it is not possible to incorporate fully bond portfolios and portfolios of unlisted assets into a mean-variance-based risk forecast, these asset classes can usually be approximated by including some listed proxy. For bonds this can be a bond index that is close to the actual portfolio, and direct property can be included using a mix of bonds and equities. The results are not perfect, but better than the alternative of omitting the asset classes altogether or, worse, bypassing the risk forecasting process.

The danger of omitting risk forecasts is that, without some quantification and analysis of portfolio risk, the investor cannot be sure that all the risk in the portfolio is intentional and therefore associated with extra return. Unintentional risk merely contributes to portfolio volatility. Having been quantified, it therefore must be either managed or eliminated by hedging.

IMPLEMENTATION OF SHORT-TERM ASSET ALLOCATION

Short-term asset allocation is sometimes called tactical asset allocation, designed to exploit short-term asset return forecasts to achieve returns above those for the long-term benchmark, typically over a period of three to six months.

How this portfolio is put in place depends on whether asset allocation is conducted as a specialist activity, as an overlay or as part of a balanced mandate.

The **specialist asset allocation manager**, having determined the short-term asset allocation, instructs the custodian and each of the specialist asset class managers of the change in allocation, and when it is to take place. It is important to give each manager adequate notice, taking into account the size of the required transaction, liquidity of the market concerned and settlement periods.

In the case of a **balanced mandate**, the investment manager decides the short-term mix, and so instructs his or her sector managers to adjust the amount in each sector portfolio accordingly. The balanced mandate manager is subject to the same liquidity and settlement conditions, but can coordinate the efforts of asset class managers more easily, so the details of the transaction are largely invisible to the investor.

Normally each sector manager will decide the best way of effecting the required purchases and sales. For relatively liquid instruments such as bonds, equities and money market instruments, the process is fairly simple and is soon completed. Less liquid investments such as real property and unlisted equity can pose some problems. Most specialist managers of these asset classes maintain a balance of liquid assets to facilitate implementation, but a large change in allocation can necessitate liquidating assets.

For **overlay mandates** the process is quite simple, necessitating only some transactions in derivative instruments while the physical portfolio remains unchanged, invested in physical assets, usually in the long-term allocations. The physical asset class managers may not even be aware of the short-term decisions being made.

The overlay manager typically holds most of the **frictional liquidity** of the fund, normally about 10% of the value of the overall fund. Frictional liquidity is the amount held by all portfolios in short-term deposits and other liquid instruments to meet unforeseen cash requirements, such as minor redemptions and other miscellaneous cash requirements. The overlay manager uses this cash to meet margin calls on derivatives positions.

Constructing the overlay to meet short-term asset allocation specifications is relatively simple for those asset classes with established futures markets, such as equities and bonds, but things become more complicated for asset classes such as real property and direct equity. In these cases, the overlay manager's choice is to seek some kind of over-the-counter derivative, such as a forward agreement or an asset swap, or try to synthesize the required asset using combinations of exchange-traded derivatives. For example, property exposure is often synthesized using a mix of equity and bonds. This technique is not ideal, as the returns achieved tend to be at best an approximation of the return to real property portfolios, but can yield acceptable results for most portfolios.

Even for the 'easy' asset classes, the task can be complicated by **basis risk**. Basis risk is the risk that the derivative instrument chosen will not deliver the same return as the physical assets it is meant to replicate. For example, most equity futures contracts are based on a well-diversified hypothetical portfolio (index) of shares. If the actual portfolio does not resemble exactly this hypothetical portfolio, then the overlay manager may be using apples to replicate pears. There is no simple solution to this; one approach is to stipulate, for all asset classes, mandates that resemble the hypothetical, in other words, indexed portfolios. If the investor is confident of the investment managers' abilities to deliver above indexed returns, this solution is clearly inappropriate, as it foregoes these extra returns. Another, partial solution is to instruct the sector manager to tell the overlay manager what is in the physical portfolio. The overlay manager can then judge what mix of derivatives contracts can minimize the inevitable basis risk. This is similar to the solution described above to replicate asset classes without futures contracts.

Examples 4.12.1 to 4.12.3 are simplified examples of how futures contracts might be used to effect a short-term asset allocation shift over a five-month period. Physical assets are held in the long-term allocation, which is shown

EXAMPLE 4.12.1 *Short-term allocation shift using futures and forwards*

Asset Class	Asset Class Benchmark	Long-term Allocation %	Short-term Allocation %	Required Transactions %	
US Fixed Interest	US Treasuries	25	10	Sell	15
US Equities	S&P500	35	45	Buy	10
UK Equities	FTSE AllShare	10	15	Buy	5
European Equities	Euro STOXX	10	15	Buy	5
Japanese Equities	TOPIX	15	10	Sell	5
Cash	Cash	5	5	Sell	0
Total		100	100		40

Source: Thomson Financial Datastream, FTSE, Salomon Smith Barney, IDC

together with the desired short-term asset allocation. Not all the asset class benchmarks have liquid futures contracts, so some substitutions are necessary:

- The FTSE100 contract is used to represent the FTSE Allshare.
- The DAX contract is used to represent euro STOXX.
- The Nikkei 225 is a more practical and liquid contract than the TOPIX, even though the latter is more suitable as a broad-based benchmark for Japanese equities.

Based on a portfolio value of USD1 000 000 000 and maintaining foreign currency exposure equal to the face value of futures held in each currency – a currency neutral position – the transactions to implement the short-term asset allocation shift are as in Example 4.12.2.

The face value of futures to be bought and sold is calculated as the face value of the asset class to be traded, adjusted for the face value of each futures contract, the futures point value and the exchange rate. For example, the required number of FTSE100 contracts is calculated as follows:

$$\text{Number of contracts} = PV \times UKE \times GBP/(FT100 \times pv) \tag{4.3}$$

Where:

PV = portfolio value
UKE = percentage allocation to UK equities
GBP = GBP/USD exchange rate
FT100 = current FT100 physical index

EXAMPLE 4.12.2 *Transaction summary – start of period*

		Number	Face Value $
Buy 5-month Futures:	S&P500	151	110 318 360
	FTSE100	198	49 972 547
	DAX (Germany)	118	50 132 508
Buy Spot Currency	GBP/USD		49 972 547
	Euro/USD		50 132 508
Sell 5-month futures	US Treasuries	1506	150 041 156
	Nikkei 225	642	49 962 156
Sell Spot Currency	JPY/USD		49 952 156
Net Futures Bought or Sold			420 103

Source: Thomson Financial Datastream, FTSE, IDC, Salomon Smith Barney

pv = FT100 futures point value

$$\begin{aligned}\text{Number of contracts} &= 1\,000\,000\,000 \times 5\% \times 0.6173/(6231.93 \times 25)\\ &= 30\,865\,000/155\,798.25\\ &= 198.11\end{aligned}$$

Since only whole contracts can be transacted, this rounds to 198. Working backwards, the face value of UK equities thus transacted is:

$$\begin{aligned}\text{Face value transacted} &= 198 \times 25 \times 6231.93/0.6173\\ &= \$49\,972\,547\\ &= 4.9973\%\end{aligned}$$

The effective face value, 4.9973%, is not the same as the target face value of 5%. This problem is unavoidable, and must be taken into account when evaluating this means of effecting short-term asset allocation, particularly when relatively small values are to be transacted. Where many asset classes are included, the differences usually offset each other, but still should be quantified, since they will contribute to unwanted return volatility.

Note that, to maintain currency neutrality, foreign exchange needs to be transacted commensurate with the face value of futures transacted. Thus the change in allocation to UK assets of 4.9973% is accompanied by an equivalent transaction to GBP.

To revert to the long-term allocation, the manger reverses the above trades, as set out in Example 4.12.3.

Note that this time the face value of currency traded does not exactly match the face value of futures bought and sold. This is because the change in the value of the currency is not the same as the change in value of the futures contracts.

EXAMPLE 4.12.3 *Transaction summary – end of period*

		Number	Face Value $
Sell 5-month Futures	S&P500	151	110 928 375
	FTSE100	198	55 285 238
	DAX (Germany)	118	63 977 242
Sell Spot Currency	GBP/USD		49 714 832
	Euro/USD		46 946 780
Buy 5-month Futures	US Treasuries	1506	143 743 507
	Nikkei 225	642	59 377 913
Buy Spot Currency	JPY/USD		56 014 625
Net Futures Bought or Sold			27 069 435

Source: Thomson Financial Datastream, FTSE, IDC, Salomon Smith Barney

The investment manager is reversing previously open positions, so the number of futures contracts transacted is identical to that traded previously, while the amount of foreign exchange traded matches the foreign amount already transacted, leaving a zero balance for both futures and foreign currency, with all profits and losses denominated in the base currency.

USE OF DERIVATIVES

In some circumstances, there are advantages in replacing all physical assets with derivatives, in which case the portfolio itself is managed in the same way as an asset allocation overlay, with the physical assets of the portfolio held in cash rather than the long-term allocation portfolio. This approach confers a number of benefits:

- It can be very cost effective, saving on transaction costs both for asset allocation resets and within asset classes. It can virtually eliminate management fees for individual asset classes. Custodian fees are greatly reduced because there are fewer transactions.
- Resetting asset allocation to benchmark can coincide with rolling futures positions from one expiry month to the next, further reducing transaction costs.
- Manager risk can be controlled because the risk of individual asset classes underperforming their benchmarks is virtually eliminated, since each asset class is effectively managed as an indexed portfolio.

- Because futures markets are more liquid than markets for physical assets, changes in asset allocation are very easy to implement.

The main disadvantage is that the choice of asset classes is limited to those with viable futures markets. This can rule out some of the more interesting asset classes, such as direct equity, small capitalization stocks and emerging markets. It also forfeits the benefits of extra returns from security selection within asset classes.

As with asset allocation overlay mandates, close attention must be given to ensuring that no unintended exposure to asset classes and foreign currency results. This is particularly important if a hedge to base currency is required, as all profits and losses in foreign asset classes are denominated in these currencies, while the hedged amount remains constant.

ONGOING MANAGEMENT

The processes for ongoing management depend on the type of mandate and the tolerance for deviations between actual portfolio weightings and target allocations. Because different assets in the fund grow and shrink at different rates, the actual allocation can quickly deviate from the target allocation.

A balanced mandate typically specifies that asset classes need to be rebalanced when the difference between actual and target allocations exceeds a certain, predefined limit, such as 5% or 10%. The investment manager inspects the allocations at regular intervals to ensure that this guideline is adhered to, and effects adjustments as and when required. Alternatively, the mandate may specify that the target asset allocation be restored at predefined time intervals, such as each three or six months, with the investment manager automatically adjusting the asset allocations to match the target on the specified dates.

As the balanced mandate manager sells and buys physical assets to reset the portfolio, it is important to allow reasonable tolerance between actual and target allocations, and time intervals that are not too short. This can help to reduce the cost of asset class reallocations by allowing the investment manager to coincide some of the required transactions with natural cash flows, such as new investment in the fund, redemptions and accrued dividend and coupon income.

If asset allocation is by means of a specialist mandate, the asset allocation manager needs to instruct each sector manager when an asset reallocation has taken place. Each asset class manager will then invest or divest the amount indicated by the asset allocation manager by buying or selling physical assets. It is important to allow enough time for transactions to be conducted in an orderly way, taking into account liquidity and settlement times in each market. While futures can often be used to manage asset class exposure during allocation changes, they do not fill the gap entirely, so some thought must be directed at potential problems in executing the asset allocation.

The job of the overlay manager is quite a bit simpler because physical assets remain unaltered, usually at the long-term allocation, while all short-term adjustments are made using derivatives. Typically, the mandate stipulates the maximum allowed difference between actual and target allocations or the time interval for resetting the allocation to target, with the overlay manger automatically transacting the necessary derivatives. The issues remaining are to ensure that there is always enough cash to meet margin calls and to manage the lumpiness in cash balances resulting from profits and losses realized on expiry of futures contracts, and ensuring that open futures and forward contracts match the overlay specifications.

When investing new funds and liquidating in response to fund redemptions and reallocations, the issues are as for implementing changes in asset allocation. Unless otherwise instructed, the investment managers buy or sell assets in proportion to the current holdings of their portfolio. Similarly, the overlay manager must alter each derivative position exactly in proportion to current holdings to ensure that the current fund allocation is not altered unintentionally.

ADMINISTRATION

For balanced and specialist mandates, administration is very straightforward because the assets are nearly all held in physical securities. Administration of asset allocation is simply the sum of the administration of individual asset classes.

The asset allocation overlay presents some interesting complications because of the lumpiness of the cash flows that are generated by derivatives. This lumpiness arises from the fact that derivatives contracts expire regularly and need to be renewed, usually by replacing them with identical positions in the next expiry month, a transaction known as a 'futures roll'. This process converts unrealized profits and losses into realized profits and losses, which take the form of cash, which may need to be repatriated or reinvested.

VALUATION

As for administration, valuation for asset allocation purposes is straightforward for both balanced and specialist managers, because it is simply the sum of each of the asset classes.

EXAMPLE 4.13 *Valuation of short-term asset allocation overlay*

Contract	Bought or Sold	Number of Contracts	Face Value in Local Currency	Face Value in Base Currency	Unrealized Profit/Loss in Local Currency	Unrealized Profit/Loss in Base Currency	Realized Profit/Loss in Base Currency
US Fixed Interest	Sold	1506	143 743 483	143 743 483	–6 297 649	–6 297 640	
US Equities	Bought	151	102 841 435	102 841 435	8 086 940	8 086 940	
UK Equities	Bought	198	31 494 595	50 756 801	2 809 895	4 528 437	
European Equities	Bought	118	47 133 309	47 241 966	16 696 785	16 735 276	
Japanese Equities	Sold	642	5 781 725 527	56 484 228	–296 197 613	–2 893 685	
GBP/USD							–263 116
Euro/USD							–3 205 759
JPY/USD							–6 103 210
Total						20 159 319	–9 572 086

Source: Thomson Financial Datastream, FTSE, IDC, Salomon Smith Barney

For overlay mandates, the physical portfolio is often the long-term asset allocation and is valued as simply the sum of its asset classes. The value of the overlay is simply the sum of unrealized and realized profits and losses on derivatives. The physical portfolio and the overlay together make up the value of the fund:

Total fund = physical + overlay
= long-term allocation + short-term asset allocation

Example 4.13 shows an end of period valuation for the tactical asset allocation shift described in Examples 4.12.1 to 4.12.3.

This shows the portfolio with $20 159 319 in unrealized profits on futures transactions, and a loss of $9 572 086 on currencies. The value of the overall portfolio is therefore the sum of these two figures plus the value of the physical portfolio.

This example is simplified by the fact that there were no realized profits or losses on futures positions. In practice these simply would be added to the unrealized profit and loss.

PERFORMANCE MEASUREMENT AND ATTRIBUTION

The objective is to compare the portfolio's performance with that of the long-term allocation or benchmark. The contribution of short-term asset allocation to portfolio return is the difference between short-term and long-term asset class allocations times the return to each asset class, as illustrated in Example 4.14.

For the asset allocation overlay, the end value of the overlay is divided by the starting value of the physical portfolio to give the overlay's contribution to portfolio return.

The portfolio returned 10.51% compared with the benchmark return of 10.79%, a negative variation of 0.28%. The contribution of short-term asset allocation was 1.88%, which was due mostly to the reduction in the allocation to domestic fixed interest, which delivered a below benchmark return of –4.01% for the period. This positive contribution was partially offset by below benchmark allocation to Japanese equities, which did better than the overall portfolio, giving an asset allocation effect of –0.99%.

Performance measurement is in practice nearly always made more complicated by cash flows to and from the portfolio during the investment period, usually resulting from new investment or redemptions. When this happens, the return period is split so that there is a pre-cash-flow return period and a post-cash-flow return period. Returns are calculated for each period and

EXAMPLE 4.14 *Return contribution for short-term asset allocation*

Asset Class	Short-term Asset Allocation %	Long-term Asset Allocation %	Over/ Under %	Return to Asset Class in Base Currency %	Asset Class minus Benchmark Return %	Asset Allocation Effect %
US Fixed Interest	10	25	−15.00	−4.01	−14.80	2.22
US Equities	45	35	10.00	10.58	−0.21	−0.02
UK Equities	15	10	5.00	10.26	−0.52	−0.03
European Equities	15	10	5.00	24.79	14.00	0.70
Japanese Equities	10	15	−5.00	30.56	19.77	−0.99
Cash	5	5	0.00	0.00	−10.79	0.00
Total	100	100	0.00	10.79	0.00	1.88

EXAMPLE 4.15 *Return calculation*

Portfolio value at start of period	$10 000 000
Portfolio value end of period	$15 000 000
Cash flow	$2 500 000
Portfolio value immediately prior to cash flow	$12 000 000

$$R = (15\,000\,000/(12\,000\,000 + 2\,500\,000)) \times (12\,000\,000/10\,000\,000) - 1$$
$$= 1.0345 \times 1.2000 - 1$$
$$= 1.2414 - 1$$
$$= 24.14\%$$

compounded to give the return for the overall investment period, as set out in Example 4.15. This method of calculating return is known as **money-weighted.**

$$R = (PV_t/(PV_{cf} + cf)) \times (PV_{cf}/PV_{t-1}) - 1 \qquad (4.4)$$

Where:

R = portfolio return
PV_t = portfolio value at end of period
PV_{cf} = portfolio value immediately prior to cash flow

cf = cash flow
PV_{t-1}= portfolio value at start of period

An important aspect of performance evaluation is quantifying the risk of the portfolio. Optimization of the short-term asset allocation gave a forward-looking estimate of tracking error of 3.22%, which can now be compared with the observed tracking error. For each month, the benchmark return is subtracted from the portfolio return. These differences are then squared, and the squares totalled and divided by the number of returns to give the portfolio variance. The square root of the variance is the monthly tracking error, which, when multiplied by the square root of 12 gives the annual tracking error. Example 4.16 illustrates how this is done.

- The sum of squared variations is 0.1270%.
- 0.1270% divided by 12 observations is 0.0106%.
- The square root of 0.0106% is 1.03%. This is the monthly tracking error.
- The annualized tracking error is 1.03% times the square root of 12, which gives 3.56%.

The observed tracking error is thus slightly higher than the expected tracking error.

EXAMPLE 4.16 *Observed tracking error*

Date	Portfolio Value	Benchmark Value	Portfolio Return %	Benchmark Return %	Variation %	Variation Squared %
31 12 1998	100.00	100.00				
31 01 1999	101.87	101.59	1.87	1.59	0.28	0.0008
28 02 1999	98.93	99.37	−2.89	−2.19	−0.70	0.0049
31 03 1999	101.81	103.21	2.90	3.86	−0.96	0.0092
30 04 1999	105.85	106.12	3.98	2.82	1.15	0.0133
31 05 1999	101.82	103.12	−3.81	−2.83	−0.99	0.0097
30 06 1999	106.02	106.74	4.13	3.51	0.62	0.0038
31 07 1999	105.23	107.47	−0.75	0.68	−1.42	0.0203
31 08 1999	105.39	107.83	0.15	0.34	−0.18	0.0003
30 09 1999	104.13	107.77	−1.19	−0.05	−1.14	0.0130
31 10 1999	108.93	111.70	4.60	3.64	0.96	0.0092
30 11 1999	111.20	114.32	2.08	2.35	−0.27	0.0007
31 12 1999	118.19	119.17	6.29	4.24	2.05	0.0418
Total			18.19	19.17		0.1270

PITFALLS

The biggest danger is defining a long-term allocation that is not suitable to the requirements of the fund. This can be the result of having chosen inappropriate asset classes or from misjudging the long-term return and risk characteristics of the asset classes. If this happens, the chances are that the fund will have chronic funding problems, which may give rise to the temptation to take an unhealthy amount of risk to make up the shortfall. There is no way to ensure that this does not happen, but testing for robustness of long-term allocations can help. This involves changing each of the assumptions in turn to see what impact they have on the resulting portfolio allocation.

Short-term asset allocation is also very sensitive to asset class return forecasts, it is therefore a good idea to review constantly forecasts in light of what is actually happening. This means posing the question 'what is going right?', as well as the frequently asked one 'what went wrong?'

Many otherwise well-constructed portfolios suffer because the investor has misjudged the impact of currency volatility. It is essential to give as much attention to the effects of possible currency movements as to returns forecasts in traditional asset classes, either by actively managing currency risk or hedging it to base currency.

For asset allocation overlays, there is the risk that the derivatives being used by the overlay manager do not correspond to the assets held in the underlying asset classes. This represents a source of risk that needs to be quantified and managed.

CASE STUDY

Some of the issues surrounding asset allocation are illustrated by the approach taken by a large public pension fund. Taking advantage of the size of the fund, the managers sought to invest in a wide range of asset classes. These included:

	%	%
Domestic equities	25	
Passive		10.0
Active Industrials		5.5
Active Resources		3.0
Active Listed Property Funds		1.5
Active Direct Equity		5.0

	%	%
International Equities	15	
Passive		8.0
Active		4.0
Emerging Markets		3.0
Domestic Fixed Interest	15	
International Fixed Interest	10	
Money Markets	5	
Cash	5	
Commercial Property	10	
Rural Property	5	
Infrastructure	10	

The long-term strategic benchmark asset allocation was carried out by the fund's managers in collaboration with the fund's consulting actuaries, and incorporating the econometric analysis provided by the fund's own economists and their advisors. Short-term asset allocation was delegated to a specialist manager, with management of individual asset classes also delegated to specialist managers. Implementation of short-term decisions was the responsibility of the asset allocation manager, who sent instructions to individual asset class managers.

The fund managers were aware that, being a very large fund as well as the major pension fund for government employees, it was very visible. Major investment decisions were sometimes subject to public scrutiny.

The fund was thus obliged to invest heavily in domestic equities. This proved to be the source of some of its difficulties. The sheer size of the fund meant that a traditional, active investment portfolio would be very difficult to manage efficiently. Finding enough underpriced stocks to buy would be close to impossible because, to make a difference to the fund's performance, it would have to buy controlling interests in many of them. Otherwise the fund would be limited to holdings in the largest stocks, compromising its scope for diversification. The fund's managers adopted two tactics to cope with the difficulty of size in the domestic equity market.

1. Core–satellite. This effectively meant splitting up the domestic equity mandate into several mandates, each with a very specific objective. As the name implies, a large proportion is invested in a 'core' portfolio, which is an indexed fund, designed to track the domestic equity market by buying each stock in index proportions. The manager charged with managing the core is expected to deliver a low-risk, low-cost exposure to the equity market. The core was the largest component of the domestic equities portfolio.

2. Complementing the core were four 'satellite' portfolios, defined as industrial stocks, resource stocks, listed property and direct equity. The equity benchmark comprised 30% resource stocks, 55% industrials and 15% listed property. As these broad sectors had consistently low correlations with each other, it made sense to treat them as separate asset subclasses.

The benchmark for each mandate was a sub-index of the overall equity market, such that together they comprised the broader equity market against which the core manager and the overall domestic equities asset class was evaluated.

Six features of this structure bode well for its success:

1. The sums invested with individual satellite investment managers were small enough that the managers could invest in a wide range of individual securities, thereby increasing their opportunities for superior returns without taking very large stakes in small companies.
2. The managers were expected to be aggressive in deviating from their respective benchmarks. The fund could afford a high level of risk in the satellite portfolios because the core portfolio provided a buffer.
3. Because there was no overlap between the satellite mandates, the fund did not run the risk that individual portfolios would either compound each other or cancel each other out, resulting in an unintended indexed portfolio.
4. Splitting domestic equities into asset subclasses effectively adds more scope to add value by varying allocation to the various asset subclasses.
5. Splitting the domestic equity portfolio up reduced the fund's manager risk; the risk to the portfolio caused by an investment manager being unable to fulfil the requirements of his or her investment mandate.
6. By investing a significant proportion of domestic equities in an indexed portfolio, management fees are substantially reduced because indexed portfolios attract significantly lower management fees than do active portfolios.

After initial success of the core–satellite approach for domestic equities, the same approach was applied to international equities. Although size did not pose the same problem for this portfolio, the core–satellite approach conferred a number of benefits to this sector too, such as fee reduction, reduction of manager risk, creation of additional subsectors, enabling the choice of highly specialized investment managers as well as adding value by fine-tuning the allocation between international equities subclasses.

By investing in unlisted equity, the fund added another asset class, increasing materially the potential for very attractive investment returns. Normally a direct equity portfolio would be invested in a number of different enterprises. In this case, the fund took a large stake in a major tourist development. This created some serious problems for the fund because, being unlisted, and a substantial proportion of the fund (5%), changes in its valuation materially impacted the performance of the overall fund.

Although the early experience in direct equity was not altogether happy, it was recognized that the fund needed to depart from conventional investments if it were to achieve the returns required to meet its obligations. The fund therefore diversified into emerging market infrastructure projects, such as dams in China and highways in Indonesia. Being long-term in nature, with a predefined return range, such investments can be very effective at diversifying a large portfolio. One of the main benefits is that the fund gains exposure to potentially fast appreciating currencies. Of course, the danger in long-term projects of this nature is the exposure to sovereign risk, and currencies that can depreciate even faster than they appreciated. For example, the government in the target country may decide to arbitrarily and retrospectively limit the returns paid to foreign investors, as happened in China in the early 1990s, or it may impose a tax or limit on foreign exchange transfers, as happened in Malaysia in the late 1990s, or become the subject of a coup, as in Indonesia.

CHAPTER 5

Portfolio Protection

Before reading this chapter, readers not familiar with options theory and markets might take a quick look at Appendix 5, which is devoted to options.

APPLICATIONS

Managers of funds that cannot afford to lose money over a given period, or that need some known minimum return to regain an acceptable level of reserves, may consider some kind of portfolio protection or capital guarantee. The two are often thought of as different species, but they are really cousins. A capital guaranteed fund is a fund with a guaranteed minimum return of 0%.

Portfolio protection can be incorporated into the fund's asset allocation or applied as an overlay. Either way, most portfolio protection is a temporary measure and so is effected as part of the fund's short-term asset allocation.

All portfolio protection is in fact a type of insurance in that it transfers some of the risk of the portfolio to the provider of the insurance or protection. As with any other type of insurance, reduced risk is always associated with some cost, whether it is in the form of an initial payment or foregone future returns, and the cost of the insurance is not recouped if it turns out not to have been needed. In the same way, your house insurance premium was 'wasted' if your house did not burn down. The cost of insurance always depends on the value of the goods insured, how likely is the event insured against, such as fire, theft or negative returns, the period covered and the excess or deductible. In portfolio protection terms, these are the amount of the investment to be insured, the riskiness of the investment, the period of protection and the minimum return required.

Just as wooden houses are more expensive to insure against fire than brick houses, a volatile investment costs more to protect than a more stable one. In general, it is considerably cheaper to protect a diversified portfolio than an individual asset class or security because the former is nearly always less volatile.

Portfolio protection works by some application of option theory. An option is the right, but not the obligation, to buy or sell something at a given price on a given date. The right to buy something is called a **call option** and the right to sell something is called a **put option**.

In buying portfolio protection, the investor buys the right to cash compensation for portfolio losses resulting from adverse market outcomes.

Portfolio protection can comprise either a bought put option, which gives the investor the right to sell the investment at a given price, or a bought call option, giving the right to buy, thus protecting against price rises. The put option is used in conjunction with an existing portfolio, while the call option is in lieu of the portfolio.

The portfolio plus put arrangement in some ways resembles a tactical asset allocation overlay in that the physical portfolio remains invested as normal, with the put option effected as an overlay, concurrently providing the required insurance by means of a cash settlement equal to the difference between the portfolio's market value and the agreed minimum value, otherwise referred to as the exercise price. Above the contract minimum, the value of the put option is zero.

The call option replaces the physical portfolio. It is itself valueless below the specified portfolio value, while above that value the investor receives a sum equal to the difference between the portfolio's market value and the agreed minimum. Economically, there is no difference between the two arrangements, except that they incur different transaction costs and, in most jurisdictions, taxes.

Example 5.1 shows the outcome for both strategies under four different market scenarios. Scenario 1 is strong market appreciation, scenario 2 is a moderate market appreciation, scenario 3 is a stable market, and scenario 4 shows what happens if the market drops sharply. This example ignores transaction costs, so the hold physical and buy put strategy appears to cost slightly less than it would in practice because of the relatively high cost of transacting physical assets. Costs for options transactions are usually negligible.

For each scenario the difference between the two strategies is minimal. Both benefit from market appreciation but are protected against falls. The apparent difference results from the fact that the number of options purchased does not give a face value exactly the same as the starting portfolio, with the result that interest income and dividends do not exactly offset the price difference between

EXAMPLE 5.1 *Hold shares and buy put options versus sell portfolio and buy call options*

Market Data				
Length of Period in Days	153			
Initial Value of Equities Held	$100 000 000			
At Start				
Short-term Interest Rates	7.50%			
Dividend Yield	1.50%			
S&P500 Physical	1 328.7			
S&P500 Futures	1 362.1			
Point Value of Futures	$500			
Option Exercise Price	1 375.0			
Estimated Volatility	25%			
Call Option Price	79.55			
Put Option Price	92.41			
At End	Scenario 1	Scenario 2	Scenario 3	Scenario 4
Market Move	25%	5%	0%	−25%
S&P500 Physical	1 660.9	1 395.2	1 328.7	996.5
S&P500 Futures	1 660.9	1 395.2	1 328.7	996.5
Hold Physical and Buy Put Option				
Number of Put Options Purchased	151			
Face Value of Options	$100 318 360			
Option Premium Paid	$6 976 727			
Value of Equities Held	$125 000 000	$105 000 000	$100 000 000	$75 000 000
Value of Put Option	$0	$0	$3 494 140	$28 573 730
Cost of Option	$6 976 727	$6 976 727	$6 976 727	$6 976 727
Interest Income	$0	$0	$0	$0
Dividend Income	$628 767	$628 767	$628 767	$628 767
Value of Portfolio	$118 652 040	$98 652 040	$97 146 180	$97 225 770
Sell Physical and Buy Call Option				
Number of Call Options Purchased	151			
Face Value of Options	$100 318 360			
Option Premium Paid	$6 005 663			
Proceeds of Sale of Equities	$100 000 000	$100 000 000	$100 000 000	$100 000 000
Value of Call Option	$21 585 450	$1 521 778	$0	$0
Cost of Option	$6 005 663	$6 005 663	$6 005 663	$6 005 663
Interest Income	$3 143 836	$3 143 836	$3 143 836	$3 143 836
Dividend Income	$0	$0	$0	$0
Value of Portfolio	$118 723 623	$98 659 951	$97 138 173	$97 138 173

call options and put options. In both cases, the portfolio is very slightly under-protected, so the precise difference in the two outcomes is affected by whether the market goes up or down.

THEORY

Portfolio protection relies on option theory. The most common applications use some variant of Black–Scholes option pricing technology, which is described in some detail in Appendix 5. Portfolio protection can take the form of an option purchased on market or **over-the-counter**, or the investment manager can create it by means of a process known as option replication. Options replication is in fact a carefully defined mix of the risky assets to be protected and the risk-free asset, or cash. Creating and managing replicated options is usually carried out by investment managers specializing in this activity. The risky asset in this mix is structured to resemble as closely as possible the asset allocation of the protected portfolio. It can consist of physical assets, but in practice is usually made up of futures, which significantly reduces its cost and allows short sales, which are required to replicate bought put options. Using futures contracts in lieu of physical assets can introduce basis risk, the risk that the return to the portfolio of futures is different to that of the underlying portfolio, but basis risk is usually preferable to incurring the high costs of transactions of physical assets.

The proportion invested in risky assets in the **replicated option** is known as the **option's delta**. The option delta is also the change in value of the option corresponding to a small change in the value of the underlying portfolio. When the value of the underlying investment is the same as the value at which it is protected (the agreed minimum value of the portfolio), the option is said to be **at-the-money** and the option delta is about 0.5, so risky and riskless assets each make up 50% of the portfolio replicating the option. As the value of the option increases, so does the delta, until the replicating portfolio resembles the investment being protected. As the value of the option decreases, the delta does too, until the replicating portfolio comprises 100% cash. Replicating a bought call option requires that risky assets be bought, while replicating a bought put option means selling risky assets. In either case, the replicating portfolio is buying in a rising market and selling in a falling market.

Because the delta, and therefore the mix of risky and riskless assets in the replicating portfolio, changes constantly, it is often called a **dynamic hedge**.

The main difference between an option purchased on market or over-the-counter and a replicated one is that the cost of the purchased option is known at the outset, while the cost of the replicated option can be only estimated in advance. To protect a physical portfolio with replicating put options, the investment manager may choose to pay the protection provider a fixed fee at the start

EXAMPLE 5.2 *Cost of option versus equity participation*

Market Data				
Length of Period in Days		153		
Initial Value of Equities Held		$100 000 000		
At Start				
Short-term Interest Rates		7.50%		
Dividend Yield		1.50%		
S&P500 Physical		1 328.7		
S&P500 Futures		1 362.1		
Point Value of Futures		$500		
Estimated Volatility		25%		
At End	Scenario 1	Scenario 2	Scenario 3	Scenario 4
Market Move	25%	5%	0%	−25%
S&P500 Physical	1 660.9	1 395.2	1 328.7	996.5
S&P500 Futures	1 660.9	1 395.2	1 328.7	996.5
Structure 1				
Participation Rate	100%			
After Market Appreciation of	0%			
Exercise Price	1 350.0			
Number of Call Options Purchased	151			
Face Value of Options	$100 318 360			
Call Option Price	90.88			
Option Premium Paid	$6 861 077			
Cash Collateral Held	$100 000 000	$100 000 000	$100 000 000	$100 000 000
Value of Call Option	$23 472 950	$3 409 278	$0	$0
Cost of Option	$6 861 077	$6 861 077	$6 861 077	$6 861 077
Interest Income	$3 143 836	$3 143 836	$3 143 836	$3 143 836
Value of Portfolio	$119 755 709	$99 692 037	$96 282 759	$96 282 759
Structure 2				
Participation Rate	50%			
After Market Appreciation of	0%			
Exercise Price	1 350.0			
Number of Call Options Purchased	75			
Face Value of Options	$49 827 000			
Call Option Price	90.88			
Option Premium Paid	$3 407 820			
Cash Collateral Held	$100 000 000	$100 000 000	$100 000 000	$100 000 000
Value of Call Option	$11 658 750	$1 693 350	$0	$0
Cost of Option	$3 407 820	$3 407 820	$3 407 820	$3 407 820
Interest Income	$3 143 836	$3 143 836	$3 143 836	$3 143 836
Value of Portfolio	$111 394 766	$101 429 366	$99 736 016	$99 736 016

continued on next page

Structure 3				
Participation Rate	100%			
After Market Appreciation of	5%			
Exercise Price	1 425.0			
Number of Call Options Purchased	151			
Face Value of Options	$100 318 360			
Call Option Price	60.07			
Option Premium Paid	$4 535 267			
Cash Collateral Held	$100 000 000	$100 000 000	$100 000 000	$100 000 000
Value of Call Option	$17 810 450	$0	$0	$0
Cost of Option	$4 535 267	$4 535 267	$4 535 267	$4 535 267
Interest Income	$3 143 836	$3 143 836	$3 143 836	$3 143 836
Value of Portfolio	$116 419 019	$98 608 569	$98 608 569	$98 608 569

of the option period, in which case the manager bears the risk of the actual cost of replicating the option exceeding the amount paid for it. Otherwise the investor may choose to pay the ongoing cost of the replicated option. Paying the investment manager a fixed fee for protection has the advantage that the investor can ask a number of managers to quote prices for the protection, and choose the most attractive. Professional protection managers have a significant cost advantage over individual investors, because they can aggregate the hedge programs of different portfolios. This can significantly reduce both the cost and risk of replicating options, an advantage that is hard to overstate for a fund that is close to its minimum funding requirements.

One way of modifying the cost of portfolio protection is to choose an option **participation rate** of less than 100%. The participation rate is the percentage of the portfolio that is protected. Choosing a participation rate of less than 100% reduces the cost of protection simply by providing less protection, similar to buying half an insurance policy. The other way of reducing the cost of protection is to choose protection that cuts in at a higher value for a call, or a lower value for a put, effectively raising the threshold at which the option takes effect. For example, the investor might choose to forego the first 5% of any market rise, and to participate fully in appreciation above 5%, or alternatively, participating straightaway but receiving only half the returns delivered by the market.

Example 5.2 compares three portfolio protection structures under the same scenarios as in Example 5.1. The three protection structures are:

- a simple call option covering all the portfolio (the same as the bought call option in Example 5.1)

- the same call option covering only half the portfolio
- a call option with full participation that becomes effective only after a small rise in the market.

Example 5.2 shows that less than full market participation can be quite cost effective. The third structure is most effective if the market moves sharply up, as in scenario 1, which is almost the same as for full participation. The second structure can also save costs, and gives at least some participation for all positive market moves.

OPTION PRICING

The most commonly used method for pricing options is the **Black–Scholes** formula. To use Black–Scholes to calculate the price or **premium** of an option and to estimate the delta for the replicated option, the following information is required:

- The value of the underlying investment.
- The value at which the option takes effect, otherwise known as the **exercise price.**
- The time to expiry of the option or the **exercise date.**
- The risk-free interest rate.
- The **volatility**, or riskiness, of the underlying investment.

Increase in	*Call Price*	*Put Price*
Value of underlying investment	up	down
Exercise price	down	up
Time to expiry	up	up
Risk-free interest rate	up	up
Volatility of underlying investment	up	up

Option pricing technology makes a number of assumptions about asset returns, which, when violated, can change the cost of the option. The first of these is that both the interest rate and portfolio volatility will not change during the life of the option. Although these assumptions are frequently violated, most replicated options are robust enough to endure all but the most extreme departures from theory. More important are the assumptions of zero transactions costs and continuous asset price movements. Because most replicated options require frequent transactions, paying transactions costs can significantly add to the cost of protection. And because asset prices, and therefore portfolio values, sometimes change abruptly, rather than in the smooth series of infinitely small increments assumed by the theory, the actual cost of replicating an option can be much higher than the theoretical cost. Differences of 10% between closing prices and opening prices the following day are not uncommon in some markets. Such **gapping**, or **jump risk**, can cause the actual cost of the replicating strategy to significantly exceed the estimated cost. While theory requires that the investor adjust the replicating portfolio simultaneously with changes in value of the underlying, in reality the investor always lags behind the market, which usually means buying at a higher price and selling at a lower price than is predicted by the theory. This effect is demonstrated in the next example.

Example 5.3 shows that, starting from the point where the actual and the replicated option intersect, a change in the price of the underlying asset will always result in a higher price for the actual option than the replicated option. For example, starting with a futures price of 1362.1, both the actual and replicated options are valued at 90.88, with a delta of 0.55. A 10% increase in the futures causes the actual call option value to increase to 178.90, with a new delta of 0.77, while the value of the replicated option increases by 55% of the change in the futures price to 166.36 (90.88 + 0.55 × (1498.4 – 1362.1). A fall in the futures price has a similar effect, reducing the call option price to 34.26 and the value of the replicated option to 15.39. The more volatile and the more gaps in the value of the underlying investment, the more dramatic is this effect.

EXAMPLE 5.3 *Actual versus replicating options*

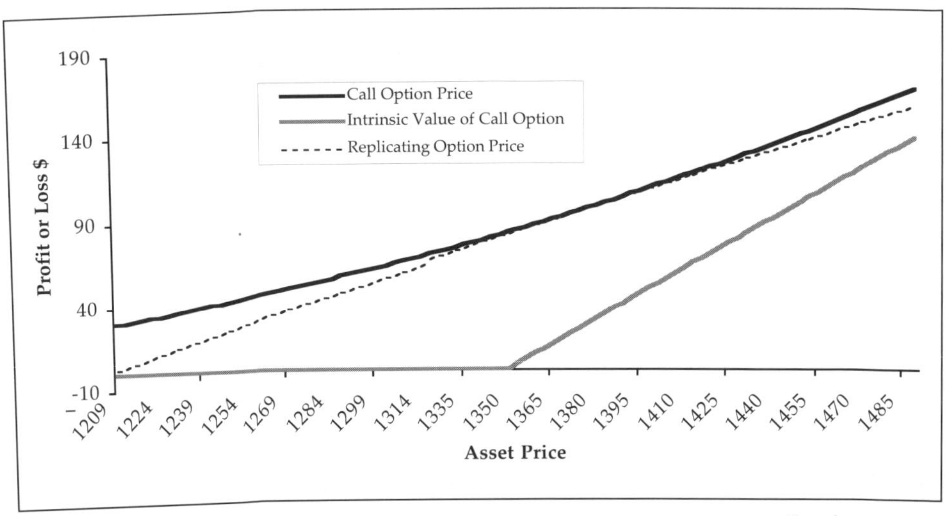

continued on next page

Market Data	At Start	After Market Move of 10%	After Market Move of −10%
Length of Period in Days	153	153	153
Initial Value of Equities Held	$100 000 000	$100 000 000	$100 000 000
Short-term Interest Rates	7.5%	7.5%	7.5%
Dividend Yield	1.5%	1.5%	1.5%
S&P500 Physical	1328.7	1461.6	1195.8
S&P500 Futures	1362.1	1498.4	1225.9
Point Value of Futures	$500	$500	$500
Option Exercise Price	1350.0	1350.0	1350.0
Estimated Volatility	25%	25%	25%
Call Option Price	90.88	178.90	34.26
Call Option Delta	0.55	0.77	0.30
Value of Replicating Option	90.88	166.36	15.39

In practice, replicated options always lag behind real ones, as the investment manager manually adjusts the delta of the replicating portfolio by placing buy and sell orders in the underlying investment. For small changes in the value of the underlying, the lag is barely noticeable but for large changes the replicating portfolio can suddenly be rendered significantly over- or underinvested in the underlying investment, with the result that the portfolio is temporarily under-protected and the necessary adjustment is carried out at a less attractive price, increasing the cost of protection.

An alternative option replicating technology is called Constant Proportions Portfolio Insurance, or **CPPI**, developed by Fisher Black, one of the authors of Black–Scholes. Its principal advantage over the more widely used Black–Scholes technology is that it can deal with large and frequent gapping. CPPI does not require a forward estimate of the volatility of the underlying portfolio, but protects against a single prespecified event, such as a reoccurrence of the market crash of 1987. It is conceptually simpler than Black–Scholes: the required proportions of risky and risk-free assets can be estimated on the back of an envelope.

CPPI works by always holding just enough risk-free assets to allow the portfolio to deliver an acceptable return (the **floor**) in a predefined, adverse market scenario, or 'crash'. Because the investor decides the nature of the crash, it can be tailored to provide exactly the protection required.

Example 5.4.1 shows that CPPI holds enough defensive assets to ensure that the interest income, at 7.5% over the 12-month period, will compensate for a fall of 25% in the value of the risky assets, delivering a minimum return of 0%.

EXAMPLE 5.4.1 *Constant proportions portfolio insurance (CPPI)*

Market Data	
Length of Period in Days	153
Length of Period in Years	0.42
Starting Value of the Portfolio	$100 000 000
Short-term Interest Rates	7.50%
Minimum Return Required	0.00%
Protect Against a Fall in the Value of Risky Assets of	25%

The allocation to risky assets, for a 12-month protection period would be calculated as:

$$RA = (1 + \min - i)/(1 - i - c) \tag{5.1}$$

Where:

RA = risky assets
min = minimum return required
i = the exponent of the interest rate
c = crash test

which in this case is:

$$\begin{aligned} RA &= (100\% + 0.00\% - e^{0.075})/(1 - e^{0.075} - 25\%) \\ &= 23.75\% \end{aligned}$$

Working backwards, after an immediate fall of 25% in the value of the risky asset, the portfolio's value is calculated as:

$$\begin{aligned} \text{Portfolio} &= \text{value of risky assets plus value of riskless assets} \\ &= \$1\,000\,000 \times (23.75\% \times (1 - 25\%) + (1 - 23.75\%) \times e^{0.075}) \\ &= \$1\,000\,000 \times (17.82\% + 82.18\%) \\ &= \$1\,000\,000 \end{aligned}$$

Example 5.4.2 shows the CPPI allocations for a 153-day protection period.

The protection manager reviews the portfolio constantly to ensure that it is achieving its objectives. If the market falls, the proportion of the portfolio held in risky assets decreases, as Example 5.4.3 shows.

EXAMPLE 5.4.2 *CPPI: asset allocation*

Structure of Portfolio	At Start $	Allocations %	Crash Test Allocation $	%
Risky Assets	11 327 947	11.33	8 495 960	8.50
Riskless Assets	88 672 053	88.67	91 504 040	91.50
Total	100 000 000	100	100 000 000	100

A 10% fall in the value of the risky asset over a three-month period shows that the allocation to risky assets has fallen from 21.18% to 19.22% of the portfolio. Meanwhile the defensive assets have earned interest, increasing their weight from 78.82% to 80.78%. The expected value of the portfolio at the end of the protection period is still above $100 000 000, as the combination of interest earned and expected makes up for the losses incurred by the risky asset.

One of the major shortcomings of CPPI is that it is **path dependent**. This means that the future value of the portfolio at any time depends on what has happened so far. If markets exhibit a sharp fall early on in the protection period, the portfolio divests a large proportion of its risky assets. If these then rise sharply, the portfolio's ability to participate in the price appreciation is reduced.

EXAMPLE 5.4.3 *CPPI: asset allocation adjustment*

Return to Risky Assets	−10%		
Time Elapsed	25% or 3 months of 12-month protection period		
	New Portfolio Values $	**New Portfolio Weighting %**	**New Crash Test $**
Risky Assets	12 460 742	12.24	9 345 557
Riskless Assets	89 371 725	87.76	91 504 040
New Portfolio Total	101 832 467	100.00	100 849 596
Interest Not Yet Earned	978 614		978 614
Total	102 811 080		101 828 210
Reset Minimum Return	**Reset Portfolio Values $**	**Reset Portfolio Weighting %**	**Reset Crash Test $**
Risky Assets	8 957 034	8.71	6 717 775
Riskless Assets	93 854 047	91.29	96 093 305
Reset Portfolio Total	102 811 080	100.00	102 811 080

On the other hand, if the risky asset increases its value early in the protection period, then the investor has the choice of maintaining the existing level of protection or effectively 'locking in' the gains by setting a new, higher floor. Staying with the same level of protection affords the portfolio a higher level of participation of further appreciation in the risky asset, with the possibility of losing all gains to date if the market subsequently falls. Resetting the floor means reducing the portfolio's exposure to the risky asset, so limiting its participation in further gains, but ensuring a higher minimum return for the portfolio.

BLACK–SCHOLES VERSUS CPPI

The first task of the investor is to decide how much and what type of portfolio protection to put in place. Whether to choose a Black–Scholes approach or some other kind depends largely on the type of markets the portfolio is exposed to. If the markets are subject to frequent gaps, especially those that happen overnight, then some kind of CPPI is indicated. If the markets have traded options, then Black–Scholes might provide a better solution.

The fund's sensitivity to low returns usually indicates what level of protection is required. For example, the fund may be unable to tolerate any negative returns at all. A small positive return would then be set as the minimum allowable, so that even after paying for protection, the overall return will be zero or better. If the fund can tolerate a small negative return (loss) then the minimum return can be set accordingly. The higher the minimum return required, of course, the costlier is the portfolio protection.

IMPLEMENTATION

Both Black–Scholes and CPPI can be implemented as a replicated call option, effectively replacing a physical portfolio, or as a put option overlay, in parallel with the physical portfolio. If comprising a replicated call option, protection can theoretically be effected using either physical assets or derivatives, although in practice it is nearly always done with futures to minimize transactions costs. On the other hand, using futures contracts exposes it to potential basis risk, in which respect, implementing portfolio protection overlays is similar to asset allocation overlays. The overlay manager needs to know some of the characteristics of the underlying portfolio so that he or she can adjust the derivatives positions to minimize basis risk.

The dynamic hedge is arguably the most important part of both Black–Scholes and CPPI. A successful dynamic hedge requires planning both the initial implementation and the details of ongoing management of the hedge. This means first of all deciding the precise mix of risky and riskless assets, and defining rules by which subsequent adjustments should be effected. Decision rules need to be clear and very well thought out. For example, should the hedge be adjusted daily, or twice daily, come what may? If so, the fund may be carrying out small, unnecessary transactions, while delaying more fundamental adjustments necessitated by intra-day market gyrations. On the other hand, the mere passing of time may require hedge adjustments even in static markets. Many dynamic hedge adjustments are triggered by market moves of a specified size, say 2 or 5%. This often works very well, provided the trigger point is well chosen. Too small a price interval may expose the hedge to too much trading, often in alternate directions, exaggerating the effect of market zigzags. If the trigger interval is set too large, the hedge will be in danger of lagging behind trends in the market, which can also be very expensive.

Both Black–Scholes and CPPI portfolio protection can be complemented by purchasing actual options, either exchange traded or over-the-counter. These can be expensive, but do reduce the risks associated with managing dynamic hedges, so many protection managers are constantly on the lookout for keenly priced options that can smooth or reduce the cost of the dynamic hedge. Being specialists in this activity, they are in a good position to spot such opportunities, and sometimes to command very competitive prices.

ONGOING MANAGEMENT

As with asset allocation overlays, portfolio protection requires adept use of futures and other derivatives, with close attention to currency positions and cash balances to ensure that there is always enough liquidity in the portfolio to meet all margin requirements.

An important requirement of managing portfolio protection is that the decision rules governing adjustments to the dynamic hedge be closely observed. In most programs this is stimulated primarily by shifts in the prices of assets in the underlying portfolio, but can happen simply with the passage of time. Rebalancing too often can subject the portfolio to very high transaction costs and the risk of **whipsawing**, the risk of always being behind a zigzagging market. This happens when a small price rise requires the manager to buy that asset class. He or she does so only to see the price drop again, requiring the same asset to be sold, probably at a lower price. Trading losses and transaction costs thus accumulate, escalating the cost of protection.

In response to this dilemma, some managers choose to exercise discretion in applying decision rules. This can work if the discretion is very limited, but can suffer from sometimes-imperfect judgement on the part of the protection manager. The real skill is to set the decision rules to suit the conditions of the asset class markets themselves.

The protection overlay manager, like the asset allocation overlay manager, must communicate regularly with the manager of physical assets to ensure that the protection program is always appropriate to the underlying portfolio. This includes being kept informed by the portfolio manager of the underlying portfolio of significant flows of funds to and from the portfolio and changes in the portfolio composition.

The task of keeping the protection program synchronized with the underlying portfolio is obviously simplified if the underlying portfolio allocation is the same as the fund's long-term asset allocation. If a short-term asset allocation overlay is also in place, the potential for communication failures between overlay and investment managers is greatly increased.

Sharp market appreciation may present the opportunity to reset the level of protection, giving the benefit of locking in market gains while still enabling the investor to enjoy further market growth, albeit at a slightly lower participation rate. Resetting the level of protection is achieved, for both Black–Scholes and CPPI, simply by recalculating the required mix of risky and risk-free assets using the higher protection threshold, and implementing the required net changes in the appropriate futures and options.

CURRENCY MANAGEMENT

As with asset allocation overlays, the protection overlay manger's job is to ensure that no unintended currency risk results from the portfolio protection programme. So for positions in foreign derivatives contracts, he or she must monitor the balances of initial and variation margins to ensure that the overall position is currency neutral. Foreign futures contracts can give a partially hedged currency position, because the initial margin is often held in local currency, while the rest of the initial face value of the position can remain in base currency. Unrealized futures profits and losses are in local currency.

Keeping precisely this balance means constant monitoring and frequent adjustment of foreign currency using currency forwards. It is usually a good idea to try and coincide the settlement date of currency forwards with the expected roll of foreign futures positions, since the fact of rolling the futures to the next expiry date often necessitates some foreign currency adjustments, as unrealized profits and losses become realized. If the investor requires a hedged return, then profits can be repatriated when they are realized, and the hedge closed out.

ADMINISTRATION

Portfolio protection shares almost identical administration issues with asset allocation overlays, but with significantly more transactions. Thus the protection manager must pay attention to the valuation and composition of the underlying portfolio and lumpiness of cash balances resulting from expiry of futures contracts.

VALUATION

As with the short-term asset allocation overlay, the value of the portfolio protection program is simply the sum of realized and unrealized gains and losses on derivatives positions.

If protection is implemented using an option on a basket of risky assets, as in Example 5.5.1, then the value of the protection is the estimated value of the option on the basket. The portfolio value is the value of the physical portfolio plus the value of the option. Examples 5.5.2 and 5.5.3 illustrate valuations of a replicated put option and CPPI.

EXAMPLE 5.5.1 *Valuation of bought put option*

Bought Put Option		%
Exercise Price	$100 000 000	
Exercise Date	31 07 2000	
Put Option Value	$290 507	0.29
Initial Cost of Put Option	$3 195 264	3.20
Cost of Protection	−$2 904 757	−2.90
Value of Protected Portfolio	$108 035 952	8.04
Value of Unprotected Portfolio	$110 940 709	10.94

EXAMPLE 5.5.2 *Valuation of replicated put option*

Initial Option Delta	−48.28%
Current Option Delta	−5.34%

Asset Class	Futures Contract Used	Current Portfolio Weight %	Unrealized Profit & Loss on Futures in Base Currency $	Realized Profit & Loss on Futures in Base Currency (est) $	Realized & Unrealized Profit & Loss on Futures in Base Currency $
US Fixed Interest	US Treasuries	−1.15	54 362	225 812	280 174
US Equities	S&P500	−1.86	−160 668	−589 115	−749 782
UK Equities	FTSE100	−0.53	−56 267	−239 752	−296 018
European Equities	Dax (Germany)	−0.60	−144 326	−745 311	−889 637
Japanese Equities	Nikkei 225	−0.94	−57 626	−202 522	−260 149
Cash					
Cost of Protection	−$1 915 412	−1.92			
Value of Protected Portfolio	$109 025 297	9.03			
Value of Unprotected Portfolio	$110 940 709	10.94			

Source: Thomson Financial Datastream, FTSE, IDC, Salomon Smith Barney

EXAMPLE 5.5.3 *Valuation of CPPI*

Minimum Return Required	0%
Protect Against a Fall in the Value of Risky Assets of	25%
Initial Exposure to Risky Assets	23.75%
Initial Exposure to Riskless Assets	76.25%
Sum of Risk plus Riskless Assets	100.00%

Asset Class	Futures Contract Used	Initial Portfolio Values in Base Currency $	Current Portfolio Values in Base Currency $
US Fixed Interest	US Treasuries	5 938 389	5 689 139
US Equities	S&P500	8 313 745	8 967 497
UK Equities	FTSE100	2 375 356	2 627 885
European Equities	Dax (Germany)	2 375 356	3 031 341
Japanese Equities	Nikkei 225	3 563 034	4 234 515
Cash		77 434 120	79 868 522
Total		100 000 000	104 418 898
Interest Not Yet Earned			9 485 755
Cost of Protection		−2 963 943	−2.96%
Value of Protected Portfolio		113 904 652	13.90%
Value of Unprotected Portfolio		110 940 709	10.94%

Source: Thomson Financial Datastream, FTSE, IDC, Salomon Smith Barney

PERFORMANCE MEASUREMENT AND ATTRIBUTION

Evaluating portfolio protection involves posing two questions, corresponding to design and implementation:

- How appropriate to the fund's objectives was the technique employed?
- Was the protection effective at the lowest cost possible?

The overall cost of protection is the difference between what the portfolio actually returned and the return to its long-term asset allocation. Ex post evaluation of the suitability of the program selected and whether it actually provided the required protection at the lowest possible cost can be quite tricky. For example, if the program comprises replicating options using Black–Scholes technology, the actual cost of the program can differ from the initial estimate, either because markets were more volatile than expected, there was basis risk between the futures used to apply the dynamic hedge and the assets in the underlying portfolio, or because the dynamic hedge-reset decision rule was inappropriate, or not applied with sufficient discipline. Often it is a combination of these, and separating out the different effects is an ungainly task, sometimes requiring analysis of individual trades.

CPPI suffers the same problems, plus that of path dependency, although this effect is relatively easy to tease out because the investor can easily see what the allocation to risky assets was at the start of a market uptrend.

PITFALLS

The biggest danger associated with portfolio protection is choosing the wrong model and protection level to protect the portfolio. This can result in the portfolio being over- or underprotected, or being protected against the wrong thing altogether. The only way to avoid this is to ensure that the minimum return is unambiguous and applies to the appropriate markets – usually all the asset classes in which the portfolio is invested. The investor also needs to be sure that the participation rate will allow the portfolio enough benefit from rising markets.

For protection programs comprising Black–Scholes dynamic hedges, the next biggest pitfall is underestimating the cost of protection. This is usually the result of underestimating the frequency and size of gaps in asset prices.

Dynamic hedges also suffer from misspecification of the hedge-reset criteria. This is related to the problem of underestimating volatility and gapping. Failure to follow the hedge-reset criteria can happen at any time, even when markets behave as forecast, and the criteria are appropriate. Such failure can be associated with lack of experience, or a badly constructed chain of command within the protection manager's portfolio management organization.

THE 1987 MARKET CRASH

Portfolio protection, or portfolio insurance, as it was then known, is thought by many people to have been a major, if not the main, cause of the stock market collapse of October 1987. Although convenient, this explanation is inaccurate and diverts attention from other, more valid, explanations of what happened. The co-villain of portfolio insurance is of course the market for derivative instruments and, in particular, share price index futures, such as S&P500 futures.

Knowing something about how portfolio insurance and share price index futures work can help to understand the role they played in 1987.

Observers often note that share price index futures tend to be more volatile than the underlying index of physical shares. From this it is sometimes concluded that the futures market contributes to volatility in the underlying market for physical shares. It is true that futures markets can be more volatile than the underlying physical market, but it does not follow that they cause stock market volatility. If anything, the opposite is the case. The volume of futures transacted each day is often several times the equivalent value transacted in the underlying physical market. There are a number of reasons for this:

- Futures contracts have much lower transaction costs than physical investments, so many investors, particularly short-term speculators, invest in futures instead of physical investments. Arguably this reduces the volatility of the underlying physical market.
- It is easy and cost efficient to sell futures contracts short. By contrast, selling shares you don't already own can be very expensive, and in many markets is illegal. At any time there are just as many open sold futures contracts as bought ones. The relative ease of speculating on a market downturn ensures that both bulls and bears have equal say and therefore apply equal force in the futures market, which is not the case in the physical. The effect of this is, if anything, to temper wild swings in the market.
- Futures markets are open for longer periods than physical markets. For several hours each day, futures markets are open while physical markets are closed. Investors needing to adjust a position in the physical are therefore often obliged to use futures as an interim measure. The futures market can therefore absorb market volatility that is not apparent in the physical market

simply because it is not open. Without the futures market, most of this extra volatility would happen in the physical market as soon as it reopened.

If it were the case that futures markets increased volatility in the underlying physical market, then one would expect that markets without futures contracts would be less volatile than markets with futures. This is not obviously the case.

One reason people 'blamed' portfolio insurance for the crash was because they find it disquieting that professional investors blindly follow instructions that are generated by computers. This is understandable until one considers that other investors follow, just as blindly, investment advice from, for example, astrologers, celebrities and technical advice based on apparent patterns described by previous asset price movements. The fact that the advice comes from a computer is less worrying than the fact that investors follow it blindly. Both astrology and technical advice can easily be programmed into a computer without changing their nature.

The role of computers in portfolio insurance is to generate the option delta, which determines the mix of risky and riskless assets that most closely replicates an actual option on a portfolio. The delta can be very sensitive to a change in the value of the underlying portfolio, so most market movements dictate a change in the mix of risky and riskless assets. For all bought options, an increase in the price of the risky asset requires that those assets be bought, so that a replicated bought call eventually holds 100% in the underlying risky asset. The same price increase requires a reduction in the sold position replicating the bought put, so that it would eventually hold 100% in cash.

Just as replicated bought options require purchases of risky assets in response to a rise in their price, a price fall stimulates sales. If enough investors are following a similar strategy, this can cause a further fall, stimulating further sales, and so on. To the extent that portfolio insurance was, at the time of the 1987 crash, very popular, it certainly contributed to the market's fall.

The trading pattern required by portfolio insurance is almost identical to that for **margin trading**. Margin trading is borrowing money to invest, whereby the investment itself secures the loan. If the value of the investment falls below the amount of the loan, the lender demands that the investor pay the difference. Should the investor fail to do so, the lender can sell the investment. So a fall in price stimulates a sale, which can cause a further fall in price, and so on. Since the volume of share purchases funded by margin loans on the eve of the crash far exceeded the volume of portfolio insurance outstanding, it follows that margin trading probably contributed far more to the severity of the downturn than portfolio insurance.

CASE STUDY

The classic application of portfolio protection is a medium-sized company pension fund. It is a defined benefit fund, and, due to a combination of lower than expected returns and a higher than expected number of payouts, its reserves are adequate but low. As with many such funds, its charter does not allow it to borrow.

A number of retirements with significant payouts are anticipated in the next five years or so, but the majority of the other members are relatively young. It is therefore necessary to structure the fund to participate in growth markets while protecting the capital for members about to retire. The trustees would like to avoid any negative returns until enough reserves are accumulated to provide a significant safety net. Portfolio protection is thus indicated. The question is how much and what type to choose.

The trustees listened to the advice of their consultant and decided that it was prudent to protect against negative returns. Setting the minimum return at zero meant that a small negative return might result, as the cost of protection must be deducted. The trustees estimated that their members would probably find this acceptable, since an investment environment that caused negative returns would cause all investment funds to do badly. So the fund could in fact tolerate a small negative return for one, perhaps even two, out of the five years, so long as the five-year result was positive.

An overlay was decided on, as the managers wanted to avoid the cost and disruption of liquidating the physical portfolio, which otherwise was delivering satisfactory results relative to its benchmark.

Choosing the type of protection was not quite so simple. The trustees had listened to the arguments by various protection overlay managers extolling the virtues of Black–Scholes, CPPI and complex options that could give a customized outcome over the five-year period. While they offered some advantages, the trustees decided against customized, complex options because of their cost, and the difficulty of explaining their advantages to the fund's members.

So it came down to Black–Scholes replication or CPPI. Approximately 50% of the portfolio to be protected was invested in domestic equities or in international assets. The domestic equity market is famous for its overnight gaps, in which a 10% discrete price jump is not uncommon. The currency is similarly affected, despite being quite heavily traded.

Such high occurrences of gapping indicated CPPI. The initial protection period was set at one year, with a review at the end of that time. The function of the review was to determine, in light of the overall returns of the 12-month period and the consequent level of reserves, whether a further protection period was required.

Having decided on a CPPI program to give a minimum return for one year of 0% by means of an overlay program, the next decision was to estimate what kind of financial markets disaster needed to be protected against. The understanding of course was that the more severe the disaster, the more expensive would be the final cost of protection. On the other hand, insufficient protection could subject the fund to negative returns if a major financial collapse occurred. Like many people, the fund's managers considered that a 1987-style collapse was a reasonable proxy for a worst-case outcome, and that they could be forgiven for not foreseeing anything worse. Thus the plan was to protect against a fall of 25% in all asset classes.

The expected cost of the protection program also favoured CPPI. The CPPI manager expected the protection to cost about 2% of the face value protected, while Black–Scholes was estimated to cost about 3.5%. It was recognized that neither protection technology could say for sure in advance what the cost of protection would be, consequently some extra negative return was indeed possible, although this would most likely be very small.

With either protection program, it was definitely better value to protect the portfolio overall than to protect its individual asset classes. This was due to the effects of diversification. A well-diversified portfolio is always less volatile than single asset classes. In this case the risk of the portfolio, as measured by its recent return volatility, was 8.60%, compared with the weighted average volatility of the component asset classes, of 11.85%. The cost of protection is commensurately lower, 2.16% versus 2.97%. Example 5.6 illustrates this effect.

As the fund was required to hold most of its worth in the assets comprising its long-term allocation, any protection program had to be implemented by means of an overlay program.

The fund's managers were also impressed by the fact that CPPI technology made it easy to explain how the protection would work, so that the nature and extent of the protection was clear even to the most sceptical of its members.

The CPPI manager had considerable experience managing both Black–Scholes and CPPI, and had found that, in general, a daily review of the dynamic hedge was sufficient most of the time. In addition, intra-day changes in the portfolio's valuation of 1% should trigger an adjustment of the hedge. In very volatile markets, reviews were carried out twice daily, and in extreme market conditions monitoring was continuous. In practice this meant that the portfolio would be subject to regular reviews in the same way as existing programs under management by them, so the process for ongoing monitoring was well established and reliable.

Example 5.7.1 compares various protection methods. The trustees were proved right in their choice of CPPI, as this combination easily outperformed the other alternatives available to them. Interestingly, the markets in which the portfolio was invested turned out to be much less volatile than expected, so a

EXAMPLE 5.6 *An option on a basket of assets versus a basket of options*

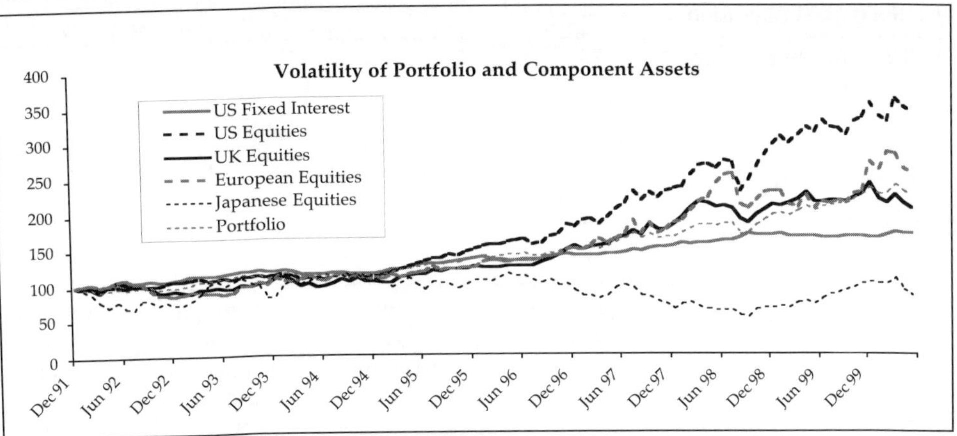

Source: Thomson Financial Datastream, IDC, JP Morgan, Salomon Smith Barney, FTSE

Portfolio Value	$100 000 000
Length of Option in Days	153
Exercise Price of Option	$100 000 000

Asset Class	**Benchmark**	**Strategic Benchmark Weighting %**	**Estimated Asset Volatility %**	**Option Price $**
US Fixed Interest	US Treasuries	25	4.16	260 589
US Equities	S&P500	35	12.84	1 125 560
UK Equities	FTSE AllShare	10	13.40	335 646
European Equities	Euro STOXX	10	14.86	372 175
Japanese Equities	TOPIX	15	23.30	874 966
Cash	JPM 1 month MM	5	0.32	
Total			11.85	2 968 936
Portfolio			8.60	2 155 357

replicating put option would have given a better result than an ordinary put option with the same exercise price and date.

Example 5.7.1 also shows that the unprotected portfolio did better than either the put or the replicating put strategies, because the volatility of the underlying portfolio, at 3.51%, was much less than the expected volatility of 8.60%. Had they declined in value by more than the expected cost of protection (3.19%) then

EXAMPLE 5.7.1 *Comparison of protection methods*

Portfolio Asset Allocation	%
US Fixed Interest	25
US Equities	35
UK Equities	10
European Equities	10
Japanese Equities	15
Cash	5

	Unprotected Portfolio	Portfolio Plus Put Option	Portfolio Plus Replicated Put Option	Portfolio Plus CPPI
Start Date	01 Jun 99	01 Jun 99	01 Jun 99	01 Jun 99
End Date	01 Jun 00	01 Jun 00	01 Jun 00	01 Jun 00
Interest Rate	7.50%	7.50%	7.50%	7.50%
Expected Portfolio Volatility	8.60%	8.60%	8.60%	8.60%
Actual Portfolio Volatility	3.51%	3.51%	3.51%	3.51%
Crash Test	n.a	n.a	n.a	−25.00%
Portfolio Start Value	$100 000 000	$100 000 000	$100 000 000	$100 000 000
Minimum Return Required	n.a	0.00%	0.00%	0.00%
Expected Cost of Protection	n.a	$3 186 691	$3 186 691	$3 186 691
Actual Cost of Protection	n.a	$3 186 691	$327 269	$0
Portfolio End Value	$98 974 250	$96 813 309	$99 672 731	$104 040 358
Return 12 Months to June 20	−1.03%	−3.19%	−0.33%	4.04%

any kind of protection would have worthwhile. Example 5.7.2 illustrates the comparison between the unprotected portfolio and three protection methods.

The unprotected portfolio is significantly more volatile than any of the protected portfolios, so if the trustees at any time were wondering if protection was a waste of money, they only needed to consider how they would have thought in October 1999. More interestingly, the graph shows clearly that from October 1999 to March 2000, both the replicated put option and the unprotected portfolio gave better results than did CPPI. This is because of the low participation rate given by CPPI.

EXAMPLE 5.7.2 *Comparison between unprotected portfolio and three protection methods*

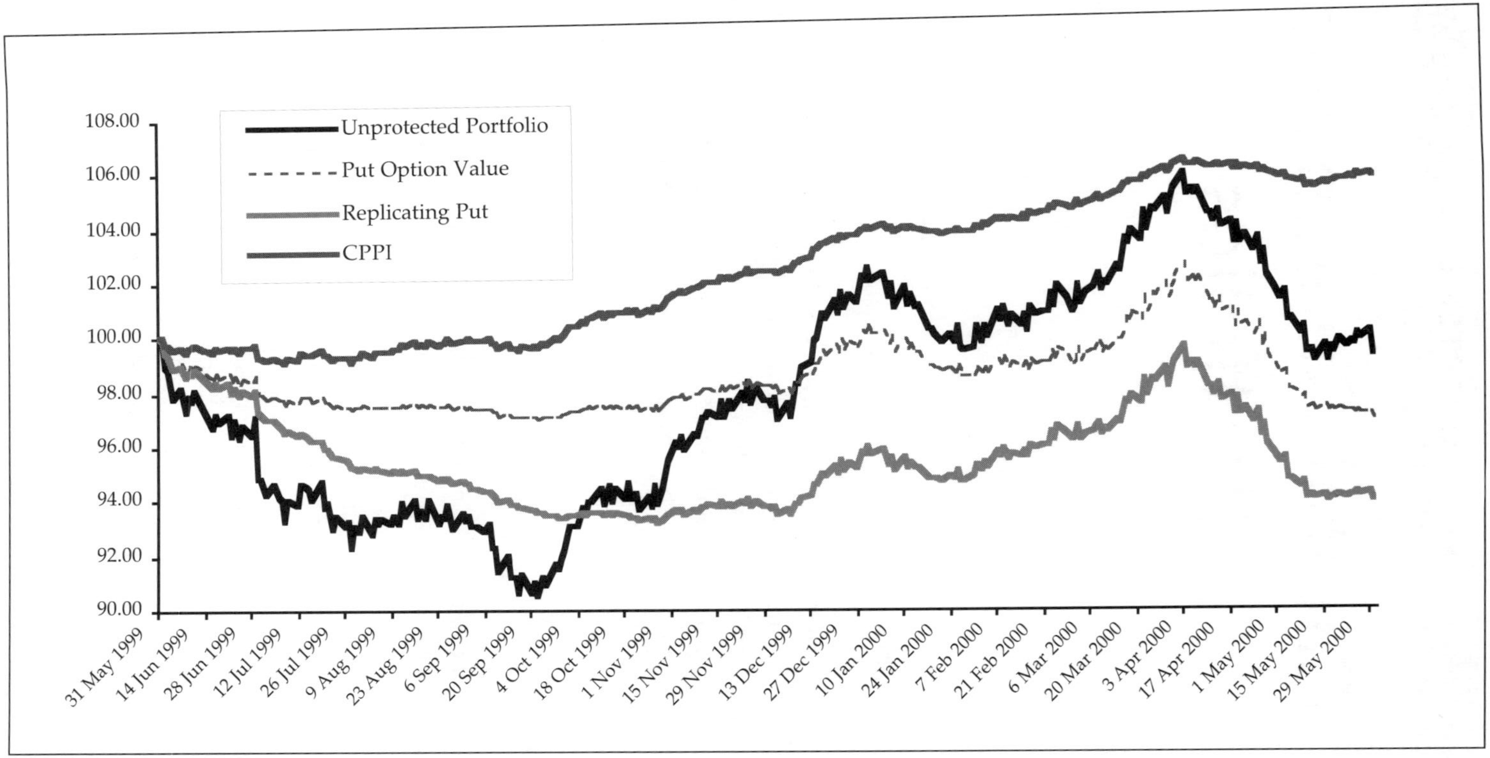

CHAPTER 6

Capital Guaranteed Portfolios

APPLICATIONS

Capital guaranteed portfolios can cover a wide variety of investment products. They are often, but not always, marketed to individual investors who want to preserve the nominal value of their investments while enjoying the returns to growth, or risky, assets. But the same investments can easily be applied to larger portfolios, or wherever there is the need to preserve capital.

THEORY

In principle, a capital guaranteed portfolio is simply a protected portfolio with a minimum return of zero, with the difference that the institution offering the capital guarantee undertakes to compensate the investor should the underlying investment return be negative. The institution thus puts its own capital at risk. It may then purchase some kind of portfolio protection to protect its own capital, or it may decide that the risk is worth running, in which case it will normally set capital aside as a reserve against the possibility of the investments losing money. Indeed, in many jurisdictions it is required to do so.

Much of this is invisible to the investor, who sees only the contract guaranteeing the return of the original investment plus some interest or dividend payments linked to a market, or a basket of risky markets such as equities and bonds.

EXAMPLE 6.1 *The cost and price of a guarantee*

	Investment Grade Institution %	Non-investment Grade Institution %
Expected Annual Investment Return without Capital Guarantee	15.00	15.00
Cost of Guarantee per Annum	3.00	3.00
Value of Guarantee per Annum	4.50	3.50
Expected Annual Investment Return with Capital Guarantee	10.50	11.50
Margin to Institution per Annum	1.50	0.50

One important difference between capital guarantees and portfolio protection concerns when the minimum return is guaranteed. The latter may simply ensure that the redemption value of the investment at maturity is at least as great as the sum invested, while the former can provide continuous guarantee for a set investment horizon. In other words, the investor receives at least his or her original capital plus any investment returns, even in the case of early redemption of capital.

The investor accepts that the returns to a guaranteed investment will be less, most of the time, than an investment fund without a guarantee, with the return differential constituting the price of the guarantee.

One of the things determining the price of a capital guarantee is its reliability. A bank with a very high credit rating is unlikely to default on such a guarantee, while an institution with a lesser credit rating may not have the ability to be so reassuring, and so will be unable to command as high a fee for the guarantee.

Other things being equal, the institution with a superior investment rating has a competitive advantage in offering such products because it can command a higher price for its guarantee while paying the same market prices as its competitors to offset the risk. This is illustrated in Example 6.1.

In either case, the institution providing the investment will make its own estimation about how it will protect its own capital against the event that markets do not deliver the desired results. It will decide whether it is more cost efficient to buy protection in the marketplace, to apply some kind of option replication strategy, or risk capital. Either way, the investor needs to judge whether the price charged for the guarantee is a good reflection of the value of the guarantee or whether the institution is likely to fail to honour that guarantee.

The return delivered by a capital guaranteed fund is in general less than the return to a similar fund without the guarantee, the difference reflecting the 'cost' of the guarantee. If the return appears higher than this, then the institution may be taking on an unsafe amount of investment risk, thereby possibly compromising its own ability to underwrite the guarantee.

IMPLEMENTATION

If the institution has decided to guarantee the portfolio value using some kind of portfolio protection, it can implement this by obtaining competing quotes for protection from several different protection providers, and choosing the most attractive proposal, exactly as for portfolio protection.

If it decides to use its own capital to guarantee all or part of the investment, then it must decide how much capital to set aside as reserves, invested in low-risk, short-term investments.

How much to set aside depends on the riskiness of the investment portfolio to be guaranteed, the investment horizon, the interest rate and whether the guarantee applies throughout the life of the investment or only at the end.

The institution may well choose some kind of option technology to estimate what sum constitutes an appropriate reserve. This makes sense, given that the capital guarantee has many features of an option.

The calculation for the capital reserve requirement, shown in Example 6.2, is based on the same principle that applies to either Black–Scholes or CPPI:

$$CR = 1 - (1 + \min - i)/(1 - i + c) \tag{6.1}$$

Where:

CR = risky assets
min = minimum return required
i = the exponent of the interest rate
c = estimated worst case

which in this case is:

$$\begin{aligned} CR &= 100\% - (100\% + 0.00\% - e^{0.075})/(1 - e^{0.075} - 10\%) \\ &= 56.22\% \end{aligned}$$

EXAMPLE 6.2 *Estimated capital requirement for various asset allocations*

	100% Bonds	50% Bonds, 50% Equities	100% Equities
Maturity in Years	1.00	1.00	1.00
Current Interest Rate	7.50%	7.50%	7.50%
Minimum Return Required	0.00%	0.00%	0.00%
Estimated Volatility	8.00%	12.00%	18.00%
Estimated Worst Case	–10.00%	–15.00%	–25.00%
Estimated Capital Reserve Requirement	56.22%	65.82%	76.25%

If the fund provides the capital guarantee for early redemption as well as at the maturity of the investment, then the appropriate level of reserves or capital required is higher to cover the early redemption contingency. Most option price calculations assume that early redemption will never happen so do not accommodate this event. Actuarial estimations are often used to project early redemptions, but these can have at most limited accuracy because early redemptions of a capital guaranteed investment are more likely in extreme circumstances, such as acute liquidity shortages, very adverse market conditions, or where the quality of the capital guarantee is under question.

If the capital guarantee is to be underwritten with a replicated option or some other dynamic hedge, it is necessary to establish the appropriate decision rules for maintaining the hedge, including when the hedge is to be renewed. The issues applying to these decision rules are the same as those for portfolio protection.

CURRENCY MANAGEMENT

As most capital guarantees are expressed in the base currency of the investor, currency management is not generally a major issue, except in so far as foreign assets are held in the underlying investment portfolio. If so, this risk may be dealt with specifically by setting in place a currency hedge, usually taking the form of foreign currency sold forward. Alternatively, currency risk may be incorporated into the overall risk of the fund, and offset by either purchased options, replicating options or allocation of additional capital.

ONGOING MANAGEMENT

The level of ongoing management required for a capital guaranteed fund depends on how the guarantee is to be effected. The simplest case is where the guarantee is matched by options purchased in the marketplace. In this case, the only requirement is to carry out regular valuations of both the option and the portfolio to ensure that the option is indeed performing its intended function. If early redemption is guaranteed, then its likelihood must be re-estimated from time to time to ensure that contingent reserves remain adequate.

Where a replicating option portfolio offsets the guarantee, the dynamic hedge needs to be monitored and adjusted by applying the decision rules established prior to implementation.

If capital has been set aside, it is necessary to monitor the risk of the underlying investment to ensure that the capital allocation for the guarantee is still enough to underwrite the guarantee, as illustrated in Example 6.3.

Reserves are initially about 71% of the value of the portfolio, with the remainder invested in equities and bonds. The figure of 71% is calculated by applying the CPPI formula with a worst-case assumption of a simultaneous fall in the value of equities and bonds of 15% and a 5% chance of early redemption. Both disappointing and favourable outcomes after three months are shown. The first is a fall in equities and bonds of 25% and 10% respectively. The value of the overall portfolio, taking into account interest yet to be earned on reserves, is still above its initial value but the percentage held in reserves is higher, reflecting both the fall in value of equities and bonds and the higher reserve requirement due to the shorter investment horizon – with less interest income to offset further falls in equity and bond values.

The combination of adverse market conditions and an early redemption can have a serious impact on the fund. The fall in the market value of the fund reduces the amount held in risky assets from 29.20% to 25%. A redemption at this point would reduce the overall value of the fund, because it would reduce the capital base from which to recover the initial value of the remaining investors' units. The effective return required to achieve this would be commensurately increased.

Those who redeemed their investment would have retained the nominal value of their investment while foregoing the possibility of greater returns in the future. On the other hand, investors who stayed invested now need to live with a more conservative asset allocation adopted by the investment manager to ensure preservation of the nominal value of their investment.

EXAMPLE 6.3 *Portfolio liquidation values*

Initial Portfolio Value	$100 000 000
Maturity in Years	1.00
Minimum Return per Annum	0.00%
Portfolio Mix (% Equities)	50.00%
Interest Rate	7.50%
Estimated Volatility	12.00%
Estimated Worst Case	−15.00%
Likelihood of Early Redemption	5.00%
Initial Reserves (Liquid Assets)	$70 822 918
Equities	$14 588 541
Bonds	$14 588 541
Total	$100 000 000

	Liquidation Value 1 Disappointing Market Returns	Liquidation Value 2 Favourable Market Returns
Time Elapsed in Years	0.25	0.25
Time Remaining in Years	0.75	0.75
Return to Equities	−25.00%	25.00%
Return to Bonds	−10.00%	10.00%
Value of Reserves	$72 163 376	$72 163 376
Equities	$10 941 405	$18 235 676
Bonds	$13 129 686	$16 047 395
Total	$96 234 467	$106 446 447
Interest Accruable on Reserves	$4 175 526	$4 175 526
Total with Unearned Interest	$100 409 994	$110 621 972
Effective Minimum Return Required	3.91%	0.00%
Reserves Required	$87 778 869	$82 137 508
As a Percentage of Portfolio Value	87.42%	74.25%

ADMINISTRATION

Capital guaranteed portfolios require impressive administrative resources, since, in addition to the administrative issues of protected portfolios, they must incorporate the functions required for unitized (pooled or comingled) funds that are offered to individual investors. Otherwise, administration for capital guaranteed portfolios is as for any other multi-asset class portfolio.

VALUATION

As with protected portfolios, the valuation of a capital guaranteed portfolio is simply the sum of the market value of all component assets, including physical assets, profits and losses on derivatives and interest earned and accrued on reserves.

PERFORMANCE MEASUREMENT AND ATTRIBUTION

Similarly, performance is measured in the same way as for any other portfolio. That is, it is the current portfolio valuation divided by the starting valuation minus one. If there has been a capital call, this is treated as a new deposit to the fund, using the principle of time-weighted cash flow. Early redemption is treated as any flow of capital out of the fund.

Attribution analysis can be carried out as for an ordinary portfolio to ensure that the underlying investment is delivering the best balance of risk and return.

PITFALLS

In addition to the standard pitfalls of portfolio management, the capital guaranteed portfolio is acutely susceptible to liquidity management issues. These can result from an unforeseen volume of early redemptions, or they can be caused by unusually adverse investment conditions, including a sharp fall in the interest paid on cash.

If the capital guarantee is offset by purchased options, then this risk is largely neutralized, although there remains the very small risk that the seller of the options may default. This risk is identical to the credit risk embedded in the capital guaranteed fund. In the unlikely event that this does happen, then the institution issuing the capital guarantee bears the cost. If that institution also fails to deliver on its guarantee, then the cost is borne by the investor. This is an extreme scenario, but is by no means impossible, especially in conditions of extreme market stress.

CASE STUDY

The market conditions favourable to offering capital guaranteed funds are often not the same as those giving rise to demand for such funds, and vice versa. Investors seek the reassurance of a capital guarantee in times of market volatility. These are the very conditions that make capital guarantees difficult to offer at attractive rates.

In the late 1980s such conditions prevailed in many markets. Following a long period of expansion, returns to equities were volatile, with the long uptrend having given way to general uncertainty. Interest rates were high, and a negative yield curve prevailed, meaning that short-term interest rates were higher than long-term interest rates. Most economists agree that negative yield curves are generally unlikely to last for very long, but in this case they would have been proved wrong: the curve had been negative for more than five years, and many people were beginning to believe that this had become the normal state of affairs.

A lively local options market encouraged some innovative upstart investment managers to offer funds with guaranteed minimum returns. Most of these funds were constructed on the safest of grounds, that is, they invested the portfolio in long-term, low-risk assets, and used part of the (relatively safe) interest income to buy options on equity instruments. They were therefore able to guarantee that the fund would always earn the long-term interest rate less the cost of the option plus appreciation in the local equity market. At the time, the minimum return turned out to be in the order of 7–8% per annum (10–11% annual interest income less 3% per annum for the equity options).

The success of these funds sparked competition and, unsurprisingly, some of this came from one of the traditional investing institutions, which saw that they were in danger of losing some of their market share. They responded by offering capital guaranteed equity products of their own. To ensure that theirs would be more attractive to investors, they offered higher minimum returns.

Although aware that this strategy could prove very risky, the risk was considered worth taking because, following one of the longest periods of stock market appreciation in living memory, they held reserves against their traditional investment products of unprecedented dimensions. It was intended to use these reserves to make up any shortfall in returns between what they had promised their investors by way of capital guarantees and what was actually achievable in the market. So no offsetting options or other risk control measures were thought necessary, and none were implemented. Because equity markets had delivered star-spangled performance of late, it was decided to invest heavily in the domestic equity market. About 70% of the fund was thus allocated, with the rest invested mostly in short-term bonds.

It was estimated that a call on the institution's capital was unlikely, as this would only happen if both interest rates rose and the equity markets failed to deliver attractive returns.

The fund was, unsurprisingly, a hit. The combination of attractive, guaranteed minimum returns, the promise of positive equite returns and the reassurance of a long-established and well-respected investment manager was irresistible to many investors.

So it was on a grand scale that things went wrong when they did. Launched early in 1990 with approximately 70% invested in equities and no strategy to underwrite the capital guarantee, Example 6.4 tells the story.

EXAMPLE 6.4 *Market conditions 1988–90*

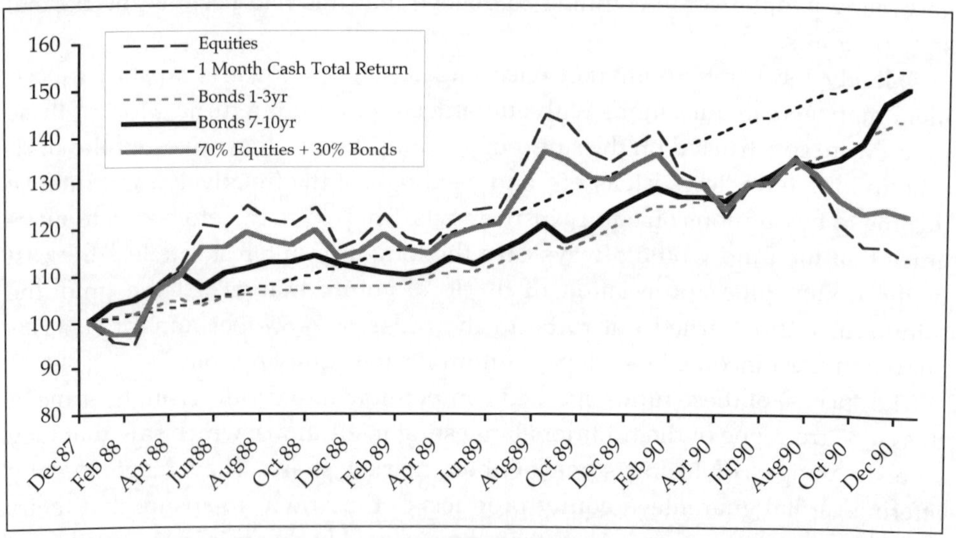

	1986–87		1988–89		1990	
	Annual Return %	Volatility %	Annual Return %	Volatility %	Annual Return %	Volatility %
Equities	18.43	126.39	17.64	59.40	−17.52	38.93
1 Month Cash Total Return	16.88	37.05	15.68	47.23	16.24	29.14
Bonds 1–3yr	17.59	35.14	10.80	30.03	18.00	34.83
Bonds 7–10yr	19.68	36.39	12.44	27.08	19.30	38.57
70% Equities + 30% Bonds	18.18	96.06	15.65	48.81	−7.83	20.55

Source: Thomson Financial Datastream, Salomon Smith Barney, JP Morgan

The returns delivered by the markets in the ensuing few years were not extraordinary. Following very encouraging returns in 1988 and 1989, equity markets, although volatile in 1990, eventually delivered very disappointing results thus denying that source of return At the same time, bond yields fell, giving a positive return to the part of the portfolio held in bonds, but reducing interest earned on reserves and increasing **reinvestment risk**. Long bond yields fell more rapidly than did yields on short bonds, so the fund's strategy of investing mostly in short-term bonds failed to capture the full benefit of holding bonds.

Having guaranteed returns close to 10% per annum, the investment return of –7.8% left a shortfall of about 17%. Given the success of the fund in terms of funds under management, the value of the shortfall was a significant sum, even in the context of a large and well-established institution.

The institution survived, but not before there was open talk of government intervention and an orchestrated purchase by another large financial institution.

CHAPTER 7

Passive Asset Allocation

What if the resources are not available to implement and monitor an effective short-term asset allocation program? One solution is to simply leave the portfolio weightings at the long-term allocation. This is effectively a passive approach to asset allocation.

APPLICATIONS

Passive asset allocation can be used in conjunction with active or passive management of individual asset class portfolios, or a combination of these. It can be implemented as part of a balanced mandate, or as a specialist mandate, with individual asset classes managed separately by specialist sector managers.

There are two main reasons for choosing passive asset allocation. One is to save money. Passive asset allocation, like other forms of passive investing, attracts lower management fees because it does not rely on expensive economic or security research. This can reduce the annual management fee burden by as much as 20 or 30 basis points (0.20–0.30%). In addition, the passive approach saves money by reducing transaction costs. A typical diversified fund will trade up to 30% of its value each year just implementing changes to short-term asset allocation. If all this trading is carried out using physical assets – and for a large part of most portfolios there is not much choice – then this turnover can cost the fund up to 1% of its value each year.

The other main reason for choosing passive asset allocation is that the investor believes either that extra returns cannot be achieved from actively managing asset allocation, or that, even though investment managers are skilled at forecasting asset class returns, they are unlikely to add sufficient value to cover the additional management fees and transaction costs required to implement active short-term asset allocation.

Cost is the reason often given by small pension funds for choosing passive asset allocation. Investment management fees are normally quoted as a percentage of the value of the investment, but the investment management company does not take its eye off the dollar value of the fee, as the cost to the investment manager is similar, regardless of the size of the fund. A fund of ten billion dollars may be quoted an annual management fee of 0.03% while the same investment strategy for a 50 million dollar fund attracts a fee of 0.60%. By opting for passive management the large fund shaves its fee to, say, 0.02% per annum, while the small fund reduces it to perhaps 0.30%, a much more meaningful reduction, especially when it comes to preparing the annual report to members.

Small to medium pension funds often find that passive asset allocation can reduce manager risk too. Because small funds are more likely to hire a small number of managers with balanced mandates (rather than a larger number of specialist managers), they are more prone to manager risk. Passive asset allocation removes one of the main sources of manager risk: that of poor short-term asset allocation decisions.

Since, for small funds, individual mandates can be very expensive, the strategy is ideal, allowing them to maintain their own mandate, rather than buying units in a large pooled investment vehicle.

THEORY

The theory of passive asset allocation derives from the theory of efficient markets. Passive asset allocation relies on the assumption that there is little value to be gained, after costs, from trying to outperform the fund's long-term asset allocation by forecasting short-term returns to asset classes. Even if it were feasible to regularly predict returns, the cost in terms of economic and sector research of deriving the forecasts, coupled with the transaction costs of implementing short-term asset allocation, outweigh any possible economic benefits.

Alternatively, the investor may take the view that some markets are more efficient than others, choosing passive asset allocation combined with passive asset class management for asset classes where active returns are hard to achieve, for example because of very high transaction costs; and active asset class management for asset classes in which investment managers have enough skill to warrant the additional cost. For example, the investor can combine active management of domestic equities with passive for international equities, if the investor takes the view that there is less scope for 'beating the market' where one is less familiar or where a competitive advantage cannot be demonstrated.

IMPLEMENTATION

Most funds with passive asset allocation hold most of their portfolios in physical assets, either as part of a balanced mandate or with specialist asset class managers.

If a balanced mandate, the investment manager implements the required asset allocation and instructs individual asset class managers to invest actively or passively according to mandate specifications. The other approach, separating asset allocation and asset class management, requires defining a specialist asset allocation mandate to calculate and monitor actual asset allocation. For the specialist mandate, the investment manager determines the amount for each asset class and advises the custodian and each asset class manager of the sum to be invested. The custodian effects the required transfers to implement individual asset class investments.

It is important to establish the rules for rebalancing the portfolio, specifying either the time intervals at which the asset allocation should be reset to benchmark, the maximum allowable deviation between actual and benchmark allocation, or some combination of the two.

If asset classes are allocated strictly according to benchmark, then the expected tracking error due to asset allocation is theoretically zero. If the mandate allows some variation from benchmark allocation, some estimate of expected tracking error is required. Overall actual portfolio tracking error must include this with any tracking error resulting from return variations within asset class portfolios, taking into account covariances between asset classes.

CURRENCY MANAGEMENT

The issue to decide is how much exposure to foreign currency is desirable, with three approaches possible:

- Passive foreign currency exposure, or currency neutrality, where the amount held in each currency exactly matches the value of the assets held in that currency.

- Zero exposure to foreign currency, where all foreign currency held for purchase of foreign assets is hedged to base currency by selling forward the same amount of foreign currency.
- Manage foreign currencies as a separate asset class.

Most passive asset allocation strategies adopt either currency neutrality or hedging to base currency. Active currency management is not incompatible with passive asset allocation, but would normally be undertaken as a separate, specialist mandate.

USE OF DERIVATIVES

Actual asset allocation fluctuates over time as each asset class delivers different rates of return. Futures and forward contracts are used routinely to facilitate periodical rebalancing, to manage cash flows and for managing foreign currency exposure.

Another approach is to use futures to invest the whole portfolio, with the physical assets of the fund held entirely in cash. This strategy can be applied to active as well as passive allocation, of course, although asset class management is necessarily passive. Implementation of this portfolio works in the same way as an asset allocation overlay with physical assets held in cash instead of the long-term asset allocation portfolio. This approach confers a number of benefits:

- It can be very cost effective, saving on transaction costs for asset allocation resets and eliminating transaction costs within asset classes. Custodian fees are greatly reduced because there are fewer transactions.
- Resetting asset allocation to benchmark can coincide with rolling futures positions from one expiry month to the next, further reducing transaction and administrative costs.
- Manager risk is controlled because the risk of individual asset classes under-performing their benchmarks is virtually eliminated.
- Because futures markets are more liquid than markets for physical assets, changes in strategy are very easy to implement.

The main disadvantage is that the choice of asset classes is limited to those with viable futures markets, potentially ruling out some of the more interesting asset classes, such as direct equity, small capitalization stocks and emerging markets. Using derivatives eliminates the potential to earn extra return from security selection within asset classes. Each asset class is effectively an indexed fund. For small portfolios, the requirement to buy only whole numbers of futures contracts can mean that required asset class allocations often cannot be achieved precisely. This adds risk to the portfolio that must be quantified and managed.

As with asset allocation overlay mandates, close attention must be given to foreign futures holdings to ensure that no unintended exposure to foreign currency results.

ONGOING MANAGEMENT

The most important question to answer when designing the ongoing management of passive asset allocation is how often to rebalance the portfolio to its benchmark asset allocation. The choice is whether to rebalance at fixed intervals in time, such as every six months, or to rebalance when a prespecified mismatch is reached, for example when any actual asset class allocation is more than 5% from the benchmark allocation. Most passive asset allocation mandates specify a mixture of both, so that the portfolio is rebalanced, say, every six months, with more frequent rebalances if and when any asset class weighting differs from the benchmark by, say, 5% or more. The mandate can also specify that natural cash flows be used to effect ongoing rebalances whenever possible.

The frequency of resets, and the size of the allowable mismatch should reflect the investor's tolerance of deviation from long-term asset allocation, and likely transaction costs, which are determined largely by the asset classes themselves. For example, a large allocation to domestic fixed interest and equities implies low average trading costs, while a significant investment in less liquid assets, such as small capitalization equities and direct equity, implies higher transaction costs. The availability and use of futures contracts can further reduce transaction costs by smoothing resets and managing liquidity.

If asset classes are managed separately by specialist sector managers, the asset allocation manager receives regular reports from asset class managers and the custodian, providing details of asset class holdings, and determines when a reset to benchmark allocation is required. Having calculated the necessary adjustments to each asset class, he or she then instructs the custodian or trustee to transfer funds between sector managers, with corresponding advice issued to each manager, alerting them to the change in the value of assets in their charge.

Example 7.1 shows a typical portfolio starting on 31 December 1991 at the long-term asset allocation. By the end of June 1992, the actual portfolio allocation had deviated noticeably from the benchmark, so a rebalance was called for. The last row shows the purchases and sales required for each asset class. For

EXAMPLE 7.1 *Rebalancing passive asset allocation*

Asset Class	US Fixed Interest	US Equities	UK Equities	European Equities	Japanese Equities	Cash	Total
Long-term Asset Allocation	25%	35%	10%	10%	15%	5%	100%
Initial Portfolio Value	$25 000 000	$35 000 000	$10 000 000	$10 000 000	$15 000 000	$5 000 000	$100 000 000
30 Jun 92	$25 519 865	$34 248 965	$10 426 192	$10 686 000	$10 888 816	$5 189 924	$96 959 761
Effective Portfolio Allocation	26.32%	35.32%	10.75%	11.02%	11.23%	5.35%	
30 Jun 92 Rebalanced	$24 239 940	$33 935 916	$9 695 976	$9 695 976	$14 543 964	$4 847 988	$96 959 761
Purchases (Sales) of Assets	–$1 279 924	–$313 048	–$730 215	–$990 024	$3 655 148	–$341 936	$0

this rebalance, the portfolio turnover required was 3.59% of the portfolio value. The average cost of transactions was about 0.44%, and the cost to the portfolio of this rebalance was about 0.05%.

ADMINISTRATION

Other things being equal, the administration of portfolios with passive asset allocation is more straightforward than for actively managed portfolios, because the number of transactions required by passive management is usually much smaller than for active management.

As with other portfolios, the approach to administration depends much more on whether the asset allocation is managed as part of a balanced mandate or as a series of specialist asset class mandates. This determines how much communication between investment managers is appropriate, and how much intervention by the custodian is required.

VALUATION

The most important consideration for valuing the portfolio is whether the portfolio is managed as a single, balanced mandate or as a series of specialist asset class mandates with an asset allocation overlay.

For a balanced mandate, the portfolio value is simply the sum of the market values of its components. These are mostly physical assets with market-based valuations or some kind of estimation of the valuation. If there is an asset allocation overlay, then unrealized profits and losses on derivatives also form part of the valuation.

PERFORMANCE MEASUREMENT AND ATTRIBUTION

For a balanced mandate, the return to the fund is the end value of the portfolio divided by the start value minus one. For individual asset class mandates, the return to each asset class is the end value of each portfolio divided by the start value minus one. When weighted by the percentage allocation to each, individual asset class returns should add up to give the fund return. In other words, the sum of the end values of the asset class portfolios divided by the sum of the

EXAMPLE 7.2 *Return to the portfolio and asset classes*

Asset Class	Allocation %	Start Value $	End Value $	Return %	Weighted Return %
US Fixed Interest	25	25 000 000	25 652 646	2.61	0.65
US Equities	35	35 000 000	34 343 032	−1.88	−0.66
UK Equities	10	10 000 000	10 445 258	4.45	0.45
European Equities	10	10 000 000	10 686 358	6.86	0.69
Japanese Equities	15	15 000 000	10 904 426	−27.30	−4.10
Cash	5	5 000 000	5 198 474	3.97	0.20
Total	100	100 000 000	97 230 193	−2.77	−2.77

start values of the asset class portfolios minus one should give the same answer, as in Example 7.2.

The portfolio return of –2.77%, calculated as $97 230 193/$100 000 000 – 1, is the same as the sum of the returns to the individual asset classes weighted by their allocation.

One of the benefits of passive asset allocation is that, because the return variance due to asset allocation is negligible, all variation should, at least in theory, be due to return variance within asset classes. It remains only to discover how much variation has occurred within each sector. Even so, it is inevitable that actual portfolio allocations do vary slightly from benchmark and, under some circumstances, the return effect of this difference may require quantification. If so, the procedure for doing so is simply to calculate for each asset class the difference between the actual and benchmark allocation and multiply this by the difference between the appropriate sector benchmark return and the portfolio benchmark return.

Example 7.3 shows the results of performance attribution estimates for a portfolio with passive asset allocation and a mixture of passive and active sector management. Domestic assets are managed actively, while foreign assets are managed passively. The portfolio delivered a negative return of 2.77% over the period, beating the benchmark return of –3.04% by 0.27%.

The analysis shows that nearly all of this outperformance came about because the returns to the portfolio sectors were better than the benchmark return, most notably for US fixed interest, where the portfolio delivered 2.61% compared with the benchmark sector return of 2.08%. The difference of 0.53% is multiplied by the benchmark asset allocation of 25% to give a contribution to

EXAMPLE 7.3 *Attribution analysis for passive asset allocation with active and passive sector management*

Asset Class	Long-term Asset Allocation %	Asset Class Return %	Benchmark Return %	Over/Under %	Contribution to Portfolio Return %
US Fixed Interest	25	2.61	2.08	0.53	0.13
US Equities	35	−1.88	−2.15	0.27	0.09
UK Equities	10	4.45	4.26	0.19	0.02
European Equities	10	6.86	6.86	0.00	0.00
Japanese Equities	15	−27.30	−27.41	0.10	0.02
Cash	5	3.97	3.80	0.17	0.01
Total	100	−2.77	−3.04	0.27	0.27

overall portfolio performance variation of 0.13%. Adding the sector variations together shows that these explain nearly all the portfolio's performance variation from benchmark.

In this portfolio there was also some slight variation from benchmark asset allocation, contributing 0.0022% to the overall portfolio return variation. This variation is estimated as the difference between portfolio and benchmark average asset class allocation times the difference between asset class benchmark return and overall benchmark return. Most of the asset allocation return variance is due to a slight underallocation to Japanese equities, which, when multiplied by the large return difference between this asset class and the benchmark overall, contributed 0.0025% to return variance.

Because portfolios with passive asset allocation are supposed to have little or no return variation due to asset allocation, many investors choose not to bother with detailed attribution analysis. This is understandable, but may be a mistake. For one thing, it assumes that the manager responsible for asset allocation has been abiding strictly to the terms of the mandate, which may or may not be the case. For another, it can, in the case of a single balanced manager mandate, camouflage some serious sectoral performance variation. For example, an overall outperformance of 1% may be informally attributed to keen domestic stock picking. This is a comfortable explanation, but it may conceal shortcomings, such as unintended risk exposures that could be highlighted by attribution analysis.

If there is material variation between actual and benchmark return, it can help to calculate tracking error as a means of quantifying the portfolio's risk. It should be borne in mind, however, that tracking error is a portfolio-wide measure, incorporating risk within asset classes as well as from asset allocation. While it is feasible to attribute return variation to asset allocation and security selection within asset classes, this is not easily done for tracking error.

PITFALLS

The active/passive debate is continuing and fierce. But applying passive asset allocation to a portfolio highlights another aspect of asset allocation in general, which is the selection of the long-term asset allocation. If the long-term allocation of the fund is badly conceived, the resulting problem becomes much more visible with passive asset allocation than with active because there is less scope for active returns to provide camouflage.

If, over an extended period, a fund fails to meet its return objectives, the fund's managers need to ask the question: is the long-term asset allocation appropriate? It is possible to estimate what the return to the long-term asset allocation would have been over any given period, but this will give only an estimate, because 'virtual' portfolios based on historical (usually month-end) return data cannot accommodate cash flows occurring at odd intervals, transaction costs and other frictions. By contrast, a real portfolio managed to the long-term asset allocation highlights the suitability of the long-term benchmark and provides a more effective benchmark.

Of course, this is not a pitfall unique to passive asset allocation; active asset allocation is equally prone to the problems caused by a poorly conceived long-term asset allocation. The converse is equally true. A fund with passive allocation cannot incorrectly attribute failure to meet its objectives to poor short-term asset allocation if the source is really an inappropriate long-term allocation.

CASE STUDY

This is a corporate pension fund of about USD80 million. The company is in fact a subsidiary of a major multinational corporation in the food manufacturing sector, but the laws of the land in which this subsidiary operates demand that it provides each employee with an individual pension account. There are 800 employees, many of whom are nearing retirement. It is anticipated that the fund will continue to decline in value as members retire, taking with them significant lump sum payments and reducing the size of the fund.

The same laws demand that a board of trustees oversees the fund, and that this board of eight trustees be made up at least 50% by representatives of the members themselves. Because of the time commitment required by board membership, the company observed a policy of 'revolving' board membership, whereby each member trustee was elected by the fund membership to serve on the board for two years. Thus two new members were elected to the board every year.

The secretary of the board, a full-time position, was therefore always concerned with educating member trustees. He found this to be a double-edged sword. While new member trustees tended to be naturally suspicious of derivatives and quantitative investment techniques, the constantly changing board composition meant that the fund's investment structure was always being scrutinized from a new and different point of view. To achieve the best investment results, given its size and the necessity of containing costs, the fund needed to be as flexible as possible in its attitude to investment alternatives. The secretary recognized the potential contribution of derivative-based strategies to cost control for such a fund. Bearing in mind the suspicion of derivatives harboured by many members, he was keen to ensure that a high level of discipline was applied to the management of the fund in general, and especially to those aspects of the fund where derivatives were used.

What concerned the secretary, even if it was less on the mind of the other trustees, was the risk of poor manager selection. He realized that poor investment performance was perfectly achievable without the help of derivatives. Of course, the best way to reduce manager risk is to hire multiple managers, but the scope for this is limited in a fund that is small and shrinking. The fund was invested in six asset classes, as shown in Example 7.4.1.

EXAMPLE 7.4.1 *Long-term asset allocation*

Asset Class	Long-term Asset Allocation %
US Equities	25
International Equities	20
US Fixed Interest	20
Listed Domestic Property	15
Inflation-linked Bonds	10
Small Stocks	10
Total	100

Given that the smallest sectors were at most only $8 million, specialist mandates were out of the question, except by buying units in pooled investment vehicles. Even this would turn out to be expensive, because it would necessitate a specialist asset allocation mandate to coordinate asset allocation, which might cost at least 0.5% of the fund's value each year, and would be unacceptable to the fund's members.

The only workable solution was to split the fund into a number of balanced mandates. The consultant suggested that three of these would be enough to provide the required manager diversification. To try to minimize the likelihood of active asset allocation strategies cancelling each other out, and thus delivering effectively an indexed fund with active fees, the consultant suggested that one mandate be managed using passive asset allocation and passive asset class management. The other two mandates were defined respectively as **conservative** and **aggressive** active. Managers were selected primarily according to track record and demonstrated competence in each investment style. They were also required to manage as much as possible of the portfolio in individual accounts rather than via units in pooled vehicles. This was to satisfy the fund's requirement that its assets should be held, wherever possible, directly in the name of the fund. Most managers were able to provide this service for most asset classes. The exceptions were international equities, inflation-linked bonds and small stocks, which together comprised 40% of the long-term allocation. The portfolio was simply too small to enable these asset classes to be managed as individual accounts by each manager.

The passive manager was able to offer three of the six asset classes as passively managed individual portfolios, but the portfolio was too small to manage international equities, inflation-linked bonds and small stocks in this way. International equities were invested by buying units in the investment manager's pooled fund, which was passively managed, but only actively managed pooled vehicles were available for inflation-linked bonds and small stocks. Therefore these sectors were managed actively within the passive mandate. Example 7.4.2 summarizes how each asset class was managed within each mandate.

All three mandates specified the same benchmark allocation. The conservative active portfolio was given a target return of 3% per annum above the benchmark. The aggressive mandate sought 5%. The performance of the fund over four years is set out in Example 7.4.3.

With a return of 9.63% per annum for the four years to December 1997, the passive part of the fund comfortably outperformed both active parts. In fact, only during 1994 did the conservative active part of the fund do better than the passive strategy. The tracking errors measuring the ongoing variance from benchmark of the portfolio's performance are roughly consistent with the return results, although it should be said that both look a bit conservative. The

EXAMPLE 7.4.2 *Portfolio structure*

Asset Class	Passive		Conservative Active		Aggressive Active	
Percentage of Fund	**40%**		**30%**		**30%**	
US Equities	Passive	Individual	Active	Individual	Active	Individual
International Equities	Passive	Pooled	Active	Pooled	Active	Pooled
US Fixed Interest	Passive	Individual	Active	Individual	Active	Individual
Listed Domestic Property	Passive	Individual	Active	Individual	Active	Individual
Inflation-linked Bonds	Active	Pooled	Active	Pooled	Active	Pooled
Small Stocks	Active	Pooled	Active	Pooled	Active	Pooled

conservative portfolio's tracking error of 1.43%, for example, implies that the fund would only deliver the target 3% above benchmark about once every 40 years. Two-thirds of the time it will be within the range of the return to the long-term allocation plus or minus 1.43%. Similarly, the aggressive portfolio, while slightly more aggressive, is quite unlikely ever to deliver 5% outperformance. Its tracking error indicates that it will outperform the return to the long-term benchmark by 1.88% one year in six, or 16% of the time, and will outperform by 3.76% one year in 40 (2.5% of the time). It is worthwhile noting, too, that the tracking error of the overall fund was measured at 0.81%, considerably less than the weighted average of the tracking errors of the component portfolios, which is 1.06%, illustrating the fact that the variance of the component funds offset each other to some extent, so that overall portfolio risk is reduced by engaging three managers with different investment mandates. But since aggregates and averages can conceal as much as they reveal, closer inspection of the results is warranted. A rudimentary attribution analysis tells an interesting story.

Example 7.4.4 gives an idea of what is going on. It indicates that the conservative manager indeed added value from asset allocation, but not enough to cover the transactions costs of implementing asset allocation changes. The aggressive manager failed to add value from either asset allocation or stock selection over the four-year period, although there were periods of outperformance within the four years. The problem was again transaction costs. The aggressive shifts in asset allocation turned out to be very costly to implement.

Both active portfolios suffered at some point from poor stock selection, and closer inspection shows that this was nearly always in international equities. Both managers had a policy of actively managing currency risk. In practice, this often consisted of hedging foreign currency exposures to base currency: investment managers are often too optimistic about the prospects for the home

EXAMPLE 7.4.3 *Portfolio returns*

Percentage of Total Fund		Benchmark	Passive Asset Allocation 40%		Conservative Active 30%		Aggressive Active 30%		Total Portfolio 100%	
		Return	Return	Variation	Return	Variation	Return	Variation	Return	Variation
4 Years to December 1997		9.69	9.63	−0.06	9.50	−0.20	5.35	−4.35	8.21	−1.48
3 Years to December 1997		15.51	15.45	−0.07	14.63	−0.89	10.73	−4.79	13.67	−1.84
2 Years to December 1997		14.37	14.33	−0.04	13.51	−0.86	11.62	−2.75	13.21	−1.16
1 Year to December 1997		16.35	16.33	−0.02	17.00	0.65	13.37	−2.99	15.66	−0.70
Tracking Error			0.16		1.43		1.88		0.81	
2.5% Chance of Outperforming by			0.33		2.86		3.76		1.61	
Calendar	1996	12.42	12.36	−0.06	10.12	−2.30	9.89	−2.53	10.82	−1.60
Calendar	1995	17.83	17.71	−0.12	16.89	−0.94	8.97	−8.86	14.60	−3.23
Calendar	1994	−6.06	−6.11	−0.04	−4.56	1.50	−9.27	−3.21	−6.64	−0.58

EXAMPLE 7.4.4 *Attribution analysis*

Summary Attribution Analysis 4 Years to December 1997

Return Contribution by Manager	Passive %	Conservative %	Aggressive %	Total %
Asset Allocation	0.04	0.70	−0.28	0.16
Stock Selection	0.00	0.23	−0.23	0.02
Transaction Costs*	−0.10	−0.81	−2.18	−1.00
Residual	0.00	−0.32	−1.65	−0.67
Total	−0.06	−0.20	−4.35	−1.48

* Asset allocation only. Transaction costs associated with stock selection are included in sector performance.

currency. During the period in question, this turned out to have been a disastrous policy, as the home currency delivered negative returns against most major currencies during the period.

A final word of caution on the attribution analysis carried out here. This was quite rudimentary, designed only to identify the most important return effects. As it was based on month-end data only, it did not take into account the impact of cash flows, or the actual prices at which assets were bought and sold, and so ignores much of those influences on the portfolios.

CHAPTER 8

Quantitative Models for Domestic Equity Portfolios

APPLICATIONS

It is a rare investment portfolio that invests nothing in domestic equities. Even if all the signs point to a falling market, nearly all portfolios will retain a significant share in their home market, and it is accepted wisdom in the investment management industry that an investment manager will have difficulty retaining credibility without some expertise in the domestic equity market.

Most domestic equities portfolios are benchmarked to a local, broad-based equity index. In the USA the most popular is the S&P500. In Britain, it is the FT Allshare. There are enormous incentives to achieve returns superior to these benchmark indices. Not only is the manager's credibility often at stake, but overall portfolio performance too. Because domestic equities usually comprise such a large proportion of any investment portfolio (typically 25% to 60%), the impact of the returns to this sector tends to affect strongly those of the overall portfolio.

THEORY

The importance of domestic equities is that they impute the expected growth of the domestic economy. By anticipating economic growth, they respond to the likely future changes in the fortunes as opposed to merely reflecting current economic conditions. Investing in domestic equities therefore buys a share in this future growth.

The principal inputs to portfolio construction after defining the benchmark, are return forecasting and risk management. Most quantitative investment managers apply a combination of modelling techniques, including CAPM to forecast returns, while mean-variance is generally used to forecast risk.

DEFINING THE BENCHMARK

One of the most important aspects of equity investing is selecting a benchmark. The purpose of the benchmark is:

- To set a target return that reflects the opportunities in the domestic equities market. The benchmark is the quantifiable representation of the asset class in the context of the overall portfolio.
- As a point of comparison by which the returns achieved by individual domestic equities investment managers can be evaluated.

RETURN FORECASTING

Unsurprisingly, there are thousands, if not tens of thousands, of 'unique models' for predicting share price behaviour. Most fall into one of the following categories, and this section will attempt a brief discussion of each:

- Technical analysis, trend models and momentum models.
- Dividend discount models.
- Single stock models.
- Ratio models.
- Arbitrage pricing theory.
- Industry models and macroeconomic models.
- Factor models.
- Mean-variance models with consensus earnings forecasts.

The first five categories can be thought of as 'bottom-up' stock selection models. They focus on evaluating individual assets, on the premise that the portfolio return is but the sum of the returns to each of its components. The latter three categories combine bottom-up and top-down portfolio construction. They rely on variations of the capital asset pricing model, incorporating the principle that each stock's return can be analysed in terms of its relationship with markets and market-related variables. This approach implicitly recognizes the interactive effects of different assets on portfolio risk.

Technical analysis, trend analysis and price momentum models

The **technical analysis, trend analysis** and **price momentum** models have been around for a long time. The idea is that share prices can be predicted by studying patterns of earlier share price movements. Share price histories are presented as a line or a series of points on a graph. The analyst looks for evidence of patterns with known sequences in an attempt to predict the next price move.

Efficient market adherents scoff at this technology, insisting that if it were that easy, the share price would very quickly adjust to achieve the predicted price, so the pattern would instantly disappear. The case in favour of using charts of historical price movements **(charting)** is described in an article by Andrew Lo et al. in the *Journal of Finance*, August 2000.[1]

Example 8.1 shows five years of monthly price history, from which a technical analyst might draw conclusions from the zigzag pattern evident in early 1998 or the dramatic twin peaks in early 1999 to predict subsequent price movements.

Another variation on trend models is momentum models. These models also use historical price data presented as a line on a graph, with the addition of a **moving average**, which is the average price over some recent period, say one

EXAMPLE 8.1 *Technical analysis*

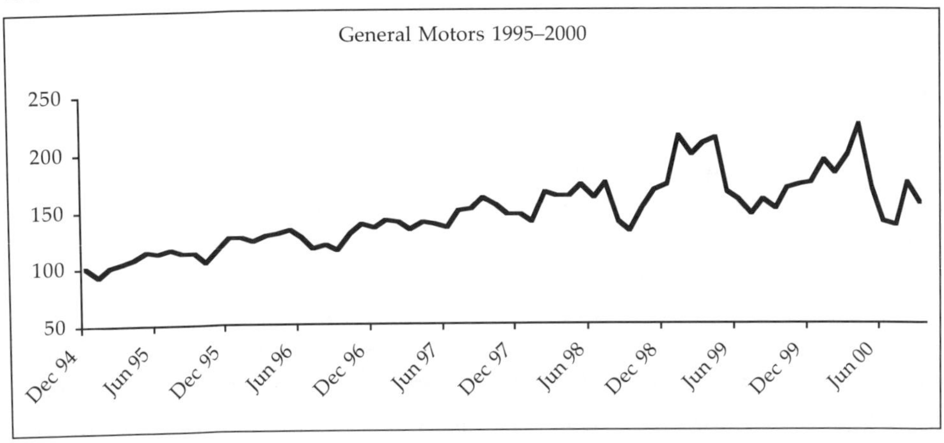

Source: IDC

EXAMPLE 8.2 *Analysis of momentum*

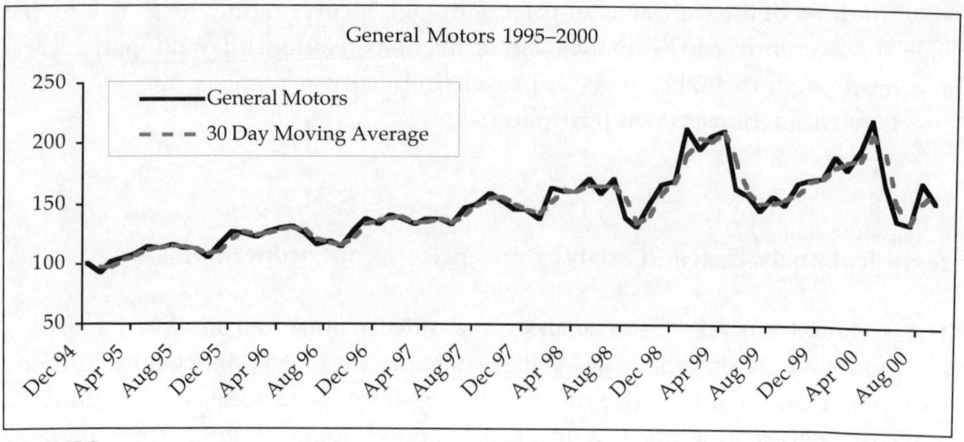

Source: IDC

month. When the price line and the moving average line intersect, a change of trend is indicated, which is interpreted as a signal to either buy or sell the stock.

Example 8.2 shows such buy and sell signals: for example, where the price line for General Motors crosses the moving average on the way down just prior to September 1998, a sell is indicated. Not long after that the two lines intersect in the other direction, which is taken as a buy signal. The chart demonstrates that momentum analysis does not always give a good indication of the strength of the buy or sell signals, for example there are a number of conflicting signals in late 1999 and early 2000.

While few investment managers admit to basing important investment decisions on technical analysis, many mangers find charts useful for short-term decisions, such as timing of purchases and sales.

Dividend discount models

These are the simplest of the so-called fundamental models designed for analysing equities, relying on projections of the profitability of the firm. They are based on the assumptions that, first, the firm will ultimately pay its entire worth to its shareholders in the form of dividends. These dividends will be paid periodically for the life of the firm, at the end of which the firm will be either wound up or sold, the proceeds going to shareholders. The second assumption is that these dividends are reasonably predictable. The stream of dividends thus forecast is then discounted to give a present value equivalent. The discount rate is an interest rate that reflects the risk of the firm.

EXAMPLE 8.3 *Dividend discounting*

Current Dividend	$2.00
Annual Dividend Growth Rate	2.00%
Discount Rate p.a.	7.50%
Assumed Time Horizon in Years	100
Present Value of Last Dividend in Horizon	$0.01
Present Value of Future Dividends	$38.90

The theory behind this model is impeccable. The current value of the firm is, by definition, the value in current money of what investors will ultimately receive from it. Bonds are priced in exactly the same way. The problems in applying it to shares arise because future earnings are very difficult to predict in practice and the correct discount rate is difficult to identify because the risk of the firm changes in unpredictable ways. There are other shortcomings too, for example the model cannot predict the potential for the firm to be taken over, with the associated price premium; and it cannot predict short-term price movements.

Example 8.3 shows the effect of discounting over 100 years. The present value of the last dividend in the analysis is $0.01 ($2.00 \times ((1 + 2\%)^{100} / (1 + 7.5\%)^{100}$), as opposed to the current dividend payment of $2.00. The dividend is assumed to be growing at 2% per year, and the applicable interest rate is 7.5%, adding up 100 years of discounted dividends indicates a current value for the share of $38.90.

Single stock models

This is a means of estimating the future profitability of the firm. The analyst effectively builds a model for the individual company based on information gathered from meetings with directors and knowledge about the firm and the industry in which it operates.

Example 8.4 shows the relationships between the costs to which the firm is subject, the revenue possible and the resulting profitability. The analyst can then change the inputs to see what effect these will have on the firm's profitability. For example, if long-term interest rates rise by 0.5%, earnings per share reduce from $2.18 to $2.17, while if hourly labour costs rise to $9.00 per hour, earnings per share go down to $0.61.

Stock modelling is often combined with dividend discount models, ratio analysis and, to the extent that at least some of the inputs to the stock model are macroeconomic variables, macroeconomic analysis.

EXAMPLE 8.4 *A simplified single stock model*

Inputs to the Firm		Outputs	
Number of Shares on Issue	15 000 000	Market Price per Unit	$15.75
Current Share Price	$50.00	Units Sold	105 000 000
		Capacity Utilization	87.50%
Short-term Interest Rate	4.50%	*Total Revenue*	$1 653 750 000
Long-term Interest Rate	6.50%		
Flat Rate of Corporation Tax	40.00%	Materials Costs	$367 500 000
Fixed Labour Costs	$15 000 000	Labour Costs	$684 375 000
Hourly Labour Costs	$8.50	Marketing Costs	$535 000 000
Hours of Labour per Unit	0.75	Administration Costs	$8 500 000
Fixed Marketing Costs	$10 000 000	*Operating Costs*	$1 595 375 000
Unit Cost of Marketing and Sales	$5.00		
Administration Costs	$8 500 000	Operating Profits	$58 375 000
Actual Capital Investment	$55 000 000	Interest Costs	$3 800 000
Actual Working Capital	$5 000 000	Tax	$21 830 000
Units Production Capacity	120 000 000		
Raw Materials Costs per Unit	$3.50	*Net Profit*	$32 745 000
		Earnings Per Share	$2.18
Market Price per Unit	$15.75		
Units Sold	105 000 000		

Ratio models

These use balance sheet information to predict profitability. The advantage of this type of analysis is that it allows large numbers of securities to be analysed simultaneously. Unlike single stock models, which involve painstaking analysis of individual securities, the analyst can simply purchase balance sheet information from a data supplier, such as a stock exchange, load it into a model and derive a list of promising assets that can then be researched in more detail. The advantage of accessing a large list of candidate assets should not be understated and, if the analyst's predictions about which stock characteristics will outperform are correct, the outcome is a very powerful portfolio.

Examples of ratios used for forecasting profitability are:

- **Price to book** is the ratio of the market price of the share to its book value (usually the price at which it was issued, adjusted for stock splits and other relevant corporate actions).

- **Payout ratio** is the ratio of the dividend paid per share and the earnings per share for the same period.
- **Gearing ratio** is the ratio of total debt to the market value of the company (measured as total debt plus market value of total equity). It can be expressed as D/(D+E).
- **Debt to equity** is the ratio of total debt to the market value of total equity. It can be expressed as D/E.
- **Dividend yield** is the ratio of dividends paid annually to the market price of the share.
- **Earnings yield** is the ratio of annual earnings per share to the market price of the share.
- **Interest cover** the ratio of total earnings (usually EBIT) to interest payable over the same period.
- **EBIT** Earnings before interest and taxes.

The problems are not too difficult to spot. First, it is not at all easy to predict which ratios characterize the winners. If it were, the share price of candidate stocks would adjust automatically to eliminate the effect. There is also the problem of data reliability. Balance sheet data is, in most places, either inadequate or misleading or both and, being updated infrequently, it is not even timely. To say that the portfolio is investing heavily in high price to book stocks may not be helpful if the book value is calculated only once a year, or is based on uncertain data.

This kind of model can be very useful for a portfolio that is seeking some characteristic based on ratios, such as higher than average dividend yields. High yield stocks are usually identified not only by a higher than average payout ratio, but also by some overt company policy. But by itself this does not help to identify the most profitable stocks, as dividend payout is not a good indicator of profitability.

Arbitrage pricing theory (APT)

APT is based on the observation that the value of any asset is the sum of the value of its parts. This is helpful when a listed company owns parts of other listed companies. The value of the parent company should be the sum of the value of its holding in subsidiaries plus the value of any operations it carries on directly. If there is a discrepancy between the fair price thus estimated and the price at which the securities are traded, there exists an opportunity for arbitrage, or risk-free profits. To exploit the arbitrage opportunity, the investment manager buys the underpriced assets and sells the overpriced assets in offsetting quantities. When market prices converge to their fair relationship, the investor reverses, or unwinds, the position.

In Example 8.5, the market value of the company is $171 250 000 000, or $68.50 per share. It has direct operations with an estimated value of $94 000 000, a very small percentage of the company's overall worth. Most of its value is in its holdings of other listed companies, here known as subsidiaries #1 through #5. The sum of the market value of these holdings and the direct operations come only to $147 716 250 000, or $59.09 per share. This would imply that the parent company is overpriced relative to its subsidiaries.

The investor can make a risk-free profit by buying the subsidiaries, in proportion to their 'weighting' in the parent, and selling shares in the parent company. The transaction will be reversed when the market price and the theoretical price of the parent company are the same or similar. This strategy will yield similar profits regardless of the direction of the overall market. The only risk is that the value of the direct operations is underestimated, increasing the theoretical value of the parent, and reducing commensurately the potential gains to the strategy. For this to eliminate the profitability of this particular strategy, however, the subsidiaries would need to be worth many times more than the value attributed them, which is unlikely.

The appeal of APT is that it is independent of any other market condition, and relies on conceptually fairly simple analysis. Because it is so simple, and relatively unambiguous, opportunities for true arbitrage do not come along very often.

Industry models and macroeconomic models

Industry models and macroeconomic models form part of top-down portfolio construction, the process of forecasting the outcomes of macroeconomic variables, such as budget deficits and economic growth rates, then modelling the likely impact on sector and industry group returns, and the stocks within them. For example, a forecast increase in fuel prices is usually good news for the energy sector, but bad news for transport stocks. The object of these models is to use historical return data to quantify the relationship between each macroeconomic or industry variable and each asset, and to quantify the relationships between the variables themselves.

EXAMPLE 8.5 *Arbitrage pricing theory*

	Shares on Issue	Market Price of Shares $	Market Valuation $	Valuation Estimate $	Percent Owned by Parent %	Value of Parent Holding $	Percentage of Theoretical Value of Parent %
Parent Company	2 500 000 000	68.50	171 250 000 000		100	147 716 250 000	100.00
Direct Operations #1				58 000 000	100	58 000 000	0.04
Direct Operations #2				36 000 000	100	36 000 000	0.02
Subsidiary #1	2 150 000 000	45.50	97 825 000 000		52	50 869 000 000	34.44
Subsidiary #2	980 000 000	75.00	73 500 000 000		58	42 630 000 000	28.86
Subsidiary #3	850 000 000	62.25	52 912 500 000		32	16 932 000 000	11.46
Subsidiary #4	730 000 000	98.50	71 905 000 000		25	17 976 250 000	12.17
Subsidiary #5	1 050 000 000	91.50	96 075 000 000		20	19 215 000 000	13.01
Theoretical Share Price of Parent Company		59.09					

For example, the expected return of stock i might be driven by macroeconomic variables x and y, as follows:

$$Er_i = a_i + b_{ix} \times (Er_x - Er_f) + b_{iy} \times (Er_y - Er_f) + e_i \quad (8.1)$$

Where:

Er_i = the expected return to stock i
a_i = alpha of stock i
b_{ix} = the covariance, or beta of stock i to factor x
Er_x = the expected return to factor x
Er_f = the expected risk-free rate of return
b_{iy} = the covariance, or beta of stock i to factor y
Er_y = the expected return to factor y
e_i = random, specific risk of stock i

This says that the expected return to stock i is equal to:

- The alpha of stock i, which is the amount by which the stock is over- or underpriced
- plus the beta (covariance) of stock i to macroeconomic variable x times the difference in the expected return to macroeconomic variable x and the expected risk-free rate of interest
- plus the beta of stock i to macroeconomic variable y times the difference in the expected return to macroeconomic variable y and the expected risk-free rate of interest
- plus some random variable or error, which also can be thought of as the diversifiable risk.

Again, the theory is impeccable, and in practice can work quite well too. The problems arise because macroeconomic and industry returns tend to be quite difficult to forecast in practice, and the method is very sensitive to unforeseen events, such as changes in economic policy, which can alter the relationship between variables as well as the variables themselves.

It is also more difficult than is sometimes imagined to model the sensitivity of individual firms to macroeconomic variables. Take, for example, a gold producer. A company that does nothing else but extract gold could be thought of as being influenced primarily by the world price of gold and the currency in which the stock is priced. But what if the company sells its gold production forward and hedges its currency exposure? What is left to affect its profitability and therefore its share price? Just extraction costs and interest rates. The difficulty is that such a company is not obliged to follow a set policy on hedging production and currency, but may carry out these activities on an ad hoc basis, so its true sensitivities to gold, currency and interest rates are simply not knowable in advance.

Macroeconomic and industry models work better in some markets than in others. Many stock exchanges do not require companies to give detailed accounts of their businesses. Analysts are thus left to guess the mix of revenue streams and cost structures that impact on the ultimate profitability of firms.

An advantage of this approach is that it can be applied just as effectively at the level of the portfolio as for individual stocks. Thus the investment manager can construct a portfolio incorporating the precise macroeconomic and industry sensitivities to best exploit his economic forecasts.

Factor models

The theory behind factor models is similar to industry and macroeconomic models. They are based on the premise that external events impact the returns to any security. Factors can be anything for which a price or return series can be generated. For domestic equities portfolios, industry groups are probably the most commonly used factors, but more unconventional factors have been successfully applied. So if the event can be forecast, and the likely impact of the event on security returns is known, then the return to the asset can also be forecast. For example, a two-factor model, using factors x and y might give the following expected return algorithm:

$$Er_i = a_i + b_{ix} \times (Er_x - Er_f) + b_{iy} \times (Er_y - Er_f) + e_i \quad (8.2)$$

Where:

Er_i = the expected return to stock i
a_i = alpha of stock i
b_{ix} = the covariance, or beta of stock i to factor x
Er_x = the expected return to factor x
Er_f = the expected risk-free rate of return
b_{iy} = the covariance, or beta of stock i to factor y
Er_y = the expected return to factor y
e_i = specific risk of stock i

This says that the expected return to stock i is equal to:

- the alpha of stock i, which is the amount by which the stock is over- or under-priced
- plus the beta of stock i to factor times the difference in the expected return to factor x and the expected risk-free rate of interest
- plus the beta of stock i to factor y times the difference in the expected return to factor y and the expected risk-free rate of interest
- plus some specific, random variable or error, the diversifiable risk.

The principle is the same as for macroeconomic models. The difference is how the factors are defined.

Most factor models bypass the step of analysing company operations, revenues, costs and so on. They look at historical return data for the important relationships that drive security returns.

The advantage of this approach is that it allows a large number of assets to be analysed together. Indeed, the technique is most often used to estimate the sensitivities of a portfolio. The most obvious disadvantage is that relationships change over time. This turns out not to be fatal, however. A competent investment manager will be able to recognize patterns that are ongoing and those that are in the process of change or are obsolete, and make the appropriate adjustments. For such a manager, quantifying such relationships is less error prone than relying on current balance sheet and business operations data that may be of uncertain quality and provenance, and much less open to scrutiny.

A more important challenge with factor models has to do with choosing the right factors. A very elegant solution is to conduct a **principal components** analysis. This is a statistical process that uses the return history for a stock or a portfolio to identify important relationships occurring during a given period. This process can be very successful in explaining nearly all the factors influencing the behaviour of a stock or portfolio. The problem is that the results can be difficult to interpret. Being simply the output from a statistical process, they may not correspond to anything in the observable world. The analysis does not assign meaningful names to the factors, they are identified simply as Factor A, Factor B and so on. What may look like an interest rate factor, for example, may turn out to be a hybrid interest rate and currency factor. The other problem is that apparent sensitivities change significantly over time as the data set rolls forward, so that this month's measured sensitivities may not correspond to last month's. For an investment manager implementing a clearly articulated investment strategy, this can be a fatal shortcoming.

So most factor models predefine their factors, that is to say, they identify which factors are likely to be important, then measure stocks and portfolios against them to see how important they turn out to be. For a domestic equities portfolio, probably the most straightforward approach is to use industry groups as factors and measure the sensitivity of each stock to its industry group. If the industry groups are well defined, this will provide a reasonable basis for stock selection and portfolio construction. If they are ill-defined, then the result will be unsatisfactory.

It is important to note that the industry exposures in a portfolio may bear little resemblance to its industry allocations. The latter are simply the percentage of the portfolio's value in each industry category, while the former measure the sensitivity of the portfolio to changes in the fortunes of industries. For example, a gold producer who has sold forward all gold production is still included in the gold industry group, but has virtually no exposure to the fortunes of that industry. Its beta to the gold industry group can therefore be expected to be small.

The following characteristics are desirable in factors:

- Together they should explain as much as possible of the total portfolio or security return.
- The number of factors should be limited, probably to three or four dozen at most.
- They need to be intuitive: having a tilt towards factor A is unhelpful. So the factors need to be something one can talk about, such as industries, interest rates or currencies.
- Because of the mathematics underlying factor models, the factors need to have an unambiguous return series associated with them. The gold price is an example of a factor with an official closing price each day, giving unambiguous returns. Commodity baskets are less helpful because there is no single, widely accepted basket with unambiguous prices.
- Most importantly, the factors should be **statistically independent** (**orthogonal**): it is not a good idea to have overlapping factors.

Most factor models try to improve on simple industry groupings, and there is considerable controversy about which is the best approach. It is probably fair to say that in so far as choosing the right factors is concerned, the best solution is one that is most tailored to the market in question, which may or may not be simple industry groups.

Sometimes the factors that are important to a security or portfolio are at first surprising. Example 8.6 is an analysis of the sensitivity of a portfolio comprising the FTSE Allshare, which is composed only of UK pound denominated stocks, to non-UK currencies. The overall volatility of the portfolio is 13.00%. The beta of the portfolio to the currency indicates the degree to which the portfolio will move relative to a given move in the currency. This portfolio is almost as sensitive to US dollars as it is to its home currency.

EXAMPLE 8.6 *Portfolio exposures to currencies*

	Beta of Portfolio to Currency	Contribution to Portfolio Variance %
Euro	−0.5180	2.13
Japanese Yen	0.2612	5.85
UK Pound	0.6292	0.00
US Dollar	0.6276	10.33
Australian Dollar	0.3548	8.69
Canadian Dollar	0.5856	7.06
Swedish Krona	0.2968	3.75
Swiss Franc	−0.1262	0.51
Central America	0.0649	0.27
Asia	−0.0297	0.06
South African Rand	0.0041	0.00
South America	0.0526	0.26
Total Currency		38.92

Source: QUANTEC

More important is the right-hand column, which shows the importance of each currency to the portfolio's marginal risk. This is random risk and can be in either direction, corresponding to the error term at the end of the CAPM and factor model equations, so it is the risk that investors would like to eliminate. For this domestic portfolio, nearly 40% of its diversifiable, non-systemic risk is due to exposures to foreign currencies. This risk, if unintentional, is not contributing to portfolio return. Having been quantified, it must be either managed or eliminated by hedging it.

Having defined the factors most pertinent to a portfolio, the next step is to forecast returns for the factors. These forecasts are in principle very similar to and no easier to forecast than macroeconomic variables, so it is often here that one encounters the weak link in applying factor models to the portfolio construction process.

Mean-variance models with consensus earnings forecasts

These models use similar technology to factor models. The difference is that factor models emphasize the relationships of securities to factors and of factors to each other, while consensus earnings forecast models place more emphasis on forecasting profitability of individual securities. Mean-variance processes are then applied to estimate and manage the risk of the portfolio.

This approach takes forecast asset returns from published earnings forecasts, generated by most large broking houses and commercial forecasting agencies, and uses them to identify assets that are apparently mispriced relative to their expected risk. This is close to a pure application of the principles of modern portfolio theory, incorporating the notion of the efficient frontier of risk and return.

Example 8.7 shows, for each stock in the S&P500 index, a measure of expected return and risk. The diagram shows typical clustering, in this case of expected returns between –5% and +15%, with risk between 5% and 15%. Most of the stocks lying within this cluster area can be considered to be close to their fair value, but stocks outside the cluster are more likely to be either too dear or too cheap. Since it is expected that risk and return should be positively related, it would be normal to see the cluster slope upwards to the right. It is partially evident here. Once stocks leave the cluster in the lower left-hand corner, they seem to follow an upward-sloping pattern, with considerable mispricing of individual assets.

Assets showing expected returns greater than, say, 20% with risk less than, say, 25% are candidates for greater scrutiny, as they appear to be too cheap.

EXAMPLE 8.7 *Risk and return*

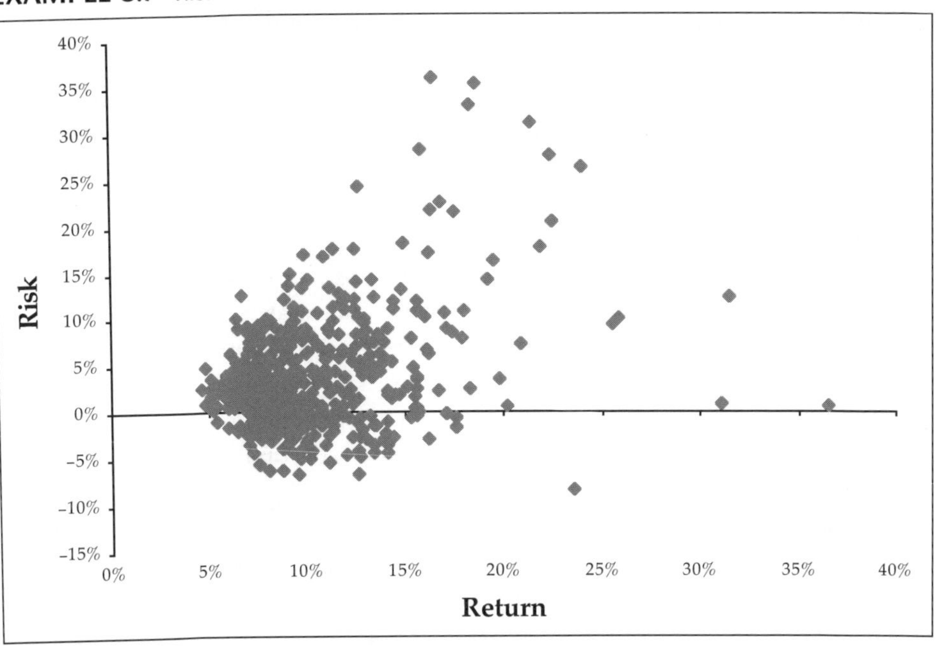

Source: Thomson Financial Datastream, IDC

Similarly, there are a number of high volatility, low expected return stocks that may well be overpriced. These securities can be investigated in detail to determine if a genuine mispricing exists. The advantages of this type of modelling are that the initial analysis can cope with very large numbers of assets, allowing the more labour-intensive research effort to be targeted very accurately. This makes it suitable for both domestic and international equity portfolios.

A major shortcoming of this approach is that earnings forecasts by stockbrokers tend to have a built-in bias. Stockbroking analysts are famously optimistic about the prospects for the companies they analyse. This optimism can sometimes be compounded if the broker's investment banking arm is providing advice to the company in question. Despite 'Chinese walls' designed to separate the two activities, brokers rarely jeopardize lucrative advice mandates by issuing pessimistic forecasts for those companies

RISK FORECASTING AND MANAGEMENT

The objective of forecasting, analysing and managing risk is to gain as much understanding as possible of the sources of risk in a portfolio. Since only undiversifiable risk contributes to return, any unnecessary risk in the portfolio is a potential drag on its performance and should be identified and eliminated wherever possible.

Investors are becoming increasingly aware of the value of forecasting risk as a complement to forecasting return. This is partly the result of increased accountability of investment managers, and with it the requirement that they explain their investment results together with the reasons for any deviation from forecast, and partly because consulting actuaries, advising their clients, are demanding forward-looking risk estimates.

Tracking error has come to be the most popular, indeed, the standard measure of forward-looking risk. Because forecast tracking error is based on mean-variance analysis and therefore relies on a covariance matrix, it is determined by the choice of factors on which covariances are based. Inappropriate factors will result in inaccurate risk estimates. Inaccurate risk estimates result in misallocation of risk. If risk is misallocated, it cannot be managed effectively, with the consequence that intentional and unintentional risk become confounded.

Example 8.8 shows tracking error estimates for a portfolio comprising S&P500 stocks, based in USD, using three different risk-factor models, each giving a different estimate of tracking error, as well as a different explanation of its sources.

EXAMPLE 8.8 *Forecast tracking error: sectors, industry groups and currencies as factors*

	Sectors as Factors %	Industries as Factors %	Currencies as Factors %
Expected Tracking Error	17.17	16.87	14.88
Comprising:			
Market	95.46	92.91	50.49
Currencies			39.27
Sectors	1.27		2.72
Industries		5.10	
Others			5.28
Specific Risk	3.26	2.00	2.24
Total	100.00	100.00	100.00

Source: Thomson Financial Datastream, QUANTEC

Risk management can be incorporated in the portfolio construction process or it can be conducted as a separate exercise. Which approach is adopted depends largely on how return is forecast, and how portfolio construction and analysis is allocated between members of the investment management team. Incorporating risk management in the portfolio construction process inherently recognizes the interdependence of risk and return, while managing risk separately usually implies that return forecasts are of primary importance.

Whichever approach is adopted, it is important that risk management be carried out on a portfolio-wide basis, because portfolio risk is not simply the sum of the risks of the components, but is determined by the correlations between the elements of the portfolio. Ideally, this omnibus risk measure includes some analysis of the sources of the portfolio's risk, which should then be checked for consistency with the analysts' return forecasts and, if applicable, forecasts of macroeconomic events. For example, if the portfolio risk analysis identifies an exposure to oil prices, this should be consistent with oil price forecasts and forecast returns to oil-price-sensitive stocks.

CURRENCY MANAGEMENT

For most domestic equities portfolios, currency management is not an issue because the assets are all held in the base currency of the portfolio, but there may be exceptions. For example, where stocks have multiple listings, some domestic stocks may be bought on overseas exchanges in foreign currency, or stocks may be listed in the domestic exchange in foreign currency. This is unlikely to occur often, but it would necessitate hedging the unwanted currency exposure, requiring attention to associated liquidity and foreign exchange settlement issues.

It is possible, however, for a domestic equities portfolio to be exposed to foreign currency even without any multiple or foreign currency listings. Consider Ericsson, the Swedish maker of mobile phones. Although denominated in Swedish krona, the company's operations and profit sources are global. With increasing globalization of companies, the same can be said for many others. Example 8.9, which shows the foreign currency exposure of five well-known equity indices illustrates this effect. The same can be said of almost any major market.

Example 8.9 shows that in each of the five markets, between 30% and 50% of typical portfolio return volatility can be attributed to foreign currency risks.

Investment managers are becoming increasingly cognizant of this effect, but foreign currency risk analysis is some way yet from being a universally accepted component of domestic portfolio construction.

IMPLEMENTATION

Since one of the main objectives of using quantitative models for stock selection is to encourage a disciplined approach to portfolio construction, it is critical that the investment process is clear as to when the model should be run, what data should be used, how the results are to be interpreted and what action should follow. Predefined decision rules should stipulate when assets are to be sold as well as bought, how long the position should be held, what additional return is anticipated and what loss can be tolerated.

How assets are actually bought and sold depends on the type of model used for their selection. For example, most of the top-down models require assets to be bought and sold as **basket trades** because such models frequently indicate simultaneous readjustments to the holdings of a large number of assets. Bottom-up models are more likely to require purchases and sales of isolated assets, so traditional implementation methods can be used.

Brokerage and commission charges vary widely from market to market, with some markets prescribing brokerage rates. Brokerage is usually applied on a sliding scale, with the per-share rate declining with the number of shares traded or as the value of the transaction increases. Most large markets allow brokerage to be negotiated between broker and investor, while others are at a stage of

EXAMPLE 8.9 *Foreign currency exposures within domestic portfolios*

Portfolio	DJ EUROSTOXX 50		SMI		FTSE Allshare		TOPIX		TSE 300	
Benchmark	Euro Cash		Swiss Francs Cash		UK Pounds Cash		Japanese Yen Cash		Canadian Dollar Cash	
Base Currency	Euro		Swiss Francs		UK Pounds		Japanese Yen		Canadian Dollar	
Portfolio Variance	229.45%		319.49%		168.98%		329.75%		256.24%	
Portfolio Tracking Error	15.15%		17.87%		13.00%		18.16%		16.01%	
	Beta of Portfolio to Currency	**Contribution to Portfolio Variance %**	**Beta of Portfolio to Currency**	**Contribution to Portfolio Variance %**	**Beta of Portfolio to Currency**	**Contribution to Portfolio Variance %**	**Beta of Portfolio to Currency**	**Contribution to Portfolio Variance %**	**Beta of Portfolio to Currency**	**Contribution to Portfolio Variance %**
Euro	−0.2212	0.00	0.1136	0.68	−0.5180	2.13	−0.6624	1.99	−0.7243	18.82
Japanese Yen	0.2332	5.21	0.3634	8.48	0.2612	5.85	1.0040	0.00	0.3372	−1.47
UK Pound	0.1257	2.37	−0.5022	−5.89	0.6292	0.00	0.4761	3.41	0.1301	−2.17
US Dollar	0.8623	26.31	0.9392	23.72	0.6276	10.33	0.1824	1.18	−1.3258	17.79
Australian Dollar	0.2910	4.96	0.3352	3.49	0.3548	8.69	0.8880	21.49	0.3498	4.40
Canadian Dollar	0.4838	4.10	−0.0476	−0.13	0.5856	7.06	0.2981	1.99	2.0244	0.00
Swedish Krona	0.4440	5.02	0.6398	5.20	0.2968	3.75	0.4091	3.58	0.6368	5.95
Swiss Franc	−0.4573	2.43	0.3498	0.00	−0.1262	0.51	0.1730	−0.27	−0.4843	2.15
Central America	0.0801	0.29	0.0902	0.26	0.0649	0.27	0.0855	0.26	−0.0055	0.00
Asia	−0.0308	0.04	−0.0361	0.04	−0.0297	0.06	0.0111	0.00	−0.0094	0.00
South African Rand	0.0324	0.02	0.0406	0.05	0.0041	0.00	−0.0474	0.06	0.0446	0.06
South America	0.0555	0.23	0.1549	1.23	0.0526	0.26	−0.0013	0.00	0.0325	0.08
Total Currency		50.98		37.12		38.92		33.70		45.63

Source: Thomson Financial Datastream, QUANTEC, STOXX, FTSE

transition, during which brokers are obliged to levy prescribed rates, but may be allowed to offer a 'rebate' for large or very simple transactions.

In most markets, brokerage is quoted as a percentage of the value of the transaction, while others present it as a value per share or as a sum for the overall transaction. Brokerage for physical equity transactions ranges from as little as $25 for a transaction to over 1% of its face value.

Many markets are still subject to taxes and duties on share purchases and sales. These can be significant: up to 0.5% on the value of the purchase or sale, or both.

USE OF DERIVATIVES

Nearly all investment managers use share price index futures contracts to help to manage the liquidity of their domestic equity portfolios. Many routinely keep 5 to 10% of the portfolio in liquid instruments, covered by share price index futures contracts to meet ongoing cash requirements, such as rights take-ups and small, frequent cash outflows.

The standard application of derivatives is to 'equitize', or expose to the equity market, cash accumulated from dividends received or small cash inflows to the portfolio, until enough cash is accumulated to warrant purchasing a block of physical stock.

CORPORATE ACTIONS

Equity portfolios are frequently affected by corporate actions. Corporate actions occur when companies make changes to their capital base. They can be as simple as declaring and paying a dividend, or a complex exchange of capital with another company as part of a merger or takeover. The effect of a corporate action on the value of a company can be complex, or it can be zero.

Take, for example, a stock that is trading at $50.00 when it announces that it will pay a dividend of 50 cents per share. The dividend itself does not directly impact the value of the share, so, other things being equal, the price of the share after the dividend has been paid will be $49.50. The investor still has an investment worth $50.00, but now 50 cents of it is held in cash. Similarly, a company, trading at $65.00 may announce a two-for-one **stock split** or **bonus issue**. This simply means that the number of shares on issue will double. Because the overall value of the firm is unchanged, the value of each share will halve, to $32.50.

A **rights issue** is a bit more complicated, because the value of the firm will increase when investors take up their rights. Rights are, economically speaking, call options on the shares of the firm. The amount by which the firm's value increases depends on the amount raised by the rights issue (the number of rights taken up multiplied by the take-up price of each right) and what the company plans to do with the extra cash. A typical rights issue will look something like this:

Announcement Date	1 October 1998
Share Price at Announcement Date	\$56.50
Number issued	one-for-four
Ex-rights Date	16 November 1998
Rights Start Trading	1 December 1998
Rights Exercise Date	30 June 1999
Rights Exercise Price	\$55.00

Shareholders are each allocated rights in proportion to their holdings of common stock as at the close of trading on 16 November 1998 (the ex-rights date). 'One-for-four' means that for every four common shares held, the holder is allocated one right. Between 1 December, 1998, when the rights begin trading, and 30 June 1999, when the rights expire, rights holders are entitled to either sell their rights or hold them as a continuing investment in the company. When the rights expire, rights holders choose either to exercise or abandon their rights. In this case, rights holders will exercise their rights if the common share price is trading above \$55.00 on 30 June 1999, paying \$55.00 to convert each right held into one common share.

The value of the company has increased by \$13.75 (\$55.00/4), the amount of new capital paid in by investors converting their rights to common stock. When all rights are converted, the number of shares on issue increases by 25%. If the shares are trading at \$58.00 immediately prior to the rights exercise date, the share price after all rights are exercised is \$57.40 $((4 \times 58 + 55)/5)$.

Share buy-backs became increasingly common during the 1990s. They are potentially the most complicated of all corporate actions. In principle, a firm with a sizeable cash balance will buy back its shares when they are trading below book value. This has the effect of reducing the number of shares on issue without reducing the overall value of the firm. If the shares really are underpriced, then the firm makes a profit, benefiting shareholders. Share buy-backs are not universally applauded because investors often want to know why the firm doesn't simply pay a dividend or, better still, develop a strategy to invest the cash for superior returns.

Share buy-backs can indicate other characteristics of the firm too, for example if the firm had previously issued large numbers of **employee stock options**. The idea behind issuing stock options to employees and management is to align the interests of these groups with those of the company and therefore its shareholders. By giving staff a direct stake in the firm, the thinking goes, they will be motivated to put in extra effort to maximize the ongoing value of the company. Options are preferred to common stock because the latter can decline in value much more than the former, so constituting a potential 'stick' when the objective was to provide only a 'carrot'. But issuing stock options to staff can have some questionable side effects. For example, when employees wish to exercise their stock options, the firm is obliged to either issue more shares, which it may not be entitled, or willing, to do. If this is the case, it is obliged to buy shares in the market. Naturally, companies with many employee stock options on issue will prefer not to wait until the last moment to buy stock, but will 'stockpile' when it is perceived that those shares are trading relatively cheaply.

Many companies reward their management with stock options. Normally such options have fairly tight restrictions as to how and when they may be exercised, but when the options become exercisable, management can be faced with a conflict of interests because they, arguably, have some control over the company's prospects and therefore the price of common stock. When they exercise their options, it is in their interests that the share price be as high as possible, so that they can then sell those shares for a profit. Buying back the company's shares in the market is one way of temporarily boosting the share price to this end. In these cases, issuing stock options to managers may not align their interests with those of other shareholders.

ONGOING MANAGEMENT

The most important aspect of ongoing management is to ensure that the chosen model or models are applied consistently over time. If established prior to implementation, then ongoing management should be a semi-automatic process. Even so, a system of monitoring needs to be put in place as a failsafe to ensure that all rules are indeed being rigorously observed, and tolerances are not breached.

Most investment managers conduct regular reviews of models and portfolios to spot potential problems early. These reviews also provide the opportunity to identify events that may change the assumptions on which the analysis is based and to take corrective action.

Other ongoing management issues concern liquidity and derivatives management and ensuring that the portfolio is always fully invested according to mandate specification. Most investment managers, recognizing that transactions can be a significant drag on returns, seek to achieve economies by coordinating, where possible, portfolio adjustments with natural cash flows.

ADMINISTRATION

With few, if any, foreign currency exposures to complicate things and only fairly rudimentary use of stock index futures contracts, administration of domestic equities portfolios is typically very simple, requiring only fairly basic custodian and settlement services. Administrative systems need to coordinate settlement and confirmation of transactions according to local market conventions and, naturally, the complexity and cost of this increases with the number of transactions, so very frequent cash flows or rebalances increase the administrative burden. Most domestic equity administrative systems accommodate some tax accounting, for example by providing rudimentary analysis of dividend tax credits and capital gains liabilities.

VALUATION

Domestic equity portfolios are usually very straightforward to value using a simple mark to market process, with the value of the portfolio equal to the market value of its components plus unrealized derivatives profits and losses. Most investment managers use valuations based on the day's closing price, although some managers choose to value their portfolios slightly before the close, or even using the day's opening prices. If so, the investor needs to take a good deal of care in comparing the performance of such portfolios with those of their competitors. Equity markets can exhibit surprising volatility within a trading day, so the timing of the valuation can have a measurable impact. It is also important to ensure that the share price index futures contracts are valued at the same time as the physical equities, and that the face value of the exposure they represent is correctly calculated. Calculating the correct face value for a futures contract is described in Appendix 3.

Another complication can arise if one or more stocks within the portfolio has been the subject of a corporate action, such as a dividend, rights issue or a stock split. Sometimes the share price is erroneously recorded as **ex-dividend**, while the valuation fails to record receipt of the dividend.

In the event of a two-for-one stock split, for example, this will result in the value of the shares held in that particular company as showing half their actual value. When a stock goes ex-dividend, the value of the shares held goes down by about the value of the dividend. There will be a corresponding increase in the amount held in liquid instruments, which usually shows as 'sums accrued' or 'dividends accrued'. There should also be an entry in the portfolio valuation reflecting any tax credits due as a result of the dividend. If the amount of the dividend fails to show in the liquids part of the portfolio, the value of the portfolio will be understated. Once spotted, this error is easily rectified, but if not corrected can distort return calculations.

PERFORMANCE MEASUREMENT AND ATTRIBUTION

Performance measurement for domestic equity portfolios is basically a matter of comparing the value of the portfolio at the end of the investment period with its value at the beginning, with time-weighted adjustments for cash flows occurring during the period.

Example 8.10 shows portfolio and benchmark returns measured for two consecutive months. The returns themselves say very little about whether or not the portfolio is performing to mandate, as each period appears to tell a different story. For this reason, portfolio returns are usually accompanied by risk measures, usually observed tracking error. The observed tracking error for this portfolio is 0.44% to 30 June 1996 and 0.40% to 31 May 1996.

Most attribution analysis models seek to explain performance variation in terms of natural asset categories within the portfolio. The most popular is to use sector or industry groups, but this is not the only approach.

If the portfolio has been constructed using, for example, a factor-based stock selection model, then there is a compelling argument to apply the same factor approach to performance attribution. This would allow the investor and the

EXAMPLE 8.10 *Return measurement*

Period	Portfolio %	Benchmark %	Difference %
to 30 June 1996			
3 Months	1.92	1.82	0.10
6 Months	3.93	3.82	0.12
12 Months	15.53	15.81	−0.28
2 Years	22.74	22.42	0.32
to 31 May 1996			
3 Months	0.00	0.09	−0.09
6 Months	6.68	7.07	−0.40
12 Months	16.63	17.05	−0.42
2 Years	18.25	18.18	0.07

investment manager to evaluate the success or otherwise of the manager's factor-based strategy.

Some attribution systems allow analysis at the level of individual securities. This would show, in the case of the lost dividend for example, that that security appeared to underperform the same security in the benchmark, highlighting the problem immediately.

PITFALLS

The pitfalls of using quantitative stock selection techniques generally fall into one of the following categories:

- Model risk.
- Misinterpretation of results.
- Limitations of historical data.
- Unreliable balance sheet data.

Model risk is the risk of choosing a model that is:

- Inappropriate.
- Misspecified.
- Requires input that the investment manager cannot reliably provide.

This can happen if the model was developed originally for another market or another style of investment. For example, a model developed for leading stocks cannot be expected to produce results of the same quality for portfolios of small capitalization stocks. The next potential problem is model misspecification. Most models are developed and tested on historical data. If its at-first very promising results came from an atypical period in the past, it will fail to deliver the results expected of it in the future. This problem occurs surprisingly often. The practice is sometimes known as **data-mining**, because the analyst has, in effect, wittingly or unwittingly, chosen the test period to best flatter the model. Other data periods, including the one when the model was investing real money, can yield less impressive results. Model risk also covers those occasions when the model requires input that the manager is not very good at providing. For example, for a macroeconomic model to work, the manager must have access to very good macroeconomic research.

Misinterpretation of results also happens surprisingly often. The model may appear to give clear insights into the relative valuation of an asset or portfolio construction, when in fact the results are open to several interpretations. Probably the most common error is where an asset appears to be underpriced relative to its risk, when in fact it is the risk that is being underestimated. Results can also be misinterpreted if there has been an error in the data. The problem of misinterpretation is most acute when a model is used as a **black box**. In other words, when the investment manager does not fully understand all the relationships that drive the model.

Limitations of historical data are generally quite well understood by quantitative investment managers. Not only are historical data prone to errors, but also, even when the integrity of the data is impeccable, there is room for healthy scepticism about what period of history is most appropriate, and to what extent historical data can be used to forecast the future.

Unreliable balance sheet data, surprisingly, is less well accepted as a problem for quantitative models. Balance sheet data has two main flaws. First, it is released infrequently, and second, it can be very misleading. With the exception of the USA, many stock market regulators do not require high degrees of detail and accuracy in company reports, so the standard of information contained in company reports and other reports to shareholders is not of a high enough quality to use in return and risk modelling. Most companies are required to produce reports only once or twice a year, and not necessarily very soon after the end of the reporting period. Because many stock selection models have their origins directly or indirectly in the USA, where company data tends to be timely and accurate, they tend to assume high quality balance sheet data and to underemphasize the problems caused by inadequate or inaccurate data in other markets.

CASE STUDY

Stock selection models benefit from parsimony. Some of the simplest stock selection models can turn out to give impressive results over successive return periods.

The Australian economy, most people recognize, is a resource-based economy. The local stock market index, widely used by local investors as the benchmark for domestic equities, is the All Ordinaries Index (AOI). The AOI is made up of stocks classified as either industrials or resources. The proportions by market capitalization are roughly 70% and 30% respectively, and the two

EXAMPLE 8.11.1 *Comparison of return and volatility for Australian All Ordinaries, All Industrials and All Resources indices*

To December 1995	All Ordinaries Total Return		All Industrials Total Return		All Resources Total Return	
	Return %	Volatility %	Return %	Volatility %	Return %	Volatility %
1 Year	20.19	11.51	24.94	9.21	11.69	18.48
2 Years	4.77	13.59	4.49	12.49	5.49	18.97
3 Years	16.85	14.28	15.34	13.22	20.33	19.43
5 Years	15.91	13.79	16.03	13.41	15.96	17.78
10 Years	12.85	20.82	13.53	20.13	11.76	25.87
15 Years	12.56	20.52	17.18	18.86	7.31	26.41

Source: Thomson Financial Datastream

sectors behave quite differently. The resource sector is characterized by low returns and high volatility, and is dominated by a small number of jumbo stocks favoured by offshore investors. Other stocks in the sector are plagued by chronic lack of liquidity, which further increases their volatility. The global stock market, by contrast, comprises only about 10% in resource stocks.

For the Australian market to justify having so much more in resources than the rest of the world, Australian resources must have a diversifying effect with respect to the industrial sector that is peculiar to Australia. There seemed to be little evidence for this and, as the AOI nearly always delivers lower returns and higher volatility than an industrials-only portfolio, some tests were run to see what the effect would be of varying the mix of industrials and resources.

From Example 8.11.1 it would appear that the best solution would be simply to exclude resource stocks altogether, but a closer look at the data suggested that this might be unacceptable to investors. The returns to 1993 and 1994, set out in Example 8.11.2, show that, in some market conditions, resource stocks can greatly outperform industrials, so an industrials-only strategy would sometimes disappoint.

So what proportion of industrials to resources gives the best risk-return balance across all test periods? The conclusion drawn was that the global proportion would probably be a good place to start. So the same calculations were carried out using a portfolio comprising 90% resources and 10% industrials, with the results shown in Example 8.11.3.

The risk-return trade-off for the four hypothetical portfolios is illustrated graphically in Example 8.11.4.

EXAMPLE 8.11.2 *Comparison of return and volatility for Australian All Ordinaries, All Industrials and All Resources indices: 1993 and 1994*

	All Ordinaries Total Return		All Industrials Total Return		All Resources Total Return	
	Return %	Volatility %	Return %	Volatility %	Return %	Volatility %
1993	45.36	13.47	40.53	12.71	56.55	18.00
1994	−8.67	14.35	−12.61	13.23	−0.37	19.31

Source: Thomson Financial Datastream

EXAMPLE 8.11.3 *Results for Australian All Ordinaries, All Industrials and All Resources indices and 90/10 portfolio from 1996 to 1999*

	All Ordinaries Total Return		All Industrials Total Return		All Resources Total Return		90/10 Portfolio Return	
	Return %	Volatility %	Return %	Volatility %	Return %	Volatility %	Return %	Volatility %
1996	14.60	8.60	19.82	9.27	4.11	11.31	18.22	8.91
1997	12.23	16.72	24.57	16.77	−17.23	20.99	19.76	16.69
1998	11.63	11.46	17.47	11.16	−11.22	21.78	14.45	11.17
1999	16.10	11.42	10.77	10.54	49.80	27.53	14.50	11.01
1996–99	13.63	12.41	18.05	12.35	3.47	22.29	16.71	12.30

Source: Thomson Financial Datastream

EXAMPLE 8.11.4 *Risk-return trade-off for Australian All Ordinaries, All Industrials and All Resources indices and 90/10 portfolio from 1980 to 1999*

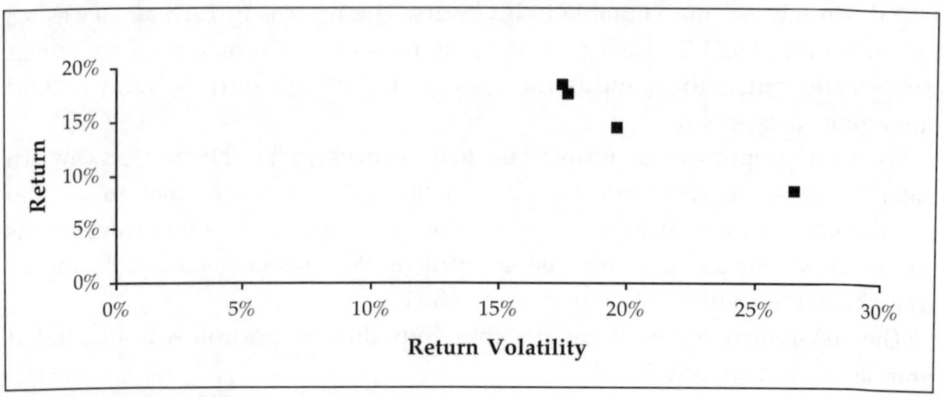

Source: Thomson Financial Datastream

The 90/10 portfolio and the All Industrials Index are quite close together, showing a very high return to risk ratio. The All Ordinaries shows a slightly lower return with higher risk, while the position of the All Resources Index suggests that the long-term rewards to this portfolio by itself cannot justify the return volatility.

So the 90/10 strategy was adopted. No other stock selection was required, or even seen as desirable, so each sector was managed as an indexed portfolio. The problem with this strategy was its simplicity; since all its value was in the insight underpinning the model, it was both very easy for other investment managers to copy, and difficult to demand significant management fees.

The second problem was easily overcome using performance-based fees. The investor would pay indexed portfolio fees plus a proportion of the amount by which the portfolio did better than the AOI. This arrangement was subject to a 'catch-up' clause, whereby any underperformance would have to be matched by subsequent, equal outperformance before the performance-based fee could be reactivated.

The first problem was much less tractable. To demonstrate ongoing value added, the investment manager sought to develop a 'switching mechanism' to forecast periods when resources were indeed likely to do better than industrials. The portfolio would then 'switch' to the benchmark 70/30 allocation.

Development of the switching mechanism turned out to be much more difficult to do. After considerable research using historical data, a factor-based model emerged based on a number of macroeconomic indicators and resource price indices. The model was shown to have some predictive value on past data, but was not subject to sufficient live testing – using current prices – to be proved of unambiguous value. In fact, the switch signal was never activated, and the portfolio remained at its initial 90/10 allocation. The good news was that portfolio returns delighted the members and the trustees of the fund, not to mention the investment manager. It soon had a number of imitators.

Example 8.11.5 summarizes the results for two years. The portfolio initially suffered from its underexposure to resources, thus invoking the catch-up clause in the calculation of performance-based fees. The underperformance of the quarter to March 1996 was recuperated in subsequent periods before the manager could claim further fees based on performance.

Note

1. Andrew Lo, Harry Mamaysky and Jiang Wang, *Journal of Finance*, August 2000, cited in *The Economist*, 19 August 2000, p. 76.

EXAMPLE 8.11.5 *Actual portfolio performance 1996 to 1997*

Period: 3 Months to:	Value of Portfolio $	Notional Value of All Ordinaries $	Difference $	Base Fee $	Performance Fee $	Cumulative Fees Paid $	Cumulative Net Return to Investor $	Compared to the All Ordinaries $
Dec 95	60 000 000	60 000 000	0			0	60 000 000	0
Mar 96	61 105 808	61 173 623	−67 815	48 884	0	48 885	61 056 923	−116 700
Jun 96	62 702 232	62 294 637	407 595	50 161	84 945	183 992	62 518 241	223 604
Sep 96	66 075 261	64 169 829	1 905 432	52 860	476 358	713 210	65 362 051	1 192 222
Dec 96	70 931 340	68 758 415	2 172 924	56 745	543 231	1 313 186	69 618 154	859 739
Mar 97	72 107 887	69 343 172	2 764 715	57 686	691 179	2 062 051	70 045 836	702 664
Jun 97	82 502 382	78 840 729	3 661 653	66 002	915 413	3 043 466	79 458 916	618 187
Sep 97	86 797 908	80 730 271	6 067 637	69 438	1 516 909	4 629 814	82 168 095	1 437 824
Dec 97	84 946 879	77 166 380	7 780 499	67 958	1 945 125	6 642 896	78 303 983	1 137 603

CHAPTER 9

Quantitative Models for International Equity Portfolios

APPLICATIONS

Investors' attitudes to investing in international equities vary widely. Many people consider the investments available in their home market provide more than adequate opportunities to earn handsome returns. It is also sometimes argued that investing overseas deprives local enterprise of much needed investment capital. Trustees of pension funds may also argue that, because the liabilities of the fund are denominated in the home currency, it makes sense to offset these with assets similarly denominated.

It is certainly true that investing internationally introduces risks and costs that do not obviously apply to investment in domestic equities. But there are very good reasons to invest outside one's home market. The most important is to increase diversification. Stock markets perform differently from each other, and because of this they are important sources of diversification, providing the opportunity for a much superior return for a given level of risk. Taken individually, foreign markets may appear very risky, as investors in emerging markets discovered to their costs during the 1990s. Taken together, they can significantly enhance the risk-adjusted returns to an investment portfolio. While the argument for evaluating returns relative to some liability can be compelling, it is absolute return levels that are needed to meet the fund's eventual obligations.

Example 9.1 illustrates the fact that, most of the time, the international portfolio delivers higher returns with lower volatility of returns than a broad-based domestic portfolio.

EXAMPLE 9.1 *Risk and return for domestic and international portfolios*

	S&P500		MSCI World	
	Annualized Return %	Risk %	Annualized Return %	Risk %
1970s	1.60	15.89	2.74	13.96
1980s	12.59	16.32	15.78	14.62
1990s	15.31	13.36	9.62	13.94
1998	26.67	20.56	22.78	18.79
1999	19.53	12.58	23.56	11.67
2000	−10.14	17.25	−14.05	13.94

Source: Thomson Financial Datastream, MSCI

The other important reason is that most domestic portfolios already have considerable international exposure. This comes from the fact that many firms derive significant proportions of their incomes from outside the home economy. Because the constituents of most domestic portfolios have international risks, so also must the portfolio. There are sound reasons to recognize and manage this risk and, once the decision has been taken to do so, there is little logic in limiting the investment opportunity set of the portfolio to those assets with listing on the home stock market.

THEORY

The main objective of investing in international equities is to seek expanded investment opportunities and to fine-tune risk control through diversification. With the increase in investment opportunities comes a variety of ways of analysing and selecting assets, constructing the portfolio and managing its risks.

How much extra investment opportunity and diversification potential is achievable is determined first of all by what universe of international equities the portfolio is selected from. For example, should the portfolio be limited to large stocks in developed markets, or should small stocks and emerging markets be included too? It is tempting to select countries that one is familiar with, such as neighbours and countries sharing a language, but this risks defeating the purpose of investing internationally, which is to broaden horizons, and may best be achieved by venturing further abroad.

As a rule, a broader investment universe is preferable to a narrower one, but if cost is a consideration, then the fund may need to confine its range of investments. The minimum practical size of investment depends on the country and the investment instruments available, but in practice most funds are able to invest in at least several developed and emerging markets, with only large funds having complete flexibility to include a wide range of small markets in their opportunity set.

DEFINING THE BENCHMARK

The choice of international benchmark should reflect the investor's investment universe and be investable, meaning that it should be possible for the investor to actually invest in all the component securities in their benchmark allocations. Most investors prefer benchmarks that are widely used, as this incorporates some element of peer-group benchmarking without the worst difficulties of overtly using peer-group portfolios as benchmarks. An important distinction between international equity indices is how they allocate to countries, which can be either by gross domestic product (GDP) or market capitalization. GDP allocation has the advantage that it is not affected by stock market valuations and can be said to represent the contribution of each economy to world output. On the other hand, it can result in large allocations to countries with relatively small stock markets, with the consequence that investability can suffer. Market capitalization inherently applies any mispricing of markets relative to each other. Because it gives greater allocations to markets that are overpriced, it builds in inferior returns. Nevertheless, the most popular international equities benchmarks apply market capitalization.

RETURN FORECASTING

For most investors, forecasting returns is the most important aspect of investing in international equities. While in theory all methods for forecasting returns to domestic equities are equally valid for international equities, in practice most investment managers adapt some kind of top-down approach, such as ratio analysis or factor analysis that allows screening of large numbers of stocks. The task becomes interesting very quickly as international differences in industry structures, regulations and accounting conventions make cross-country comparisons complicated. For example, comparing an European bank with a US-based bank is not like comparing two European banks because they are subject to completely different regulations. From the enactment of the Glass-Steagall Act of the 1930s until quite recently, US banks have been obliged to be either a money centre, investment bank or a regional lending bank. European banks have been free to mix their business.

Likewise, comparing Japanese companies and western ones with similar business mixes can be challenging because Japanese accounting conventions differ strongly from most western ones.

Different markets are dominated by different industries. There are few gold explorers in the UK, for example, while Japan is not known for its pharmaceutical industry, and Switzerland is. Anyone looking for an aerospace industry in Australia is going to be disappointed.

In order to devise a coherent strategy for investing in international shares, the investor must decide the following issues:

- Categorize assets by country, industry or some hybrid categorization.
- Include emerging markets in the global portfolio, as a separate asset class, or omit them altogether.
- Apply global factors.
- Include currency forecasting and management in the international equity portfolio or treat currencies as a separate asset class.
- Include risk management in the return forecasting and portfolio construction process or manage risk separately.

Categorize assets by country, industry or some hybrid categorization

How assets are categorized within the portfolio is important as it determines how security return forecasts are generated, and hence how securities are selected.

Ideally, the international equity portfolio should be constructed, analysed and managed without categorizing assets at all. Unfortunately, this approach poses problems of its own because of the scale and scope of the task. The necessity of dividing the job of evaluating, analysing, implementing and managing a portfolio with tens of thousands of investment possibilities means that many heads are needed. Because of the level of skill and specialization required, lines of responsibility need to be carefully defined. There is no unambiguous best formula for achieving this, so the investor needs to evaluate the structure that makes sense, given the investment objectives, the skills available, the costs and tolerance for risk.

Country-by-country categorization is superficially the simplest, as most investors think in terms of country of domicile. After all, most companies are based somewhere. If the company's head office is in Berne, it is a Swiss company. If it is based in Toronto, it is Canadian. The big advantage of this approach is that it allows the world to be viewed simply as the sum of its countries, allowing any of the return forecasting approaches described in Chapter 8 to be applied. This approach can also have the appeal that many markets are dominated by one or two industries, such as gold and diamond production in South Africa, pharmaceuticals and banking in Switzerland, communications in Finland, and so on. Country-by-country categorization can thus act as a proxy for industry categories. Another advantage of this approach is that the country category can usefully indicate something about the tax and regulatory environment. US banks are different to banks in other parts of the world, for example, because they have grown up in a different regulatory environment.

It also enables the investor to categorize emerging markets easily, as they are just another group of countries. But this way of thinking is at best limited, and at worst may misrepresent the real opportunities open to the international investor. Perhaps the worst danger of the country-by-country approach is that it can encourage the assumption that the currency of denomination of an asset is the dominant characteristic of the security. For example, it assumes that a security categorized as Swiss has more in common with other Swiss stocks than with similar stocks domiciled elsewhere. Assets with multiple currency exposures are arbitrarily assigned a single currency exposure that may bear little relationship to what actually drives their returns. This can cloud the global view and result in missed opportunities. There are other ways of including emerging markets.

An even more serious shortcoming of the country-by-country approach is that country exposure can be taken to equal currency exposure. In other words, it is easy to assume that all Swiss assets have exposure only to Swiss currency.

Example 9.2 illustrates how country allocations in developed markets, based on market capitalization, have changed over time, reflecting faster growth in some stock markets than in others.

Industry-by-industry categorization can yield impressive results because it avoids the most arbitrary outcomes of the country-by-country approach, based on the location of a company's listing. The industry in which a company has its main operations is a much more salient feature of the company than the location of its main listing. For example, saying that a company is an oil producer is a sensible definition, whether it is based in the UK, the US or elsewhere is unim-

EXAMPLE 9.2 *Categorization of international portfolio by country*

Country/Region	Weight 2000 %	Weight 1995 %	Country/Region	Weight 2000 %	Weight 1995 %
Belgium	0.40	0.70			
Finland	1.30	0.30			
France	5.50	3.60			
Germany	4.10	3.90			
Ireland	0.30	0.20			
Italy	2.20	1.30	Switzerland	3.40	3.40
Netherlands	2.70	2.30	Total Europe	33.50	28.50
Portugal	0.20	0.00			
Spain	1.40	1.00	Canada	2.40	2.20
Eurozone	18.10	13.30	United States	50.60	40.80
			North America	53.00	43.00
Austria	0.10	0.20			
Denmark	0.40	0.50	Australia	1.30	1.50
Norway	0.20	0.30	Hong Kong	1.00	1.80
Sweden	1.30	1.20	Japan	10.70	23.40
United Kingdom	10.00	9.60	Malaysia	0.00	1.20
Other EU	12.00	11.80	New Zealand	0.10	0.20
Total EU	30.10	25.10	Singapore	0.50	0.70
			Asia Pacific	13.60	28.80
			World	100.00	100.00

Source: MSCI Perspectives

portant. Similarly, British Telecom has more in common with Deutsche Telekom than with, say, Cadbury Schweppes. The industry group approach also forces an active view of currency exposure. Because the investor needs to convert all asset values to a common currency in order to carry out even the most rudimentary analysis of returns, the temptation to equate currency of denomination with currency of returns and risk is very much reduced. Instead, the investor is forced to think separately about the effects of currencies on portfolio returns.

However, there are limitations to the pure industry-by-industry approach. Defining industry groups and assigning securities to them is difficult when the nature of the business carried out changes, and the industries in which they operate change too. This is by no means insurmountable: the job of the investment manager is to keep abreast of such developments, to interpret their significance and exploit the opportunities that they present.

A more intractable problem is that not all industries are global or even international. Some are stubbornly local. Classifying a security as retail is not especially helpful: it needs to be defined as UK retail or Japanese retail, because retailing is by its nature a local operation.

Stocks spanning several industry groups pose a bigger problem to portfolio and stock analysts. The most popular solution is simply to select the sector that represents the bulk of the company's sales. It would be better, most people would agree, to choose the sector providing the biggest contribution to profitability, but this can be hard to identify because companies are not always required to give information about sector-by-sector profitability. To do so implies disclosing details of cost structures by industry, and most companies are understandably reluctant to do this. Even if it were practical, allocating a company to an industry group according to its largest profit contributor would still result in some degree of misallocation.

Industry-based approaches do not lend themselves to all forecasting methods. Those that are most amenable to industry-based analysis include single stock models, arbitrage pricing theory (APT), macroeconomic, factor and other mean-variance approaches.

One of the implications of applying industry-by-industry stock categorization is that emerging markets must be integrated into the main international equities portfolio, placed in a special asset class or omitted altogether from the investment portfolio. Most investors adopting the global industry approach tend to focus on developed markets, with emerging markets as a separate asset class. The shortcoming of this approach is that the distinction between emerging and developed markets is itself arbitrary and changeable. Countries such as Portugal, Greece, Israel, South Africa and Taiwan have legitimate claims to be members of both groups. Consider the number of West European and North American automobile manufacturers with operations in South America and Eastern Europe. Many emerging markets' telecommunications firms are listed in New York as well as in their 'home' market.

Example 9.3 shows how international industry allocations in developed markets have changed over time.

Include emerging markets in the global portfolio, as a separate asset class, or omit them altogether

The argument for treating emerging markets separately is that they sometimes seem to behave as a group. The first strong evidence of this was during the 'Asian

EXAMPLE 9.3 *Categorization of international portfolio by industry*

Industry Group	Weight 2000 %	Weight 1995 %	Industry Group	Weight 2000 %	Weight 1995 %
Energy Sources	5.40	5.90			
Utilities	3.60	5.00			
Energy	9.00	10.90			
Building Materials	0.60	1.20			
Chemicals	1.70	3.50			
Forest Products and Paper	0.40	1.20			
Non-Ferrous Metals	0.50	1.10			
Steel	0.20	1.10	Broadcasting & Publishing	2.60	2.00
Misc. Materials & Commodities	0.20	0.80	Business & Public Services	7.80	4.00
Materials	3.60	8.90	Leisure & Tourism	1.30	1.60
			Merchandising	4.50	4.60
Aerospace & Military Equipment	0.90	0.90	Telecommunications	7.80	5.00
Construction & Housing	0.40	1.20	Transportation – Airlines	0.50	0.60
			Transportation – Road & Rail	0.60	1.20
Data Processing & Reproduction	1.80	2.10	Transportation – Shipping	0.20	0.40
Electrical & Electronics	4.90	3.80	Wholesale & International Trade	0.30	0.70
Electronic Components	6.30	2.10	Services	25.60	20.10
Energy Equipment & Services	0.50	0.30	Banking	10.00	13.20
Industrial Components	0.80	1.50	Financial Services	4.40	2.60
Machinery & Engineering	0.90	2.00	Insurance	5.40	4.20
Capital Equipment	16.50	13.90	Real Estate	0.80	1.50
			Finance	20.60	21.50
Appliances & Household Durables	1.10	1.40	Multi Industry	3.50	2.70
Automobiles	1.80	2.70			
Beverages & Tobacco	2.40	3.80	Gold Mines	0.10	0.30
Food & Household Products	2.40	3.70			
Health & Personal Care	12.40	8.50			
Recreation & Other Consumer Goods	0.90	1.20			
Textiles & Apparel	0.20	0.30			
Consumer Goods	21.20	21.60	**Total**	**100.00**	**100.00**

Source: MSCI Perspectives based on the old MSCI classification system CII (Country Industry Indices) which was discontinued as of the close of 13 July 2001. It has now been replaced by the Global Industry Classification Standard (GICS SM), developed jointly by MSCI and Standard & Poor's

Crisis' that began in late 1997. Many large investors had begun to hold portfolio investments in countries where they had little previous investing experience. These investments were viewed as highly speculative for various reasons.

South and Central American investments could have been thought to be subject to difficult economic regimes, having had a history of unstable macroeconomic policies, so their prospects for growth could have been thought of as uncertain. Eastern Europe could have been thought of as being subject to political risks and corruption, with a shaky legal environment and the legal rights of investors subject to some compromise. Asia had demonstrated the capacity for extraordinary growth, but western-style stock market regulation was in most places deemed inappropriate to the dynamism driving profits. Meanwhile, the combination of a selective application of market-based asset valuation with state sponsored intervention gave rise to a misinterpretation of investment risks by many investment managers, with the result that the investments turned out to be more risky than had been anticipated.

Although the economic forces driving growth in each region was quite different, Latin America, Eastern Europe and Asia were grouped together in the minds of many European and North American portfolio investors, mainly because they were unfamiliar to them. When it was perceived that South East Asia was less sound than had been assumed, all regions suffered the sell-off.

The problem with treating emerging markets as separate from other markets is that the distinction is often arbitrary and open to interpretation, and that countries increasingly breach the categorization criteria.

At the time the 'Asian Crisis' hit in 1997, for example, Morgan Stanley Capital International (MSCI) classified Malaysia as a developed market (having been given that status in 1993). By the end of the crisis, it again considered it an emerging market. The criterion had been set by the index provider well in advance, and had been respected, reinforcing the point that objective criteria are sometimes unavoidably arbitrary and therefore subject to being breached.

What defines a market as emerging as opposed to developed is very much open to debate. It may be simply that the stock exchange on which it is listed is not subject to an acceptable amount of regulation, or it might just mean that there is very little information about the stocks listed on it. Many assets thought of as emerging have more in common with developed market assets (think of some South American telecommunications stocks) than with other assets listed in their home markets. By the same token, many stocks listed in developed countries derive a significant part of their value from operations in parts of the world regarded as emerging. For example, most oil producers have significant operations in sub-Saharan Africa and the Middle East. Big airlines form joint ventures all over the world, as do privatized utilities and telecommunications companies. Example 9.4 sets out countries usually considered to be emerging markets.

EXAMPLE 9.4 *Categorization of emerging markets portfolio by country*

Country/Region	Weight %	Country/Region	Weight %
Greece	4.86		
Hungary	0.76		
Poland	1.14		
Turkey	2.54		
Russia	1.91	Argentina	1.38
Czech Republic	0.51	Brazil	10.43
Emerging Europe	11.72	Chile	3.26
		Colombia	0.28
Hong Kong	6.39	Mexico	9.78
Taiwan	15.37	Peru	0.30
Thailand	1.50	Venezuela	0.41
India	7.03	*Latin America*	25.84
Indonesia	0.88		
South Korea	9.23	Israel	5.19
Malaysia	6.83	Jordan	0.13
Philippines	1.07	*Middle East*	5.31
Sri Lanka	0.03		
Pakistan	0.27	South Africa	8.50
China	0.04		
Emerging Asia	48.63	*Emerging World*	100.00

Source: MSCI Perspectives Emerging Market Indices

As western investors become more familiar with investing in such regions, and as these markets mature, the frontier between emerging and developed will inevitably be breached more frequently. There is thus a strong argument for including emerging markets portfolios in the overall international equity portfolio.

Apply global factors

Yet another approach is to avoid classification by country or industry and use global factors. The principle is the same as a factor model applied to a domestic equity portfolio, with the difference that the portfolio potentially contains many times more securities in it and the factors chosen must have relevance to the global portfolio as opposed to the domestic market. Although computationally complex, this approach has a number of benefits:

- It avoids the arbitrariness of security categorization, removing the most confounding influences on return and risk analysis.
- It encourages an innovative approach to return forecasting, as forecasts are generated according to global principles rather than within country or industry boundaries.
- It can highlight the portfolio's exposure to global effects that would otherwise remain hidden.
- It can highlight the real currency exposures of the portfolio, encouraging an active approach to currency management.
- By eliminating country and industry boundaries, it can allow enormous flexibility in defining and applying the global factors that are most appropriate to the portfolio in question. Thus it gives the best scope for fine-tuning the choice of factor, giving potentially the best risk analysis.

The global factor approach is becoming increasingly popular as markets become more and more global. Of a typical international equity portfolio, most is made up of stocks either with multiple listings or operations diversified across several or many countries. The problems of misallocation of risk associated with traditional portfolio classification are thus becoming both more acute and less acceptable.

Include currency forecasting with asset forecasts, or treat currencies as a separate asset class

The importance of currencies to portfolio returns is hard to overstate. The investor might apply impeccable analysis to gain high quality forecasts of individual asset returns, but lose money because the currency went the wrong way, or the opposite might happen.

Even experts agree that forecasting currency returns by applying fundamental analysis is a hazardous occupation. Economists agree broadly on the factors to which exchange rates should respond, such as economic growth within the currency zone, the structure of interest rates, current and forecast inflation rates and so on, but most also agree that these factors persistently fail to produce forecasts of exchange rates that are even vaguely accurate.

Choosing the best approach to currency management depends on how many currency groups there are in the portfolio and how securities are categorized, such as country-by-country, industry-by-industry, and whether emerging markets are included. There are three broad approaches to currency management:

- Currency neutral, or passive currency management.
- Hedge to base currency.
- Active currency management.

The simplest approach is known as **currency neutral**, or passive currency management, whereby the amount of each foreign currency held exactly matches the nominal value of assets bought in that currency. The investment manager simply has to ensure that there is always enough of each currency to effect required purchases and to meet any obligations resulting from corporate actions. Similarly, dividends can be reinvested in the currency in which they are received.

A portfolio that is **fully hedged to base currency** shares some of the features of the currency neutral strategy, in that just enough foreign currency is purchased to enable the purchase of foreign assets. The hedged position differs in that foreign currency is then sold forward to neutralize or hedge away the foreign currency risk. The manager must closely monitor the balance in each currency group to ensure that the value of forward exchange contracts is providing the appropriate hedge. This is not as straightforward as it sounds, as the values of equity holdings rise and fall while the face value of the currency hedge remains the same. The investor and the manager must agree how much discrepancy between the value of the foreign investment and the currency hedge can be tolerated, and at what intervals the hedge should be adjusted. For example, the investor might agree to a maximum discrepancy of 1% of the overall portfolio value, which is easy to manage for small countries, but trickier for big ones. Alternatively, the tolerance might be set to a percentage of the benchmark allocation to that currency, or some other criterion selected. In each case, the tolerance for discrepancy should be augmented by regular review at preset time intervals.

Active currency management seeks to exploit extra returns and risk control from forecasting currencies and increased opportunity for diversification. This strategy requires constant monitoring of actual versus forecast currency returns. Predefined decision rules are indispensable to ensure that profits are realized, losses contained and maximum risk tolerances are not exceeded.

The volume of currencies traded throughout the world exceeds the 'underlying' trade in goods and services and investment flows by staggering orders of magnitude. The vast bulk of exchange rate transactions occur between banks, which are using their shareholders' money to speculate on future currency movements. Currency speculation is different from speculation in stocks and bonds in that the outcome is a zero sum game. In other words, the gains to one participant are offset equally by losses to other participants. This fact, together with the difficulty of analysing currency movements, leads many investors to put currency management in an investment class of its own. This can then be placed in the hands of a specialist currency manager, who is given the brief to earn a positive return from trading currencies.

The logic behind separating currency management by putting it in the hands of a specialist or adopting a policy of hedging it away altogether is compelling. It leaves the international equity investment manager to concentrate on

EXAMPLE 9.5 *Foreign currency exposure of a portfolio with a nominal currency hedge*

Portfolio	DJ EUROSTOXX 50 Currency Hedged			
Benchmark	DJ EUROSTOXX 50			
Base Currency	Euro			
		Absolute		**Relative to Benchmark**
Portfolio Variance		2.44%		1.30%
Portfolio Tracking Error		1.56%		1.14%
	Beta	**% Contribution to Risk**	**Beta**	**% Contribution to Risk**
Euro	−0.0859	0.00	0.0735	0.00
Japanese Yen	0.1980	3.57	−0.0099	1.73
UK Pound	0.1904	3.12	−0.0617	17.13
US Dollar	0.6975	17.24	−0.0019	0.39
Australian Dollar	0.1756	2.07	−0.0093	0.54
Canadian Dollar	0.6766	5.51	−0.0098	0.23
Swedish Krona	0.2550	1.98	−0.0023	0.04
Swiss Franc	−0.2894	1.00	−0.0250	0.62
Central America	0.1269	0.72	−0.0130	1.38
Asia	0.0000	0.00	−0.0004	0.00
South African Rand	0.0000	0.00	−0.0016	−0.02
South America	0.1177	0.91	0.0043	0.21
Total Currency Risk		36.12		22.24

Source: QUANTEC, STOXX

deriving the best possible returns from selecting portfolios of international equities. At the same time, it is important to recognize that return to equities cannot be entirely dissociated from currency movements because companies nearly always derive some part of their profits from currency-related events.

Although the portfolio in Example 9.5, based in euros, has all its nominal foreign currency risk fully hedged, the inherent foreign currency risk within companies leaves it quite vulnerable to foreign currency volatility. Measured in absolute terms, the 'hedged' portfolio has significant exposure to US dollars, while relative to an international equity benchmark, it is exposed to UK pounds. Currencies contribute 36.12% to the total absolute risk of this portfolio and 22.24% relative to the equity benchmark. Even with currency fully hedged, the portfolio has significant foreign currency exposure. This is due to the exposures inherent in the stocks making up the portfolio, and highlights the potential advantage of measuring and managing this risk.

Include risk management in the return forecasting process or manage risk separately

The sources of risk to international equities portfolios are complex and varied, so there are many different approaches to risk management and control. How the investor combines return management and risk control is influenced by how portfolio construction is divided between members of the international equities team, and whether currency management is delegated to a specialist manager or integrated into the portfolio itself.

One of the functions of risk management is to estimate the tracking error of the portfolio. This is important not only because consultants require it, but also for use by the investment manager. Without some meaningful quantification of risk, it is impossible to manage. If it is neither quantified nor managed, portfolio risk is contributing to return variation without contributing to returns. Intentional and unintentional risk become confounded. The most widely used measure of risk, the tracking error forecast, relies on the covariance matrix, so it is sensitive to the choice of risk factors on which the covariance matrix is based. Because the way assets are categorized within the portfolio affects the way in which risk factors are selected, this categorization also determines the reliability of the tracking error estimate and sources of tracking error. Given the scope for errors, many investment managers subject their portfolios to two or more risk analyses, using different models, effectively obtaining a 'second opinion'. The benefits of this are that it provides more insight into the sources of portfolio risk and ensures that both models are subject to scrutiny.

It is important that the risk of the international equities portfolio is estimated on a portfolio-wide basis. It is tempting, for example, to estimate the risk of each country portfolio and add these together. This will give misleading results because country risks are not additive. The covariance matrix underpinning the risk estimate should reflect the global nature of the portfolio.

Ideally, the tracking error forecast should include some analysis of the sources of the portfolio's risk, which should then be checked for consistency with analysts' return forecasts, and the investor's own forecasts of important macroeconomic events.

IMPLEMENTATION

One of the main advantages of using quantitative models for stock selection is that they can encourage a disciplined approach to portfolio construction, incorporating predefined decision rules and risk control. In view of this, it is critical that the investment process is clear as to when the model should be run, what data should be used, how the results are to be interpreted and what action should follow. Predefined decision rules should stipulate when assets are to be sold as well as bought, how long the position should be held, what additional return is anticipated and what loss can be tolerated.

Obviously, the issues associated with implementing the international equities portfolio depend on how the portfolio is constructed, and what assets are included in it. For the most part, implementing an international equity portfolio is similar to a domestic one with the addition of purchasing and possibly hedging foreign currency. Equities are bought through international brokers in the home market or through local brokers in the target market. Orders can be placed individually or collectively as basket trades. Nevertheless, there are material differences in the costs and conventions of dealing in international markets, including issues relating to:

- brokerage
- duties
- taxes
- custodian costs
- settlement
- registered versus bearer stock
- foreign ownership restrictions.

Brokerage charges vary widely from market to market. Some markets still have regulated brokerage rates that brokers and other agents are obliged to charge. Generally these are applied as a sliding scale, with the per-share rate of brokerage declining with the number of shares traded or as the value of the trade increases. Most large markets allow brokerage to be negotiated between broker and investor, while some markets are in some stage of transition, during which brokers are obliged officially to charge list prices for transactions, but privately may agree to a 'rebate' for transactions that are very large or simple to execute.

In most markets, brokerage rates are expressed as a percentage of the face value of the transaction, while others, notably the USA, quote brokerage as a value per share or as a sum for the overall transaction.

To give an idea of the range of brokerage rates possible: discount brokerage can be obtained for as little as $25 per transaction or full service brokerage can be more than 1% of the face value of the transaction, even for wholesale investors.

Many markets are still subject to **duties** on share purchases and sales. These can be significant: up to 0.5% on the face value of the purchase or the sale, or both.

Foreign investors may be subject to **taxes** that do not apply to local investors. These may be levied differentially according to the nature of the assets held, for example assets in some industries may be treated differently to assets in other industries. More frequently, the amount of tax payable will depend on how long the asset has been held. In addition to these taxes, dividends may be subject to withholding taxes.

Custodian costs tend to be considerably higher for international investments than for domestic portfolios, reflecting the increased complexity of administering international assets. Custodian costs are normally negotiated between the investment manager and the custodian, with the investment manager working with both. Custodian fees may be levied as an annual fee covering predefined services, as a simple face value of the portfolio or as a fee per transaction, or some combination of all these. The basic service offered by custodians is to arrange settlement of transactions, but can be much more extensive than that, covering accrual and receipt of dividends and coupons, handling cash flows, managing cash balances, portfolio valuation and reporting.

Although the custodian arranges **settlement** of foreign share transactions, the investment manager needs to be aware of settlement rules and practices in each market in order to manage liquidity. Most large markets have established rules defining the maximum time interval for share settlements, usually five to ten days, although some markets have reduced it to three. If there is no maximum settlement period, the investment manager should make provision with the broker to guarantee settlement within a given time. Extended settlement delays can be very costly if they cause a delay in reinvestment of sale proceeds, and can lead to even further complications if the portfolio includes complex currency hedges or other derivatives positions.

Related to settlement is the question of **registered versus bearer stock**. This is not a feature of all markets, but the distinction still exists widely. Holders of registered shares are identifiable on the share register, while bearer shares are not: the share belongs to whoever has possession of the share certificate, no different from a fifty-dollar bill. Many companies issue both kinds of stock in parallel, in which case the two types of shares are priced differently, attracting different rates of return. The implications are significant for takeover activity and also for dividends, not to mention tax. In some regimes, investors in bearer shares are required to register them in order to be entitled to dividends.

Foreign ownership restrictions can seriously bias the construction and implementation of international equities portfolios. Many markets still limit the type of shares that can be held by foreigners. Some, for example, limit the voting rights exercised by offshore investors, so companies wishing to attract foreign investment are obliged to issue non-voting or limited-voting shares in parallel with normal shares for domestic investors. Non-voting shares are usually priced differently from the ordinary kind, usually attracting lower returns.

Other markets limit the size of the investment by foreigners in some industries that may be deemed strategic or otherwise politically sensitive. Banking and media often fall into this category.

The complexity and costs of implementing portfolios of international equities has understandably given rise to a number of attempts to make it simpler and cheaper for western investors. For example, companies based in countries with costly or restricted market practices may simply list their shares on some developed stock exchange. Many choose a listing in either London or New York, which can be very expensive for the company concerned. Another way is to set up a trust in a developed market, the sole assets of which are shares in a company whose shares are otherwise difficult or expensive to buy on its home market. The trust holds the shares indefinitely, and units in the trust are traded on the market where it is listed, thus the rules and settlement procedures of the developed market apply. **American Depository Receipts (ADRs)** and **Statutory Deposit Receipts (SDRs)**, both traded in New York, are examples of such securities.

Yet another approach is to form a trust, often referred to as an **Exchange-traded Fund** (**ETF**), that invests in a diversified portfolio made up of the companies listed in a particular country. As with ADRs and SDRs, the trust is listed on a developed exchange, allowing investors to invest cheaply in a less developed market, with the familiarity of transactions on the developed exchange. The trust indefinitely holds the shares of the target market, and investors gain exposure to the developing market simply by buying units in the trust. Some are actively managed so that the investor gains not just the return to the market in question, but also some performance variation resulting from security selection within the market. Other such trusts guarantee indexed fund-like performance, so the returns to the investor reflect the market return only.

Apart from the obvious benefits of simpler settlement procedures, with associated savings in custodian fees, these trusts may, depending on how they are set up, go some way to overcoming the worst limitations of foreign ownership, such as tax penalties. Obviously, these arrangements need to be evaluated on a case-by-case basis, as tax rules and therefore the benefits offered by the trust vary widely according to regime and investor.

ONGOING MANAGEMENT

The most important aspect of ongoing management is to monitor the efficacy of the portfolio strategy. That is, the investor needs to be sure that the assumptions on which the portfolio was constructed continue to hold true. This is no trivial task because of the amount of information that needs to be assimilated and the number of individual portfolio managers and analysts whose efforts need to be coordinated.

Most managers have systems of regular meetings at which portfolio compositions are reviewed in light of the most recent information. These are usually supplemented with special meetings when unusual events occur, such as unforeseen wars, government defaults and so on.

Because of the complexity of most international equities portfolios, it is important to establish, at the implementation stage, decision rules quantifying the portfolio's tolerances for losses and the risk of losses. These will help to indicate when some kind of adjustment is required to the portfolio holdings, or the assumptions underlying the current portfolio strategy. For example, the investment manager may specify re-evaluating a strategy when actual returns fall outside a prespecified return range, or the extent to which model inputs and assumptions can change before the model needs to be rerun.

This part of ongoing portfolio management can be largely automated, so that the manager's computer system provides constant checks on the critical balances within the portfolio, and sends a message to the appropriate managers when a prespecified limit has been breached. Nevertheless, many investment managers prefer a regular review, whereby the model and portfolios are subject to human inspection.

Whichever criterion is used, such 'early warning' mechanisms can be a powerful addition to any quantitative strategy, as they can help to minimize the possibility of damage due to human error. In general, however, they should be regarded as complementary to the human input to ongoing management, rather than a substitute.

Cash flow management

An important aspect of ongoing management for international equity portfolios is simple liquidity management. As with domestic portfolios, cash must be invested when it is accrued, and the manager must ensure that he or she is always informed of cash as it arrives in the portfolio or is accumulated from dividends or other corporate actions. Given the relatively high transaction costs for most international equity portfolios, there are considerable savings to be derived by equitizing cash flows using futures contracts until physical shares can be bought and sold in economic quantities. For the domestic equities manager, there is one cash balance for each portfolio to think about, but for the international equities manager, there is a separate cash balance for each currency in which the portfolio is invested, amounting to perhaps 15 or 20 separate cash accounts to monitor. He or she therefore needs a well-devised system to keep track of fund movements and to ensure that the portfolio is fully invested, but never overinvested. The services of the custodian are crucial in delivering regular reports on the composition of the portfolio, including cash balances and accruals.

USE OF DERIVATIVES

It is virtually impossible to imagine investing in international equities without using derivatives. In fact, many investors choose to use only derivatives, eschewing as far too costly all investment in physical assets outside the home market. This approach can give a very cost effective exposure to international equities, but is limited both by the inability to derive extra returns from security selection within countries, since each country is effectively an indexed portfolio, and restricts investment to those countries with suitable derivatives markets.

Nearly all international equity portfolios use derivatives, even if only to manage liquidity. In addition to this function, derivatives can be used to fine-tune currency exposures and to implement short-term changes in country allocations. This kind of adjustment follows the same rules and procedures as the adjustments to short-term asset allocation described in Examples 4.12.1 to 4.12.3. More complex strategies might employ asset swaps to exploit anomalies between tax regimes or transient inefficiencies in the relative prices of assets in different markets.

ADMINISTRATION

International equities portfolios present a different set of administration issues from domestic portfolios. Not only is administration made more complex by different settlement conventions and regulatory environments in different countries, but also different tax regimes, and the interaction of each tax regime with that of the investor's home country. For these reasons, most investors and investment managers engage a global custodian to centralize, as far as possible, all the administrative aspects of running an international equities portfolio.

Many custodians engage local firms of custodians on contract in some countries to exploit economies and gain access to local knowledge of market conventions. If the custodian is doing a good job, the administration should appear seamless to the investor, in that he or she will not be aware of individual cash movements, and the participation, as agents of the custodian, of many individual financial institutions.

VALUATION

The custodian often provides this service for the investor and the investment manager. The principles underlying portfolio valuation are no different than for domestic equities portfolios with the addition of physical foreign currencies. The value of the portfolio is usually calculated as the sum of the market value of each individual holding. The value of each holding is the number of shares held, multiplied by the price at which they can be sold and converted to base currency at a specified exchange rate.

Most valuation reports show the value of each holding in both its local currency and the portfolio's base currency. The sum of the base currency values shows the portfolio's holding in that currency, and the sum of these, together with any cash holding, is the value of the portfolio, as shown in Example 9.6.

PERFORMANCE MEASUREMENT AND ATTRIBUTION

The return to the portfolio is calculated as the value in base currency at the end of the period divided by the value at the start of the period minus one, with adjustment for funds flowing to or from the portfolio during the return period. By themselves, portfolio and benchmark returns for discrete periods say little about the portfolio, as results can change abruptly from one period to the next.

EXAMPLE 9.6 *Portfolio valuation*

Valuation Date	30 November 2000		
Portfolio	International Equities		
Base Currency	US$		

Portfolio Summary	$	**Base Currency** $	%
Physical Equities		151 688 046	85.17
Equity Futures		18 788 167	10.55
Total Equities	170 476 213	170 476 213	95.72
Money Market		25 528 174	14.33
Accruals		885 790	0.50
Net Money Market	6 740 007	6 740 007	3.78
Total Portfolio		178 102 009	100.00
Canadian Dollar		5 429 168	3.05
Euro		20 320 833	11.41
Japanese Yen		9 193 214	5.16
Swedish Krona		2 690 480	1.51
Swiss Franc		3 390 653	1.90
UK Pounds		17 959 952	10.08
US Dollars		119 117 708	66.88
Total Portfolio		178 102 009	100.00
Automobiles		2 415 797	1.59
Banks		1 724 273	1.14
Business Services		13 319 015	8.78
Computers		10 531 371	6.94
Electrical		20 241 899	13.34
Energy		7 222 851	4.76
Food Manufacturing		3 812 134	2.51
Health		4 267 421	2.81
Household Appliances		1 471 305	0.97
Insurance		5 132 769	3.38
Leasing & Consumer Credit		3 505 206	2.31
Leisure & Tourism		1 491 526	0.98
Media & Communications		3 466 086	2.29
Oil & Gas		4 709 320	3.10
Pharmaceuticals		15 954 745	10.52
Stores & Retail		6 427 173	4.24
Telecommunication		45 995 156	30.32
Physical Equities		151 688 046	100.00

By contrast, the observed tracking error of the portfolio can provide a more stable measure of the portfolio's variation from benchmark, and has the advantage that it can validly be compared with the forecast tracking error to obtain some insight into consistency of performance.

Because returns by themselves provide so little information, portfolio attribution is a very important exercise, especially for international equities portfolios, where it is necessary to quantify the contribution of foreign currency exposure to portfolio return variance. The principles are the same as for domestic equities, in that the portfolio is decomposed into chunks, which can be countries, industry groups or other factors, to see which ones contributed significantly. What distinguishes an international portfolio is that each asset has a local currency return and a base currency return, with the difference being approximately the currency effect.

In Example 9.7 the overall portfolio returned –8.18% compared with –6.30% for the benchmark. Physical equities returned –9.55%. Of the 3.25% (9.55 – 6.30) return variation, –2.03% could be attributed to industry-related variance, while

EXAMPLE 9.7 *Single period performance attribution*

Period	31.10.2000 to 30.11.2000	%
Portfolio	International Equities	–8.18
Benchmark	MSCI World	–6.30
Variation		–1.88
Portfolio Return in Local Currencies		–1.58
Currency Effect		–0.30
Physical Equities		–9.55
Variation from Benchmark		–3.25
Industry Allocation Effect		–2.40
Stock Selection within Industries		0.37
Total Industry-related Variance		–2.03
Unexplained Variation for Physical Equities		–1.22
Value Added by Trades		–1.03
Country Allocation Effect		–0.65
Asset Allocation within Countries		–0.75
Total Country and Currency-related Variance		–1.40
Unexplained Variation for Portfolio		–0.48

country-related attribution explained –1.40%. Portfolio turnover during the month was 0.26%. The overall impact of trading activity was –1.03%.

The weighted portfolio returns in local currencies amounts to –1.58%, indicating that currency effects largely offset each other, resulting in a net impact of –0.30% to the portfolio overall.

PITFALLS

Perhaps the most dangerous pitfall associated with investing in international equities is not investing enough. Not only are there enormous benefits in terms of increased risk-adjusted return through diversification and greatly increased investment opportunities, there are also significant economies of scale in international investing. Because the global market for equities is larger than any single domestic market, even the largest institutional investors can achieve exposures to stocks or groups of stocks that can contribute meaningfully to their overall portfolio return.

While any categorization of assets is necessarily arbitrary, there needs to be some kind of classification simply to order data and allocate the tasks of managing the assets on a day-to-day basis. One example of misleading asset classification is the distinction between developed and emerging markets. Many assets are listed in both types of market, and so can be arbitrarily classified as one or the other, and risk being in both groups, so investors may unwittingly double their intended exposure. The other problem is that assets and whole countries move from one category to the next, and sometimes back again, often changing the composition of the benchmark as they do. Investors may thus be forced to conduct substantial portfolio adjustments to comply with the investment mandate, thus incurring significant costs with no discernible benefit to the portfolio.

Inappropriate categorization of assets can cause the portfolio's risk to be seriously misestimated. International investing opens up considerable opportunities for enhanced return, but this is associated with an increase in the sources of risk. If managed properly, this directly allows greater control of risk, if not it can result in increased risk. The investor needs to be confident that risk management is both adequate and appropriate.

Administrative and regulatory traps are often the dangers that prevent investors venturing abroad, or limit their exposure outside their home market. Custodians operating in multiple markets should be able to provide some reassurance in this area, as should stockbrokers executing the transactions.

Currency demands particular attention if the investor is either hedging the portfolio's currency exposure to base currency, or the portfolio makes significant use of derivatives contracts in international markets. The danger is that the portfolio becomes over- or underexposed to a particular currency, which can result in an increase in portfolio risk for which there are no compensating returns.

CASE STUDY

This is a pooled trust designed to give exposure to developed markets with minimal non-market risk. Thus it was not designed to anticipate high performing countries or industries, but to be a kind of indexed fund. The benchmark for the fund was a recognized index of developed country equities. The investors in this trust chose it because it was very cheap to trade. The **bid–ask spread** (the difference between the purchase and sale price) of units was set at 0.5%, compared with 1.5% with 2.0% for other indexed international equity trusts.

The way this trust was able to maintain such a small bid–ask spread was by keeping its own transaction costs very low. To minimize transaction costs, the manager held share price index futures instead of physical shares. Every time an investor placed new funds with the trust, the trust's manager would therefore buy international assets to expose the new funds to international equity futures instead of physical equities. When funds were withdrawn, the manager sold futures instead of physical international assets. The transaction costs for the trust were therefore close to the bid–ask spread of the trust.

Because most of the physical assts of the fund were held in short-term interest-bearing instruments, the fund could earn additional returns by investing in short-term investment grade bonds and bills rather than simply holding cash deposits. Such instruments carry some credit risk, and so earn a higher rate of interest than do bank or government-backed deposits. However, the credit risk is generally quite small and, with diversification of issuers and countries, the portfolio-wide risk could be expected to be minimal. It was expected that the fund could earn as much as 0.50% per annum from this source.

The other source of extra return was assumed to come from rolling futures contracts from one settlement month to the next. The portfolio manager, being able to calculate the 'fair' value of the difference in price from one settlement month to the next, would monitor the spread and execute the required trade when the tradable spread was advantageous. Spread trading could earn between 0.20% and 0.50% per annum.

Investing in futures rather than physical shares limits the countries in which the portfolio could invest to those with suitable futures markets. Most major

EXAMPLE 9.8.1 *Composition of the international indexed portfolio and benchmark*

	Portfolio %	Benchmark %
Australia	1.56	1.48
Austria		0.30
Belgium	0.76	0.72
Canada	2.50	2.38
Denmark		0.43
Finland		0.12
France	4.14	3.93
Germany	4.17	3.96
Hong Kong	1.76	1.67
Ireland		0.00
Italy		0.96
Japan	25.78	24.50
Netherlands	2.12	2.01
New Zealand		0.18
Norway		0.19
Portugal		0.00
Singapore		0.78
South Africa		0.09
Spain		1.17
Sweden		0.76
Switzerland	2.93	2.78
UK	11.88	11.29
USA	42.42	40.31
World	100.00	100.01

markets were included, as shown in Example 9.8.1. Country allocations were maintained as closely as possible to benchmark, with consideration for regional allocations. For example, the shortfall in Singapore was compensated by overweighting Japan, and the lack of futures contracts in smaller European countries was compensated by increased allocations in UK, Germany, France, the Netherlands and Switzerland. Example 9.8.1 shows the country allocations of the portfolio and its benchmark.

For the first four or five years of its life the trust worked splendidly. Not only were transaction costs low, but custodian fees were kept to a minimum because the number of transactions was much reduced – 11 each time the portfolio required rebalancing, compared with an average of about 1000 for a portfolio of physical shares. The problems began in early 1992, as illustrated in Example 9.8.2, when the fund began to deliver below benchmark returns. The unit holders became restless and started demanding explanations.

A detailed performance attribution was carried out, which showed that the performance problem had a number of sources, including a mismatch in its allocation to individual markets, and the fact that, within markets, the portfolio did not match the benchmark return. It was also significant that the benchmark assumed the full benefit of dividend tax credits even though the fund, as a foreign investor, was not able to earn these credits.

Example 9.8.3 shows that country allocation effects contributed to underperformance in 1993, 94, 96, 98 and 99, mainly due to the lack of futures contracts in countries such as Spain, Italy, Finland, Sweden and Singapore. Security selection within countries contributed to underperformance in the USA, the UK and Japan, where the share price index contract on which futures contracts are based underperformed the benchmark index in those countries.

EXAMPLE 9.8.2 *Performance of the international indexed portfolio and benchmark: 1992–96*

Twelve Months to:	Portfolio %	Benchmark %	Variation %
31 12 1992	−6.52	−3.31	−3.21
31 12 1993	15.92	22.67	−6.75
31 12 1994	4.67	6.31	−1.64
31 12 1995	19.47	22.63	−3.17
31 12 1996	11.10	13.01	−1.91
31 12 1997	8.48	12.39	−3.91
31 12 1998	19.03	21.43	−2.41
31 12 1999	26.79	30.75	−3.96
31 December 1991 to, Annualized:			
31 12 1992	−6.52	−3.31	−3.21
31 12 1993	4.10	8.91	−4.81
31 12 1994	4.29	8.04	−3.75
31 12 1995	7.89	11.51	−3.62
31 12 1996	8.53	11.81	−3.28
31 12 1997	8.52	11.91	−3.39
31 12 1998	9.96	13.22	−3.26
31 12 1999	11.94	15.28	−3.34

EXAMPLE 9.8.3 *Summary attribution analysis of the international indexed portfolio*

	Country Allocation Effect %	Security Selection Within Country %	Residual %
31 12 1992	0.67	−0.40	−3.48
31 12 1993	−0.98	−1.38	−4.39
31 12 1994	−0.32	0.13	−1.45
31 12 1995	0.34	−1.08	−2.43
31 12 1996	−0.60	−0.25	−1.06
31 12 1997	0.67	−1.15	−3.43
31 12 1998	−0.82	−0.77	−0.82
31 12 1999	−0.81	−2.03	−1.12

Sources of Variation		Contribution to Return Variance %	Sources of Variation		Contribution to Return Variance %
Country Allocation					
1993	Spain	−0.24			
	USA	−0.24			
	Singapore	−0.14			
	Italy	−0.14			
	Others	−0.22			
1998	Italy	−0.61			
	Spain	−0.39			
	Others	0.19			
1999	Finland	−0.96			
	Sweden	−0.42			
	Others	0.57			
Security Selection			*Security Selection*		
1992	USA	−0.73	1997	USA	−0.91
	UK	−0.37		Germany	−0.16
	Others	0.70		Others	−0.09
1993	USA	−0.56	1998	USA	−1.20
	Japan	−0.55		Others	0.43
	UK	−0.41	1999	USA	−0.99
	Others	0.13		Japan	−0.86
1995	USA	−0.97		Germany	−0.17
	UK	−0.16		Others	−0.01
	Others	0.05			

CHAPTER 10

Optimized Stock Selection Models

An optimizer is a computer program that uses a combination of share price history data and the relationships between those histories to estimate the most efficient portfolio allocations possible. An efficient portfolio is one that gives the best possible expected return for a given level of risk, or conversely, the lowest possible risk for a given expected return.

APPLICATIONS

Most quantitative investment processes employ the use of an optimizer to assist at some stage in the portfolio construction process, usually in conjunction with some other investment management technology, such as return forecasting models. Some investment managers rely solely on the optimizer to choose an 'optimal' portfolio for them, while others use quite different technology for portfolio construction, simply applying an optimizer for risk forecasts.

Optimizers can be used both for asset allocation and security selection, with the former applying simpler technology than stock selection optimizers.

Pension fund consultants increasingly expect investment managers to provide tracking error and other risk forecasts, and optimizers are used for this purpose, with many managers using their optimizer only to report risk estimates to consultants.

To analyse the risk of an existing or proposed portfolio, the investment manager enters the portfolio and benchmark allocations. The optimizer calculates the forecast risk of the portfolio, together with some analysis of the sources of tracking error.

To construct a new equity portfolio or rebalance an existing portfolio using an optimizer, the investment manager typically enters the following data:

- The existing portfolio and benchmark allocations. Portfolio allocations can be represented as the number of shares held, holding value or percentage of total portfolio value. Benchmark holdings are represented as percentage holdings.
- The universe of permitted investments.
- Forecast returns for each asset in the portfolio and benchmark.
- Any constraints to which the portfolio is subject, such as the total number of assets or maximum exposure to industry groups.

The program identifies a series of efficient portfolios, together with expected risk and return for each portfolio, as well as interesting information about each, such as how likely it is to exceed some target return. The investment manager chooses the portfolio with the desired risk and return characteristics.

THEORY

The underlying theory is derived from Markovitz mean-variance theory. This is closely related to modern portfolio theory and the capital asset pricing model, which is based on the idea that the higher the return expected of a portfolio, the more risk will need to be assumed to earn that return.

Mean-variance theory differentiates between diversifiable and non-diversifiable risk; the importance of the distinction being that only non-diversifiable risk attracts extra returns. Thus investors are interested to know how well diversified their portfolios are and, by extension, if they are achieving the best possible balance of risk and return.

While the return to a portfolio is simply the weighted sum of the expected returns to its components, the portfolio's risk is not. Risk can be thought of as the likelihood of some adverse event taking place, such as a negative return. As with the rolling of dice, where the likelihood of a double one ten times in a row is not simply ten times the likelihood of a single occurrence of a double one. The chance of hurricanes occurring simultaneously in Washington DC and Geneva is not the sum of the likelihood of a hurricane occurring in either place. So the likelihood of the prices of two assets dropping sharply at the same time is not simply the sum of the likelihood of them falling independently.

The science of estimating portfolio risk rests on the ability to estimate the chances of two events occurring at the same time. In the case of asset price movements, this is the correlation or covariance between the returns to two assets. The covariance is estimated using past asset returns to derive a single number to describe the relationship between the two assets. A covariance of +1.0 indicates that the two assets move together: a 10% move in the price of one asset will be accompanied by a 10% move in the same direction of the other asset. A covariance of zero means that they are unrelated, while a covariance of –1.0 means that they have offsetting returns. A covariance of 1.2 indicates that a 10% move in the price of the first asset will be accompanied by a 12% move in the same direction of the price of the second.

While historical returns do not provide an infallible prediction of future covariances, they usually do give the most practical solution, in view of the difficulty of forecasting covariances and the relative stability of historical relationships between asset returns.

If the covariances between each of the components of a portfolio are known, or can be accurately estimated, then the extent to which the risks of the components offset each other can also be calculated, and an estimation of the portfolio-wide risk obtained. In a portfolio comprising only a small number of assets, this is a relatively simple task. A portfolio of ten assets, for example, implies a ten by ten covariance matrix. The imperatives of statistics mean that this must be supported by at least eleven return observations to achieve a meaningful result. No problem here. But most equity portfolios comprise dozens or hundreds of assets, giving rise to potentially enormous logistical data problems and computational complexity. The output for a 200 stock portfolio, for example, would be difficult to compute, let alone verify or interpret.

Markowitz's model requires the investor to forecast, for each asset in the portfolio and benchmark, the return and risk for the investment horizon, as well as the covariances for each pair of assets. For most equity portfolios, this implies a large number of forecasts and a correspondingly high probability of error.

In 1963 William Sharpe introduced the notion of an index as a proxy for the overall market. This greatly simplified the calculations required, as the investor now needed only to estimate expected returns for the overall market, with individual assets' returns and risks estimated in terms of their relationship, expressed as the covariances, or betas, to the market proxy, plus some alpha, which is some fixed amount by which the asset is under- or overpriced relative to the market.

This model is described by the equation already set out in Chapter 3:

$$r_i = a_i + b_i \times (r_m - r_f) + e_i \qquad (10.1)$$

Where:

r_i = expected return to asset or portfolio i
a_i = alpha: intentional or active risk to the asset or portfolio
b_i = beta: the relationship of the asset or portfolio to the market
r_m = the return to the market
r_f = the risk-free rate of return
e_i = residual or error: incidental risk of the asset or portfolio

Sharpe's innovation was welcomed, but most investors recognize that it oversimplified things a little, as forces other than the market can affect the behaviour of asset prices. Some of the complexity of asset price movements could be recaptured by introducing multiple risk factors to replace the single (market) factor that Sharpe had proposed. Optimizers based on this approach are collectively known as 'multi-factor models'.

Factors, which are also referred to as risk factors, can be described as a series of returns that are external to, and have stable and predictable relationships with, the returns to assets within a portfolio or investment universe. Transport stocks, for example, can be expected to routinely respond to changes in the oil price. Thus the oil price might be used as one external factor to help to describe the behaviour of all transport stocks.

The importance of factors is that they reduce the size of the covariance matrix. Using multiple factors necessitates quantifying the covariances between the factors as well as the covariances or betas of each of the stocks to each of the factors.

OPTIMIZERS FOR ASSET ALLOCATION AND STOCK SELECTION

The difference between optimizers for stock selection and asset allocation is that the stock selection problem is a choice between a large number of available assets (several hundred to several thousand), while the asset allocation problem is a choice between, at most, 20 or 30 asset classes. Therefore, for asset allocation it is not necessary to look for factors to reduce the size of the covariance matrix because this is already of a manageable scale. Optimizers for asset allocation therefore create the entire covariance matrix, thus observing the direct relationships between each pair of asset classes. This brings two advantages. The first is that, by not having to choose the right factors, it eliminates an important source of potential error. The second is that the relative simplicity of the computations can allow a great deal of increased flexibility in the software itself, giving the investment manager more scope to refine the computational procedures.

ESTIMATING THE RISK FACTOR MODEL

For stock selection models, the factors applied might include the returns to the market in which the portfolio is invested, the returns to sector, industry and sub-industry groups. They might also include the returns to groups of assets based on common characteristics such as market capitalization, dividend yield and other balance sheet items.

Most factor models try to identify likely candidates for risk factors before applying them to a portfolio analysis. This gives the outcome intuitive appeal and consistency from one period to the next. Another approach is principal components analysis, by which factors are derived directly from portfolio and benchmark return data, giving a potentially very effective explanation of the sources of risk. There are some shortcomings, however. The first is that, since the program simply seeks the most salient relationships, the analysis results in factors without names. It is then up to the investment manager to interpret these and give some economic explanation of them. This can be more easily said than done, and there is almost inevitably a strong element of subjectivity in the interpretation of the results. The second problem with principal components analysis is that, because the factors are derived directly from the data, relatively small changes in data can alter the results achieved. This means that, from one month to the next, the apparent factor sensitivities of the portfolio can change, even with no change in the composition of the portfolio, giving the impression that either the portfolio or the model is unstable.

These shortcomings are unfortunate in that they exclude a very powerful analytic tool from most investment portfolio analyses. Principal components analysis is still widely used by investment bankers and investors seeking to construct an equity portfolio to match an equity index over a short investment horizon, say a few days or weeks.

Most stock selection optimizers for investment management therefore use some kind of predefined factors. The choice of factors, and how they are arrived at, is what most distinguishes between optimizer models. There are some (to mathematicians, at least) important differences between computational procedures but, for the purpose of interpreting the results, they are less important than the choice of factors.

CAPM allows the possibility that each asset and portfolio has an alpha. Alpha is the risk-free return to the asset or portfolio, the amount by which the asset is mispriced. Alpha is zero for a fairly priced asset. The alpha of the portfolio is the weighted sum of the alphas of the assets in the portfolio, which is the same as saying that the portfolio return is the weighted sum of the returns to its components.

Domestic equities portfolios are usually assumed to have relationships with the market in which they are traded as well as industry groups and other common factors, and each of these relationships can be described by a beta, or covariance of the portfolio to that factor. That component of the asset's price movements not associated with markets, industries or other identifiable factors is known as the specific risk of the asset. Portfolios and assets can have betas to a number of markets, industries or other factors. They also have some price fluctuations that are unique, which are described collectively as specific risk, residuals or error. Here is the formula for a two-factor model.

$$Er_i = a_i + b_{ix} \times (Er_x - Er_f) + b_{iy} \times (Er_y - Er_f) + e_i \qquad (10.2)$$

Where:

Er_i = the expected return to portfolio or stock i
a_i = alpha of portfolio or stock i
b_{ix} = the covariance, or beta of portfolio or stock i to factor x
Er_x = the expected return to factor x
Er_f = the expected risk-free rate of return
b_{iy} = the covariance, or beta of portfolio or stock i to factor y
Er_y = the expected return to factor y
e_i = random specific risk of portfolio or stock i

This says that the expected return to stock i is equal to:

- the alpha of stock i, which is the amount by which the stock is over- or under-priced
- plus the beta of stock i to factor times the difference in the expected return to factor x and the expected risk-free rate of interest
- plus the beta of stock i to factor y times the difference in the expected return to factor y and the expected risk-free rate of interest
- plus some error.

Most factor models apply more than two factors, frequently three or four dozen. The group of factors used to create a covariance matrix supporting an optimizer is often referred to as a factor model or a risk model because the factors are designed to explain the variance in the portfolio returns, or risk. Desirable characteristics of risk factors include:

- The factors need to be **relevant** to the portfolio and the market in which it is invested. If they are not, then the relationship of the stocks to the factors (the betas) will be near zero, and the resulting portfolio will not have the desired characteristics.
- They need to be **intuitive**. This is especially important if the portfolio has a significant exposure to one of them. The model should allow the investor to be able to say something about how the portfolio will respond to events in the real world.

- **Observable** factors tend to have more appeal than abstract factors. They reinforce their intuitive appeal, and also are more amenable to data verification. Returns to size, for example, can be observed simply by comparing the returns to published indices of large capitalization stocks with small capitalization stocks within a market. By contrast, it is difficult to compare the total return of high dividend yield stocks with low dividend yield stocks. To achieve the latter, a dedicated index of high dividend yield stocks needs to be created.
- They should be **statistically independent**, meaning that they should have covariances of zero with each other. This just means that they should not overlap: to the extent that factors overlap they are redundant. The ideal is a small number of completely uncorrelated factors.
- They need to have **reliable data** to support them. Reliable, unambiguous data is important because the covariance matrix relies on a series of monthly returns. Problems will occur if the basis of the return calculations changes over time, for example in the way the factor returns are calculated, or if the investor lacks confidence in the source of the factor covariance estimation.
- There should be **not too many** of them. Too many factors can greatly increase the computational complexity of the optimizer, as well as the difficulty of interpreting the results. And of course, the more factors there are, the more possibility of computation or data errors.

Ideally, the risk model should be customized to the portfolio and the market in which it is invested. This is rarely practicable because of the quantity of computations and complexity of the analysis that underpins most risk models. And both portfolios and markets change over time as economies restructure, old industries are transformed or decline and new ones grow. A small number of privatizations can change completely the profile of a market.

A number of optimizer systems are available commercially, although many investment managers choose to develop their own. The advantage of in-house developed optimizers is that they can be customized to a greater degree to the requirements of the investment managers' portfolios. This benefit is greatest for highly specialized investment managers, for example those investing purely in a particular region or stock category. The disadvantage is cost and reliability. Optimizers require a great deal of analysis, management, data, programming and maintenance, which can be carried out more efficiently by a specialist provider.

Of the commercially available optimizers designed for single-market stock selection, a number of approaches present themselves. They broadly divide into those using industry groups as factors and those applying stock characteristics identifiable from balance sheet information to construct factors.

Individual stock characteristics, such as size by market capitalization, dividend yield, debt to equity and price to book ratios, can define highly effective risk factors, particularly in markets where investors use these characteristics as part of their investment analysis and return forecasting process. Stocks thus grouped behave similarly, and the resulting covariance matrix can explain a large proportion of the return variance of the portfolio. This approach to defining risk factors is most powerful when customized to a particular market or portfolio. For example, the kind of stock characteristics important in a resource-based economy are different from those of an economy based on heavy, secondary industry, and different again from one dominated by finance and services. Factors that are irrelevant to the portfolio do not add, and potentially misdirect, information. Dividend yield, for example, is a poor factor for use with Japanese equities because they are characterized by low dividend yield. Nor need it be confined to accounting information: factors can be defined to match any approach to portfolio construction.

One problem with balance sheet information is that it can be hard to come by, and in many markets is unreliable and not timely. Because of important differences in accounting conventions, risk factors based on accounting information can render comparisons between markets invalid. The consequence is that, while potentially useful in constructing single market portfolios, models based on balance sheet information have limited application for international equity portfolios.

Related to this is the problem that risk factors derived from accounting data tend not to be observable. Because independent index or data providers do not generally publish them, the optimization supplier must create and maintain him or herself the risk factor return series. This means that there is no independent check on the computational accuracy of the factor returns, potentially raising questions about their reliability. Another is that some optimization specialists can succumb to the temptation to apply the same risk factors to different markets, putting in doubt their validity. Many investment managers compensate for this shortcoming by adjusting the confidence that they place in the results, effectively accepting at best a very limited risk analysis, and at worst a very misleading one.

The other main approach is to use industry groups as proxies for risk factors. The advantage is that it is much less labour intensive than the stock characteristic approach, and so is less prone to errors of analysis and data processing. Probably the biggest advantage is that industry groups, because they are defined by the local stock exchanges, are likely to embed a reasonable amount of local knowledge about the structure of the market, and so can lend relevance to the risk factors. Return series to locally provided industry groups are frequently published, in which case the factors are observable and their reliability is open to scrutiny.

The industry groups as factors approach also can be very effective if locally defined industry groups are selected on the basis of their statistical independence and ability to explain portfolio variance. Individual stocks can then be assigned to industry groups on the basis of this observed relationship. The result is that the industry groups underpinning the optimizer may not correspond precisely with those published by the local index provider.

Nevertheless, industry groups as factors have a number of shortcomings, the first of which is that industry groups are often poorly composed, and securities assigned to them arbitrarily. Securities spanning several industry groups are usually allocated to the industry from which they derive most of their sales. Allocation on the basis of profit would probably be more valid, but the required information is usually unavailable to achieve this categorization reliably. The second shortcoming is that the industry group approach does not lend itself easily to fully customizing the risk covariance matrix to individual portfolios. Cross-country comparisons of portfolio analyses based purely in industry groups need to be made with care. While there are undoubtedly many unambiguously global industries, such as energy, pharmaceuticals and automobile manufacture, many industries are stubbornly local. There is, as yet, no global building materials industry, nor is retail a global activity. Arguably, the differences between regulations in various countries limit the extent to which banking can be considered a global industry.

THE RELATIONSHIP BETWEEN STOCK SELECTION AND ASSET ALLOCATION

A popular way of constructing a portfolio is first to allocate the portfolio to different asset classes and then to select individual assets within each asset class. A typical portfolio asset allocation is described in Example 10.1. Optimizers can be used during either stage of portfolio construction.

Once asset allocation has been defined, individual sector managers are told their new allocation and instructed to proceed with stock selection. Before implementing individual asset class portfolios, it would be useful to quantify the risks and exposures of the overall portfolio. For example, is the underexposure to US autos nullified by the overexposure to Japanese autos? Or is the global exposure to the finance sector within the investor's desired limits?

The two-tiered, country-by-country process of portfolio construction is usually adopted for its compelling procedural logic, and because it facilitates dividing the analytic and managerial work fairly evenly and according to specialist skills. It might not, by itself, result in the best portfolio construction or

EXAMPLE 10.1 *A typical portfolio asset allocation*

Universe of Assets Includes	Long-term Asset Allocation %
Domestic Fixed Interest	15
International Sovereign Debt	5
Domestic Corporate Debt	10
Domestic Equities	30
Developed Markets Equities	10
Emerging Markets Equities	5
Real Property	15
Cash	5
Foreign Currency	5
Total	100

the best understanding of the investment opportunities available and it almost certainly gives a misestimation of the risks of the portfolio.

Few if any markets operate in isolation. Companies are competing across more and more international frontiers, and so are deriving an increasing share of their revenues from outside their country of domicile. More and more companies identify their principal competitor as some company located on the other side of the world. For example, Novartis does not merely compete with Roche, but also with AstraZeneca, Glaxo Wellcome and Pfizer. It is becoming increasingly popular for companies to emphasize their international nature by listing their shares in several markets. These are not necessarily just Goliaths such as DaimlerChrysler and BP Amoco; plenty of minnows of Asian, European and Latin American origin seek listings in the USA and elsewhere.

Companies with international operations make up the bulk of most international and even domestic equity portfolios. These stocks pose serious problems for the traditional, two-tier portfolio construction technique. To begin with, they are assumed by the process to be sensitive only to events within their country of domicile. This means that stocks must be arbitrarily assigned to one or another country in which they operate or are listed, and this arbitrary classification can alter the collective risk profile of the entire portfolio. At least as important is the question of currency. The two-tier approach can encourage the view that the only currency to which a stock is exposed is its currency of denomination, which can be changed arbitrarily. This assumption is clearly an oversimplification: most equities have multiple currency exposures.

Given the volatility and potential contribution to portfolio risk and return of foreign currencies, many investors prefer to manage or even hedge their currency exposure. This task quickly becomes meaningless if the true currency exposure of the portfolio is unknown.

Example 10.2 shows two portfolios, each comprising Swiss stocks from a single industry. The banks portfolio has a beta of 0.71 to the Swiss franc, while the pharmaceuticals portfolio has a beta of only 0.19 to the Swiss franc. This means that both portfolios will move in the same direction as the Swiss franc against other major currencies, but banks are much more responsive than pharmaceuticals, which are more responsive to changes in the euro and US dollar. This is an unsurprising result when one considers that a large part of Swiss banks' operations are concerned with domestic banking, while pharmaceuti-

EXAMPLE 10.2 *Foreign currency exposure in two domestic portfolios*

	Swiss Banks		Swiss Pharmaceuticals	
	Beta of Portfolio to Currency	**Contribution to Portfolio Risk %**	**Beta of Portfolio to Currency**	**Contribution to Portfolio Risk %**
Euro	0.2207	1.60	0.6082	6.07
Japanese Yen	0.1281	3.02	0.1802	4.42
UK Pound	−0.2457	−3.31	−0.2782	−5.02
US Dollar	0.4368	12.76	0.5869	19.26
Principal Currency		14.08		24.74
Australian Dollar	0.2114	3.25	0.1885	2.32
Canadian Dollar	0.1381	0.89	0.5906	4.73
Swedish Krona	0.3354	3.02	0.1137	0.55
Swiss Franc	0.7129	0.00	0.1893	0.00
Secondary Currency		7.17		7.61
Central America	0.0887	0.70	0.0000	0.40
Asia	−0.0201	0.00	0.0000	0.00
South African Rand	0.0000	0.00	0.1107	0.00
South America	0.0344	0.00	0.0000	0.00
Emerging Currency		0.70		0.40
Total Currency Risk as a Percentage of Total Portfolio Risk		21.95		32.74

Source: Thomson Financial Datastream, QUANTEC

cals companies are much less concerned with their 'home' market. Of random specific risk, both portfolios are subject to risk against the US dollar, which contributes 12.76% and 19.26% respectively to portfolio risk, or tracking error. Foreign currencies contribute between one-fifth and one-third to the overall risk of these 'domestic' portfolios.

APPLYING GLOBAL FACTORS

One way around this dilemma is to apply a global risk model, eliminating the country of domicile from the portfolio construction and analysis process. To do this, all equities are analysed as if they belong to a single, global market, which means identifying risk factors that have global relevance, as opposed to factors that are relevant to a single market. The distinction is not trivial. Take, for example, industry groups. Not all industries have global relevance, even if they exist in nearly all markets. The road transport industry exists in most markets, but it is hard to think of a global road transport industry. It is an activity that is local by its nature. By contrast, chemical production and aeroplane construction are undeniably global, even if some companies in these industries operate only in one country.

Because markets do not operate in vacuums but as part of a global economy, a global risk model cannot be constructed simply as the sum of country models.

An important aspect of global models is dealing with currencies. Obviously all prices and return calculations need to be converted to a single base currency before any other computations can be carried out. A by-product is that this operation highlights the importance of foreign currency exposure. Dispensing with the assumption that currency of denomination is equal to currency of risk can yield important insights. The investment manager is forced to quantify the relationships of the portfolio with a range of currencies. Analysing the currency sensitivity of Rolls-Royce can produce interesting results. Example 10.3 shows influences of currencies on the returns to Rolls-Royce. Three views are presented:

- Absolute, showing the factors to which Rolls-Royce returns are sensitive compared to cash.
- Relative to UK equities, showing the factors contributing to return differences between Rolls-Royce and the UK equity market.
- Relative to global equities, showing the factors contributing to return differences between Rolls-Royce and the global equity market.

EXAMPLE 10.3 *Currency sensitivities of Rolls-Royce from a UK pound base*

	Absolute		Relative to FTSE Allshare		Relative to MSCI World	
	Beta of Portfolio to Currency	Contribution to Portfolio Risk %	Beta of Portfolio to Currency	Contribution to Portfolio Risk %	Beta of Portfolio to Currency	Contribution to Portfolio Risk %
Euro	0.1823	0.26	0.5449	0.95	0.5172	0.31
Japanese Yen	−0.2339	0.38	−0.5432	4.81	−0.6069	6.75
UK Pound	0.2415	0.00	−0.3422	0.00	0.0885	0.00
US Dollar	0.8101	3.69	0.3405	0.48	0.0011	0.00
Principal Currency		4.34		6.24		7.05
Australian Dollar	0.0734	0.22	−0.2825	0.74	−0.3240	1.36
Canadian Dollar	0.7134	1.59	0.2584	−0.07	−0.0425	0.06
Swedish Krona	−0.1665	−0.12	−0.4643	0.79	−0.6117	1.68
Swiss Franc	−0.7655	1.37	−0.4957	0.27	−0.2445	−0.06
Secondary Currency		3.06		1.73		3.04
Central America	0.0000	0.00	−0.0621	0.06	−0.0426	0.02
Asia	0.6382	6.29	0.6805	7.75	0.6352	6.46
South African Rand	0.0000	0.00	−0.0092	−0.01	−0.0214	−0.02
South America	0.0000	0.00	−0.1136	0.10	−0.0550	0.01
Emerging Currency		6.29		7.90		6.48
Total Currency Risk		13.69		15.86		16.57

Source: MSCI, QUANTEC, IDC, FTSE

In absolute terms, the stock is more sensitive to both Canadian and US dollars than to UK pounds, with betas of 0.71 and 0.81 respectively; while relative to UK and global equities, the euro is more important in explaining returns. The stock can therefore be said to have a mismatch to these factors meaning that its returns are driven in part by these currencies. The contribution to portfolio variance indicates the sources of the random component of the return equation, corresponding to the error, or specific risk term. The analysis shows that both Asian currencies and the US dollar contribute to random return variance in absolute terms, while relative to other equities, Japanese yen are a bigger contributor.

Adding interpretation to these outcomes requires judgement and knowledge of the markets involved. For example, the fact that the Canadian dollar contributes more to Rolls-Royce specific risk in absolute terms than relative to either stock index reflects the differential sensitivities to the Canadian dollar of Rolls-Royce and the other components of those indicies.

The importance of global risk models is becoming increasingly accepted as investors and investment managers experience the limitations of the country-by-country approach. Their advantage is that they can provide a useful and often novel insight into the forces likely to affect the portfolio's returns and return variability. But it is a long way from being widely implemented, and there are some good reasons for this.

The global approach effectively merges the asset allocation and stock selection parts of portfolio construction. This merging can introduce some inconvenient problems of analytic and computational complexity and it can be hard to fit into established portfolio construction procedures.

Moreover, defining global factors is not straightforward. Not only is the process computationally complex, but a good deal of intuition is also required to determine what factors have truly global relevance. There is no reason to believe that the same set of global factors are equally relevant to all global equity portfolios, for example portfolios designed to benefit from a fast-growing world economy respond to different factors than those designed to benefit from slower growth.

Less accepted is the relevance of global factors to purely domestic equities portfolios. This is understandable, yet there is plenty of room to argue that the global model can be as important for domestic portfolios as for international ones.

PORTFOLIO RISK ANALYSIS

The objective of risk analysis is to quantify each source of portfolio return variance, both compared to both cash (absolute variation or volatility) and an equity benchmark (relative variation or tracking error). Factor-based optimizers rely on the equation given earlier in this chapter. For a two-factor model:

$$Er_i = a_i + b_{ix} \times (Er_x - Er_f) + b_{iy} \times (Er_y - Er_f) + e_i \quad (10.2)$$

Where:

Er_i = the expected return to portfolio i
a_i = alpha of portfolio i
b_{ix} = the covariance, or beta of portfolio i to factor x
Er_x = the expected return to factor x
Er_f = the expected risk-free rate of return
b_{iy} = the covariance, or beta of porfolio i to factor y
Er_y = the expected return to factor y
e_i = random variation specific to portfolio i

Investment managers conduct risk analysis to quantify the sensitivity or betas of the portfolio to each factor in the risk model and the amount of random variation to which the portfolio is subject. This is also known as the tracking error, when measured against the benchmark, and the volatility when measured in absolute terms. Random variation is the risk for which there is no expected return, so most investors would prefer this risk to be zero. In practice, however, most investment mandates stipulate quite large tracking errors, which are usually misnomers, as they include the hoped-for alpha. Because alpha is impossible to predict accurately, it is bundled with the tracking error estimate.

Multi-factor risk models are able to quantify the component of tracking error that derives from factor exposures. These estimates should not be confused with portfolio factor betas, the difference being that, while betas indicate the direction of the risk, the random variation can be in either direction.

Example 10.4 shows a typical global factor analysis of the tracking error of the S&P500 against the MSCI US index. Factor betas refer to the relationship of the portfolio to each factor relative to the benchmark. The contribution to variance is how much of the portfolio's tracking error is due to each factor. It shows that factor betas play a minor role in determining return variation between the two indices, indicating that both the S&P500 and the MSCI US are largely influenced by the same factors. The total tracking error of the S&P500 against the MSCI US is 1.07%, with a significant contribution from the energy-related factor. This is mostly due to the S&P500 holding in Royal Dutch Petroleum, a stock that is not included in the MSCI US index. Reducing this holding would reduce the tracking error of the portfolio. Where there is a negative contribution to tracking error, as for example in basic industries and resources, an increase in exposure to that factor can be expected to reduce tracking error. Together, the factors in

EXAMPLE 10.4 *Factor beta versus contribution to portfolio risk*

Portfolio	S&P500
Benchmark	MSCI US
Base Currency	USD
Portfolio Variance	1.14%
Portfolio Tracking Error	1.07%

Factor	Beta	Contribution to Portfolio Risk %	Factor	Beta	Contribution to Portfolio Risk %
Euro	0.0289	3.42			
Japanese Yen	0.0044	0.57			
UK Pound	−0.0304	1.01			
US Dollar	−0.0029	0.00			
Principal Currency		4.99	Asian Tigers	−0.0006	0.01
			Australia/NZ	−0.0038	0.02
Australian Dollar	−0.0138	1.30	Belgium	0.0012	−0.02
Canadian Dollar	0.0139	−0.05	Denmark	0.0026	0.06
Swedish Krona	−0.0096	0.28	Finland	0.0012	0.04
Swiss Franc	−0.0008	−0.01	France	0.0010	0.00
Secondary Currency		1.52	Germany/Austria	−0.0012	0.00
			Hong Kong	0.0012	0.07
Central America	−0.0008	0.00	Ireland	−0.0016	0.09
Asia	−0.0018	0.01	Italy	0.0012	0.06
South African Rand	0.0064	0.37	Japan	−0.0030	0.09
South America	0.0152	2.08	Latin America	−0.0002	−0.01
Emerging Currency		2.46	Netherlands	−0.0038	0.19
			Norway	0.0060	0.30
Global Equity	−0.0053	0.24	South Africa	−0.0002	0.00
Global Bond	−0.0052	0.03	Singapore	0.0060	0.49
Global Market		0.26	Spain	0.0009	−0.01
			Sweden	−0.0021	−0.02
Energy-related	0.0211	5.24	Switzerland	−0.0049	0.03
Basic Industries & Resources	−0.0150	−3.42	UK	−0.0241	1.27
Industrials	0.0188	6.12	US/Canada	−0.0067	−0.08
Autos	0.0038	0.57	Regional/Local		2.57
Consumer Staples	0.0062	0.97			
Pharmaceuticals	−0.0278	8.10	Factor Risk		37.72
Financials	0.0270	7.53	Specific Risk		62.28
Computers & Telecoms	−0.0022	0.80			
Global Sector		25.91	Total Risk		100.00

Source: Thomson Financial Datastream, MSCI, QUANTEC

this analysis explain 37.72% of the portfolio tracking error, with the remaining 62.28% specific to the portfolio.

PORTFOLIO CONSTRUCTION

To use an optimizer to construct a portfolio, the investment manager provides the following information:

- Existing portfolio and benchmark allocations. Portfolio allocations can be represented as the number of shares held, holding value or percentage of total portfolio value. Benchmark holdings are represented as percentage holdings.
- The universe of permitted investments.
- Forecast returns for each asset in the portfolio and benchmark.
- Any constraints to which the portfolio is subject, such as total number of assets or maximum exposure to industry groups.

The starting portfolio might be some existing portfolio, the benchmark portfolio or cash. Because the optimizer works by making small changes to the existing portfolio, the composition of the starting portfolio is important. An investment manager seeking to adjust an existing portfolio would prefer to start with that portfolio and look for the smallest required changes to reach optimality.

The investment manager must indicate which securities can be held, allowing securities to be excluded because they are embargoed or because they are difficult to buy or incur very high transaction costs.

The investment manager usually provides forecast returns for each security. If these are omitted, the optimizer assumes that all securities have equal returns and so will seek the minimum risk portfolio, which is suitable for an indexed portfolio.

Most optimizers recognize that investors may wish to put limits on the shape of the portfolio that emerges from the program, or on the path to that portfolio. These requirements are dealt with by means of constraints on the optimization process or outcome. For example, the investor might want to limit the percentage of the portfolio held in any one asset, or the requirement might be to never have more than double the benchmark allocation in any industry group. A frequent constraint is to limit the total number of assets in the portfolio or cap the total turnover allowed. Most optimizers also allow investors to assign transaction costs and compute the cost of implementing any optimal solution. They usually also allow total transaction costs to be capped too.

The important thing to remember is that every constraint imposed on the optimization moves the resulting portfolio further away from the best risk-return position. Too many or too severe constraints can result in a portfolio that has little or no chance of delivering the risk and return outcome required.

Example 10.5 illustrates a set of holding constraints that might be found in a typical equity mandate. The objective is to keep the portfolio allocations reasonably close to the benchmark weights. Such constraints can indeed help to control the risk of the portfolio, but it is important that they are consistent with the investor's objectives.

The optimization summary in Example 10.5 shows that keeping the portfolio allocations close to benchmark limits the portfolio's range of risk and return outcomes. Not only high-risk, high-return but also low-risk, low-return outcomes are excluded by the constraints.

The most important inputs to the optimization process are the returns forecast for each asset. Optimizers are very sensitive to the overall level of forecast return but even more sensitive to the differences in the returns forecast for each asset.

Return forecasts have at least two components. The first is the alpha for each asset. This is the amount by which the asset is mispriced, with a positive alpha indicating that the asset is underpriced and a negative alpha indicating that it is overpriced. The other component is the return forecast for each factor in the return model. Strictly speaking, it is also necessary to forecast the beta of each asset to each factor, but in practice most investment managers apply some estimate based on historical beta calculations.

Many investment managers prefer simply to assign rankings of expected returns to the optimization. This can be perfectly adequate for the purpose of finding optimal portfolio allocations and forward estimates of portfolio risk, but of course the calculation of the portfolio expected return will be missing.

Because optimizers rely heavily on past asset and factor return data, the source of the data and how it is processed can have an important effect on the outcome. Most optimizer systems available commercially are supplied with data, which is updated periodically. Optimizer providers usually buy the data from recognized data vendors and then apply some kind of data cleaning process to eliminate obvious errors before using it to calculate returns for assets and risk factors. Data errors do creep in, however, so it is the responsibility of the investment manager to scrutinize the results for reasonableness and if necessary inspect intermediate calculations and source data.

However, the potential problems of such heavy use of historical data are not limited to errors in the data. There is the implicit assumption that the past is a reasonable indicator of the future. It is widely accepted that this is not the case for asset returns, but many if not most investment managers accept that there is some stability in the relationships (betas and covariance matrices) linking assets

EXAMPLE 10.5 *Constrained and unconstrained optimization*

	Original Portfolio %	Benchmark Portfolio %	Expected Return %	Minimum Holding %	Maximum Holding %
American International	7.00	10	−0.05	7.50	12.50
AOL Time Warner	8.16	10	−11.58	7.50	12.50
Citigroup	9.16	10	1.50	7.50	12.50
Exxon Mobil	11.21	10	−2.50	7.50	12.50
General Electric	17.65	10	18.00	7.50	12.50
Intel	7.61	10	5.00	7.50	12.50
IBM	7.43	10	−5.64	7.50	12.50
Microsoft	13.30	10	5.00	7.50	12.50
Pfizer	10.01	10	12.00	7.50	12.50
Wal-Mart	8.47	10	15.00	7.50	12.50
Portfolio	100.00	100	3.67		
Optimization Summary	**Efficient Portfolios Minimum Risk**				**Maximum Return**
Unconstrained Optimization					
Relative Return	0.000	3.582	7.164	10.745	14.327
Tracking Error	0.000	2.828	5.863	9.962	17.490
Constrained Optimization					
Relative Return	0.000	0.458	0.916	1.374	1.832
Tracking Error	0.000	0.362	0.732	1.200	2.259

Source: IDC, QUANTEC

and risk factors. These relationships certainly are not stagnant, however, and the question arises whether it is better to use only recent history, which is more relevant to the present and arguably the future, or to use longer history, which covers more economic cycles and so is more likely to reflect a wider range of conditions that may prevail over the investment horizon.

For most purposes, five years of monthly observations seems to work, although for portfolios with many assets, or risk models with many risk factors, a longer period is called for. Very few optimization problems warrant as much as ten years of data, however, and most investment managers would agree that this period covers far too much structural change in markets to have much relevance for any forward-looking analysis.

Where a long history is applied to the optimization, many investors seek to minimize the confounding effect of the earliest observations by applying differential importance to the observations, with the most recent events given the heaviest weights, and the importance of earlier observations diminishing and eventually disappearing. The advantage is that events in the distant past that were very extreme fade out rather than dropping off abruptly, enhancing the overall stability of the risk analysis from one period to the next.

CURRENCY MANAGEMENT

One of the advantages of using optimizers to construct portfolios and analyse risk is that they enable the investor to incorporate currency management as part of the overall portfolio. This can be very powerful because the investment manager can apply separate return forecasts for assets and currencies, thus taking full advantage of the diversifying effects of investing in a wide range of instruments. The optimizer allows the investment manager to stipulate the required extent of currency risk for the overall portfolio. One of the most frequently used constraints in the optimization is to specify limits to foreign currency exposures, including currency hedges if desired.

USE OF DERIVATIVES

Portfolio optimization is perfectly compatible with futures, forwards and swaps, but standard optimizers are incompatible with options. Forwards, futures and standard swap contracts all have return distributions that ultimately resemble those of physical assets. That is, their returns are approximately normally distributed around the expected return, with about an equal possibility of the return being greater or less than the expected return. This is a necessary assumption for optimizers. Options are not compatible because, by their very nature, the likelihood of returns being either better or worse than expected are eliminated depending on whether the option is a call or a put. Their return distribution is thus said to be truncated or asymmetrical, and it is this asymmetry that is incompatible with optimization. Many hybrid instruments, such as convertible bonds, are incompatible with optimizers for the same reason.

When including forwards, futures and swaps the investment manager needs to ensure that the necessary adjustment to cash holdings is effected to accommodate the face value of the instrument. It may also be necessary to adjust the expected return if the derivative is above or below its estimated fair value.

ONGOING MANAGEMENT AND ADMINISTRATION

Optimizer programs are usually easy enough to maintain because the provider usually undertakes to update the data and all calculations at regular intervals, usually monthly. The investment manager needs to update expected returns for each asset, as well as the allocations of the portfolios and benchmarks.

Modern software technology allows data updates to be carried out in a few minutes with minimal risk of mishap. The internet has greatly simplified the required data transfers, improving the timeliness of routine analyses.

PERFORMANCE MEASUREMENT AND ATTRIBUTION

The two main functions of optimizer programs are both forward looking, helping to construct portfolios and forecast portfolio risk. By themselves, optimizers do not tell the investor anything about why the portfolio behaved as it did over previous return periods.

Fortunately, the standards of systems built for performance attribution and analysis are improving rapidly, and are increasingly designed to complement forward-looking risk analyses and portfolio optimization. In addition to attributing performance variation to asset classes, sectors and industry categories, many systems are now able to quantify the contribution of factor mismatches to portfolio return variation.

REVERSE OPTIMIZATION

One of the most frequently cited shortcomings of optimizers is that they are very sensitive to changes in input data, especially forecast returns. Many investors have noted with frustration that even quite small changes to forecast returns can result in dramatic changes in 'optimal' portfolio weights. They conclude that the results can hardly be optimal if they are so easily changed, and so regard with scepticism all results from portfolio optimizers.

Examples 10.6.1 to 10.6.3 show the effect of a relatively modest change in the expected returns on an optimization outcome. The second optimization shows greater concentration of allocations in the low-risk portfolios and quite different allocations to high-risk portfolios. This result is due to the interaction of forecast returns and stock and factor covariances.

EXAMPLE 10.6.1 *Effect of changed forecast returns on optimization*

Security	Forecast Returns #1 %	Forecast Returns #2 %
American International	−0.05	1.25
AOL Time Warner	−11.58	5.00
Citigroup	1.50	−2.25
Exxon Mobil	−2.50	5.00
General Electric	18.00	5.00
Intel	5.00	−6.00
IBM	−5.64	−7.00
Microsoft	5.00	10.00
Pfizer	12.00	7.00
Wal-Mart	15.00	10.00

EXAMPLE 10.6.2 *Optimization with forecast returns #1*

Optimal Portfolios	Minimum Risk %	%	%	%	Maximum Return %
American International	10.00	3.90			
AOL Time Warner	10.00	8.26	6.20	0.28	
Citigroup	10.00	8.91	4.78		
Exxon Mobil	10.00	2.59			
General Electric	10.00	21.67	35.05	53.51	100.00
Intel	10.00	10.85	11.87	11.04	
IBM	10.00	7.25	1.77		
Microsoft	10.00	9.52	8.85	6.26	
Pfizer	10.00	14.13	16.17	12.73	
Wal-Mart	10.00	12.93	15.32	16.18	
Number of Holdings	10	10	8	6	1
Relative Return (% pa)	0.00	3.58	7.16	10.75	14.33
Tracking Error (% pa)	0.00	2.83	5.86	9.96	17.49
Tracking R-Squared (%)	100.00	98.21	92.33	77.95	48.31
Portfolio Trade-off: Sharpe Ratio	0.32	1.27	1.22	1.08	0.82
Incremental Trade-off: Lambda	0.00	1.17	0.97	0.65	0.31
Absolute Return (% pa)	3.67	7.25	10.84	14.42	18.00
Absolute Risk (% pa)	21.02	21.15	20.90	19.89	23.41

Source: IDC, QUANTEC

EXAMPLE 10.6.3 *Optimization with forecast returns #2*

Optimal Portfolios	Minimum Risk %	%	%	%	Maximum Return %
American International	10.00	5.61			
AOL Time Warner	10.00	10.96	11.79	10.70	
Citigroup	10.00	7.38	3.66		
Exxon Mobil	10.00	12.26	14.06	6.88	
General Electric	10.00	11.76	13.54	5.02	
Intel	10.00	7.72	4.14		
IBM	10.00	3.64			
Microsoft	10.00	12.85	15.87	22.87	39.97
Pfizer	10.00	13.38	17.29	22.33	
Wal-Mart	10.00	14.44	19.64	32.20	60.02
Number of Holdings	10	10	8	6	2
Relative Return (% pa)	0.00	1.80	3.60	5.40	7.20
Tracking Error (% pa)	0.00	2.90	5.89	9.81	18.64
Tracking R-Squared (%)	100.00	98.09	92.30	81.13	53.67
Portfolio Trade-off: Sharpe Ratio	0.34	0.62	0.61	0.55	0.39
Incremental Trade-off: Lambda	0.00	0.57	0.52	0.30	0.15
Absolute Return (% pa)	2.80	4.60	6.40	8.20	10.00
Absolute Risk (% pa)	21.02	20.84	20.98	22.53	27.35

Source: IDC, QUANTEC

Most investment managers find the covariance explanation unhelpful, because it offers only a vague explanation of what is going on. Insight can be added by turning the process around.

The two things that go into the optimizer, return forecasts and covariance forecasts, are themselves estimates at best. Then the investment manager presses a button and out comes a set of portfolio allocations to two or more decimal places. Because the program calculates only precise numbers, it is not capable of handling forecast ranges, even though it is ranges that really concern the investment manager.

One way to accommodate the reality that returns are rarely forecast as exact numbers, but usually as ranges, is to reverse the optimization process. This is done by putting in the portfolio allocations and asking the optimizer what returns for the assets in the portfolio are implied by the allocations. If the 'implied' return is within the investor's range of expectations, then the current portfolio allocation is acceptable. If the implied return is higher than the investor's range, then the allocation to that security should either be reduced or the range of forecast returns revised.

EXAMPLE 10.7 *Reverse optimization*

	Implied Return %	Expected Return %
American International	4.53	−0.05
AOL Time Warner	3.80	−11.58
Citigroup	1.95	1.50
Exxon Mobil	10.13	−2.50
General Electric	−6.64	18.00
Intel	−11.26	5.00
IBM	4.77	−5.64
Microsoft	9.03	5.00
Pfizer	−5.60	12.00
Wal-Mart	7.16	0.00
Portfolio Values	5.18	5.18

Source: IDC, QUANTEC

Reverse optimization can thus provide a useful check on the consistency of the investor's forecasts and portfolio construction.

Example 10.7 illustrates the difference between expected and implied returns. The investor has forecast a return of –0.05% for American International, but to justify the current portfolio allocation the investment manager would need to expect a return of about 4.53%. Either the expected return estimated needs to be modified or the holding in that asset class sharply reduced. In some cases, notably Citigroup and possibly Microsoft, it is possible that the implied return is in fact within the range of expected returns, although the two appear quite different at first glance.

PITFALLS

As with any computer program, optimizers are subject to the 'garbage in, garbage out' **(GIGO)** rule. Data errors, the source of most problems, fall into three broad categories: simple data errors, data processing errors and forecasting errors.

Simple data errors are hard to avoid. A typical global optimizer program obtains price and return data on tens of thousands of securities and indices from several hundred suppliers. Unsurprisingly, some suppliers are more reliable than others, and most data supplier intermediaries and optimizer providers run routine 'cleaning' programs. These might seek out, say, zero index returns, zero values or returns that are abnormally high. They cannot detect all data errors, so some errors creep through to the analysis.

Data processing errors can also be a source of concern. These might be simple bugs that creep into the calculations, a flaw in the design of the program, or, more serious still, a flaw in the mathematical model underpinning the optimizer. The first can originate from a simple change in a security identifier, which might result in that asset being attributed inappropriate factor betas. Once identified, this is easily solved. Program design flaws are usually also easy to fix. They might arise because a shortcut was applied to some part of the calculations that, with the data available at the time, was thought to have no impact on the results of the computation, but with changed market conditions and new data turned out to be material. Once identified, these are also often easily fixed. The third type of data processing error is of course the hardest to identify, and so is the hardest to rectify. Problems with model specifications usually only become apparent over time, as the investment manager notices that the results predicted by the optimizer are frequently wide of the mark. Since all risk models are to some extent misspecified, it is often impossible to say with certainty to what extent the model is to blame for unintended results. At this point, considerable judgement must be exercised. If the model is seriously flawed, a new approach is almost certainly warranted. Unfortunately, because the model sits at the core of many portfolio construction processes, a change in optimizer model can require a rethink of the basis on which returns are forecast and portfolios constructed, conceivably leading to a change in investment strategy.

The optimizer also relies on forecasts of expected return for individual assets. If these are inaccurate, the portfolio constructed using the optimizer has little chance of achieving its objectives. These errors are by their nature impossible to identify until it is too late.

Pitfalls associated with raw data, data processing and forecasting are made much worse if the mistakes are hard to find. Some optimizer programs make it easy for users to find mistakes, others make it harder. This is an important distinction. If the investment manager relies on the optimizer for meaningful risk analysis or portfolio construction, not knowing how the results were obtained, or if there are errors in the input or intermediate calculations, can result in poor portfolio construction.

Interpreting the results is an important part of the optimization process. Sometimes this is not a trivial exercise. For example, in unusual market conditions, the optimizer might give quite unexpected risk analysis. The investment manager needs to appreciate the limitations of the model being used, as well as how data is used to generate the results. Interpretation can be aided by a system that allows inspection of input data as well as intermediate calculations.

CHAPTER 11

Indexation

Indexation, also known as passive investment, is a method of investment management designed to deliver the same returns as a given benchmark, with no attempt at better returns through security selection.

APPLICATIONS

The largest group of indexers is made up of pension plan sponsors and trustees, mutual funds and insurance companies. Indexation first became popular with long-term investors in the USA where nearly 30% of these funds' investments are indexed. In the UK the figure is closer to 20%, and it is beginning to become popular in Continental Europe and Asia.

Interest in indexation was first raised by academic research into the relative performance of equity managers, which indicated that few, if any, active managers consistently did better, after fees had been deducted, than the S&P500 – the market in which they invested. This seemed to suggest that active equity management represented poor value for money, and that indexation, with modest but reliable performance, was a better alternative.

The main appeal of indexation is that it is an efficient way of investing large funds, with:

- controlled risk, meaning low specific risk
- minimized transaction costs
- minimized market impact.

Portfolios in any asset class can be indexed, and even asset allocation can be managed passively. However, indexation is most frequently applied to domestic and international equity portfolios.

THEORY

Indexation starts with the principle that markets are broadly efficient. That is, there are no opportunities to make excess returns from buying underpriced and selling overpriced assets. Returns can only be improved by assuming more market risk.

It is not necessary to believe this to find advantages in indexation. Because indexation creates a low maintenance buy and hold portfolio, its costs compare favourably with an actively managed portfolio. Naturally, the importance of this advantage depends on the costs of trading the component securities, for example a portfolio of domestic equities with a turnover of 30% costs from 30 to 80 basis points (hundredths of 1%) each year in transactions costs. By contrast, indexed portfolios typically trade less than 10% per year. For an international portfolio, the cost advantage is greater, because both trading and custodian costs are significantly higher than for domestic portfolios.

The indexed portfolio has another cost advantage over the actively managed portfolio, that of low management fees. The manager passes on to the investor the saving from not having to conduct expensive research and analysis of individual securities. As one would expect, management fees vary widely between markets and between managers. For a domestic equity portfolio, the difference in management fees between active and indexed portfolios can be as much as 0.5% per year, or 50 basis points. For an international equities portfolio, the difference is about 35 basis points.

As well as costing less, indexed portfolios are less risky. While both portfolios win and lose according to the market in which they are invested, the active portfolio runs the additional risk that the securities it has bought will do better or worse than the market. In contrast, the indexed portfolio reflects only the market performance without the excitement of bets placed on individual securities.

It is the job of armies of analysts to find and apply all the important information driving security returns. If all assets within a market were indexed, then this information would not be used; it would be wasted, with the result that prices would not trade at their fair price. In such a world, the indexed portfolio manager would soon have no business, because all rational investors would not allow the valuable information to be wasted, rather they would use it to invest in such a way as to achieve better than market returns.

The indexed portfolio can be successful only within a market that is kept efficient by the efforts of active portfolio managers, enjoying something of a free ride, benefiting from all this feverish activity and the resulting market efficiency, while incurring only a fraction of the costs and risks in doing so.

There are a number of reasons for investing in indexed portfolios, including:

- As part of a core–satellite investment strategy.
- To reduce costs and increase the efficiency of a global portfolio.
- As part of an asset swap transaction.
- To exploit opportunities for stock index arbitrage.

Large funds farm out management of their portfolios between several, sometimes dozens, of asset managers all operating in the same market. This leads to the problem that the use of multiple managers within a market can result in the sum of all these active managers' investment decisions amounting to a very large indexed portfolio for which the fund pays active fees. This is known as a **closet index** and is clearly not in the investor's best interests.

The investor can overcome this problem by adopting what has come to be known as the 'core–satellite' approach. Within any given market, the fund invests a core of 50 or 60% of its assets in one indexed portfolio, with the rest allocated to a small number of satellite portfolios consisting of active managers with mandates to aggressively manage their portfolios. Satellite portfolios can include hedge funds, long–short portfolios and other alternative investments. This approach, if effected properly, has a number of advantages:

- The active portfolios are more likely to meet their given objectives because achieving better than market returns is much easier for small to medium portfolios than for large ones.
- It reduces the likelihood of running a closet index because each satellite portfolio can be assigned a distinctive mandate.
- It facilitates the inclusion of hedge funds and other alternative investments in the overall portfolio structure.
- It recognizes the reality that all conventional portfolios consist of the benchmark plus a long–short portfolio representing the allocation differences between the portfolio and the benchmark.
- It minimizes the problem of market impact which otherwise would limit the investment manager's ability to assume the risks necessary to achieve acceptable returns.

- It facilitates the identification and reward of better than market performance by active managers.
- Overall management fees are reduced because the bulk of the portfolio attracts very low fees.

Global asset managers find indexation an attractive means of gaining cost effective exposure to international markets. There are two ways in which indexation can improve the efficiency of global portfolio management. The first is that by simply indexing the securities within each target market, management resources can be focused on the choice of which countries to invest in. Empirical research into the performance of globally diversified portfolios shows that approximately 70% of the variability of returns is attributable to selection of markets, with only 30% due to security selection within markets. Logically, therefore, the global manager will devote management resources to that aspect of the fund which is likely to deliver the best results, that is, country selection and allocation. At the same time he or she eliminates the complexities of trying to manage portfolio specific risk in individual markets – often in an awkwardly different time zone. This leaves time to focus on optimizing and managing the risks attributable to the markets themselves and allocating between them. Indexation offers the additional benefits of minimizing management, transaction and administration costs.

The second way is to combine indexation with **asset swaps**. This is very useful to global managers who are subject to domestic tax. It works by arranging for a financial intermediary to swap the return on one asset, or basket of assets, for another. The global investment manager receives, over a fixed period, usually one, two or three years, the return to an agreed international asset or basket of assets. The manager pays the return to domestic assets plus a margin. The benefit to the global manager is that, although the portfolio is effectively invested internationally, physical assets can be held domestically and so earn tax credits on dividends. Part of this benefit is given up in the form of the margin paid to the intermediary, but part is retained by the fund. Structured correctly, this can be a most efficient means of global investing for a taxable investor.

DEFINING THE BENCHMARK

Defining the benchmark is arguably more important for an indexed portfolio than for an actively managed one because the benchmark provides the major, if not the only, source of risk to the portfolio. Desirable features for the benchmark of an indexed portfolio are:

- It must meet the investment objectives of the investor. Usually this means that it must give a broad coverage of the market in which it invests. In some instances, this may necessitate designing a customized benchmark either within a recognized asset class or as a composition of different asset classes or parts of asset classes.
- It should be investable. In other words, the securities that make up the benchmark should be freely traded on a recognized exchange.
- Availability of derivatives is a big help. For the purposes of liquidity management and periodic rebalancing, there is an enormous advantage in selecting a benchmark on which futures contracts are traded. This is not always possible even for domestic equity portfolios, and is often not available for international asset classes.
- Public quotation reduces ambiguity. While it is preferable to identify a benchmark that is quoted publicly, customized or less widely recognized benchmarks can work well provided the components are publicly quoted. This allows independent computation of benchmark performance by the investor, investment manager and custodian, so avoiding confusion about the relative performance of the portfolio.

The steps to setting up an indexed portfolio are:

- set the target level of tracking error
- determine the type of portfolio construction
- decide rebalancing rules
- plan implementation.

Target tracking error

How much tracking error the portfolio can tolerate is determined by the size and purpose of the portfolio and how difficult and costly it is to achieve close to zero specific risk.

Ideally, the indexer will aim for zero tracking error, which, combined with a beta of exactly one, theoretically gives perfect benchmark returns. But this ignores transaction and other costs, which can have a significant effect on the outcome. There is usually a trade-off between tracking error and transaction costs, whereby improved tracking error comes only with increased costs. The investor is nearly always better off with some tracking error because this flexibility can help to reduce the other costs of the portfolio. The impact on portfolio return of tracking error can be either positive or negative, while the impact of transaction costs is always negative.

Portfolio construction

Having determined the benchmark and its tolerance for tracking error, the indexer must now decide the best way to go about portfolio construction. The inputs are:

- the benchmark
- the tolerance for tracking error
- the purpose and expected life of the index portfolio – long or short term
- the form of the existing portfolio – cash, shares and so on
- estimates of transaction costs for each security
- beta estimates for each security.

It is important to note that the process does not require any security return forecasts. Indexation implicitly assumes that, because all assets are fairly priced, forecast returns are zero and therefore superfluous. Instead, the indexer is seeking the lowest possible specific risk or tracking error.

The first part of this process is to decide whether to fully replicate the benchmark index or adopt a sampling approach, and, if the latter, how many securities to include in the sample. Full replication is the process of simply buying every security in precise index proportions, while sampling is where only some securities are bought.

The choice is usually determined by the portfolio's tolerance for tracking error and the structure of the benchmark. If the benchmark is made up of a great number of securities, sampling is almost certainly the right approach. If there are only a few dozen securities in it, then full replication could be the answer, provided each component is sufficiently liquid and trading costs are not too high.

Full replication gives portfolio performance that is very close to, but not identical with, the benchmark. The difference stems from the fact that all benchmarks change their components from time to time and the replicating indexer must follow suit. Unlike the benchmark, the portfolio is subject to trading costs, which, together with administrative costs, have a negative impact on performance, ensuring that the fully replicated portfolio always returns less than the benchmark to which it is 'identical'. Sampling incurs a larger tracking error but lower rebalancing and administrative costs, because there are fewer securities to trade and changes in the benchmark can be followed less rigidly. The objective of the sampling indexer is to minimize this tracking error, delivering portfolio performance with variations from benchmark which are not only small, but are positive as often as they are negative.

There are a number of approaches to sampling, including random sampling. We will concentrate on only two: stratified sampling and optimized sampling, which are often applied in tandem.

Stratified sampling is where the benchmark is broken up into bite-sized chunks and securities selected from each chunk to make up a portfolio. In the case of a domestic equities portfolio, the bite-sized chunks usually correspond to industry groups, with the result that the allocation to each industry is the same for the portfolio and the benchmark. An international equities index may start with a country-by-country approach, while a property portfolio may seek to separate the index into different property sectors, such as commercial, industrial and residential. For fixed interest one might approach the task by looking at various credit exposures within the benchmark.

For example, to construct a 100 stock portfolio to track a benchmark comprising 500 stocks, the simplest approach would be simply to select the 100 largest stocks by market capitalization. This portfolio is called TOP100 and will often give satisfactory results, although stratified sampling, which is more computationally complex, usually gives a more robust outcome.

The indexer then notices that the benchmark is divided into 50 industry categories. Since it makes sense at least to try to match industry allocations to the benchmark, the indexer decides to select 100 stocks according to industry categories.

The first step is to decide which stocks to select. Obviously the largest stock in each industry group should be included. (If the number of industry groups exceeded the number of stocks, that is, there were more than 100 industry groups, then one stock would be selected from each of the 100 largest industry groups by market capitalization.) The next step is to select the next largest stock from each industry group, taking care to select only stocks that are actually liquid.

Then the indexer must determine the allocation to each security. Industry groups are allocated according to their weight in the benchmark index. Within industry groups, stocks are allocated according to their relative weight within the industry. Individual stock allocations are therefore different from their weight in the benchmark index.

The 100 stock portfolio selected by this process is called SAMP100. Example 11.1.1 shows the composition of the benchmark and the two portfolios.

EXAMPLE 11.1.1 *Stratified samples*

	Benchmark		TOP100		SAMP100	
Industry Group	**Weight %**	**Number of Stocks**	**Weight %**	**Number of Stocks**	**Weight %**	**Number of Stocks**
Aerospace and Defence	1.26	7	1.12	2	1.27	2
Airlines	0.25	4	0.00		0.25	1
Auto Components	0.94	13	0.69	1	0.28	1
Automobiles	0.27	1	0.38	1	0.28	1
Banks	7.17	28	7.33	11	7.20	5
Breweries and Distillers	0.44	3	0.56	1	0.45	1
Brokerage	0.25	2	0.00		0.25	1
Business Services and DP	7.00	26	8.20	5	7.04	3
Chemicals	1.84	15	1.84	3	1.85	2
Computers	5.21	20	5.99	6	5.24	6
Conglomerate	1.39	12	1.00	2	1.40	2
Construction Materials	0.05	1	0.00		0.05	1
Contracting and Construction	0.09	4	0.00		0.09	2
Electrical and Electronic	8.48	27	10.42	7	8.52	2
Electrical Instruments	1.42	14	0.60	1	1.43	3
Energy Equipment and Services	0.82	6	0.45	1	0.82	2
Food Manufacturing	2.97	14	2.38	2	2.98	2
Food Retailing	0.91	5	0.76	2	0.92	2
Gold	0.13	4	0.00		0.13	1
Health and Personal Care	7.34	33	7.78	9	7.37	4
Household Appliances	0.11	4	0.00		0.11	2
Household Products	0.34	2	0.41	1	0.34	1
Industrial Components	0.63	5	0.48	1	0.64	1
Insurance	4.13	23	3.28	3	4.15	2
Investment Services	1.32	5	1.43	2	1.33	2
Investment Trusts	0.44	1	0.61	1	0.44	1
Iron and Steel	0.08	5	0.00		0.08	2
Leasing and Consumer Credit	4.10	8	5.31	4	4.12	2
Leisure and Tourism	1.43	11	1.27	2	1.44	2
Machinery and Engineering	0.39	7	0.00		0.39	2
Media and Communications	2.29	14	1.92	3	2.30	2
Metal Fabricators	0.11	1	0.00		0.11	1
Miscellaneous	0.46	5	0.00		0.46	2
Miscellaneous Basic Industries	0.06	3	0.00		0.06	2
Miscellaneous Consumer Goods	0.93	4	1.02	1	0.93	1
Miscellaneous Financials	0.30	3	0.00		0.30	2
Miscellaneous Transport	0.37	4	0.00		0.37	2
Non-ferrous Metals	0.48	5	0.42	1	0.48	1

continued on next page

	Benchmark		TOP100		SAMP100	
Industry Group	**Weight %**	**Number of Stocks**	**Weight %**	**Number of Stocks**	**Weight %**	**Number of Stocks**
Office Equipment and Copiers	0.18	3	0.00		0.18	2
Oil and Gas	6.61	24	7.09	5	6.64	4
Paper and Forest Products	0.49	10	0.00		0.49	2
Pharmaceuticals	7.27	11	9.63	6	7.31	3
Property	0.06	1	0.00		0.06	1
Railways	0.13	1	0.00		0.13	1
Recreation and Other Consumer Services	0.45	8	0.00		0.61	3
Stores and Retail	5.93	32	5.39	4	5.96	2
Telecommunications	7.96	22	9.47	8	8.00	4
Textiles and Clothing	0.13	3	0.00		0.13	1
Tobacco	1.11	3	1.41	1	1.11	1
Utilities	3.50	32	1.36	3	3.52	2
Total	100.00	499	100.00	100	100.00	100

Source: Thomson Financial Datastream

The TOP100 portfolio does not hold stocks in all industry groups and is overweight in others relative to the benchmark. By contrast, SAMP100 has industry allocations very similar to the benchmark. Both portfolios can be optimized to give an **optimized sample** and hence a more robust allocation. To show how optimization can affect a portfolio's expected risk, the two portfolios were optimized, allowing the optimizer to alter stock allocations but confining it to the same sample of stocks. The next step is to allow 20 stocks to be added from the 500 stock universe; this portfolio is called SAMP120. The results are set out in Example 11.1.2.

Stratification is an improvement on the simple TOP100 strategy, but much better results are achievable with optimization, especially if extra stocks can be added.

EXAMPLE 11.1.2 *Expected beta and tracking error – stratified and optimized sample*

	TOP100	TOP100 Optimized	SAMP100 Stratified	SAMP100 Optimized	SAMP120 Optimized
Expected Beta	1.0300	1.0000	1.0000	1.0000	1.0000
Expected Tracking Error	1.95%	0.91%	1.87%	0.85%	0.74%

Stratified sampling has intuitive appeal and gives satisfactory risk control as long as the categories are chosen well. If categories are ill chosen then risk control is liable to fail. Optimization nearly always gives more robust results than pure stratified sampling.

An endearing feature of optimizers is that they are, like all computer models, subject to the GIGO principle – garbage in, garbage out. The optimizing indexer must therefore be able to judge if the portfolio defined by the optimizer meets its objectives. The market, the benchmark, the investment objectives and constraints in the mandate determine which is the best approach for a given indexed portfolio. There is no single approach to indexation that is always better than others.

International equity portfolios can be constructed using the same methodology, either by simply optimizing the largest securities in the investment universe or by conducting some kind of stratified sampling exercise. Most indexers start with a country-by-country stratification, although global risk factors give better results for most portfolios because the result is much lower portfolio specific risk.

Rebalancing

Rebalancing rules should be set next. How often rebalancing happens depends on transaction costs and the amount of specific risk that can be tolerated: high-risk tolerance allows less frequent rebalancing because the cost of a rebalance will be justified less often by the expected reduction in tracking error. On the other hand, low-risk tolerance requires more frequent rebalances. Rebalancing will also be influenced by the frequency and timing of cash flows to the portfolio. Rebalancing costs can be sharply reduced by timing them to coincide with cash flows either in or out of the portfolio.

Implementation

Implementation of indexed portfolios usually entails a large number of small transactions. These can be placed one by one as for traditional equity portfolios, a process that is time consuming, costly and error prone for transactions such as this. Therefore, most indexers prefer to implement all the transactions simultaneously by means of a basket or block trade. Basket trades effectively transfer the risk of implementation to the broker, who quotes a fixed fee for the transaction on an all-or-nothing basis. Futures are often used to smooth the implementation process by providing short-term exposure to the required asset class, pending full implementation of the physical portfolio.

CURRENCY MANAGEMENT

For most indexed portfolios, currency can be managed in the same way as for actively managed portfolios. Most domestic indexed portfolios require no currency management at all because they have no exposure to foreign currency. Even unintentional currency exposure is negligible because the portfolio risks match very closely those of the benchmark. International indexed funds naturally need to incorporate currency management, but usually only with respect to cash flow management and periodic rebalancing. Of course, if the mandate demands that the portfolio's exposure to foreign currency be hedged to base currency, then the manager needs to ensure that unrealized profits and losses are hedged periodically, to keep foreign currency exposure within specified limits.

Currency management becomes a serious issue when a significant part of the portfolio's international investment is by means of derivatives. The investment manager must then ensure that the appropriate foreign exchange balances relating to initial and variation margins are monitored to give the currency exposures demanded by the mandate.

USE OF DERIVATIVES

As with actively managed portfolios, futures contracts are often used to facilitate implementation and usually play an important part in liquidity management for indexed portfolios. Thus they allow the manager to maintain a balance of physical liquid assets to meet short-term liquidity requirements without running the risk of being underinvested. At the same time, liquid assets, accumulating in the portfolio from, say, dividends received in cash, can be effectively invested using futures contracts, thus enabling the manager to construct physical transactions in economic sizes, so saving on transaction costs.

Indexed portfolios can be constructed entirely of share price index futures contracts. This approach is extremely cost efficient, especially for a very small portfolio or a transition portfolio. A transition portfolio is a temporary portfolio designed to give the most basic exposure to an asset class while a permanent mandate is being set up. The derivatives portfolio is managed in the same way as the derivatives component of a portfolio of physical assets, with particular attention to ensuring that the correct number of futures contracts are held at all times, and to managing the risk associated with rolling futures contracts from one futures expiry month to the next.

For many indexed portfolios, a major role of derivatives is to add value to the basic portfolio through index enhancements.

INDEX ENHANCEMENTS

Index enhancements have grown in popularity because many investors believe that markets harbour enough inefficiencies to allow extra market returns, and that indexed portfolios can be well placed to benefit from this activity. Because indexed portfolios bear a close resemblance in structure to the benchmarks against which derivative instruments, such as share price indices, are settled, and because indexing is a 'buy and hold' strategy, it can tolerate substitution of individual or groups of stock holdings by futures and options for indeterminate periods of time. Investment managers favour enhancements because they attract higher fees than plain indexing.

Enhancements come in two varieties: risk free and risky.

Risk-free enhancements

An exhaustive treatment is not feasible because so many enhancements are possible, but the main sources of risk-free enhancements are:

- mispriced derivatives – such as share price index futures and options and listed stock options
- dividend reinvestment plans
- tax anomalies.

Mispriced derivatives characterize immature markets, and markets with particularly high transactions costs. The diversity of strategies that come under this heading is very rich, so a simple specimen will be used to represent the genre. The most straightforward example is known as stock index **arbitrage**. This takes advantage of stock index futures, which are trading either above or below fair price.

Consider the investment environment in Example 11.2.1. The investment manager has two ways of investing in the stock market to the end of December:

EXAMPLE 11.2.1 *Exploiting mispriced derivatives and initial prices*

Date Now	7 July
Physical Share Price Iindex	2202
SPI Futures	2215
Expiry Date of Futures	29 December
Dividend Yield	3.2% p.a.
Interest Rate	6.8% p.a.

buy shares or buy futures and place the cash on deposit. Example 11.2.2 looks at what happens in each case.

It is important to note that the level at which the stock market closes on 29 December is irrelevant because the futures contract and the physical and the futures will by definition be at exactly the same level at that date, however, for the sake of illustration we will say that the market closes at 2210.

Example 11.2.2 shows that the investor holding cash and wishing to invest in the equity market is clearly better off using the futures contract. Another investor who already holds physical shares would sell these in favour of futures as long as the transaction costs thus incurred are less than 1.1% (3.0 – 1.9) on the round trip. Most mature markets do not allow such easy profits: share price index futures contracts tend to trade in a range – determined by transaction costs – about their fair price. Less sophisticated markets can offer rich pickings in arbitrage activity, but this often comes with exotic sources of risk such as inscrutable trading rules and Byzantine settlement systems.

Dividend reinvestment plans (DRPs) – many listed companies offer their shareholders the opportunity to receive dividends in the form of shares instead

EXAMPLE 11.2.2 *Exploiting mispriced derivatives and outcome*

Strategy	Buy Shares	Buy Futures
Profit (Loss) on Shares	8	0
Profit (Loss) on Futures	0	(5)
Dividend Income	33.8	0
Interest Income	0	71.8
Profit (Loss)	41.8	66.8
Percentage of Initial Investment	1.90%	3.03%

of cash. For the company concerned, this activity has the advantage of both reducing the effective cash paid out in dividends and encouraging new equity investment in the company because new shares are issued in lieu of cash dividends. For the investor, the attraction is that shares, which probably would have to be purchased anyway, are effectively bought with dividends foregone, saving transaction costs and adding to return if the DRP shares are issued at a discount to the price of existing shares, which they usually are.

Tax anomalies – other enhancements seek to take advantage of anomalies between tax regimes. Usually this activity centres on the fact that different classes of investor are subject to different tax treatments, especially as they relate to dividends, imputation credits and withholding tax.

The most simple strategy is where the non-payer of local tax, such as a foreign investor, sells stock to a local taxpayer immediately before the ex-dividend date and repurchases the stock immediately after. Such transactions usually have some kind of repurchase agreement attached to protect both parties from unwanted swings in the share price, and involve some sharing of the imputation benefit to give the non-local taxpayer an incentive to enter into the transaction. Alternatively, the stock may be transferred as part of an asset swap or a stock lending arrangement. The principle of transferring the benefits of dividend imputation is the same but the administrative and legal aspects may differ. The only fly in the ointment is that, in some jurisdictions, uncertainties about interpretation of the taxation law can seriously modify potential gains from this activity.

Risky enhancements

Because these enhancements add risk as well as return, it is important that the nature of the extra risk is understood and quantified. Most enhancement strategies aiming to add risk controlled return seek to exploit a judgement about which securities or groups of securities will do better than others. Normally, this judgement is the result of rigorous and sophisticated analysis, applying predefined 'rules' about when to buy and sell specified groups of assets, and a well-articulated strategy for risk control while the strategy is working, and for damage control when it is not. It is these predefined rules and strategies that differentiate enhancements from conventional active portfolio management; but the distinction can be one of degree rather than of definition.

Tilts-index enhancement strategies based on forecast returns to physical assets are often referred to as portfolio tilts, implying that the portfolio deviates only slightly – is 'tilted' away from true index proportions. The direction of the tilt can be determined by factor considerations, macroeconomic variables or active security analysis.

Factor tilts suggest a tilt to a factor that affects the performance of some stocks relative to others. An example of such a tilt would be towards growth stocks rather than value stocks. The portfolio would therefore be expected to outperform in market environments favouring emerging companies, such as those in growth industries like high technology or telecommunications. Conversely, the portfolio will underperform if sectors representing 'value' – which might include counter-cyclical stocks such as discount retailing and food manufacture – outperform the growth sectors.

Tilts that are driven by macroeconomic factors seek to exploit superior economic analysis, usually an opinion about the equilibrium level of some macroeconomic variable, such as interest rates. Thus an investor anticipating a change in the level of interest rates might favour stocks that are shown to be sensitive to interest rate changes, such as banks and financial services or very capital-intensive industries. An expected fall in oil prices might favour transportation stocks, and so on.

Options can present significant opportunities for enhancements because the investor can benefit not only from movements in the asset price but also from mispriced volatility. This is because the price of any option depends not only on the price of the underlying asset but also, among other things, on its expected volatility.

If the actual volatility of an asset is different from the volatility implied by the price of a particular option series, then the investment manager can add value by purchasing the underpriced option and replicating an offsetting option by selling or buying the appropriate quantity of physical shares, or another option series that is more fairly priced. This position must then be managed closely as changes in the share price as well as the simple passage of time will introduce new, unintended risks to the position. Even when the position is meticulously managed, the investor risks losses if the original volatility estimate was inaccurate. It is also possible to ensure that losses never exceed a predefined maximum by holding slightly more bought than sold options.

Cash enhancements can also add value to an indexed portfolio if the portfolio happens to hold enough cash, for example providing collateral for derivatives positions. Cash enhancements add value by adding two types of risk to the portfolio: yield curve risk and credit risk.

Yield curve risk is added by purchasing interest-bearing assets with more than one day to maturity. Under normal circumstances such assets earn higher rates of interest than cash simply to compensate the investor for the additional risk associated with tying up assets for a longer period. The risk to the investor is that interest rates rise in the meantime, increasing the cost of capital and the opportunity cost of not having funds to invest at a higher yield.

Credit risk is the risk that the issuer of the interest-bearing securities, the borrower, is unable to fulfil his or her obligations, or will undergo a credit 'rerating' which will cause the market value of the issued debt to fall. Adding credit risk can improve portfolio returns by increasing the interest income from interest-bearing securities. This risk can usually be controlled at the portfolio level by investing in securities from a range of borrowers, effectively diversifying much of it away.

CUSTOMIZED INDEXED PORTFOLIOS

Indexed portfolios are particularly suitable to customizing because there is no expected outperformance, or alpha, to be compromised. The investor may choose to either customize the benchmark, the portfolio or both.

Standard benchmarks are much more popular than customized ones because they are easily measured, scrutinized and are widely available. On the other hand, customized benchmarks can provide a more meaningful basis of performance evaluation, particularly if the portfolio specifications are somewhat unusual.

The most popular forms of customization relate to the level of risk or costs that the portfolio can sustain. The indexer determines the precise number of securities in the portfolio to give the required balance of expected tracking error and costs.

If the portfolio is held in a jurisdiction where differential tax treatment applies to different classes of investor, the portfolio may be customized to meet specified after-tax objectives.

Another reason to customize an indexed portfolio is if the investor has reason to impose embargoes on particular stocks, for example an ethical fund may wish to avoid the arms or tobacco industries. Customized portfolios and benchmarks are particularly useful where asset classes overlap, causing a potential double exposure to some securities. This can arise if the equity portfolio includes both large and small capitalization stocks, but where the investor needs to treat these as separate asset classes. The problem can be addressed by constructing two customized benchmarks that together equate to the original composite, or broad-based, benchmark, the first comprising the broad-based benchmark excluding some collective measure of the small stocks. The second would be the broad-based benchmark excluding large stocks.

INDEXATION OF DOMESTIC FIXED INTEREST PORTFOLIOS

Fixed interest portfolios can be indexed using either full replication or sampling. If the benchmark contains a small number of securities, then full replication is usually indicated. More securities in the benchmark indicate some kind of stratified sample.

Mean-variance optimization does not work for fixed interest portfolios because time series data for individual asset returns do not exist. The biggest difference between fixed interest and equity indexes is that fixed interest assets have a defined maturity date, while equity assets generally do not. The composition of the fixed interest portfolio and benchmark can therefore change abruptly, although usually not without notice. The indexer is thus obliged to purchase the new asset regardless of the price it commands on the day. Examples 11.3.1 and 11.3.2 illustrate a typical indexed domestic fixed interest portfolio.

This portfolio has been matched by credit quality, duration and duration within issuer. The stratified sampling process has taken no account of historical returns or their correlations; it assumes that each bond issue is fairly priced in the market and will remain close to fair price. Deviations from this rule will be the main contributor to tracking error for this portfolio, but in practice these are likely to be small as each asset in the portfolio is liquid, which helps to ensure efficient pricing.

EXAMPLE 11.3.1 *Sample indexed portfolio for domestic fixed interest*

Description	Maturity	Coupon %	Yield %	Benchmark Weight %	Portfolio Weight %
Cash					1.46
NSWTC	1 04 97	12.50	7.10	2.81	0.00
NSWTC	1 02 98	7.50	7.18	5.39	7.35
NSWTC	1 07 99	11.50	7.31	4.07	5.99
NSWTC	1 02 00	7.00	7.36	3.56	0.00
NSWTC	1 12 01	12.00	7.53	6.57	9.68
NSWTC	1 04 04	7.00	7.75	5.67	8.99
NSWTC	1 05 06	6.50	7.94	3.51	0.00
NSWTC	1 05 06	12.60	7.94	0.39	0.00
QTC	14 05 97	8.00	6.85	2.53	0.00
QTC	15 05 97	12.00	6.85	0.22	0.00
QTC	14 07 99	8.00	7.05	3.97	6.15
QTC	14 08 01	8.00	7.24	4.89	6.61
QTC	15 08 01	12.00	7.24	0.40	0.00

continued on next page

Description	Maturity	Coupon %	Yield %	Benchmark Weight %	Portfolio Weight %
QTC	14 05 03	8.00	7.40	5.22	7.07
QTC	15 05 03	10.50	7.40	0.54	0.00
QTC	14 06 05	6.50	7.60	4.52	5.22
QTC	14 09 07	8.00	7.81	2.86	0.00
SAFA	15 10 96	12.50	6.69	1.86	0.00
SAFA	15 03 98	12.50	6.82	2.20	4.16
SAFA	15 10 00	12.50	7.06	1.88	0.00
SAFA	14 01 03	10.00	7.27	1.99	2.53
TASCORP	15 03 98	12.50	6.82	1.37	0.00
TASCORP	15 01 01	12.50	7.09	1.58	3.68
TASCORP	15 11 04	9.00	7.44	0.74	0.00
TCV	15 09 97	12.50	6.78	2.16	0.00
TCV	22 10 98	12.00	6.88	3.00	7.72
TCV	15 09 99	10.25	6.96	2.54	0.00
TCV	15 07 00	12.50	7.04	2.58	5.36
TCV	22 09 01	12.00	7.15	2.19	0.00
TCV	15 10 03	12.50	7.34	2.79	0.00
TCV	15 11 06	10.25	7.63	3.40	5.39
WATC	15 01 97	10.00	6.82	1.65	0.00
WATC	1 04 98	12.00	6.93	2.35	3.51
WATC	15 04 99	9.00	7.03	2.07	3.76
WATC	1 08 01	10.00	7.24	1.89	0.00
WATC	15 07 03	8.00	7.42	2.51	5.37
WATC	15 07 05	10.00	7.61	2.12	0.00
				99.99	100.00

EXAMPLE 11.3.2 *Summary of exposure and duration*

Description	Benchmark Weight %	Portfolio Weight %	Benchmark Duration	Portfolio Duration
NSWTC	31.97	32.01	3.5705	3.5675
QTC	25.15	25.05	4.4603	4.4790
SAFA	7.93	6.69	2.4205	2.7025
TASCORP	3.69	3.68	3.1902	3.5027
TCV	18.66	18.47	3.5892	3.6280
WATC	12.59	12.64	3.3566	3.3418
CASH	0.00	1.46		
Total	99.99	100.00	3.6653	3.6662

INDEXATION OF INTERNATIONAL FIXED INTEREST PORTFOLIOS

There are two broad approaches to indexed international fixed interest portfolios. The first is to treat is as a collection of domestic indexed portfolios, in which case some combination of stratified samples can work well. A typical benchmark index, such as the Salomon World Government Bond Index, includes the 15 government bond indices of Australia, Austria, Belgium, Canada, Denmark, France, Ireland, Italy, Japan, the Netherlands, Spain, Sweden, Switzerland, the UK and the USA. While in principle the stratified sample approach will work just as well for this indexed portfolio as for the domestic fixed interest portfolio, in practice the number of securities and the volume of data to be analysed favours a more automated version of this approach.

The second approach is to use fixed interest futures contracts to achieve a broad exposure. This is suitable for a small or temporary portfolio. Its limitation is that many international fixed interest markets lack liquid futures contracts, placing a constraint on the countries in which the portfolio can invest, and a limit on its diversification.

INDEXATION OF PROPERTY PORTFOLIOS

It is generally accepted among indexers that direct property cannot be indexed because benchmarks are extremely difficult to compile, consisting of assets that are traded so infrequently that regular estimates of asset values are impossible. These obstacles have not deterred the occasional brave attempt to establish indices of direct property holdings and even derivatives markets based on these. Success has been elusive.

For this reason, property indices and property indexed portfolios are nearly always confined to listed property markets. For the serious property indexer this is highly unsatisfactory because listed property securities do not behave like property markets. This could be because direct property lacks the liquidity of listed vehicles, or because listed property securities tend to behave like equities, incorporating expected future returns to the underlying assets. Or it could be due to a combination of these plus other, unknown factors.

ONGOING MANAGEMENT

It has been said that managing index portfolios is something like patrolling the Bay of Biscay in a Sunderland (warplane) during World War II. Long periods of tedium are punctuated with bursts of manic activity, which end as abruptly as they began. As it is unlikely that any individual has first-hand experience of both occupations, the comparison must remain conjecture.

The indexer's aim is to maintain portfolio exposure close to benchmark while keeping costs to a minimum. If the portfolio is well constructed, changes in the composition of the benchmark that come about through normal price fluctuations will not cause problems, as the portfolio's composition will follow automatically.

On the other hand, changes in the benchmark that are due to external factors may need some action. The guiding principle is that if the capital structure of the benchmark or one of its components changes, then the portfolio needs to follow suit. If there is no change in capital structure, then the indexer can take no action.

Examples of day-to-day changes to benchmarks are:

- Takeovers require no action as long as the portfolio holds both the offeror and the offeree companies. The indexer will usually wait until the takeover proceeds to compulsory acquisition or the bid fails.
- Stock splits require no action because there is no change to the overall value of the company or the benchmark.
- Cash dividends are used to accumulate cash, which must be invested across the portfolio as soon as possible.
- Stock dividends are accepted in the form of physical shares, as the dividend represents an increase in the issued capital of the company.
- Share buy-backs are accepted because the issued capital of the company is contracting.
- Additions and deletions of stock from the benchmark always require action by a replicating indexer. Most additions and deletions are small stocks entering the benchmark and declining stocks leaving it. Stratified samples need only take action if the addition or deletion represents a substantial proportion of the benchmark, such as stocks created by a privatization or a large stock that merges with one that is not in the benchmark, such as a foreign company. The replicating indexer must buy or sell stock at the moment when the index change occurs, regardless of prices and costs. The sampling indexer can make a judgement about when and how to buy and sell stock.

For fixed interest benchmarks these changes are known and can be anticipated. For equities the indexer must maintain the appropriate information links, usually by subscribing to the relevant indexing service.

Cash flows need to be dealt with on a case-by-case basis. Small cash flows are treated in a similar fashion to cash dividends, in that they are accumulated as cash and equitized where possible using futures contracts until there is a large enough pool to warrant a purchase of physical stock. This stock purchase can be used to rebalance the portfolio if necessary, so helping to minimize transaction costs. If the cash flow is large, the indexer may buy physical assets outright, unless the price of the futures contract is below fair value, as in Example 11.2. Normally the indexer will view any large stock purchase as an opportunity to fine-tune the portfolio allocation and in order to keep transaction costs to a minimum.

ADMINISTRATION

Fewer transactions generally mean much simplified administration, and this can be a major source of cost saving for the investor. Indexed portfolio administration can be viewed as a slimmed-down version of actively managed portfolio administration.

The exceptions to this rule are indexed portfolios with large and frequent cash flows, and portfolios that make unusually heavy use of derivatives, for example to enhance return. Large cash flows oblige the manager to construct transactions of physical shares with correspondingly large administrative costs, as indexed portfolios tend to hold a larger number of stocks than do actively managed portfolios, and administrative charges tend to be levied according to the number of transactions.

Derivatives contracts always require frequent transactions to ensure initial and variation margins are maintained, and to adjust positions as futures and options contracts expire. Unusually heavy use of derivatives can therefore significantly contribute to administrative costs.

VALUATION

Apart from the fact that indexed portfolios tend to hold a much larger number of assets than actively managed portfolios, valuation is carried out using exactly the same principles as for actively managed portfolios in the same asset class. That is, it is the sum of the market value of each individual holding in the portfolio, in base currency, plus unrealized profit and losses on derivatives positions plus cash.

PERFORMANCE MEASUREMENT AND ATTRIBUTION

Investors who place their funds in indexed portfolios expect unspectacular results. Their investments are expected to rise and fall in value more or less with the benchmark.

The apparent performance of the portfolio depends on the particular period being measured. Consider Example 11.4.1, which sets out the results for a domestic equity portfolio. Measured to 30 June 1996, the performance of this portfolio and its benchmark looks like Example 11.4.2. The same performance measurements taken one month earlier looks like Example 11.4.3.

EXAMPLE 11.4.1 *Monthly performance of domestic equities indexed portfolio*

Month	Portfolio %	Benchmark %	Difference %	Month	Portfolio %	Benchmark %	Difference %
31 05 94	1.00	1.15	−0.15	30 06 95	0.65	0.48	0.17
30 06 94	−3.95	−4.03	0.08	31 07 95	4.91	4.91	0.00
31 07 94	3.80	3.72	0.08	31 08 95	0.80	0.94	−0.14
31 08 94	3.00	3.04	−0.04	30 09 95	0.65	0.74	−0.09
30 09 94	−4.05	−3.88	−0.17	31 10 95	−2.27	−2.34	0.06
31 10 94	1.36	1.29	0.07	30 11 95	4.43	4.43	0.00
30 11 94	−7.06	−7.23	0.16	31 12 95	2.33	2.53	−0.20
31 12 94	1.80	1.65	0.15	31 01 96	3.85	3.93	−0.08
31 01 95	−4.16	−4.25	0.09	29 02 96	0.38	0.39	−0.01
28 02 95	5.00	5.07	−0.07	31 03 96	−2.18	−2.28	0.10
31 03 95	0.02	0.07	−0.05	30 04 96	4.20	4.38	−0.18
30 04 95	7.98	7.78	0.20	31 05 96	−1.89	−1.87	−0.02
31 05 95	−1.28	−1.19	−0.09	30 06 96	−0.30	−0.59	0.29

EXAMPLE 11.4.2 *Return summary, domestic equities indexed portfolio to 30 June 1996*

Period	Portfolio %	Benchmark %	Difference %
3 months	1.92	1.82	0.10
6 months	3.93	3.82	0.12
12 months	15.53	15.81	−0.28
2 years	22.74	22.42	0.32

EXAMPLE 11.4.3 *Performance summary, domestic equities indexed portfolio to 31 May 1996*

Period	Portfolio %	Benchmark %	Difference %
3 months	0.00	0.09	−0.09
6 months	6.68	7.07	−0.40
12 months	16.63	17.05	−0.42
2 years	18.25	18.18	0.07

Neither set of results gives a good indication of the performance of the portfolio relative to the benchmark. In fact, it is not obvious that the two return summaries refer to the same portfolio. It follows that some form of continuous measurement is required to show how well the portfolio is tracking its benchmark. Because CAPM tells us that asset returns fluctuate all the time but risk characteristics are more stable, some measure of the risk is required.

When the portfolio is constructed, the investment manager generates an estimate of tracking error and beta. The beta is nearly always close to one, indicating that the portfolio will move in line with the benchmark. The tracking error is ideally zero, but in practice is usually between 0.10% and 0.50%. One of the purposes of performance analysis for indexed portfolios is to compare expected and observed tracking error.

If the portfolio exhibits very large return variation from benchmark in one or more periods, the investment manager may be called on to carry out an attribution analysis. For a domestic equity portfolio, this usually entails looking for larger than normal differences between portfolio and benchmark allocations to industry or factor groups and calculating the contribution of these to total return variation. This is a simple calculation, whereby for each industry or factor group the difference between portfolio and benchmark allocation is multiplied by the difference between the benchmark return to the group and the total benchmark return.

The other potential source of return variation comes from the composition of the industry or factor groups where this is not identical for portfolio and benchmark. The logic applied is the same: the difference between the portfolio and benchmark return to the group is multiplied by the benchmark allocation to the group.

Narrowing down the return variation to one or two industry or factor groups can be helpful. If necessary, the same principle can be applied within groups to identify individual security holdings that contributed to return variance.

The sum of industry group mismatches and return differences within industries is approximately the total portfolio return variance, with the difference due to an interaction effect.

PITFALLS

Constructing and managing indexed portfolios can look deceptively simple, and some indexed portfolios are indeed very easy to look after. This perception is associated with the continuing downward pressure on management fees.

The biggest pitfall is the expectation that one approach fits all. Often this means that the indexer goes for full replication without considering the implications for the costs of running the portfolio in question. Probably the next biggest is that of using the optimizer or other stock selection software as a 'black box'. Experienced indexers choose their optimizer according to the market to be indexed and also exercise some care about how data is sourced and results interpreted. It is important to first screen the universe of securities for investability, in order to ensure that the optimal portfolios obtained are practical and cost efficient to implement.

Once the portfolio is up and running, the indexer needs to take care to manage liquidity and to avoid unwanted portfolio turnover. Often these are two sides of the same coin, and can be dealt with by relying on the use of derivatives, such as share price index futures, to manage liquidity.

Corporate actions can occasionally cause problems by landing the portfolio with securities that are not required for diversification and merely add to transaction and administration costs. Pre-emptive action can avoid this. Similarly, large changes to the benchmark holdings, often resulting from privatized utilities or other publicly owned entities, can present the indexer with the significant challenge of buying large parcels of stock at inflated prices. These problems need to be addressed on a case-by-case basis, and require a good understanding of the structure of the underlying market.

CASE STUDY

There is often the temptation to seek to modify the indexed portfolio according to the investor's perception of what can add value to equity performance. This can, of course, add valuable insight and even enhance returns to the investment but, as often as not, it simply shackles the investment manager, restricting his or her ability to deliver stable results.

It is understandable, for example, to seek to disqualify very illiquid stocks from the investment universe. Illiquid stocks can add disproportionately to the costs of transacting and administering a portfolio, and often contribute to disappointing results because, when the manager tries to sell them in the market, the price realized can be much inferior to the last recorded market price.

However, sticking only to very liquid assets can be very restrictive, especially if the portfolio is to be held for a long time, and it is not at all easy to define the cut-off point where a stock is considered so illiquid as to be embargoed, and where it is sufficiently liquid to be included in the list of candidate assets. It is still harder to concoct a decision rule to so define assets for inclusion and exclusion.

Most indexed portfolio managers apply some decision rules, usually based on the quantity of shares actually tradable or recent volumes of trading activity, current bid–ask spreads and so on, or else they apply some kind of eye-ball scrutiny on the day of the transaction. This simply involves inspecting the activity in each suspect stock just prior to placing the order with the broker. These measures usually do the trick, but can be a bit too ad hoc for some investors, who prefer more uniform procedures in the investment process.

The danger with applying too rigid decision rules is that the manager's judgement can be bypassed, with a consequent loss of information, sometimes leading to disappointing results.

A case in point is an investor requiring a portfolio with low costs and low tracking error. Recognizing that transacting illiquid stocks can significantly increase the costs of the portfolio, it was decided to limit the number of stocks in the portfolio to 45% of the number in the benchmark index. At the time, the benchmark index held just over 200 stocks, so the mandate specified no more than 90 stocks, a constraint that was thought not to be too onerous, since the top 90 stocks represented approximately 94.5% of the benchmark by capitalization.

At the same time, the investor wanted a low tracking error for the portfolio, and again was not prepared to leave very much to the discretion of the manager. In addition to the strict limit on the number of stocks in the portfolio, the manager was expected to keep fairly closely to benchmark industry allocations, and to minimize as far as possible the inevitable size bias.

Problems began to arise when a significant expansion in the equity market resulted in an increase in the number of stocks in the benchmark, many stemming from privatization of telecommunications and airlines. After two years, the benchmark held over 300 stocks. Example 11.5 shows how the 90-stock portfolio compared with portfolios with more stocks against the 300-stock benchmark.

The combination of constraints worked against the interests of the investor, increasing risk rather than reducing it. The table shows that both tracking error and industry group mismatches increase as the number of stocks allowed decrease.

EXAMPLE 11.5 *Tracking error versus number of stocks*

Asset Class	Benchmark	150 Stocks	125 Stocks	90 Stocks
Expected Beta	1.00	1.00	1.00	1.00
Expected Tracking Error	0.00%	0.59%	0.72%	1.01%
	%	%	%	%
Aerospace & Defence	1.29	1.89	1.94	2.66
Airlines	0.24	0.00	0.00	0.00
Auto Components	0.91	0.52	0.55	0.61
Automobiles	0.27	0.34	0.40	0.00
Banks	6.69	9.20	9.80	10.27
Breweries & Distilleries	0.36	0.44	0.56	0.60
Brokerage	0.29	0.37	0.41	0.00
Building Materials	0.04	0.00	0.00	0.00
Business Services & D.P.	7.85	7.52	7.80	7.60
Chemicals	1.82	1.60	1.82	1.44
Computers	5.56	5.53	5.44	5.65
Conglomerate	1.44	2.06	2.02	1.05
Contracting & Construction	0.09	0.00	0.00	0.00
Currency	0.00	0.00	0.00	0.00
Electrical & Electronic	9.13	9.23	8.86	8.57
Electrical Instruments	1.64	1.56	1.39	0.63
Energy Service & Equipment	0.86	0.85	0.56	0.73
Food Manufacturing	2.73	2.08	2.30	2.42
Food Retailing	0.84	0.73	0.84	0.00
Gold	0.13	0.00	0.00	0.00
Health & Personal Care	6.76	6.19	5.68	5.34
Household Appliances	0.10	0.00	0.00	0.00
Household Products	0.33	0.30	0.32	0.00
Industrial Components	0.70	0.88	0.99	1.31
Insurance	3.92	3.02	2.62	2.08
Investment Services	1.40	1.42	1.54	1.90
Investment Trusts	0.41	0.52	0.54	0.78
Iron & Steel	0.09	0.00	0.00	0.00
Leasing & Consumer Credit	4.04	3.97	3.86	4.28
Leisure & Tourism	1.39	1.08	1.18	1.46
Machinery & Engineering	0.41	0.34	0.41	0.00
Media & Communications	1.58	1.96	2.34	3.39
Metal Fabricators	0.09	0.00	0.00	0.00
Miscellaneous	0.43	0.00	0.00	0.00
Miscellaneous Basic Industries	0.06	0.00	0.00	0.00
Miscellaneous Consumer Goods	1.03	0.96	0.99	1.09

continued on next page

Asset Class	Benchmark %	150 Stocks %	125 Stocks %	90 Stocks %
Miscellaneous Financials	0.31	0.00	0.00	0.00
Miscellaneous Transport	0.35	0.00	0.00	0.00
Non-ferrous Metals	0.52	0.97	1.15	1.84
Office Equipment & Copiers	0.21	0.00	0.00	0.00
Oil & Gas	6.69	9.09	9.98	10.51
Paper & Forest Products	0.50	0.58	0.40	0.00
Pharmaceuticals	7.02	6.96	6.94	7.35
Property	0.06	0.00	0.00	0.00
Railways	0.13	0.00	0.00	0.00
Recreation & Other Consumer	1.22	1.14	0.95	0.98
Stores & Retail	5.78	5.61	4.62	3.57
Telecommunications	7.72	7.95	8.15	8.72
Textiles & Clothing	0.13	0.00	0.00	0.00
Tobacco	1.08	1.08	1.13	1.14
Utilities	3.34	2.06	1.53	2.04

Source: Thomson Financial Datastream

The desire to reduce transaction costs is understandable. Transaction costs are a deadweight in the investment portfolio, and should be minimized wherever possible. But the effect of tracking error can be positive as well as negative, so while it is always in the interests of the investor to control and manage it, it is not obvious that less tracking error is always better than more.

An alternative approach is simply to relax size and cost constraints on the basis that portfolio return is measured after transaction costs, which effectively renders the liquidity constraint redundant.

CHAPTER 12

Fixed Interest Portfolios

These are made up of instruments that pay a predetermined amount of interest during their life. All interest rate investments are loans, involving a borrower and a lender (the seller and the buyer respectively). For a standard interest rate transaction, the lender has no call on the assets of the borrower, except for the amount of the loan and interest earned. The borrower, provided all repayment obligations are met, retains the right to the assets he or she owns, and so enjoys all the benefits and risks of these.

APPLICATIONS

Governments, banks, companies and individuals borrow money to fulfil liquidity or investment requirements without having to share the ownership of their assets.

Many fixed interest instruments are loans that were made initially by a bank to a company, although large companies may issue bonds or **debentures** (the same thing) directly to the public. When a bank has lent the money to a company, it records it as an asset. As with many other assets, this loan can then be resold. The bank may choose to resell it in its raw form, in which case it will describe it as Company ABC, maturity x, coupon y, and so on. The buyer of this bond from the bank knows that if Company ABC is unable to honour the loan, they may lose all or part of their investment. The bank can often sell it for a higher price if it first endorses it in some way. In endorsing the loan, the bank is effectively saying that, 'if Company ABC cannot pay up, we'll guarantee performance of the loan'. The buyer's risk is then against the bank. Either way, the loan may then be bought and sold hundreds of times before it finally matures.

Investment managers hold portfolios of interest rate instruments (loans) for many reasons:

- Sometimes they are required by regulation to hold a given amount of government bonds.
- Fixed interest is usually thought of as being less risky than, and in any case usually has a low correlation with, equities, so investors often hold bonds to modify the risk of their overall portfolio.
- Short-term fixed interest securities are often held as collateral for positions in futures, options and other derivative instruments.
- The investor may be anticipating relatively high returns to bonds.

THEORY

An interest rate, for a borrower, is a measure of the value of present versus deferred consumption. For the lender, it is the reward for delayed consumption. Any given rate of interest can be said to be determined by three factors:

- The general level of interest rates.
- The term of the loan – long-term loans usually bear a higher rate of interest than short-term loans, other things being equal. The difference between interest rates of varying maturities is described by the yield curve, an illustration of which is given in Example 12.1.
- The risk of the loan – whether the borrower will be able to repay it with interest. This includes things like whether the loan is secured against assets, what other loans the borrower already has and so on. This risk is called **credit risk**.

In modern financial markets, the general level of interest rates is mostly determined by supply and demand, which are in turn influenced by various factors. Not all economists and interested parties agree on the relative importance of the factors influencing interest rates, or even that they are all an influence. This list indicates the influences generally thought to be of some importance:

- Government policy. Governments often set some kind of reference rate for short-term interest rates. This rate has a strong impact on all other interest rates, which is one of the reasons why they do it. Interest rate setting behav-

EXAMPLE 12.1 *The yield curve*

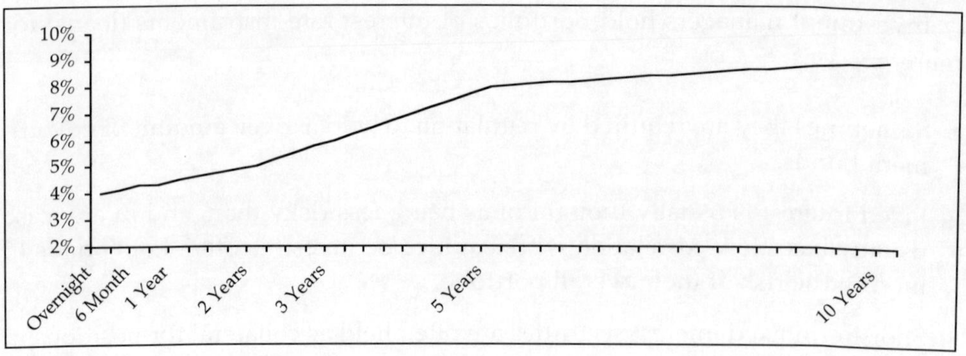

iour is usually intended as a partial control on inflation and the general level of economic activity, and historically has met with mixed success.

- Inflation is an important driver of interest rates. Investors want the value of their investment to grow at more than the inflation rate, so the real value of their investment does not decline. Inflation is so important that most economists and investment managers distinguish between the interest rate that includes inflation (the nominal rate) and the interest rate net of inflation (the real rate). The nominal interest rate is the sum of the real interest rate and inflation.

- Expected inflation, as opposed to existing, or apparent inflation is important. Investors are unlikely to be happy with a nominal interest rate that may, before the end of the loan, be less than the prevailing inflation rate.

The shape of the yield curve draws a lot of academic attention and is the cause of considerable angst for investors and borrowers. There is no universal yield curve. In practice, each currency has its own range of yield curves, each describing loans of a given risk level. For example, the yield curve for UK government bonds will be different from local government instruments, and bank and corporate bonds will each also have their own yield curves, and perhaps several of each, since banks and corporations cover a wide range of risk levels. Yield curves can move about independently of each other. Not only can interest rates rise and fall as a whole, but the difference between short- and long-term can change too. Sometimes short-term interest rates are higher than long-term rates. A number of hypotheses have been put forward to help to explain the structure and behaviour of the yield curve.

- **Expectations hypothesis**. This says that long-term interest rates reflect what short-term rates are expected to be at that point in time, allowing for the provision that they should be a bit higher to compensate for the other uncertainties that increase over time, such as expected inflation. This hypothesis is sometimes helpful when long-term rates are lower than short-term rates: it says that short-term rates are expected to fall.

- **Liquidity preference hypothesis**. Investors prefer to get their money back sooner, and so demand higher compensation for tying it up for long periods.
- **Preferred habitat/market segmentation hypothesis**. This says that the market for short- and long-term instruments is largely mutually exclusive, and so what are seen and two (or more) different yield curves.

CALCULATING THE PRICE OF FIXED INTEREST SECURITIES

Central to calculating the price of a bond are the ideas of **discounting** and compounding. Discounting is simply calculating by how much a given sum of money is worth more now than later. The interest rate determines by how much today's value is greater than next week's or next year's. For example, knowing that you will receive \$100 in one year's time is handy, but \$100 right now would be handier. If the interest for one year is 8.0%, then the value of \$100 in a year's time is as shown in Example 12.2.

EXAMPLE 12.2 *Discounting*

$$\begin{aligned}\text{Value of \$100 in one year} &= \$100/(1 + \text{interest rate}) \\ &= \$100/1.08 \\ &= \$92.59 \text{ now}\end{aligned} \tag{12.1}$$

In other words, \$92.59 invested for one year at 8.0% will result in an investment worth \$100.00. Working backwards,

$$\$92.59 \text{ now} = \$92.59 \times 1.08 = \$100 \text{ in a year's time.}$$

Discounting works as long as the interest is levied and paid in one lump at the end of the loan, in other words it attracts only **simple interest**. Securities with a single interest payment at maturity are called **discount securities**. Most loans don't work like this, but compound the interest more frequently. If the same loan has interest compounded semi-annually and is only paid at the end of the loan, the equation looks like Example 12.3.1.

EXAMPLE 12.3.1 *Compounding within one year*

Value of \$100 in one year = $\$100/(1 + i/p)^p$ (12.2)

Where:

i = the annual interest rate
p = the number of interest payments per year

Value of \$100 in one year = $\$100/(1 + 0.08/2)^2 = \$92.46$

The effective interest rate is \$8.16%, or $(1 + 0.08/2)^2 - 1$

Virtually all loans with a maturity of more than one year use some kind of compound interest, and some very short-term loans compound interest too. The same loan, with interest compounded semi-annually but with two years left to run, would be calculated as in Example 12.3.2.

EXAMPLE 12.3.2 *Compounding over more than one year*

Value of \$100 in one year = $\$100/(1 + i/p)^{p \times y}$ (12.3)

Where:

y = number of years
= $\$100/(1 + 0.08/2)^{2\times2}$
= \$85.48

The compounding factor can also be expressed as the number of days to maturity divided by the number of days in a year, so compounding an annual rate of 8.0% for 90 days can be expressed as $\$100/(1 + 8\%)^{90/365}$, or approximated by $\$100/(1 + 8\% \times 90/365)$. When using days for this purpose, it is important to respect the prevailing convention regarding the number of days in a year, since some securities are priced on the basis of a 360-day year. This is, of course, computationally a bit simpler than the 365-day convention, in which the analyst must also take care to adjust for leap years.

The ultimate in compounding is **continuous compounding**. As the name suggests, this is the idea that interest accumulates continuously during the life of the loan. Its use tends to be mostly in theoretical applications of interest rates and for pricing complex derivatives, such as options. Ironically, this is because it is much easier to calculate, since the frequency of compounding interest payments does not need to be defined. The same loan, using continuously compounded interest, would look like Example 12.4.

EXAMPLE 12.4 *Continuous compounding*

$$\text{Value of \$100 in one year} = \$100/(1 + e^{I \times y}) \quad (12.4)$$
$$= \$100/(1 + e^{0.08 \times 1})$$
$$= \$92.31$$

The effective interest rate is \$8.33%, or $(1 + e^{0.08 \times 1}) - 1$

This formula still assumes that the interest, although levied continuously, is paid in one lump sum at the end of the loan.

For most purposes, however, periodic compounding is applied and interest is paid at fixed intervals throughout the loan, so in order to calculate the price of a loan or bond, it is necessary to know when and how often interest is compounded, and when and how often **coupons** are paid.

Using the very same principles, the formula for pricing a standard bond is given in Example 12.5.

EXAMPLE 12.5 *Calculating the bond price*

$$P = v^{(f/d)} (c\,(x + a_n) + 100v^n) \quad (12.5)$$

Where:

P = the price per \$100 of the bond's face value
v = $1/(1+i)$
i = yield to maturity divided by coupon frequency
c = the periodic coupon payment per \$100 of the bond's face value
x = 0 if the bond is ex-interest, 1 if it is **cum-interest**
a_n = $(1 + v^n)/i$
f = the number of days to the next coupon date
d = the number of days from the last coupon date to the next
n = the number of complete periods from the next coupon to maturity

Ex-interest means that the next interest payment is not included in the price of the bond. By convention, there is an ex-interest period before any coupon payment and the duration of this is determined by the market in which the bond is traded. If the bond trades during this period, the original holder, not the purchaser, receives the coupon.

For example, a bond with the following characteristics:

Settlement Date:	20 January 2001
Maturity Date:	30 September 2020
Next Coupon:	30 March 2001
Last Coupon:	30 September 2000
Coupon Rate %pa	8.00%
Coupons per Year:	2
Cum-interest	0
Yield to Maturity %pa	8.35%

has a **settlement price** of $99.10 per $100 face value.

The **settlement date** is rarely the day on which the bond is transacted. Most markets have a fixed settlement cycle of one to two days, meaning that the transaction is settled one or two days later. As with foreign exchange transactions, the date on which the transaction takes place is immaterial. The settlement date and yield to maturity are what define the price actually paid.

Formula 12.5 assumes that interest is accrued on coupon dates. The **yield to maturity** is equivalent to the annual interest rate used in Examples 12.2 to 12.4. An important assumption of this bond price formula is that it assumes that the coupons are reinvested at the yield to maturity. Unsurprisingly, this is a controversial assumption, and one that many practitioners seek to improve upon. For most everyday purposes, however, this formula is used to equate a yield to maturity with a settlement price. If there are no coupons left to pay on the bond, its price is calculated as if it were a discount security.

EXAMPLE 12.6 *The bond price over the coupon cycle (cum-interest)*

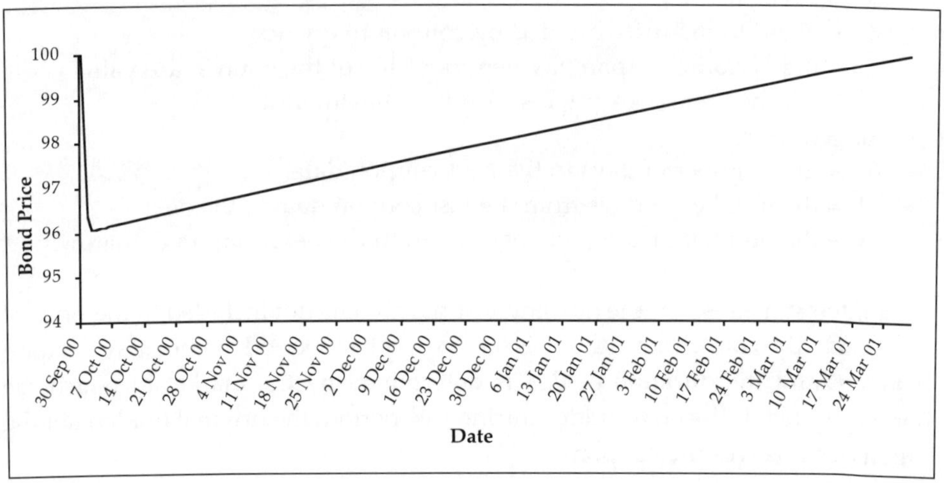

For discount securities and for bonds that pay coupons, it is important to remember that, as the yield to maturity of the bond goes up, the price goes down, and vice versa – but the relationship is not linear. The buyer of bonds is thus anticipating a fall in the interest rate underlying those bonds.

Most bond pricing exercises concern bonds that still have some coupons to pay. If the bond is priced cum-coupon, the accrued interest or coupon income is an important component of the bond's settlement value. Example 12.6 shows how the settlement value of the bond increases over the coupon period, as the value of the accrued coupon accumulates.

CREDIT RISK

The yield to maturity at which the bond is transacted is made up of the time value of money and the risk of that particular bond. The risk specific to the bond is the risk that the borrower will be unable to fulfil his or her obligations under the terms of the loan, in other words the credit risk. To help investors to assess the bond's value, most large borrowers, such as banks and large companies, are assigned a credit rating by one or more of the large credit rating agencies, such as Moody's and Standard & Poor's (Table 12.1).

These ratings effectively place each borrower within a category of risk. The categories range from government debt, which for most developed countries is considered as having almost no credit risk, through semi-government, bank, investment-grade corporate to sub-investment-grade corporate. The latter are sometimes called junk bonds.

The class in which a borrower finds itself determines how much interest it must pay above government debt of similar maturity to attract buyers of its bonds. Ratings are revised periodically, of course, but can be surprisingly sticky. The margin of interest for any given maturity between any two rating classes fluctuates according to supply and demand, with the yield difference between maturities and credit quality all subject to change. For example, a borrower of BBB (adequate) might be required to pay only 2.0% over government debt for, say, five-year loans. The following day, the market may decide that business prospects for speculative enterprises have worsened, and the yield differential may widen suddenly to 2.25%. The gap for shorter loans might have moved only by 0.10% if the market consensus was that the near term prospects for those borrowers weren't nearly so bad.

The higher the proportion of the loan to the value of the offsetting assets, the greater is the **return to equity** enjoyed by the borrower. Equity analysts call this the **leverage** of the investment. From the point of view of the lender, the higher the leverage, the higher the risk of the investment, because there is a greater

Table 12.1 Example credit ratings

Moody's	Comment	Standard & Poor's	Comment
Aaa	Highest quality	AAA	Extremely strong
Aa	High quality	AA	Very strong
A	Favourable investment attributes	A	Strong
Baa	Medium grade	BBB	Adequate
Ba	Speculative elements	BB	Less vulnerable
Caa	Poor standing	B	More vulnerable
Ca	Speculative in a high degree	CCC	Currently vulnerable
C	Lowest rating – poor prospects	CC	Currently highly vulnerable
		C	Currently highly vulnerable to non-payment

Source: Moody's, Standard & Poor's

chance of the borrower not being able to meet his or her obligations, or of the value of the assets falling below the amount owing on the loan.

Credit risk can be thought of as encompassing the riskiness of the borrower, the borrower's leverage, the time left on the loan and the potential impact on credit quality of changes in the interest rate. These items are interactive, for example a rise in interest rates may be associated with a general economic slowdown, which will affect the borrower's revenues and possibly the value of his or her assets, and thus his or her ability to repay the loan as well as his or her leverage. At the same time, if the borrower has floating rate debt, then his or her interest payments will rise, further contributing to the leverage effect.

Most investment managers think about credit risk in terms of their exposure to each borrower. For each borrower, some estimation is made of the likelihood of default, and the potential **recovery rate** if default occurs. The recovery rate is usually expressed in terms of cents per dollar.

Measuring the likelihood of default and the likely recovery rate is not straightforward, and few quantitative methods of doing so have withstood the test of time. One that has been widely used is the Z Score Method, developed by Professor Ed Altman of New York University in the 1970s. Professor Altman conducted a fairly sophisticated statistical analysis to identify relationships between balance sheet information and imminent failure of companies. From this work he quantified the importance of financial ratios that appeared to presage, with impressive reliability, loan defaults.

The practical application of this method is naturally limited. Professor Altman was working with companies with debt issued in the USA, where balance sheet information is easily available, timely and of good quality. It also happens to be the market with the lion's share of corporate debt. It is easy to imagine the Z Score being hard to apply in many other markets, where fixed interest is dominated by government and semi-government loans, and the data quality is much lower.

A more accurate estimate of credit risk can be obtained by consulting specialist credit derivatives markets, such as those for credit swaps. These markets set a 'price' on credit quality relative to safe investments such as government bonds. Because this price or 'credit spread' is determined by supply and demand, it is considered a very reliable estimate of credit quality.

It is easy to assume that the risk of a fixed interest portfolio is simply the sum of the risk of its parts, and it is only relatively recently that the analytic tools have become available to allow a more sophisticated approach, enabling estimation of credit risk of a portfolio as opposed to the sum of its holdings. The key to credit risk management is ensuring effective diversification.

One way of doing this is to apply the mean-variance optimization techniques that are widely used in equity portfolios. Such an approach could, for example, measure the portfolio's exposure to industry groups or macroeconomic events and other factors, which in conjunction with analyses of correlations between factors could lead to some useful insight into credit risk at the portfolio level.

Unfortunately, it is not nearly as simple as that because two characteristics of the fixed interest market cause problems. The first is that, unlike equities, bonds and other fixed interest instruments are not traded on exchanges. They are usually 'screen-based' or 'telephone' markets, lacking a central trading point, with no central record of traded prices for individual securities. Without a reliable record of market prices, it is all but impossible to construct a time series of asset returns on which the necessary correlation matrix can be based.

The other problem is that fixed interest securities have an inconvenient habit of maturing. In most countries, bonds are issued with a maturity of between two and ten years. Some markets boast government bonds of 30 years but these are rare, and the most liquid bond series are usually in the five- to ten-year maturity range. Mean-variance optimizers rely on at least five years of monthly return data, so many bonds mature just as they are accumulating enough data to be useful.

In isolation these problems are enormous; together they are almost fatal. One saving grace may be that most corporate issuers of bonds, and nearly all banks that issue them, also have common equity listed somewhere. It is possible that equity data could be applied to the problem, but it is early days yet, and this technology needs to be tested over time before it can be put into practice.

Equity optimizers are designed to analyse portfolio volatility, usually relative to some equity benchmark. To the equity analyst small price movements are almost as interesting as big ones, and both directions are important. By contrast, small changes in the value of a borrower's assets do not noticeably change the value of the fixed interest security, which by definition is expected to have a fixed value at maturity. The fixed interest analyst is more interested in the possibility of default, in other words, large downward movements.

Any model of credit risk also must take into account the fact that credit risk is closely related to the general level of interest rates and the shape of the yield curve. It is likely that research in this direction will improve on currently used methods of analysing credit risk, whether based on the mean-variance approach or something more closely suited to fixed income portfolios.

PORTFOLIO CONSTRUCTION

Most fixed interest portfolios are compared with some benchmark index, generally specifying a broad risk level and a range of maturities. For example, the benchmark may be confined to government issued bonds with maturities from three to five years, or it may include semi-government bonds or corporate bonds. Maturities generally range from three to twenty years, and thirty years in some markets. The benchmark is the investment manager's most important guide when setting up the portfolio.

In constructing the portfolio of fixed interest securities, the investment manager needs to decide whether to match to maturity of the benchmark and seek to add value from judicious use of credit risk, or to roughly match the credit risk and add value through judgements on maturities, or some combination of the two.

Adding value by mismatching credit risk relies on specialist analysis, usually targeted at the profitability of the borrower and resembling some kind of equity research. How much scope there is to add returns in this way depends on the benchmark and how much deviation is provided for in the mandate. For example, a government bond benchmark assumes no credit risk, while a corporate bond benchmark implies the expectation of at least some credit risk in addition to that inherent in the benchmark.

Earning extra returns by changing the maturity of the portfolio relies heavily on macroeconomic analysis, incorporating forecasts of interest rates for specific maturities. This can benefit from effective yield curve modelling, which is discussed later in this chapter.

The most attractive source of extra return comes from identifying mispriced securities. Many markets provide ample opportunities to do this, as some fixed interest securities are traded only infrequently, and prices can be inconsistent between securities of similar maturity and credit quality. There are two main sources of mispricing: the bond price may be different from the prices of bonds of similar risk level in that region of the yield curve, or it may be misallocated to the band, and therefore subject to rerating. The danger is twofold: first because the risk of the bond is misestimated, and second because the security proves very expensive to trade. The majority of mispriced securities are also very illiquid, meaning that the bid and ask prices have a large gap between them. Having bought the security at an attractive price, the investor may find that it can only be sold at a very unattractive one. The gains from having spotted a bargain can be lost in realizing the profit.

INTEREST RATE RISK MANAGEMENT

Apart from the risk that a borrower will default, there is also the risk that interest rates will behave unexpectedly. Investment managers therefore pay considerable attention to changes in the value of their fixed interest portfolios as interest rates change.

The simplest measure of interest rate risk is the portfolio value per basis point **(PVBP)** also known as the **bond volatility** or **dollar value of one point (DV01)**. As the name suggests, it measures the change in the portfolio's value if the interest rate changes by one basis point (0.01%) (Example 12.7.1).

EXAMPLE 12.7.1 *Portfolio value per basis point for two bonds*

	Bond 1	Bond 2
Face Value	$100	$100
Settlement	20 January 2001	20 January 2001
Maturity	30 September 2020	18 June 2012
Coupon per Annum	8.00%	5.75%
Coupons per Year	2	2
Next Coupon	30 March 2001	18 June 2001
Last Coupon	30 September 2000	18 December 2000
Cum-interest? (1 = yes, 0 = no)	1	1
Yield to Maturity	8.50%	6.00%
Bond Price	$97.72	$98.47
Bond Price Minus one Basis Point	$97.76	$98.51
Bond Price Plus one Basis Point	$97.67	$98.43
Portfolio Value per Basis Point per $million	$457.04	$403.59

The result is achieved by calculating the bond price twice, using yields to maturity 0.01% above and below the current yield to maturity. The difference in the cum-coupon prices is the PVBP.

Although this measure is useful for very small segments of the yield curve and for very small changes in the interest rate, it is not so helpful for larger changes in interest rates because the PVBP changes according to the interest rate, varying for different bonds within a portfolio at one point in time, and changes for the same bond as interest rates move up and down.

The **duration**, also known as **Macaulay duration,** of a portfolio gives a measure of the aggregate maturity of the bond by weighting each cash flow according to when it occurs and dividing the result by the number of cash flows. It thus gives a measure of when the instrument has paid out half its coupons, which in turn acts as a point of comparison between instruments. The duration of the portfolio is simply the weighted sum of the duration of its components.

Duration is a crude measure and, ironically for a fixed interest metric, takes no account of the time value of money. **Modified duration** does this by first estimating the present value of the cash flows, and then applying the duration formula. The modified duration is the point in time when the instrument has paid out exactly half the present value of its payouts (Example 12.7.2).

EXAMPLE 12.7.2 *Modified duration for two bonds*

	Bond 1	Bond 2
Face Value	$100	$100
Settlement	20 January 2001	20 January 2001
Maturity	30 September 2020	18 June 2012
Coupon per Annum	8.00%	5.75%
Coupons per Year	2	2
Next Coupon	30 March 2001	18 June 2001
Last Coupon	30 September 2000	18 December 2000
Cum-interest? (1 = yes, 0 = no)	1	1
Yield to Maturity	8.50%	6.00%
Interest Rate Change	0.01%	0.01%
Bond Price	$97.72	$98.47
Portfolio Value per Basis Point per $million	$457.04	$403.59
Modified Duration	4.6773	4.0986

EXAMPLE 12.7.3 *Convexity of two bonds*

	Bond 1	Bond 2
Face Value	$100	$100
Settlement	20 January 2001	20 January 2001
Maturity	30 September 2020	18 June 2012
Coupon per Annum	8.00%	5.75%
Coupons per Year	2	2
Next Coupon	30 March 2001	18 June 2001
Last Coupon	30 September 2000	18 December 2000
Cum-interest? (1 = yes, 0 = no)	1	1
Yield to Maturity	8.50%	6.00%
Interest Rate Change	0.01%	0.01%
Bond Price	$97.72	$98.47
Portfolio Value per Basis Point per $million	$457.04	$403.59
Modified Duration	4.6773	4.0986
Convexity	0.3323	0.2091

EXAMPLE 12.8 *Pull to par*

	Annual Coupon Paid Semi-annually		
Maturity in Years	6.00%	8.00%	10.00%
20	80.21	100.00	119.79
15	82.71	100.00	117.29
10	86.41	100.00	113.59
8	88.35	100.00	111.65
5	91.89	100.00	108.11
3	94.76	100.00	105.24
2	96.37	100.00	103.63
1	98.11	100.00	101.89
0	100.00	100.00	100.00

Source: Das, S. *Risk Management and Financial Derivatives, A Guide to the Mathmatics*, Sydney, The Law Book Company, 1997, p. 43

Duration is a fundamental measure of any bond or portfolio of bonds. By providing useful comparisons between bonds and portfolios, it can indicate which are more or less risky. As a rule, a portfolio with a higher duration will suffer more from an interest rate rise than a low, or short duration portfolio. This is also true of maturity: a 30-year bond is much more vulnerable to an interest rate shock than a 5-year bond. But the maturity of the bond says nothing about when the cash flows occur, and cash flows are an important component of the bond price computation. Duration therefore provides more information, but it is still limited.

EXAMPLE 12.9 *Effect on the bond price of a change in credit risk*

	Bond 1	Bond 2
Face Value	$100	$100
Settlement	20 January 2001	20 January 2001
Maturity	30 September 2020	18 June 2012
Coupon per Annum	8.00%	5.75%
Coupons per Year	2	2
Next Coupon	30 March 2001	18 June 2001
Last Coupon	30 September 2000	18 December 2000
Cum-interest? (1 = yes, 0 = no)	1	1
Interest Rate Change	0.01%	0.01%
Yield to Maturity	8.50%	6.00%
Bond Price	$97.72	$98.47
Portfolio Value per Basis Point per $million	$457.04	$403.59
Modified Duration	4.6773	4.0986
Convexity	0.3323	0.2091
Change in Credit Rating	0.25%	0.25%
Yield to Maturity	8.75%	6.25%
Bond Price	$95.47	$96.48
Portfolio Value per Basis Point per $million	$440.78	$393.28
Modified Duration	4.6169	4.0764
Convexity	0.3184	0.2033

The relationship between the PVBP and the interest rate is measured by the **convexity** of the bond. The more convex the bond or portfolio, the more the PVBP will change as yield changes increase (Example 12.7.3).

When a bond reaches maturity its value becomes equal to its par, or face value. This means that, other things being equal, as the bond matures, the discount or premium at which the bond trades will decrease and eventually disappear. This effect on the change in a bond's value is called the **pull to par**. Example 12.8 illustrates the pull to par effect for 8.0% yield to maturity.

The value of a bond also reacts to a change in the quality of its credit risk. The effect on the bond's settlement value of a given change in credit risk depends on the starting yield to maturity. In other words, the effect is not linear across all bond yields and maturities (Example 12.9).

YIELD CURVE MODELLING

Much of the theory of fixed interest portfolio management is based on the level and shape of the yield curve, and how it moves about in time. But in practice there are many different yield curves, each relating to a currency zone and, within currencies, to different risk levels. Inconveniently, yield curves tend to be difficult or impossible to observe in practice. This is because the prices at which bonds are traded tend not to be recorded officially, and some sectors of the fixed interest market trade so infrequently that the last known price may no longer be pertinent. To get around the first problem, some organizations use the idea of a panel. That is, they ask a number of banks and brokers to quote prices for a range of bonds. The prices quoted are then averaged to derive a consensus price. This is better than nothing, but suffers the problem that the panel members usually know that they are not quoting for a real transaction, and so may not bother providing a serious price. The problem of infrequently traded bonds is even less tractable. Many investors try to accommodate this by interpolating between actual prices, but this can only give approximations. There is also the problem of reinvestment risk. Yields at which bonds are traded incorporate reinvestment risk because the bond settlement price assumes that all coupons will be reinvested at the bond's current yield to maturity. Obviously this will happen rarely if ever, so it would be useful to identify a yield curve that excludes reinvestment risk.

Yield curve modelling is an attempt to fill the gaps in the observed yield curve, and to sift through the 'noisy' data in maturities where many similar bonds are traded at slightly varying prices. Yield curve modelling also tries to eliminate the reinvestment risk inherent in observed bond prices, by deriving what is known as the **zero coupon curve**. A successful yield modelling exercise will have the following characteristics:

- It will fit the available data.
- It will not be too 'noisy'. That is, it will not have too many small bumps in it. These bumps are usually a symptom of 'overfitting', and indicate that more smoothing is necessary.
- There should be consistency between the normal yield curve and the zero coupon curve. In other words, the prices of the two should not allow any arbitrage opportunities.

Deriving the zero coupon curve is a complex process using all yield curve information possible, including discount securities, futures, forward and swap prices. Forward discount factors are thus estimated and extrapolated to correct for the reinvestment risk inherent in observed bond prices.

Yield curve models usually employ some non-linear mathematical technique, for example:

- Regression can be used to find the curved line that minimizes the aggregate distance between it and observed bond yields. This is otherwise known as a **fitted curve** and is illustrated in Example 12.10.
- Cubic spline is a method that decomposes the observed yield curve to segments and then fits curves to each segment that vary only slightly from their neighbours to give a smooth overall curve.

Normally two yield curves are derived by this process for any currency: the risk-free curve, which usually comprises central government securities, and the

EXAMPLE 12.10 *A simple fitted curve*

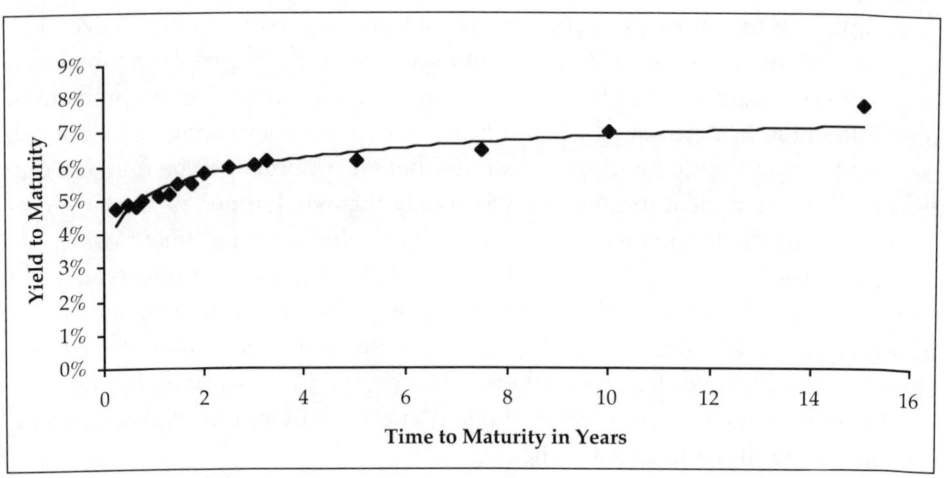

risk-adjusted swap curve, made up of non-government securities, usually banks. The latter curve is usually derived from inter-bank rates such as **LIBOR** (London Inter-Bank Overnight Rate) or a eurodollar rate, a short-term bank interest rate, as well as futures markets and swap rates where available.

Yield curve modelling is thus an inexact science, with the perfect solution often unobtainable in practice. When modelling a yield curve, there is nearly always a trade-off between market structure, data integrity, estimation accuracy, computational efficiency and cost effectiveness that requires some compromises.

It is important when applying a yield curve so derived to bear in mind the differing nature of the instruments used, in terms of credit risk, overlapping dates and the biases inherent in the prices of forwards and futures that accommodate margin requirements.

IMPLEMENTATION

Unlike most equities markets, most physical bonds are not traded on a central exchange, but on a bilateral basis between investors and brokers. Traditionally, this has been done over the telephone, although screen-based services, provided by such companies as Reuters and Bloomberg, are now widely used. In the telephone days, a buyer of a bond would ring various other brokers and investors and ask if they happen to have the required bond in the required quantity and, if so, at what yield to maturity. If not, would they have a similar bond, and so on. When a suitable bond was located at the right price and in the required quantity, the deal was confirmed either by telex or fax. Screens improve on this by allowing large investors, such as banks and brokers, to display the prices at which they are prepared to buy and sell selected bonds. The investor then rings them up and confirms the price, quantity and settlement date and the transaction is confirmed by fax or email. Although technology allows more efficient confirmation of deals, the principle of the process remains unchanged.

Important features of bond markets are:

- There is no exchange standing between buyer and seller. This means that the price actually struck for the bond is a private matter between buyer and seller. Most big bond investors and brokers, such as those providing the Reuters and Bloomberg screens, publish some traded prices, but these can be of variable quality, and do not provide a comprehensive record of transactions.
- Commissions are not levied directly, but are implicit in the bid–ask spread of the bond. The broker or bank transacting the bond profits from this difference.

- The lack of an exchange means that investors need not transact through a broker. In fact, in many markets, the bulk of wholesale fixed interest is transacted directly between investors, usually banks, with the role of the broker often to aggregate transactions for smaller investors.
- When transacting directly with the other party, the investor is taking it on faith that that party is able to honour the purchase or sale of the bond. Normally this is not a problem, and most bond traders don't think too much about it. If bank XYZ has just confirmed the sale of $10 million of US Treasuries, the investor assumes that they actually have these securities on hand to deliver. But since settlement is usually one or two days after the transaction is confirmed, there is ample time for XYZ bank to discover a rogue trader in its ranks and go bust. The investor won't have paid for the bonds yet, so the implications may not be dire. But another source of US Treasuries would be required, which might be tricky to find in a market where a major bank has just defaulted. Similarly, XYZ bank has taken it on trust that you have the means to pay for the bonds. This risk is called **counterparty risk**.
- Most fixed interest traders and investors try to control their counterparty risk by placing absolute, dollar value limits on net purchases and sales to each investor, bank and broker with whom they deal regularly. When markets were much smaller, and things moved a bit slower than they seem to today, a clerk, called a 'penciller', performed this job. Dealers would call out to the penciller every time a transaction was agreed and (usually) she would write it down on a pad and note the net position to that particular counterparty – alerting the head dealer when a limit was being approached. This function has of course been automated in most dealing rooms. The idea of managing counterparty risk might seem common sense and, for most investment managers, it is not hard to deal with. For large banks it can be very serious, particularly if transactions are being initiated, hundreds each minute, from several locations around the world and in different time zones.

USE OF DERIVATIVES

Derivatives are an integral part of nearly all quantitatively managed fixed interest portfolios. Swaps and futures are the basic derivatives, which can form the basis of options of varying complexity. Most fixed interest futures are **exchange-traded**, and therefore standardized, and are constructed around an hypothetical government bond or basket of bonds. Swaps are traded over-the-counter and can be based on any actual or hypothetical instrument. Options can be exercisable into futures or physical bonds.

The other main category of fixed interest derivatives is credit derivatives, which can be futures, swaps or options, and are usually traded over-the-counter. They are settled against the interest rate spread between different credit ratings, and allow investors to speculate on changes in credit spreads, or to hedge credit risk while retaining interest rate sensitivity. Because this market is heavily traded, it is reasonably efficient, and is often used by investment managers to obtain an objective estimate of the credit standing of a bond or bond issuer.

The simplest use of derivatives in a fixed interest portfolio is the purchase of either futures or swaps in lieu of physical bonds. This saves on transaction costs, but requires constant monitoring to ensure that variation margins and periodical settlements are managed, and that the position is rolled over when the instrument expires.

Derivatives may also be used to manage liquidity. As coupon income accumulates, for example, and other cash flows in and out of the portfolio, futures contracts can be used to ensure that the portfolio is fully invested but is not geared.

Futures contracts are often used to fine-tune the duration and convexity of a portfolio, allowing the investor to adjust the portfolio's sensitivity to changes in the yield curve without expensive sales and purchases of physical stock. Therefore they can provide an important way of responding quickly to economic news or changes in economic forecasts.

Hedging is the other main application of derivative instruments. Simple bond futures, for example, can be used to modify the interest rate sensitivity of a portfolio, leaving the credit risk intact, or the investor may want to retain the interest rate sensitivity and use credit derivatives to modify the credit risk of the portfolio.

Many bond markets present significant opportunities for arbitrage, and swaps, futures and options are used heavily to exploit such opportunities. With so many instruments available, the potential for arbitrage can be enormous and varied, allowing plenty of room for mispricing between them.

CURRENCY MANAGEMENT

For domestic fixed interest portfolios, foreign currency plays no part. Investors are increasingly seeking exposure to international bonds, however, and this obviously implies foreign currency transactions and management. There are two approaches to foreign currency management of fixed interest portfolios:

- Currency neutral.
- Hedge to base currency.

For a currency neutral portfolio, the investment manager simply needs to buy enough foreign currency to settle the bonds in each currency. The investment manager will thus have taken on the risk of the bonds him- or herself, including interest rate risk, yield curve risk and credit risk, as well as the risk of the currency in which the bonds are denominated. In this situation, there is the real possibility that the bonds themselves show an attractive return while the currency falls, giving a disappointing result overall.

If the investor is unwilling to be exposed to foreign currency risk for international bonds, the solution is to hedge the currency. To start with, this is a simple matter of selling forward the purchase price of the bonds. To do this, the investment manager needs to have some idea of how long he or she intends to hold the bonds. Then there is the question of cash flows because the coupons are received in foreign currency. Since the investment manager knows when and how much these will be, it is possible to hedge these at the time the bond is purchased, or at any time after that. When this has all been done, the bonds are still not fully hedged because their market value will change, probably continuously, so there will always be some unrealized foreign currency denominated profit and loss on them that will be unhedged. For this the investment manager needs to establish a policy of revising the hedge at fixed intervals, or when the unhedged value reaches a predefined value. When the bonds are sold, the investment manager needs to ensure that the necessary sums are repatriated or reinvested, and that the hedge is adjusted accordingly.

ONGOING MANAGEMENT

The main task of day-to-day management of a fixed interest portfolio is ensuring that the required interest rate and credit exposures are maintained. This is important because the passage of time alone will change the portfolio's sensitivities, even if the yield curve were to remain unchanged. This is usually carried out in conjunction with regular monitoring of the economic environment and reviews of return forecasts. Most managers do this at least weekly, with major reviews on a monthly basis, or following major economic events.

As with other types of portfolio, cash flows need to be managed and invested, and derivatives positions monitored.

Most quantitative managers apply ongoing yield curve modelling and other means of monitoring the price differentials between various instruments, looking for relative mispricing and other opportunities to add return. Such procedures usually conform to predefined decision rules specifying the required price differential to justify entering into a transaction, and the point at which profits should be realized.

ADMINISTRATION

With heavy use of derivatives contracts, particularly over-the-counter instruments such as swaps, credit derivatives and options on swaps, administration can be quite complex. The complexity tends to surround the non-standard nature of some over-the-counter agreements and liquidity management to maintain margins and meet periodic settlements.

On the other hand, for physical fixed interest instruments, administration has, in recent years, been greatly simplified by the establishment of central clearing and settlement houses. These institutions act as a repository of documents, so that physical bond documents do not need to be sent from seller to buyer each time the bond changes hands.

VALUATION

Valuing physical bonds and discount instruments in a fixed interest portfolio is relatively simple, and the portfolio is of course the sum of its parts. The value of each security is calculated by applying the appropriate pricing formula with current market interest rates. Complications can arise when coupons are accrued at the date of valuation, with errors potentially resulting from either double counting or omitting them. These are trivial errors and can be easily detected and remedied, and even more easily prevented. Exchange-traded bond futures contracts are even more straightforward to value because they don't have coupons. On the other hand, valuing over-the-counter derivatives can be quite complex because there usually is no relevant market price on which to base the valuation, and because many over-the-counter agreements incorporate non-standard clauses.

Non-standard over-the-counter swap or option agreements sometimes embed some unusual settlement conditions or options that can be very difficult to value, and each case needs individual attention. Options can pose other valuation problems if the option or one similar to it is not frequently traded somewhere. Most valuation models take some version of the last traded price of an asset to estimate the market value of the portfolio's holding. If the asset is not recently traded, the market price must be estimated. For bonds and discount securities, this can be calculated by applying the prevailing interest rate to the valuation formula. But options require an estimate of the forward-looking volatility of the underlying instrument, and this information can really only be derived from a relevant market transaction. If there is no information on the expected volatility of the underlying asset, then it may be necessary to extrapolate it from some similar instrument, requiring judgement and care to achieve a realistic estimate.

PERFORMANCE MEASUREMENT AND ATTRIBUTION

Measuring the return of fixed interest portfolios is no different in principle from measuring the return of other portfolios. Attribution analysis is also the same in principle, although can differ in practice because the sources of risk of bonds differ from those of equities. Ideally, the attribution analysis should answer such questions as:

- What was the impact of changes in the general level of interest rates?
- What was the impact of changes in the shape of the yield curve?
- What was the impact of changes in credit spreads?
- What was the impact of trading activity?

For international fixed interest portfolios, questions also arise about country allocation and currency effects.

PITFALLS

The most difficult part of investing in fixed interest is trying to forecast interest rates. A mistake frequently made by investment managers is to assume that interest rates will behave in future as they have in the recent past. This can lead to serious misestimation of the risk of the portfolio.

Another potential danger comes from inadequate control of credit risk. Credit risk can defy analysis, but since corporate loans can be a significant source of additional returns, a well-managed portfolio of credit exposures can significantly enhance overall portfolio returns. It is important that credit risk is adequately diversified both across categories of borrowers and across maturities.

Fixed interest derivatives can also be a source of problems. Many investors make comparisons between instruments on the basis of the implied yield to maturity. This is often adequate for instruments with very short maturities, but as maturity and duration increase, the settlement value per basis point increases dramatically, as does the change in settlement value per basis point. This can result in a transaction that appears profitable in terms of yield to maturity, but which will in fact lose money.

CASE STUDY

This case study provides an example of the last pitfall: the danger of not quantifying the possible effects of changes in terms of settlement value per basis point. It also gives one example of how investment managers analyse the relative prices of different instruments. The case revolves around an exchange-traded ten-year bond futures contract, and options on those futures. Because physical bonds are usually quoted in terms of yield to maturity, futures and options are often similarly quoted. This can cause some confusion for futures administrative systems, because settlement value increases as the yield decreases, and vice versa. To deal with this, bond futures and options contracts are sometimes quoted as 100 minus the yield to maturity. A bond future trading at a yield to maturity of 7.56% would therefore be quoted as 92.44, which should not be confused with a bond that happens to have a settlement value of $92.44 per $100 face value.

Option premia are quoted also in yield points, so an option premium of 1.00% would be quoted as 100.

As illustrated in Appendix 5, futures and options can be used to create synthetic versions of each other. A bought call option combined with a sold put option with the same exercise price will give exactly the same outcome as a bought futures contract. Similarly, a sold call option combined with a bought put option at the same exercise price will create a synthetic sold futures contract.

The implication of this is that the difference in price between the call and the put should exactly equal the difference between the current futures price and the exercise price of the options. If it does not, then there is an opportunity for arbitrage profits. The transaction in Example 12.11 appears to be an obvious winner.

This appears to be a no-risk transaction whereby the bought futures are precisely offset by the synthetic sold futures position comprising the sold call and bought put at the same exercise price. The settlement price for an option premium, however, is calculated by multiplying the DV01 by the quoted value of the option. Applying the settlement price can change the attractiveness of the transaction. What appeared to be a riskless profit of 0.70% per contract, turns out to lose $153.15 per $100 000 of bond face value instead. The pot of gold is still at the end of the rainbow.

EXAMPLE 12.11 *Put–call parity in terms of yield ...*

Face Value of Contract	$100 000	
Maturity in Years	10	
Coupon per Annum	10%	
Coupons per Year	2	
Interest Rate πChange	0.01%	
	Yield %	**Futures Price**
Current Futures Price	11.00	89.00
Exercise Price of Call Option	6.00	94.00
Call Option Premium	1.50	1.50
Exercise Price of Put Option	6.00	94.00
Put Option Premium	5.80	5.80
Strategy		
Buy Futures		0
Sell Call		1.50
Buy Put		−5.80
Exercise Call		0
Exercise Put		5.00
Outcome		0.70

... and settlement value

	Yield %	Futures Price	DV01 $	Settlement Value $
Current Futures Price	11.00	89.00	24.82	59 786.19
Exercise Price of Call Option	6.00	94.00	34.44	74 442.74
Call Option Premium	1.50	1.50	34.44	5 166.18
Exercise Price of Put Option	6.00	94.00	34.44	74 442.74
Put Option Premium	5.80	5.80	34.44	19 975.88
Strategy				
Sell Call		1.50		5 166.18
Buy Put		−5.80		−19 975.88
Exercise Call				0.00
Exercise Put		5.00		14 656.56
Outcome		0.70		−153.15

CHAPTER 13

Property Portfolios

APPLICATIONS

Many large institutional investors invest in direct property, and many more in listed property securities. This sector has consistently defied quantitative analysis, so traditional investment practices have tended to dominate.

Property is usually included in investment portfolios as a means of diversification, and because it is often seen as being linked fairly closely to economic growth. Most property portfolios are confined to the domestic market, with international property portfolios rarely seen.

THEORY

In theory, property is no different from equity. The investor buys the asset, or a share of it, and enjoys a fairly steady income flow from it as well as capital gains or losses. Property is not like fixed income, where the income stream is fixed and the final value of the investment is known at the outset.

But, in practice, the price of direct property does not behave anything like equity prices, and listed property prices do not behave like either of them. Because of this and the many other peculiarities of property investing, investment managers treat this as a completely different asset class. In fact, it could represent several asset classes, such as commercial, industrial and agricultural property, each linked to a different sector of the economy, and each with its own peculiarities.

The income derived by the owner of a shopping mall, for example, is often directly related to the revenues of the mall, so the market value of the property should correspond closely with the market value of the retailers operating there. The same principles sometimes apply to factories, warehouses and hotels. But, in each case, the relationship between the returns to the property assets and the shares of the companies occupying them tends to be much less direct than one would at first expect.

The reasons why property prices behave so differently from ordinary equities have been the subject of considerable debate. Both should reflect aspects of economic growth across various sectors of the economy, and there have been periods when both have indeed risen and fallen in tandem. But, for the most part, returns to the two sectors appear to have at best very weak links.

The difference in ownership structures prevailing in the two sectors is one possible explanation. Direct property assets tend to have only one owner at a time, and in most markets the process of buying and selling those assets is complex and time consuming. For these reasons, the assets are bought and sold infrequently – usually only once every few years. This means that the market value of the asset is rarely observed. The value can of course be estimated whenever required, but estimations are a very poor substitute for a traded price struck between a buyer and a seller in the context of competing bidders and offerors.

IMPLEMENTATION

Implementing and managing a portfolio of direct property holdings has quite a lot in common with direct equity, while a portfolio of listed property securities is implemented and managed in much the same way as a portfolio of ordinary domestic equities. This section will concentrate on the implementation of direct property.

The process of buying and selling direct property is complex, requiring a different range of skills to those demanded by trading in equities, bonds and derivatives markets. To begin with, there is considerable difference between buying an existing property and buying vacant land or an old building for redevelopment.

The case of buying an **existing building** is probably the less complex of the two. The process begins with the search for suitable acquisitions. Anyone who has bought a house or apartment to live in or for investment will know that this can take months or even years. The investment manager will begin with analysis of market trends and forecast industry profitability, with the objective of deciding the type of property most likely to deliver the highest yield, and the locality with the best prospects. This analysis should identify what features characterize the most promising investment properties. Armed with this analysis, the investment manager sallies forth, usually aided by one or more specialist search agencies, to find a number of candidate properties for more detailed consideration. Each property on the short list will normally undergo detailed evaluation, including preliminary price negotiations with the vendor and his or her agents. Sometime during this process, the short list is narrowed down, and eventually the target property is chosen.

The price is agreed usually after considerable negotiation, and the sale may embed any number of special arrangements regarding settlement of the transaction. It may even incorporate a loan to finance all or part of the sale price. Then there are the ancillary aspects, such as the naming rights, which can carry a hefty premium for an important commercial building. Many commercial property transactions also link ongoing management contracts to the sale agreement.

Once the price and other imperatives have been agreed, the real process begins and can go on for months, depending on the complexity of the title to the property and prevailing laws regarding property transactions. All this can be extremely expensive in terms of legal costs and agents' commissions, and, when transaction taxes are included, the whole transaction can cost up to 10% of the sale price of the asset. So the investor tends to hold the asset for quite a while in the hope of recovering these costs through income and capital gains.

For a **new development**, the investment manager starts by finding a suitable site for redevelopment and then making a judgement about what kind of investment will yield the best returns for the site. Finding a site is equally as complex as finding an existing building, and deciding on the sort of redevelopment most suitable to the site usually requires extensive analysis of market and industry trends. In addition, the investment manager needs to think about things such as zoning regulations, present and future, and any bureaucratic hurdles that might impede the approval of the proposed development.

In many cases, the site is purchased only after approval has been obtained for the proposed development. This greatly reduces the risk to the investor, but normally carries a significant price premium because the vendor will demand compensation for having taken the risk and expended the effort to arrange the required development approval.

Once this stage has been reached, it remains to finalize plans and contract the construction of the building. The construction needs to be closely supervised to ensure that cost and time limits are respected, so that the building can start earning income when it is expected to. Anyone who has survived the construction of a new dwelling will know what a hazardous process this can be. Large buildings are usually considerably more hazardous, especially if they are in a location that touches on local sensitivities, so political factors may also need to be taken into account.

Between buying an existing building and redeveloping a vacant site or old building, the former is much less risky and less costly in management time, but the potential rewards to redevelopment can, if the project is well managed, be very attractive.

USE OF DERIVATIVES

In general, **exchange-traded** derivatives play at most a minor role in the management of property portfolios. Exchange-traded futures and options on property and property-related assets are virtually non-existent because the price at which property changes hands is not usually published. For this reason, the derivatives contracts that do play a part tend to be over-the-counter transactions.

There are a number of ways in which these can help to manage the risk of investing in direct property. For example, during the search for the property leading up to purchase, the investment manager might purchase options to buy various properties. This can insure against a sudden surge in the price of target properties during the (often) lengthy search period, thus giving the investor enough time to carry out a thorough search without the pressure to buy hastily in order to avoid being late entering a rising market.

During the development of the property, the investment manager can incorporate options in the construction or development contract to guard against cost and time overruns. This helps to ensure that the property delivers the yield expected of it.

Once the property is functioning and earning income, there are a number of derivative-type contracts that investment managers enter into in order to maximize their return and control the risk. These contracts are usually aimed at either ensuring a steady stream of rental income or increasing the likelihood of an attractive sale price.

Commercial leases, for example, often incorporate agreements about the minimum term of the lease. These may be complemented by an agreement for lease extensions at attractive rentals. Indeed, many landlords offer attractive rental rates for extended lease periods. Obviously, the investment manager's willingness to offer such clauses depends on his or her estimation of what the future rental potential is for the property, but it is often worthwhile having the certainty of a slightly lower rental income than a potentially higher but more volatile income. Thus the investor effectively buys an option on the future income of the property.

The investment manager may also grant options to buy the property at a price that would deliver an attractive return. If the property value increases beyond that point, the buyer of the option will exercise it and the investment manager, while having forfeited a still more attractive return, has nevertheless achieved his or her target return plus the premium received for having granted the option. If the property value fails to reach the exercise price of the option, the buyer will abandon the option. The investment manager has failed to achieve the desired capital gain on the property, but has at least partial compensation in the form of the option premium received.

The other way in which derivatives can help to manage the risk and return to property investments is through swaps. These can be very useful in so far as they can help to reduce transaction costs. For example, an investment manager holding a large office building may note that economic forecasts are indicating that better returns will be earned in the future from suburban shopping malls. Rather than sell the office building and go through the expensive process of looking for and buying or building a shopping mall, the investment manager might simply agree to swap the revenue streams of the office building for those of a shopping mall. Of course, to do this, it is necessary to find another investor willing to swap the income stream of the shopping mall for that of an office building. Apart from the saving in transaction costs, the swap agreement has other benefits. For example, its maturity can be tailored to fit closely with the investors' forecasts, or it can incorporate some measure of capital gains on the two properties. At the expiry of the swap, each investor reverts to the income stream from the original, physical investment.

ONGOING MANAGEMENT

As with implementation, investments in listed property assets are managed very much the same way as a portfolio of equities, so this section will concentrate on the issues specific to managing portfolios of direct property holdings.

Most investment managers hire professional managers to look after day-to-day management of property assets. This usually takes care of routine maintenance, cleaning, insurance and dealing with the requirements of tenants, local governments and other interested parties, and leaves the investment manager to attend to strategic matters such as evaluating alternative investments and ongoing investment in the property.

The risks that need to be managed are ensuring continuity of rental income and maximizing the property's potential for capital gains. These issues are of course related: the more attractive the property is, the more rent people will be prepared to pay to occupy it, and the higher its resale potential. But even the most attractive buildings can have trouble attracting well-paying tenants during periods of very slow growth in the local economy.

Many investment managers buy insurance or options to cover themselves against the event of extended periods of vacancy, but such insurance can be expensive, covers only limited periods and is not a very good substitute for good management and well-structured lease agreements.

Maximizing the building's value is also of fundamental importance. Naturally a well-maintained and managed building is more attractive to potential buyers than a poorly managed and maintained building, but outside factors can also affect the value of the investment. These can include the type of developments taking place nearby, the availability and quality of local transport and amenities and so on. For an important investment, the investment manager needs to keep in touch with local developments and sensitivities to ensure that the local environment continues to be friendly to the investor's interests. Success in this aspect of property management not only demands a great deal of management time and effort, but benefits enormously from specialist experience.

ADMINISTRATION

During purchase, development and sale of direct property holdings, the administrative demands are generally very heavy. The details of what needs to be done depend on the nature of the property and the demands of local laws governing property transactions and development activity.

Ongoing administration during the period in which the property is held will normally be included in the management contract for the building, leaving the investment manager with little more than a supervisory role.

VALUATION

Valuation of direct property holdings is one of the most difficult aspects of this type of investment. Most other parts of the portfolio, such as equities, bonds, derivatives and listed property investments, can be valued using the most recent price known to have been traded in that asset. This is not usually possible for direct property that has not been recently traded. To get an idea of what the investment is worth, the investment manager must make some kind of estimate.

Because the valuation of the property directly affects the investment return reported to investors, the investment manager may have an interest in overestimating the worth of the investment. To avoid potential estimation error, many investors insist on an independent valuation of the investment.

The process of valuing a direct property investment follows a number of steps, designed to give a valuation as close as possible to what the property could actually sell for at that point in time. The valuer starts with a very detailed description of the property and the activities carried out in it. This description includes considerable detail about the state of the building, including any repairs that are judged to be necessary or desirable. The report also summarizes current rent and other income earned by the building, and any contractual arrangements that might affect the continuity of the income stream.

The next part of the valuation focuses on the market for similar properties. The valuer conducts research into recent sales of buildings located near the property in question, and of similar buildings over a wider geographical area. From this, some benchmark market price is estimated for a similar building in the same location, with adjustments for the particular characteristics of the property in question.

Most valuations attempt to be as scientific as possible, but inevitably the final outcome is very much influenced by judgement.

The advantage of having an independent valuer is that the valuer theoretically has no interest in the estimation, and so the valuation is likely to be fair, or at least have an equal chance of being too high or too low. The disadvantage is that such estimations are time consuming and expensive. To reduce costs, the investment manager might be tempted to employ the same valuer for successive valuation exercises, to carry out ever less frequent valuations, or both. Using the same valuer for each valuation can reduce costs, as the valuer becomes familiar with the property and its surroundings, but, over time, the independence of the estimates might become compromised, as familiarity with various interested parties develops.

The frequency of valuations can have important consequences for portfolio performance, as will be demonstrated in the next section.

PERFORMANCE MEASUREMENT AND ATTRIBUTION

Starting with guesses for valuation of direct property investments, measurement of portfolio return is even less accurate. As with other portfolios, return is the value of the portfolio at the end of the period divided by the value of the portfolio at the beginning of the period minus one. Where cash flows to and from the portfolio during the return period, the period is broken down into sub-periods. Return is calculated for each sub-period, and the results compounded to give an overall return.

EXAMPLE 13.1 *Frequency of valuation*

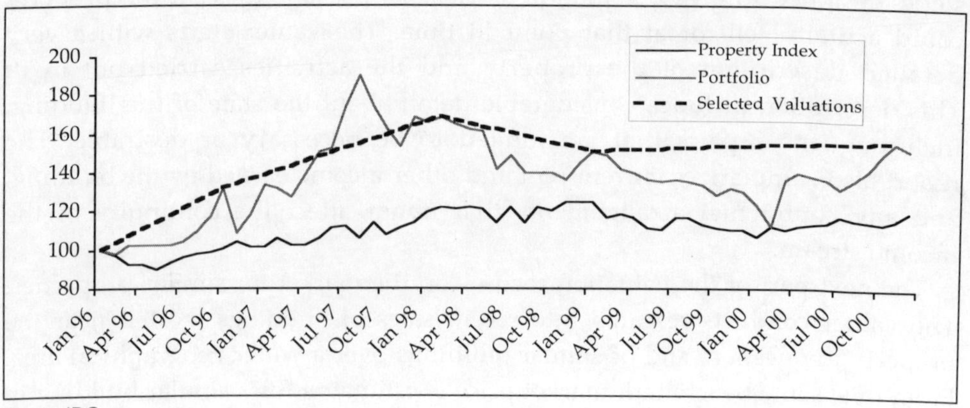

Source: IDC

Semi-annual Returns Six Months to:	Portfolio %	Benchmark %	Difference %
30 06 96	2.11	−6.26	8.37
31 12 96	16.49	8.71	7.79
30 06 97	28.32	9.33	18.99
31 12 97	10.34	2.03	8.31
30 06 98	−15.62	0.39	−16.02
31 12 98	2.47	9.73	−7.26
30 06 99	−3.61	−8.91	5.29
31 12 99	−3.90	−0.52	−3.38
30 06 00	5.41	3.81	1.59
31 12 00	11.54	4.98	6.56

Annual Returns Twelve Months to:	Portfolio %	Benchmark %	Difference %
31 12 96	18.95	1.90	17.05
31 12 97	41.59	11.55	30.04
31 12 98	−13.54	10.16	−23.70
31 12 99	−10.84	−11.98	1.13
31 12 00	17.57	8.98	8.59

Returns Based on Opportunistic Valuations Period to:	Portfolio %	Benchmark %	Difference %
31 10 96	31.58	0.38	31.20
28 02 98	28.00	21.44	6.56
31 01 99	−10.42	2.39	−12.81
30 11 00	3.49	−7.03	10.52

Equities, bonds, derivatives and listed property assets are typically valued at least monthly, and sometimes daily. Valuations of direct property are carried out much less frequently. Often the investments are not even valued at fixed intervals. In between detailed independent valuations, the property is generally assumed to have held its nominal valuation, or this nominal value is adjusted for some factor designed to adjust for fluctuations in the overall property market.

Example 13.1 illustrates the potentially distorting effects of valuing at different intervals. The return difference of 1% for 1999 disguises a fall and a rise, while opportunistic valuation camouflages even more volatility.

PITFALLS

The dangers of direct property investing are similar in principle to the risks associated with any other investment in risky assets. That is, inaccurate forecasts delivering disappointing or negative returns. The difference with direct property is that the lack of information about market prices and the time and costs of implementation leave considerably more scope for inaccurate forecasts, especially if the investment is a development or redevelopment project; and the costs of changing course are heavy and can be punitive.

Favourite changes of course include cutting costs before completion of a project because of a perceived slowdown in the local economy. Depending on the duration of the economic slowdown, this can bring a substandard project on stream just as demand is picking up. Such a project runs the risk of never fulfilling its investment objectives simply because it was not built to the original specifications. Thus a well-designed project can ultimately disappoint.

The other extreme can also be costly. There are plenty of examples of elaborate office complexes and tourist amenities developed at enormous cost in locations that have insufficient other attractions to offer in order to generate the revenues required for an adequate return on investment.

Misinterpreting local sensitivities can send otherwise well-conceived projects awry. Sometimes, the difference between success and failure is simply the effort devoted to communicating to interested parties the benefits to them of the development, and listening to and understanding their concerns.

An inappropriate revaluation policy can hurt the investment returns reported to the investor. Too frequent revaluations can be costly and, over time, can become less independent and rigorous. Revaluations carried out too infrequently can bias overall portfolio returns. This is especially dangerous if the property is part of a unit trust or mutual fund, in which units are frequently bought and sold by investors.

CASE STUDY

Consider a large tourism-related development carried out in an area of considerable natural beauty. Normally, such a development would show great earning and capital gains potential, but a few misestimations were made at the outset. The investor was a large, well-established corporate pension fund with investments spanning several domestic and international sectors, with both listed and unlisted assets.

The first estimation error was to plan for a casino in such an area. The idea of the casino was, of course, to provide higher revenues than a simple resort, both to the investor and the government. Local regulations limited the granting of casino licences, so the fact that one had been promised to this project was seen as a significant benefit to the project.

The second error was the design of the project, specifically its size. Keen to exploit the casino licence as much as possible, the project was designed to be much bigger than other tourist resorts in the area. Local residents voiced concerns that such a large development would be incongruous with existing structures, and would potentially damage the environment, which was the source of many of their livelihoods. Moreover, they were unsure about having a casino, especially such a big one, because they thought that this might affect the friendly, relaxed atmosphere of the local village, which they thought added to its appeal for visitors.

Owners of existing tourist resorts were even less happy at the prospect of a huge new competitor that could potentially undercut them by subsidizing food and accommodation from gambling income.

The project went ahead, but on a slightly smaller scale than planned. It took a lot longer to complete, and cost a lot more to build than had been planned. Various concessions to local concerns, lower than expected occupancy rates (due either to widespread public disapproval of the project or the very high accommodation rates being charged) and higher than expected operating costs resulted in lower than forecast operating profits.

The investor had planned to revalue the property annually, in keeping with its policy for its other direct property investments, but a year after the completion of the project, the independent valuation was less than the cost of the project. Then a slowdown in regional tourism resulted in negative returns to the project for the following year too. The members of the pension fund were becoming impatient.

The investor was under pressure to do something quickly. The most expedient thing to do was to carry out valuations less frequently, so a three-year valuation cycle was imposed, as luck would have it, just as regional tourism began to pick up. With the value of the project held at its last nominal valuation, it was now significantly underperforming similar projects elsewhere.

Now the pressure was to sell the property, if for no other reason than to free up funds for more promising investments elsewhere. The problem was that, for such a large investment, there were not a great number of potential buyers at short notice. The investor decided on a moderately innovative solution, which was to turn the property into a trust and list it on the stock market. This process could be achieved in a matter of months, whereas an outright sale of the property might have taken a year or more. This solution had the additional benefit that the property could be partially sold with some interest retained by the investor, leaving the potential to reap the rewards that would no doubt materialize in the longer term.

The trust was formed with the original investor owning all the units in it. These were then offered on the stock market at a price that would imply a higher valuation than the overall cost of the project. In other words, the price at which the investor was prepared to sell the units would guarantee a profit for the overall project. The problem was that hardly anybody was prepared to buy the units at that price, so most of the units stayed with the original investor. Things were becoming tense, but the investor was reluctant to sell the units at a loss because this would signal a big failure on his part to other investors, with consequent damage to his reputation.

The property was still classified in the investment portfolio as property, where it was acting as a noticeable drag on the overall returns to that sector. This could be fixed by reclassifying the investment as equity, and putting it in the much larger equity component of the fund, where its impact would be less noticeable. This did not please the equity manager, whose performance, and hence her reputation and remuneration, were to be affected by this drag on her investment returns.

Arguments ensued, with the property being moved to various different sectors, as units were gradually sold on the market. Eventually, it formed the kernel of a sector devoted to 'alternative investments', which were supposedly directed to long-term profitability, and which were not required to deliver competitive returns in the short term.

From this example, one can see how poor planning, the timing of valuations and deviations from the original investment strategy can alter the profitability of an otherwise potentially promising investment.

CHAPTER 14

Market Neutral (Hedge) Portfolios and Other Alternative Investment Classes

Before reading this chapter, it is suggested that readers not familiar with options theory and markets read Appendix 5 which is devoted to options.

Hedge funds and market neutral funds can be thought of as a subset of the class of investment called alternative investments. These investment classes have been available for a long time, but have received widespread attention in the last few years. This is probably due to the rapid growth they have experienced in the last decade, but certainly the spectacular returns achieved by some, and the profits earned for their owners and managers, have also played a part.

Alternative investment funds have grown because they fulfil the requirement for high-return, non-traditional investments that complement conventional investments in pension funds, unit trusts and mutual funds.

CHARACTERISTICS OF ALTERNATIVE INVESTMENT FUNDS

Hedge funds and other alternative investment funds are characterized more by their structure than any common element in their approach to investments. Most operate in the USA, but they are becoming very popular in Europe. Characteristics of alternative investment funds are:

- High risk, with the possibility of leverage
- Seeking absolute return, benchmarked to cash
- Specialist, boutique investment managers
- Suitable for wealthy individual investors
- High minimum investment
- Maximum fund size
- Performance-based management fees.

The first alternative investment funds were started by **boutique managers,** which are investment management firms set up specifically to manage investments sharing some clearly defined investment strategy using specified instruments, such as derivatives or unlisted investments.

Typically, they stipulated a high minimum investment: anything from half a million to ten million dollars. Setting a high minimum investment is attractive to investment managers for two main reasons. First, it attracts clients who have experience with other investments and are therefore likely to be better able to appreciate unconventional investment strategies. They are also more likely to be able to tolerate high return volatility because they have other, more stable investments in place to provide the necessary buffer.

The other attraction for investment managers of wealthy individual investors is that they are prepared to pay reasonably high fees, but the cost of management and administration are the same and administration of their accounts no more complicated or costly than for smaller sums.

Most funds also stipulate some minimum investment period, often one year to start with, with fairly long notice periods for subsequent withdrawals. These limitations allow the investment manager to maintain minimal liquidity balances, so keeping the fund fully invested most of the time.

It is common for alternative investment funds to stipulate a maximum size for the fund, beyond which no further investment is accepted. This recognizes that the most successful investment strategies accommodate only limited investment before the best opportunities disappear. It also signals outstanding success on the part of the investment manager, potentially attracting further interest in subsequent funds.

Alternative investment managers are more likely than conventional fund managers to attract performance-based fees, whereby the investor pays a regular management fee that is augmented by a share of the performance of the fund above some benchmark or minimum performance. Typically, the regular fee will be 1% to 2% of funds invested per year, with a further 10% to 20% of returns. Funds that invest in other funds (**fund of funds**) may have an extra layer of fees, in which case management fees are at the low end of this range, typically 1% and 10%.

It is not uncommon for alternative investment funds to allow leverage in their funds, allowing them to invest more than 100% of the money given to them by investors. This is the same as borrowing to increase the nominal value of the funds invested. Most conventional investment funds are not allowed to do this. It is important to remember that this is not a defining feature of alternative investment funds, as not all of them can do it, and some funds that are not alternative investment funds can and do use leverage as part of their investment strategies.

Most jurisdictions subject alternative investment funds to the same regulatory rules and scrutiny as conventional funds, and they are obliged to observe any trading and reporting rules demanded by the exchanges on which they trade. In this respect they do not differ from conventional funds.

The distinction between alternative and conventional is becoming more blurred, as conventional managers establish alternative investment subsidiaries in order to share in the continuing growth prospects of this sector, and conventional investment managers borrow some of the more successful strategies of alternative investment managers.

APPLICATIONS

Alternative investment funds were originally designed as a high-return investment for wealthy individuals to augment their traditional investment portfolios. This allowed them to participate in high-risk, high-return investment opportunities that were considered not appropriate for more risk-averse investors and conventional investment portfolios. Thus they were designed as a complement to a traditional investment portfolio, not as a substitute for one.

As the success of these funds came to the attention of a wide range of investors, so demand for them began to come from beyond their original clientele. Because many investors do not have access to the required minimum investment for alternative investment funds, there arose demand for some other way to gain access to the returns that they provide. One way of doing this is to establish a fund of funds, whereby the investor buys units in a fund that consists of units in other funds. Another way is for providers of traditional investment products, such as mutual funds and unit trusts, to include some alternative investments in their balanced portfolios. This effectively makes available to average investors the same balance of traditional and alternative investments that was previously available only to wealthy individuals.

Many large funds favour the use of alternative investments in conjunction with a passive approach to conventional asset management in a core–satellite structure. When well executed, this can result in an astute mix of attractive return investments with low overall management fees. The mix of core and satellite can be adjusted to deliver the required return and risk profile.

Many investment managers offer a mixture of conventional investments, which they manage themselves, and alternative investments, contracted out to specialist managers. Others offer a similar mixture, with both types of investment managed under one roof, but with varying degrees of separation between investment 'teams', reflecting the desired distinction between investment policies.

THEORY

Since alternative investments are designed to complement, not replace, conventional investments, it is important that the risks and returns they offer really are alternative. In other words, they should exploit investment opportunities that have little relationship with the investments found in traditional asset classes. The 'alternativeness' of the investments may be apparent from a glance at the assets selected, such as direct equity, venture capital and commodity derivatives, whereas alternative investment funds investing in listed assets often have roughly offsetting bought and sold investments, eliminating the market risk and return that dominates conventional investments.

The relationship of the alternative investment fund to conventional funds can be quantified by measuring the correlation of their returns to those of conventional funds or asset classes. If the correlation is high, say more than 0.3, or low, less than –0.3, then the investment is merely adding to or offsetting the risk of conventional investments, and is not fulfilling its purpose of exploiting completely different investment opportunities. The investor could achieve a similar result by simply adjusting his or her mix of conventional risky investments and the risk-free asset or by hedging with futures or swaps.

ALTERNATIVE INVESTMENT STRATEGIES

By their definition, the strategies employed by alternative investment funds vary considerably and, although any categorization comes with a severe health warning, the strategies followed can be described by one of the following:

- investments in listed assets
- investment in unlisted assets
- investment in other funds, or funds of funds.

In addition, of course, there will inevitably be those funds that engage in some combination of one or more of these categories.

Listed assets

Listed assets may include equities listed on stock exchanges, futures and options contracts, as well as fixed interest and currency derivatives, physical commodities traded on exchanges, commodity derivatives and exchange-traded physical fixed interest assets.

Strategies employing listed assets fall into two broad types:

- Relative value, including strategies such as:
  - Long–short
  - Market neutral
  - Convertible hedge
  - Volatility trading
  - Commodities and discretionary futures
  - Bear funds

- Event driven, including strategies such as:
  - Deal arbitrage

A short description of each strategy follows.

Relative value

Relative value strategies examine the relationships between assets to calculate the theoretical price differential between them. When this theoretical price relationship is quantified, the manager monitors market prices to identify market price differentials that diverge from it. Analysis of the liquidity of the assets then indicates whether or not an opportunity exists to exploit the apparent mispricing.

The kind of assets that an investment manager might compare is open to the manager's judgement and imagination, but they could include groups of equities with some common characteristics, such as engaging in similar business mixes. For example, the investment manager might compare the value of the businesses of two banks and conclude that the only material difference between the two is the duration of their bond portfolios. He or she could then easily work out the price implied by the duration difference for any given interest rate. If the difference in the market price of the shares of the two banks is materially more or less than the theoretical difference, then the investment manager would buy the shares of the cheap bank and, at the same time, sell short the shares of the dear bank. Knowing what the **fair price** difference is, the manager would reverse this transaction when market prices converge to their fair price differential. If the original analysis is accurate, the strategy will yield a profit regardless of the final absolute values of the shares in the two banks. In practice, many relative value strategies exploit mispricing between derivatives, or between derivatives and related physical assets.

Long–short

Long–short is the classic relative value strategy, where bought (**long**) positions in assets are closely matched against sold (**short**) positions, theoretically leaving an overall zero exposure to risky assets. Because the manager defines the relationships to be analysed and compared, there are no fixed rules as to what constitutes a sensible comparison between assets. The example above describes two banks trading in the same market, but in practice pairing across borders is likely to be more fruitful. For example, comparing two large US pharmaceutical firms is unlikely to highlight any profitable mispricing because the comparison is obvious with even rudimentary analysis, and the strategy is available to a wide range of investors, including US domestic-only mutual funds and pension plans. By contrast, comparing a US pharmaceutical with a Swiss one might be much more interesting, not only because of the complications arising from currencies of denomination, but also because the strategy is not open to US domestic-only or Swiss domestic-only investors.

Market neutral

Market neutral is a subset of long–short. The principles applied are the same, but the strategy is applied within markets, so that the theoretical exposure to each market is zero. The investment manager is free to define the market in question.

Convertible hedge

Convertible hedge is generally specific to one stock. The classic transaction is where the investment manager spots a **convertible** or **converting bond** that is underpriced relative to the underlying common stock. The simplest way to exploit this is to buy the convertible or converting instrument and sell short the common stock. The resulting position is then in a long call option in the case of a convertible instrument; or a long futures position in the stock, in the case of the converting instrument. The investment manager may decide to further enhance the value of the strategy by selling the resulting synthetic derivative. This part of the transaction can be tricky to implement because it usually needs to be done over-the-counter, and there is no certainty of finding buyers at an attractive price. For this reason, many managers leave the derivative in place, hoping to profit from its price appreciation, alternatively they can sell short a small amount of common stock, replicating a sold call option.

Volatility trading

This is often not thought of as a relative value strategy, but in all important respects it is. Rather than analyse and compare the relative prices of assets, within or across markets, the investment manager analyses the prices, usually in terms of the **implied volatility**, of exchange-traded options on a single asset. In the simplest version of volatility trading, he or she sells the expensive options while buying cheap ones. The position must be constructed carefully so that as little as possible remains by way of exposure to movements in the price of the underlying asset. This transaction, when well constructed and managed, can give pure risk-free profits, meaning that the result will be positive no matter what else happens to the underlying asset price, or the market in which it trades.

A slightly more complex version of volatility trading works by analysing long-term levels of implied volatility for options on various assets. When an option series trades at an implied volatility that is too high or too low, the option is sold or bought, and the position dynamically hedged using either other options on the underlying asset, or the asset itself. Dynamic hedging employs the same principles as portfolio protection, requiring considerable judgement and analysis, and can be very risky to execute and manage. The investment manager will therefore only undertake positions where the magnitude of the perceived mispricing is large enough to compensate for the risks.

Commodities and discretionary futures

These funds often apply some kind of relative value principle to portfolio construction. Naturally there are hundreds of ways of estimating the value of one commodity or futures contract relative to another. One technique that is fairly popular is to identify long-term relationships, for example between the prices of gold and silver, between cotton and wool or between rainfall and the

EXAMPLE 14.1 *Leverage from borrowing and bought futures positions*

Borrowing		**Futures**	
Value of Fund	$100	Value of Fund in Liquids	$100
Amount Borrowed	$25	Futures in Risky Assets	$125
Total Invested in Risky Assets	$125	Total Invested in Risky Assets	$125
Leverage as % of Fund	25%	Leverage as % of Fund	25%

price of shares in hotels and resorts. When actual price differentials deviate from their long-term differentials, the investment manager buys the cheap one and sells the dear one, anticipating that prices will return to their long-term relationship, a process known as **mean reversion**.

Most investment managers engaged in this kind of strategy conduct considerable research into the validity of the relationship. Not surprisingly, the magnitude of the long-term price differential depends on what period in time is analysed, so it is essential that any models used to calculate this are tested over various time periods. Also the speed at which price differentials revert to their long-term relationships can vary, so research must also be directed at the forces influencing this process.

Some commodities funds rely more on simple forecasts of commodities prices. These may be driven by perceived relationships with macroeconomic variables or other economic events, and the manager often employs complex modelling processes to generate the forecasts. Depending on the mandate for the fund, the manager may then apply gearing or leverage to increase the returns to the forecasts, either by borrowing money to buy more commodities or by using derivatives contracts. Derivatives can be used to gain leverage without the administrative complications of borrowing in the marketplace or from a bank. The manager simply buys commodity or other futures or options contracts with a combined face value that is greater than the total value of the fund, as set out in Example 14.1.

The sum invested in the fund is $100, but has bought futures contracts with a face value of $125, giving a leverage of 25%, the same as if it had borrowed $25 to buy $125 worth of physical investments.

Bear funds

Bear funds employ a simple strategy designed to profit from falling markets. Physical assets are invested in short-term interest-bearing securities, which provide **collateral** for short futures positions in one or more markets, profiting from a fall in the market and losing if the market appreciates. Bear funds vary according to how many and which markets are sold short, and how much gearing is allowed. For example, the face value of the futures sold short may be limited to the value of the physical investments in the fund, or the fund may be allowed to sell more, incurring higher risk with higher rewards if the strategy pays off.

Relative value strategies usually imply a zero overall exposure to risky assets. In practice, for each transaction there will often be a residual exposure, but if the fund is well managed, these should be very small and, because they are by their nature random, should diversify away at the portfolio level. These strategies are also sometimes known as **pure alpha** strategies. This term comes from the alpha in the capital asset pricing model. A 'pure alpha' strategy implies that the 'beta' or market related part of the return has been eliminated by the offsetting long and short positions, leaving only the alpha, which is the amount by which the assets are under- or overpriced.

Event driven

Event driven, such as **deal arbitrage**, is effectively another type of long–short strategy, with the important difference that they speculate on imminent market events that will change the existing price relationships within a group of assets. Even if the assets are not currently over- or underpriced, the manager bets that they soon will be, and puts in place long and short positions to exploit the impending event. Common examples of such events are mergers and takeovers, changes in regulations and other structural changes in the market.

It is commonly understood that, during the lead up to a takeover bid, the shares of the target company go up, sometimes dramatically. This can happen for two reasons. The first is because its shares were underpriced to begin with, which is perhaps the reason for it being acquired. The second is that the acquiring company often needs to pay a premium over the market price to secure a controlling interest. Numerous academic studies present extensive evidence that the price of the resulting entity often then underperforms similar assets, as the costs of effecting the merger are brought to bear on profitability, and projected synergies prove less beneficial than had been anticipated. This pattern of price relativities is what drives deal arbitrage. But since many mooted mergers and acquisitions are called off at the last minute, this can be a very risky business, with even the most careful planning and analysis resulting sometimes in losses.

Other event-driven strategies rely on changes in regulations governing an industry, or some other major structural change in a market or industry. This kind of activity has in recent years been particularly important in the airline and telecommunications industries. Sometimes the impacts of the impending changes are hard to understand, let alone quantify. This, combined with the possibility of the expected changes not taking place or being implemented in a different form, can result in considerable risk to the strategies. In general, the investment manager requires significant potential reward for undertaking the risk of event-driven strategies – depending on the estimated risk involved in each case.

Because most relative value and event-driven funds have close to zero exposure to risky assets, and are not usually subject to the same forces that drive other asset classes, they often have very low correlations to conventional investments, making them an attractive source of diversification for a balanced fund or a core–satellite strategy. The exceptions are bear funds, which are the mirror image of conventional investments. Because they effectively cancel out market risk they are not a suitable diversification for conventional balanced portfolios or core–satellite strategies.

Unlisted assets

Alternative investments based on unlisted assets can include:

- Private equity
  - Buy-outs
  - Venture capital
  - Restructuring
- Private bond
- Direct real estate
  - Agriculture
  - Forests
  - Infrastructure.

Most alternative, unlisted investments resemble conventional investments in that they usually comprise a simple bought position in physical assets, with no complicated derivative strategies or currency hedges. They are differentiated from conventional investments by high risk and high potential reward. For example, venture capital usually means investing in companies in the early stages of development, when it is far from clear that they will survive, let alone generate attractive investment returns. Similarly, buy-outs can be quite risky affairs, and the potential returns to the investor reflect this risk.

Having invested in the venture or project, the alternative investment fund holds the investment until the success of the investment is more assured, and the assets can be sold at a healthy profit. The investor thus gains from the investment's growth and its rerating as a lower risk investment.

Apart from the inherent riskiness of the projects themselves, unlisted assets carry a number of risks that do not affect listed assets to the same degree. First of all, it is difficult to hedge the risk of unlisted investments. Of course, things such as currency exposure and interest rate risk can be hedged if they can be quantified, but these measures can be expensive, and often provide only partial cover.

Not being listed, these assets cannot be sold short, so the investor is limited to buying and holding the investment. The lack of associated derivative instruments is a further limitation.

If, for some reason, the investment manager wishes to quit the investment early, the result can be very disappointing, as potential buyers may be difficult to find, and those that can be identified may demand an attractive price to assume the risk that remains with the assets.

Successful ventures can, however, yield impressive results, particularly if the outcome is that the assets are listed on a stock exchange. If this happens, the risks associated with being non-listed disappear immediately, and the investment manager can then either mix this holding with some relative value strategy, or sell it, crystallizing funds to invest in another new venture.

During the project's development, the investment manager controls the risk of individual projects by means of close monitoring of the activities of the fledgling company, or the management of the project. Risk control at this level can only be applied on a case-by-case basis, as each venture or project has its own peculiarities and risk control requirements.

At the portfolio level, risk control can be effected more systematically, usually by applying the principles of diversification. This is achieved by seeking ventures with businesses spanning different industries and markets, ideally at various stages of maturity in order to avoid sharp jumps in requirements for new funds, with maturing investments funding new ones.

Funds of funds

As the name suggests, these are funds whose principal investments are in other funds. They are often grouped with portfolios run by **managers of managers**. The difference between the two is that the fund of funds invests by buying units in funds offered by other investment managers, while the manager of managers engages investment managers to manage portfolios to customized mandates.

Thus the manager of managers has flexibility to design the mandate and hire and allocate between investment managers that the fund of funds does not. Funds of funds and managers of managers serve individual investors requiring diversification across alternative investment managers, but not wishing to commit the minimum investment required for each fund.

While the distinction between the two is not trivial, the two types of investment are similar enough to be discussed together as funds of funds.

The function of the fund of funds manager is to devise the overall investment strategy. This normally defines the type or types of alternative investments in which the fund will invest, specializing, for example, in market neutral funds for the home market or including a wide range of unlisted investments. The fund manager then scrutinizes all the alternative investment managers claiming expertize in that type of investment and allocates funds to those considered likely to give the best results.

Funds of funds can of course mix alternative investments, and allow themselves the freedom to change strategy as they see fit.

There are a number of benefits to the individual investor of using funds of funds instead of directly investing in one or more alternative investment funds, including:

- The fund of funds manager takes care of fund evaluation, seeking out the funds that are most likely to deliver the best results for the investment strategy. This process usually entails detailed analysis of the returns to each fund, its investment strategy and often its individual investments.
- Portfolio construction is carried out by the fund of funds manager. This is the process of allocating between the chosen funds to give the best possible expected return for a given level of risk. It seeks to exploit the differences in the approaches of individual funds to achieve an appropriate level of diversification that may not be available to the individual investor.
- Ongoing scrutiny of individual funds' investments is an important function of the fund of funds manager. This ensures that the funds conform to their stated investment strategies, and that the overall fund is therefore also doing what its investors expect it to.
- Access to a number of investment opportunities to which the fund has access, contributing further to diversification.
- Diversification across several or many funds reduces manager risk, enabling the fund of funds to achieve its objectives, even if one or more individual investment managers fail to achieve theirs.
- The fund of funds manager can exploit its size to negotiate significant fee reductions.

IMPLEMENTATION

Because of the variety of strategies and instruments employed in alternative investment funds, the issues surrounding implementation cover a lot of territory. Alternative investments require mastery of all the implementation techniques used by conventional investment managers, but in addition may routinely deal with others that are not always found in conventional investment portfolios.

One of the most frequently encountered implementation issues for alternative investment funds is the necessity of selling short some assets. **Short selling** is selling things that you do not already own. Short sales are routine in all derivatives markets, but when the title to a physical asset is involved, things can become quite complicated. A number of practical issues arise.

First, most stock markets impose rules and restrictions on short sales. Many markets ban the practice altogether, while others limit short selling to a relatively small number of stocks. There are usually rules about disclosure, for example the investor may be obliged to notify the exchange when a short sale has been effected, and the exchange may then keep a record so that the number of shares sold short in any company does not exceed some predefined limit.

Next, the investor may need to borrow shares for delivery because the rules of the stock exchange demand that title to the shares be presented in order to complete the transaction within a specified time, usually ten, five or two days. The investor cannot receive payment for the sold shares until he or she delivers the share certificates or the official entitlement to them. If he or she buys the shares back within this time, the requirement to borrow shares can be avoided. Borrowing shares entails finding an investor who holds shares in that company who is happy, for a fee, to lend the share certificates. These transactions usually take place via an intermediary, usually a custodian bank, which accepts a fee for arranging the transaction. The loan agreement usually stipulates the shares in question, the price at which they were borrowed, and the rent to be paid. The agreement may or may not stipulate the period of the loan, as the borrower may not know in advance how long he or she will need them. Dividends may accrue to either the borrower or the lender, according to the agreement, although some stock exchanges have rules about this too.

The lender usually demands some sort of collateral to guarantee the loan contract. The amount of collateral payable is usually calculated as a percentage of the initial market value of the stock with consideration of the perceived creditworthiness of the borrower and the scarcity of the stock in question. The amount of collateral demanded may exceed the market value of the stock, and may be augmented by some kind of variation margin, so that the borrower of the stock pays the lender or intermediary the difference between the market value of the stock and the value of the stock when it was borrowed, if the former is higher than the latter. This helps to reassure the lender that the borrower will be able to return the stock, even if its price rises significantly in the meantime.

The rent paid on a stock lending agreement depends on supply and demand for the stock and usually the prevailing interest rate. As the cost of borrowing stock can be high, the investment manager must take this cost into account when planning the investment strategy.

The main danger associated with selling shares short is that they can be difficult to buy back, for instance if demand for the stock suddenly increases. If this happens when a large number of the shares are sold short, the share price can be bid up very quickly and short sellers find themselves obliged to buy back the shares at whatever price they can, often incurring hefty losses in the process. This is known as a **short squeeze**.

Short selling is generally only available for listed assets, although the same effect can be achieved for unlisted assets using swaps.

Buying and selling unlisted instruments can involve many of the issues encountered in implementing direct property transactions. In particular, searching for investments in direct equity and bonds is labour intensive, and the legal and other costs of agreeing prices and terms of agreements can be high.

On the other hand, implementation of funds of funds can be quite straightforward once the manager's research has selected funds and decided how much of each to buy. It is then usually a matter of buying the funds on the market if the units are listed, or applying to buy units if it is an open, unlisted fund.

CURRENCY MANAGEMENT

Many alternative investment funds invest only in their home market, so currency management is not an issue. Funds buying listed offshore assets and derivatives deal with foreign currency transactions and management in the same way as do conventional funds investing in similar asset classes. Short selling foreign currency assets needs special attention, particularly if the position in that currency is net sold, that is, there is not an offsetting bought position in the currency, as this can result in an unintentional exposure in the currency. Investment managers engaging in long–short strategies across currency zones tend to manage their currency exposure on a 'net' basis. This means that, for each currency, bought and sold positions are 'netted out' against each other, so that only the remaining balance needs to be hedged or managed. This can become complicated enough, however, as the currency demands of frequent transactions, margins on derivatives positions, and short sale collateral require daily adjustments to overall foreign currency balances and hedges.

In principle, the same choices for currency management apply to alternative as for conventional investments, that is, between currency neutrality, full hedging to base currency, or active currency management if this is part of the investment manager's strategy. Either way, currency management is normally taken care of by the alternative investment manager. The investor should be aware of which policy is being pursued, however, as whatever currency risk the fund contains impacts the risk of the investor's overall portfolio.

ONGOING MANAGEMENT

The nature and complexity of ongoing management for alternative investment funds depends on the particular strategy and the instruments used in the fund. While all the same principles for ongoing management of conventional funds apply, such as continuous evaluation of the investment strategy and the underlying assumptions, alternative investment funds need to supplement these with the appropriate procedures to accommodate the ongoing management of short sales, unlisted instruments and investments in other funds.

Relative value strategies are usually monitored at least daily as managers search for opportunities to take profits, and look for early warning signs of illiquidity in the market for stocks that are sold short. Most relative value managers have devised some way of automating this routine portfolio scrutiny, so that it demands minimal management time, freeing managers to attend to identifying new profitable transactions and strategies.

Probably the most labour-intensive aspect of ongoing management of alternative investments is to do with direct equity, direct debt and direct property, especially the former. Because direct equity usually involves a shareholding in a new, or otherwise high-risk investment, it deserves continuous attention. This can involve regular scrutiny of financial and operations reports combined with meetings with the venture's managers and even visits to operations sites. The alternative investment manager may also regularly analyse the market in which the venture operates in order to maintain a good understanding of its prospects for growth.

Direct bonds and direct property demand a similar approach, although usually not in as much detail as direct equity, since the bond manager is primarily concerned with enhancing credit quality and managing the likelihood of failure; and property management entails less complexity than equities.

Funds of funds demand considerable ongoing management too. The fund of funds manager needs to monitor the portfolios of each fund to ensure that it continues to conform to the stated investment guidelines. As well as individual funds being analysed in isolation, the overall fund of funds needs scrutiny to ensure that individual funds combine to give a sensible overall portfolio with the highest expected return for the risk it has assumed.

ADMINISTRATION

As with ongoing management, the areas of alternative investment management demanding special attention are short sales, unlisted instruments and funds of funds. Most other investments are administered using conventional procedures.

Short sales need considerable administrative attention, especially if stock has been borrowed to support the position. For example, collateral and margin calls may need to be organized, as well as any other administrative procedures that the intermediary to the short sale agreement may stipulate.

Unlisted fixed interest, discount securities and most swaps usually fit into standard administrative procedures, so do not demand special attention.

Funds of funds can be reasonably uncomplicated to administer, as most of the day-to-day administration is taken care of by the managers of the funds in which the fund is invested.

VALUATION

Most investment managers value their portfolios by aggregating the most recent market values of the assets held in the portfolios. For all listed or frequently traded investments, this is straightforward. The complications really begin when the fund includes unlisted investments that are not regularly traded in a marketplace.

For these investments, most managers seek some estimate of a market valuation, often engaging the services of a professional valuer, who researches recent sales of similar investments, taking into account the peculiarities of the investment in question, and estimates a market price.

Valuing direct bonds follows a similar principle. The valuer needs to make an assessment of the credit rating of the investment, taking into account the risk of the business underlying the debt as well as any other outstanding debt or other obligations that would, in the event of the business failing, have a prior call on the assets of the firm. In other words, the valuer makes a judgement about the likelihood of the firm failing to meet its obligations, and then works out what other obligations need to be met before these particular bonds are repaid. This analysis

EXAMPLE 14.2 *Discounted cash flow*

Current Cash Flow	$2.00
Annual Growth in Cash Flow	2.00%
Discount Rate p.a.	3.50%
Assumed Time Horizon in Years	30
Present Value of Last Cash Flow in Horizon	$1.29
Present Value of Future Cash Flows	$50.23

is used to estimate an interest rate margin over the risk-free rate for bonds of that maturity, using market information for traded bonds of a similar risk level.

Direct equity is considerably more complex to value. There are various short-hand approaches, such as estimating a reasonable price-to-book ratio, or a price-to-sales ratio. These measures can give good approximations if the business resembles other firms with shares traded on an exchange. But if the business is really new, then similar, traded companies will be difficult, if not impossible, to find. For a new company in a new industry – which are the types of ventures most sought by venture capital and private equity funds – the valuation needs to be based on a comprehensive discounted cash flow analysis, also known as **net present value**, similar to the dividend discount analysis frequently applied to listed equities, and set out in Example 14.2.

PERFORMANCE MEASUREMENT AND ATTRIBUTION

Once the portfolio has been valued, return measurement is relatively simple. As with other portfolios, it is the value of the portfolio at the end of the period divided by the value of the portfolio at the beginning of the period minus one. Where cash flows occur during the period, it is broken down into sub-periods and the sub-period returns compounded to give an overall result.

Returns are calculated and reported monthly for portfolios of listed securities and assets, and of unlisted assets that are traded frequently. For portfolios with assets that are not traded, valuations may be carried out less frequently, so return periods tend to be longer.

Portfolio attribution follows the same principles as for other portfolios, in that the attribution seeks to identify sectors and holdings that have contributed most to the portfolio's return during the period.

Portfolios of listed securities lend themselves to attribution analysis at the asset class, country and sector levels, while portfolios of direct property, direct bonds and direct equity may lend themselves more to attribution analysis at the level of the individual asset.

PITFALLS

For unlisted investments, there are many potential traps to do with ongoing management of venture capital projects and other direct investments. Probably the most important is the perennial problem of not being able to sell the assets when it is desirable or necessary to do so, or of not being able to sell at a price close to that given by the last valuation.

For listed investments, the most acute liquidity problems can occur in connection with short sold stock positions. Unlike a normal bought position in an asset, where the maximum loss is the price paid for the stock, the potential losses to short positions are unlimited because there is no theoretical or actual upper limit to a stock price. Investors who sell stock short expect the price to go down, either in absolute terms or relative to some other asset or instrument. If some event in the meantime sends the price of the stock upwards, the investor often decides that the original strategy is no longer profitable, and sets about closing it by buying back the shares. Even if he or she does not decide to close the position, the decision may be forced by the weight of variation margins demanded by the stock lender. In either case, the short stock may need to be repurchased at full speed. Being a forced buyer can be worse than being a forced seller. When an asset price begins to swing sharply, many other investors follow the trend, and the price move can accelerate. Given that the stock exchange maintains, and usually publishes, records of the amount of short sales in any stock, speculators may seek to profit from the knowledge of how many forced buyers are in the market by buying the shares, knowing they will be able to sell them at an even higher price later on.

CASE STUDY

Until the dot.com boom of the late 1990s, and widespread short selling by alternative investment managers, it was accepted wisdom that stock prices nearly always rose fairly slowly but fell quite sharply, 'up by the stairs and down by the elevator' in the lexicon. This pattern can sometimes be exploited using exchange-traded options on volatile assets, such as equities. The events described here do not concern a fund open for public investment, but a private fund. Nevertheless, the strategy is of a genre that is applied by some alternative investment managers. The trader, charged with running a highly speculative portfolio (similar to a geared hedge fund), noticed that stock options on many stocks were trading at historically very high prices relative to the price of the underlying stock – their implied volatilities were in the range 40% to 80%, compared with recent levels of 20% to 30%. So he thought he would try to exploit this apparent anomaly.

His strategy was to sell at-the-money call and put options simultaneously on a number of blue-chip shares. By selling at-the-money options, the maximum option premium was earned. The risk was that the share price would move sharply up or down, in which case either the calls or the puts respectively would end up **in-the-money** and be exercised, forcing the trader to either buy shares in the market for delivery at a lower price or buy shares and resell them at a loss (Example 14.3.1).

The net option payoff in Example 14.3.2 shows that the position would be profitable as long as the shares remain above $38.37 ($50.15 – $11.78), or less than $62.03, less transaction costs.

Knowing that a significant share price move could incur a loss, and that sharp downward moves were more likely than upward ones, he decided to augment the position with short stock positions to cover the sold put options. The idea was that, if the share price moved up, there would be ample opportunity to cover the potential losses by buying back stock on the way up to offset both the sold calls. The new payoff diagram would look like Example 14.3.3, which shows that, with the short stock, the position is immune to a fall in the share price, but that an increase above $56 would start to incur serious losses.

EXAMPLE 14.3.1 *Short call and put at the same exercise price*

Current Stock Price	50.15
Exercise Price of Options	50
Implied Stock Volatility	60%
Days to Option Expiry	90
Interest Rate	8.50%
Call Price	$6.46
Put Price	$5.32
Premium Received	$11.78

EXAMPLE 14.3.2 *Short call and put at the same exercise price*

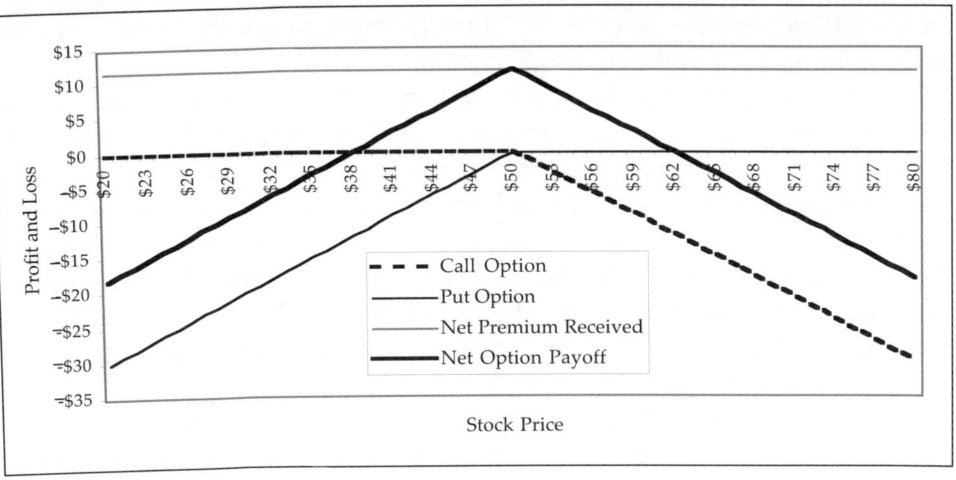

The transaction took place in an exchange operated by **open outcry**, meaning that bids and offers are communicated orally, by people standing near each other in the hall of the stock exchange. This system has operated for centuries with surprisingly little change. It is popular, and its adherents insist that it is, despite its age, the most effective way of trading large numbers of assets fairly.

Open outcry can be very labour intensive, as each transaction must be carried out individually. In this case, each transaction had three 'legs': the sold call, the sold put and the sold physical share. On this exchange, as with many

EXAMPLE 14.3.3 *Short call and put at the same exercise price with short stock position*

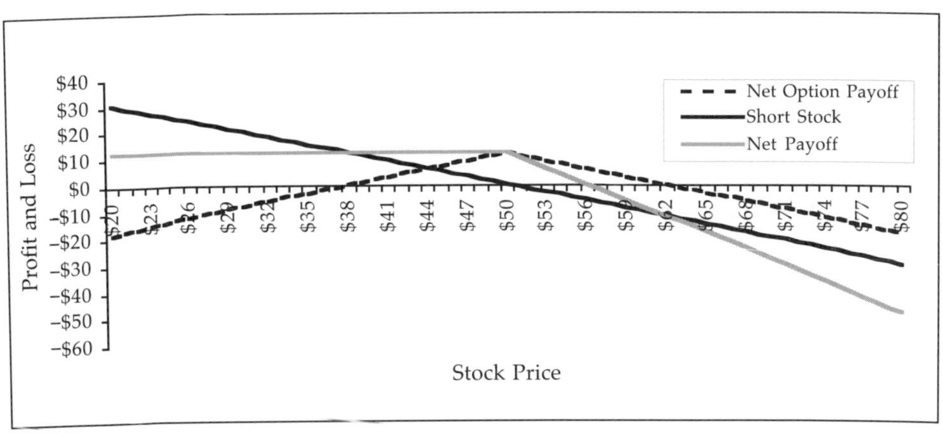

exchanges, the options are traded in a separate part of the exchange to physical shares. As the options are usually less liquid and therefore more difficult to transact, these were put in place first, the idea being to sell the shares when the options transactions had been implemented.

Selling the options took longer than expected, however, and the bell signalling the close of business sounded before the physical shares were sold. This was thought not to be a problem because, for one thing, the sold share positions were merely intended as a safety net, and not critical to the success of the strategy; and second, all the stocks in question were major companies, which could be traded on other exchanges in other time zones. The shares could thus be sold on another market within a few hours. The trader instructed his colleague to place orders to sell the shares on another market, and then left for the day, tired but happy.

More experienced traders had seen this strategy before, and had seen just how risky it could be in volatile markets. They also had seen that unusually high implied volatilities in options markets usually signalled impending unusually high volatility in the underlying securities. Some traders had even named this strategy an 'airport spread', observing that the best next move for the trader would be to head for the airport.

By coincidence, this trader was obliged, for reasons unconnected with this transaction, to travel overseas for two weeks.

Meanwhile, the colleague had had rather a busy day himself and, confident that selling parcels of leading shares would not pose a problem, thought he would leave placing the sale order until the following day, when he would have more time to calculate and check the precise quantities required. The following day, the share index opened 40% lower. The sold put options were very much in-the-money.

The trader had sold put options at an exercise price of $50 when the current share price was $50.15, obliging him, upon exercise by the buyer of the options, to buy the shares at $50, regardless of their market value. Buying at $50 and selling the shares at $30.09 incurred a loss of $19.91 per share. This transaction was highly geared because the actual exposure of the position was many times the amount of the capital required to put it in place. The **initial margin** requirements for short option positions was about $1 per option, so for each share equivalent, the transaction was backed by capital of about $2, giving a return on investment of –507%.

It is worthwhile noting that, at an implied volatility of 60%, the 40% fall in the share price was not entirely unforeseen. In fact, the trader was lucky that the bubble burst when it did; an upward price movement of the same dimension would have resulted in a loss of $31.41, or –1670%.

EXAMPLE 14.3.4 *Payoff to option strategy*

Payoff with 40% Drop in Price	
New Stock Price	30.09
Value of Call Option	$0.24
Value of Put Option	$19.16
Profit/Loss on Calls	$6.22
Profit/Loss on Puts	−$13.84
Total Theoretical Loss	−$7.62
Put Options Exercised	
Loss on Sale of Stock	−$19.19
Premium Received	$11.78
Net Loss	−$8.13

The funds invested in this fund belonged to the owners of the investment bank, who were understandably annoyed at incurring such losses, since they were not aware that they were exposed to quite this much risk. The consequences could have been much worse if the fund had been open to the public where the tolerance for large losses is more limited.

CHAPTER 15

Portfolio Transition and Transition Portfolios

PORTFOLIO TRANSITION

For pension plan sponsors, funds of funds and other investors engaging the services of investment managers, changing investment managers is time consuming and potentially very costly. Factors influencing how portfolio transition between investment managers is managed include:

- The reasons for changing.
- The mix of asset classes.
- The availability of derivatives markets.
- Whether the portfolio is managed actively or passively.

Investors change investment managers either because they are dissatisfied with the service or performance of the incumbent or in order to implement a new investment strategy or fund structure.

If the **reason for changing** is simply that he or she is not satisfied with some aspect of the service provided by the current manager, the mandate for the new manager may be identical or similar to the existing one. This being so, unless the mandate is for passive management, the new portfolio is likely to be quite different because the new investment manager will want to implement his or her 'brand' of portfolio, using his or her own research and other resources that he or she believes to be better than the competition.

If there is to be a change in investment strategy or fund structure, the following may be required:

- A change in long-term asset allocations.
- A change in asset class benchmarks.
- A shift in risk profile.
- Some combination of the above.

Changes in long-term asset allocation may imply simply increasing and decreasing allocations to existing investment managers or it may involve investment in new asset classes. Investing in new asset classes requires research into the potential contribution of the asset class to the fund's return and risk, followed by benchmark and mandate specifications and manager research, a time-consuming exercise.

Changing asset class benchmarks requires respecification of investment management mandates or modification of existing ones, and a transition period to allow the investment manager to modify the portfolio.

Shifts in risk profile sometimes necessitate appointing new asset class managers.

The mix of asset classes can be important because it impacts the transaction costs incurred if the portfolio is to be rebalanced or liquidated. It also indicates the amount of time required to carry out the transition. Listed assets and assets that are frequently traded, such as listed equities and bonds, require only a few days, although most investors prefer to allow two to three weeks, in order to allow the investment manager enough time to carry out any liquidations smoothly and cost efficiently. Unlisted, infrequently traded assets, such as direct property, may take several months if they need to be liquidated, although most investors choose to transfer these assets in-specie. An **in-specie** transfer transfers the mandate to manage the assets from one investment manager to another without any change of ownership.

The availability of derivatives markets can seriously reduce the cost and disruption of transferring from one investment manager to another, whether within the same asset class or between asset classes.

Whether the portfolio is managed passively, actively or very actively can, in some cases, impact the cost and disruption of the changeover. A passively managed portfolio being transferred from one manager to another theoretically should incur negligible costs and very little disruption, while at the other end of the spectrum, a very actively managed portfolio going to another very active mandate or a passive mandate, or a passive mandate being replaced by a very active mandate, can be expected to require considerable transaction costs and management time.

TRANSITION MANAGEMENT

Most investment management mandates are for fixed periods, with provision for renewal and minimum notice periods for the investor wishing to cancel during a mandate period or not renew at the end of the period. When changing investment managers, it is preferable to do so at the end of a mandate period. Notice periods vary according to the asset class and how long it takes to liquidate a portfolio or otherwise prepare it for transfer, with some mandates providing for as little as two weeks, others stipulating one to two months. How portfolio transition is managed depends on the nature of the old and new portfolios and the reasons for the transfer.

If the transfer is a simple **change of investment manager**, with no material change in the mandate or the benchmark, then the investor can simply request a transfer of assets in-specie. The investor can ask the new investment manager (or each candidate manager bidding for the mandate) to indicate how much of the existing portfolio must be liquidated in order to implement their proposed portfolio, and to quote on the costs of rebalancing. This can form part of the overall proposal for the management contract. Of course, it necessitates showing the candidate manager the composition of the existing portfolio (which is managed by a competitor of the candidate), justifying some sort of confidentiality clause. A transfer in cash does not encounter this problem, and the transfer can be much easier from the administrative point of view.

Some managers claim very low transfer costs for in-specie transfers because they say they can offset transactions from existing client portfolios. This may well be true some of the time, but, if the manager were to be hired for a particular style, one would have to ask why the other portfolios under management are buying the same stocks that this one is selling, and vice versa. If the portfolios are managed passively, it can be argued that selection of particular stocks is unimportant as long as the overall portfolio conforms to the desired tracking error and other specifications. But, for passive portfolios, low turnover is a desirable characteristic, so one would wonder if perhaps this is achieved by transacting existing client portfolios more frequently than is necessary, thereby incurring unnecessary transaction costs.

As a rule, in-specie transfers do not require the use of futures to smooth the transition from one investment manager to another, although the incoming manager may use them to effect subsequent rebalancing.

If the investor decides that the portfolio should be liquidated to facilitate the transfer, then the outgoing manager will be instructed to have sold all the assets in the portfolio by a particular date. Some portfolios can be sold within a few days, but for large portfolios it may be necessary to allow one or more months (for direct equity, bonds and property, the liquidation period can be many months) to avoid driving asset prices down artificially by giving the appearance of a forced sale. During the sell-down period, the portfolio will be increasingly underinvested, presenting a risk to the investor.

If the asset class in which it is to be reinvested appreciates while the portfolio is underinvested, then the fund will suffer lower returns relative to the benchmark. There are two ways of dealing with this problem. One solution is to have the new manager ready to put the new portfolio in place immediately. This hardly ever works in practice, usually because unforeseen administrative hiccups disrupt the timetable; and in any case does not deal with the underinvestment during the sell down by the outgoing manager.

The other solution is to use futures contracts if they are available. One way of doing this is to instruct the outgoing manager to buy futures contracts to cover the value of the assets being sold. The portfolio can then be transferred as a holding of cash with bought futures contracts. The incoming manager will then progressively sell the futures and buy physical assets. The remaining question is of supervision: how can the investor be sure that the outgoing manager has bought the appropriate quantity and type of futures contract? He or she has, after all, little interest in ensuring the ongoing success of the investment. Any subsequent disappointing returns can be blamed on mismanagement by the new manager, who can in turn blame the old manager for having bought the wrong number or type of derivatives. Some independent advice or oversight is desirable and may be necessary.

If the new portfolio is to be a **different asset class** from the old one, the old portfolio needs to be liquidated. This can be very expensive, but there is rarely any alternative, as in-specie transfers are not viable because the incoming manager may be unfamiliar with the assets he or she inherits, and so cannot be expected to arrange a smooth and cost efficient rebalancing. In these cases, the problem of underinvestment during the period of sell down and transfer can only be avoided using derivatives if these are available.

If **the new manager has not yet been appointed**, and the investor wishes to terminate the contract of the existing manager, then some interim solution must be sought. This problem sounds more drastic than it may be. While it is possible that the investor is so disappointed with an investment manager's service that even the most rudimentary investment management seems preferable, this happens very rarely. More often, an investor finds that a revision of investment policy or long-term strategy is imminent but not yet completed. Such a revision almost always necessitates a change in or termination of some investment management mandates. Revisions nearly always take longer than expected to complete, and investment mandates are usually agreed for periods of at least 12 months. If the investment manager's mandate is due for renewal, the investor may be reluctant to renew, knowing that it will need to be terminated mid-term – which can be clumsy and costly. He or she would prefer to seek an interim management contract rather than renew the existing mandate.

TRANSITION PORTFOLIOS

Transition portfolios can be very useful for smoothing the transfer of portfolios from one investment manager to another, wherever this transition requires the liquidation in part or whole of the old portfolio. The role of the transition manager is to ensure that the portfolio remains fully invested in the required asset classes. The transition mandate is to achieve the lowest cost and lowest specific risk investment over a short interval, with the understanding that the entire portfolio will shortly be restructured.

Transition management can control the costs and disruption of transferring assets from one investment manager to another if:

- The existing mandate must be terminated before a new manager is engaged.
- Assets must be transferred from one asset class to another.
- There is significant difference between old and new investment mandates within an asset class.

OBJECTIVES

The objectives of transition portfolios are:

- to ensure that the portfolio remains fully invested during the transition from one investment manager, or group of managers, to another
- to ensure that it is never overinvested during the transition
- to ensure that it complies at all times with the investor's investment policy and constraints
- to minimize the costs of the transition.

For in-specie transfers within an asset class, the transition manager can implement low-risk, low-cost asset management, maintaining basic exposure to the asset class with minimum cost, usually as a type of indexed portfolio.

When transferring a portfolio in cash between two or more managers within the same asset class, the transition manager can ensure that the appropriate quantity and type of derivative is used, effectively acting as a sort of referee and understudy to the outgoing and incoming managers.

For transfers between asset classes, the transition portfolio provides a sort of go-between, ensuring that the outgoing manager has implemented the appropriate derivatives contracts then selling these to buy the appropriate derivatives or physical assets in the new asset class.

IMPLEMENTATION

Transition portfolios are nearly always implemented using derivatives such as futures contracts or an indexed or other passive portfolio.

Example 15.1 illustrates a transition management mandate with a change in asset classes. The fund is switching from all active managers in domestic equities and fixed interest to a 50/50 core–satellite approach for its domestic equities, with a 10% change in asset allocation from fixed interest to domestic equities. The fund will need three months to identify and appoint two active equity managers and an indexed portfolio manager. The 10% to be moved from fixed interest to equities in the new portfolio needs to be liquidated, while the 30% remains in fixed interest, and the 60% to be transferred in equities can be transferred in specie and converted to an indexed portfolio during transition.

For Example 15.1, the role of the transition manager would be to:

1. Plan the overall transition.
2. Ensure the 10% transfer from fixed interest is liquidated and equitized, using share price index futures.
3. Determine the best mix of in-specie transfers and on market transactions to effect the transition at the lowest possible cost to the client.
4. Convert part of the equity portfolio to an indexed portfolio.
5. Plan and implement the required trades to effect the transition.
6. Ensure that the portfolio has all the necessary trades completed and settled prior to transfer to the new managers.
7. Report the transition to the client.

The transition manager needs to have extensive experience dealing in cross-market derivatives as well as the underlying assets. This means that he or she should be comfortable accepting an equity portfolio for eventual transfer into fixed interest and vice versa. Therefore the transition manager needs to be

EXAMPLE 15.1 *Portfolio transition*

Starting Portfolio	Transition Portfolio	Finishing Portfolio
40% Bonds	30% Bonds	30% Bonds
60% Equities	60% Indexed Equities	35% Indexed Equities (Core)
	10% Share Price Index Futures	35% Active Equities (Satellite)

Transaction Summary

Transition Portfolio	Sell Bonds	10%	Transition Manager
Transition Portfolio	Buy Share Price Index Futures	10%	Transition Manager
Finishing Portfolio	Sell Active Equities	60%	New Managers
Finishing Portfolio	Buy Active Equities Satellite	35%	New Managers
Finishing Portfolio	Buy Indexed Equities Core	25%	New Managers

familiar with different pricing, trading, settlement and administrative conventions, as well as estimating the appropriate foreign currency transactions to complement the portfolio if necessary.

CURRENCY MANAGEMENT

As long as the transition is between two domestic asset classes, no currency management is required, but, if either the old or new asset class has exposure to another currency, the transition manager must take into account the investor's policy regarding currency management.

Whether the investor requires currency neutrality or hedged to base currency, the currency exposure needs to be carefully managed during the transition period. This is done by implementing and managing the appropriate foreign exchange and forward foreign exchange contracts, ensuring that the foreign currency transactions implemented are giving the desired currency exposure and ensuring that all unsettled forward transactions are transferred to the new manager, usually by informing the broker and custodian.

If currency is managed actively, then the currency manager must be kept informed of changes to the portfolio composition so that overall currency risk may be maintained according to specifications.

ONGOING MANAGEMENT

Most transition portfolios are only for a few weeks or two or three months at most, but occasionally can last several months and span one or more reporting periods.

The same principles for ongoing management apply as for other portfolios in the same asset class, with special attention to cost minimization. As a special 'care and maintenance' mandate, there is usually no requirement to add returns through active management.

ADMINISTRATION

Most administrative problems arising during transition result from delayed settlement on portfolio transactions and outstanding dividend and other income accruals. For this reason, most investors instruct the outgoing manager to conduct the necessary sell down of assets and purchase of covering derivatives well ahead of the date of transfer. Most listed and frequently traded instruments have reasonably short settlement cycles, usually ten business days or less, so a notice period for terminating a mandate of three to four weeks is usually enough for this purpose. Nevertheless, there are almost always unsettled items, such as dividends and coupons accrued but not paid, other corporate actions, such as rights that need to be taken up and so on, not to mention unsettled forward foreign exchange transactions, so the process can be error prone.

It is important to ensure that the transition manager receives a detailed and accurate report of the portfolio holdings, together with any accruals and other unsettled transactions, as at the last day of the outgoing manager's mandate. This report should be prepared and verified as soon as possible to enable the transition manager to carry out the necessary adjustments and rebalancing straightaway.

This process will need to be repeated when the transition manager hands over to the incoming manager.

VALUATION

Valuation of the transition portfolio is carried out exactly the same as for any other portfolio with the same mix of assets and instruments, with special care necessary to account for all possible delayed settlement items.

PERFORMANCE MEASUREMENT AND ATTRIBUTION

Most of the issues relevant to measurement and attribution of performance of normal portfolios against their benchmarks pertain also to transition portfolios, with one or two additions.

The first is that, because the transition portfolio is expected to be in place for only a relatively short space of time, its composition may be materially different to the ongoing portfolio. For example, it often comprises a larger proportion of derivatives instruments than would the ongoing portfolio. If the benchmark is the physical asset class, it should be remembered that the transition portfolio can behave differently from the ongoing portfolio. If the only difference is that the transition portfolio is invested in derivatives, whereas the ongoing portfolio is a physical indexed portfolio, the performance variations should even out over time, so that the portfolio's return over several months will be similar to that of an indexed portfolio. If the transition portfolio is an indexed fund, while the ongoing portfolio is actively managed, then the performance difference will not even out because the transition portfolio does not earn the added returns of an actively managed portfolio.

The second modification is that the first reporting period for a new or transition manager is not counted in long-term return tables because of distortions resulting from rebalancing costs. The period thus omitted may be a month or a quarter as agreed between the investor and the investment manager. There are strong arguments for doing things this way, especially if portfolio return is a criterion by which the investment manager is to be evaluated. This should not, however, prevent the investment manager from presenting to the investor a detailed report of how the portfolio rebalancing was carried out, together with an analysis of how much it cost.

PITFALLS

Implementing a new investment strategy, or simply refining the existing portfolio composition, presents plenty of opportunities for confusion and error, so it helps if other portfolio management functions remain as stable as possible while it is happening. The role of the custodian is especially important to coordinate settlements and ensure continuity of portfolio valuations, performance measurement and so on.

One potential trap is in misspecifying the transition portfolio mandate. Because the object of the transition portfolio is to maintain continuity in the portfolio's exposure to selected asset classes, it is often assumed that the same benchmark and other specifications can apply to the transition portfolio as to permanent portfolios in the same asset class. This works well most of the time, but sometimes it is not possible to achieve a result even similar to the permanent portfolio with the limitations on cost and risk that usually apply to the transition manager. It is easy to underestimate the effect of the differences. For one thing, most transition portfolios are managed as some kind of passive or indexed portfolio, using either derivatives or physical assets. Either way, the transition portfolio cannot achieve above benchmark returns because it is not taking on enough portfolio-specific risk. The transition portfolio is therefore not a perfect substitute for the permanent portfolio in the same asset class, managed to the same benchmark.

If the portfolio is managed using derivatives, while the permanent portfolio is managed using physical assets, there will also be significant differences in the results, even if the permanent portfolio is an indexed portfolio benchmarked to the index against which the derivatives are settled. Most derivative instruments are settled quarterly, meaning that, once a quarter, the price of the derivative is precisely matched to the price of the index or benchmark asset or basket of assets. During the quarter, including the intervening month-ends, the price of the derivative contract fluctuates around the physical benchmark according to how efficiently priced the derivatives are relative to the physical, and how high transaction costs are for the physical assets. If the market is very efficient and transaction costs are low, then the price of the derivative will nearly always be close to its 'fair' value, relative to the underlying physical assets, and fluctuations will be small. If either the market is very inefficient, or transaction costs are high, there will be significant differences, both positive and negative, between the actual and 'fair' price of the derivatives, relative to the underlying physical assets. These differences translate into noticeable and sometimes confusing return variations between what was thought to be a low-risk transition portfolio and the benchmark. Unlike the active–passive distinction, where the return effect is permanent, the return impact of the derivatives–physical distinction should, if the derivatives were purchased at about fair price, diminish and eventually disappear, as the derivatives and physical prices converge.

The third, potentially hazardous aspect of transferring investment mandates from one manager to another concerns managing the outgoing investment manager. Although in the vast majority of cases, this is not a problem, it can be if an investment manager believes his or her contract to be under threat because return objectives have not been met. The investment manager may decide that there is a small chance of keeping the mandate if the return shortfall can be made up, while there is no chance of retaining the business otherwise. Therefore, the incentive for the investment manager is to take on excessive portfolio-specific risk, in the hope that this delivers enough return to close the gap.

The result may or may not be obvious to the investor, and the ploy may indeed work. But even if the return gap is made up, the investor is the loser because the portfolio has been subject to much greater risk than was intended. More dangerous still, the investment manager may conclude that the additional risk was beneficial, and maintain a similar risk profile for the future.

CASE STUDY

This is a very straightforward exercise of implementing a transition portfolio using share price index futures contracts to maintain the exposure to domestic equities of a portfolio normally managed actively using only physical equities. The portfolio had recently been restructured, with a large injection of new investment funds. The trustees and managers of the portfolio were proceeding methodically with a search for suitable investment managers for this asset class. It was envisaged that the search would take three months. In the event it took more than six months.

Assets were transferred to the transition investment manager in the form of cash. The value of the portfolio was in the vicinity of USD50 million. Because of the short-term nature of the assignment, the investor thought it appropriate to have a much shorter than usual reporting cycle. The investment manager agreed to weekly and monthly return reports because reporting a portfolio of liquids and share price index futures was administratively simple, not requiring very much management time.

Unlike the manager of a permanent portfolio, the transition manager was given no period of 'grace'. It was expected that the portfolio be implemented at the futures 'fair price' on the day the cash was transferred. This was by no means unreasonable, given the relatively small amount to be invested. The problem was that, on that day, the price of the derivatives contract traded abnormally above its fair price relative to the underlying physical benchmark index. The agreed benchmark was the physical index underlying the futures contract. While this was thought initially to be the obvious choice of benchmark, it led to serious misunderstandings.

First of all, the investment manager was obliged to buy the derivatives contracts at above fair price. From the outset, this compromised the return to the portfolio, but the investment manager concluded that this known underperformance was preferable to the unknown risk of delaying the purchase of the derivatives until a more favourable price could be achieved. In this he behaved responsibly, avoiding risk many times greater than the relatively small performance shortfall implied by the derivatives mispricing.

Derivatives contracts are often more volatile than the underlying physical assets because they tend to trade both above and below their fair price. The width of the band about the fair price is determined mainly by how high transaction costs are for the physical asset, because this dictates at what point it is profitable for arbitrageurs to enter the market and bring prices back to their fair relativities. Over the following months, the derivatives contracts exhibited higher than usual volatility, so that weekly portfolio returns bore little resemblance to the returns of the benchmark. The investor was understandably alarmed by what appeared to be a serious departure from a clearly defined mandate.

Example 15.2 summarizes the results. Futures theoretical is what the investor expected to see, and futures actual is what happened. After a disappointing start, the portfolio performed according to specification.

EXAMPLE 15.2 *Performance of a transition portfolio*

		Month to	Portfolio %	Benchmark %	Difference %
Futures Expiry Date	30 06 1999	31 01 1999	−0.22	4.10	−4.32
Interest Rate	6.50%	28 02 1999	−2.73	−3.23	0.50
Dividend Yield	1.50%	31 03 1999	4.01	3.88	0.13
		30 04 1999	4.03	3.79	0.23
Portfolio Size	$50 000 000	31 05 1999	−3.05	−2.50	−0.55
Number of Futures Bought	81	30 06 1999	6.10	5.44	0.65
Point Value of Futures	$500	Six Months	8.02	11.67	−3.65
		Annualized Tracking Error			6.68
		Excluding First Month			1.44

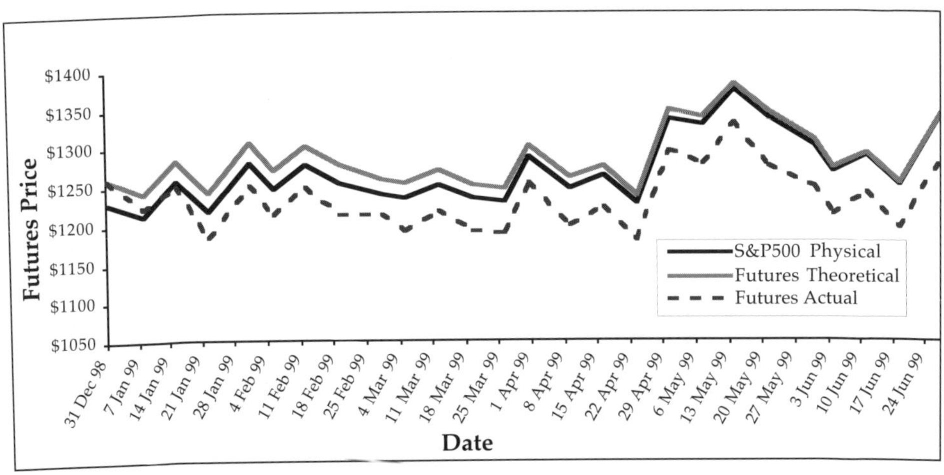

CHAPTER 16

Currency Management

APPLICATIONS

Many investors see foreign currency risk as a necessary part of investing in offshore assets, and assume that it is a risk either to be lived with, or one that can only be avoided by staying at home. Other investors see foreign currency as a separate asset class, and therefore another opportunity for extra return. This approach recognizes the sometimes weak link between the return to an asset class and the currency in which it is denominated. Sometimes asset price appreciation in local currency terms is offset by currency depreciation and vice versa. Other times, currency changes can exaggerate local currency returns.

The net result can be that the investment manager may do a fine job of selecting well-performing assets in local currency, picking stocks that do well compared with other assets in the same currency area, but find that, when converted to base currency, the returns are quite poor. All that valuable stock picking ability (and portfolio-specific risk) was wasted because insufficient attention was given to managing the currency exposure.

Example 16.1.1 illustrates this. The investor has achieved a return of 5% in local currency, but an adverse movement in the currency reduces this to 0.23% in base currency.

The only way to neutralize the portfolio's exposure to foreign currency is to run a strictly indexed, passive portfolio, so that all asset holdings are matched precisely to the benchmark. This can eliminate foreign currency exposure relative to the benchmark, and is fine if the investor is seeking a purely passive portfolio. But even this very conservative investment strategy exposes the portfolio to foreign currency risk in absolute terms.

EXAMPLE 16.1.1 *Single period return in local and base currency: unhedged*

	Start of Period	End of Period	Return in Local Currency %	Return in Base Currency %
Asset Price	$100.00	$105.00	5.00	0.23
Exchange Rate	1.1000	1.0500	−4.55	

To eliminate foreign currency exposure in an absolute sense, the investor can hedge all foreign currency back to the base currency of the portfolio. If the benchmark is also fully hedged, this can, in theory, eliminate currency risk in both relative and absolute terms. In practice, a portfolio of international assets will always have some currency risk, for the following reasons:

- Asset prices rise and fall continuously, and earn income from time to time. This means that there is always some unrealized profit and loss and accumulated or accrued income in the portfolio that is denominated in a foreign currency. Because of these, the hedge, consisting of sold foreign currency forwards, needs to be adjusted periodically. It is rarely practicable to adjust the hedge continuously so, in between hedge adjustments, there is always some exposure to foreign currency.
- When the hedge is adjusted or renewed, it is done at a new spot exchange rate, so, while the hedge may have been very effective up to the settlement of the sold forwards, the new sold forward position reflects the currency movement that occurred in the meantime. Thus, hedging can smooth out portfolio volatility due to short-term currency fluctuations and delay some currency effects, but it does not eliminate them entirely.
- The assets themselves in the portfolio have exposure to currencies other than the ones in which they are denominated. Even the components of domestic equities portfolios contain some stocks whose price is affected by currency fluctuations, either because the companies themselves have operations abroad, or because they export a significant proportion of their output or imports materials or components. In fact, foreign currency exposure can result simply from having competitors based in another currency zone.

Foreign currency exposure can be modified by hedging, or selling forward foreign currency, as in Example 16.1.2. The difference between the local currency return of 5% and the hedged return of 2.61% is the cost of the hedge.

Many investors adopt currency neutrality, understanding it to be a passive approach to currency management. This means that they buy just enough

EXAMPLE 16.1.2 *Single period return in local and base currency: hedged*

	Start of Period	End of Period	Return in Local Currency %	Return in Base Currency %	Hedged Return %
Asset Price	$100.00	$105.00	5.00	0.23	2.61
Exchange Rate	1.1000	1.0500	−4.55		
Interest Rate Local Currency	7.50%				
Interest Rate Base Currency	5.00%				
Forward Exchange Rate		1.1262	2.38		

foreign currency to cover the purchase of foreign assets. In fact, this can leave considerable exposure to foreign currency fluctuations because it does not properly account for the foreign currency exposures inherent in the portfolio's component securities.

Because currencies are volatile, with returns that can be substantially different from asset returns, their potential impact on portfolio performance can be significant. If the investor does not take an active interest in the foreign currency exposure of the portfolio, he or she may be leaving the portfolio exposed to risk for which no compensating return is being sought. This is a strong argument for either hedging or actively managing the foreign currency exposure of the portfolio.

THEORY

Because currency movements can have such a profound impact on many important aspects of the economic well-being of a country, as well as investment portfolio returns, both academics and practitioners have devoted considerable effort to try to understand what drives currency returns. These efforts have resulted in a suite of theories to explain exchange rates and their movements.

The first of these is called purchasing power parity (PPP). This says that, over the medium to long term, goods that can be traded will eventually settle at the same real price across currency regimes, so that there will be no advantage in travelling from one country to another to buy goods more cheaply. Example 16.2 illustrates PPP. Relative inflation rates between currency zones are very important to PPP, because, if inflation is high in one country and low in another, to maintain the same price in real terms, the exchange rate of the high inflation country must depreciate faster than that of the low inflation country.

EXAMPLE 16.2 *Purchasing power parity*

Currency	Exchange Rate	Original Cost of Widget	Transport Costs %	Tax Differential %	Final Value of Widget in Local Currency
US Dollars	1.0000	1.00	0.00	0.00	1.00
Australian Dollar	0.6378	1.57	15.00	0.00	1.80
Austrian Schilling	0.0711	14.06	5.00	2.50	15.12
Belgian Franc	0.0243	41.23	5.00	2.50	44.32
Canadian Dollar	0.6902	1.45	0.00	0.00	1.45
Danish Krone	0.1315	7.61	5.00	2.50	8.18
Deutschmark	0.5002	2.00	5.00	2.50	2.15
Dutch Guilder	0.4440	2.25	5.00	2.50	2.42
Euro	0.9784	1.02	5.00	2.50	1.10
Finnish Markka	0.1646	6.08	5.00	2.50	6.53
French Franc	0.1492	6.70	5.00	2.50	7.21
Hong Kong Dollar	0.1285	7.78	7.50	2.50	8.56
Irish Punt	1.2423	0.80	5.00	2.50	0.87
Italian Lira	0.0005	1979.02	5.00	2.50	2127.45
Japanese Yen	0.0093	107.04	7.50	2.50	117.75
Luxembourg Franc	0.0243	41.23	5.00	2.50	44.32
New Zealand Dollar	0.4952	2.02	15.00	0.00	2.32
Norwegian Krone	0.1209	8.27	5.00	2.50	8.89
Singaporean Dollar	0.5881	1.70	7.50	2.50	1.87
Spanish Peseta	0.0059	170.06	5.00	2.50	182.82
Swedish Krona	0.1137	8.79	5.00	2.50	9.45
Swiss Franc	0.6084	1.64	5.00	2.50	1.77
UK Pound	1.6209	0.62	5.00	2.50	0.66

Unfortunately, this simple algorithm does not even approximately explain currency movements because the two countries are almost certainly subject to different taxes and regulations, and there are plenty of other factors impacting exchange rates.

Even so, PPP does help to explain some aspects of exchange rate movements and relationships, not least the potential impact of currency devaluations on a country's rate of inflation. This relationship is reasonably well understood by economists, partly because there are numerous examples of currency devaluations being followed by a rise in measured inflation, as well as exchange rates being affected by high relative inflation between two countries. Put simply, when a currency devalues, all imported goods, including the imported components of domestically manufactured goods, rise as merchants pass on the higher cost to their customers. If there are purely domestic producers of the same goods, then they will be able to set higher prices, partially matching their competitors' price rises. While this is happening, domestic demand for imported goods will decline, reversing some of the original devaluation.

In most economies, where the price of goods is allowed to fluctuate according to supply and demand, this effect quickly becomes apparent across many sectors of the economy, so the basket of consumer goods that governments use to estimate inflation show that its price has gone up. Depending on capacity utilization, and labour market conditions, the price rise may lead to demands for increased wages, potentially leading to further inflation.

Exporters benefit from currency devaluation because the price of their goods on international markets goes down, or they can increase the price in domestic currency to keep the international price the same. Thus they earn higher profits, export more, or both. If they export more, there will be increased demand for the devalued currency, and it will start to go up again, possibly reducing inflation as it does so.

While PPP is intended to give an estimation of the long-term relationships between currencies, interest rate parity theory can give a more immediate perspective. Interest rate parity links short-term interest rates with spot exchange rates and forward exchange rates, and is illustrated in Example 16.3.

This says that the relationship between spot and forward exchange rates is driven by the relationship between interest rates in any two currency regimes, so that there is no profit to be derived by borrowing in one currency and

EXAMPLE 16.3 *Interest rate parity: calculating the forward exchange rate*

Spot Exchange Rate GBP/USD	£0.6500
GBP 90-day Interest	6.50%
USD 90-day Interest	5.00%
Time to Expiry in Days	90
90-day Forward Rate GBP/USD	£0.6524

90-day Forward Rate GBP/USD = £0.6500 × (1 + 0.065 × 90/365)/(1 + 0.050 × 90/365)
= £0.6524

EXAMPLE 16.4 *Long-term exchange rate trends*

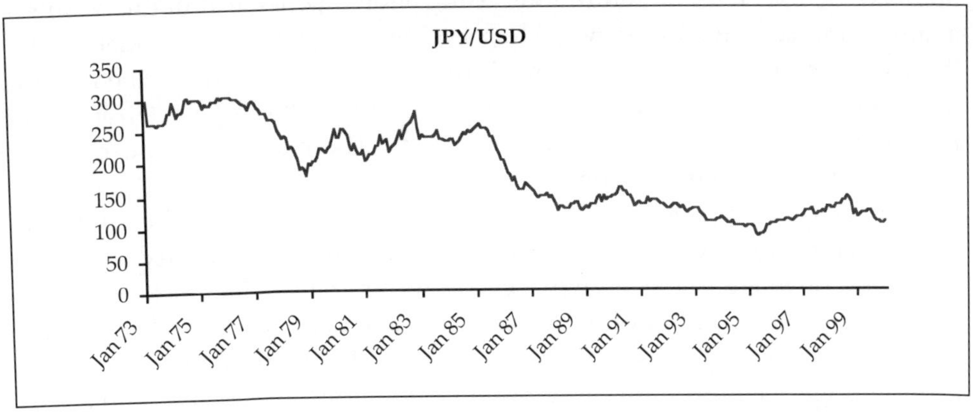

lending in another, unless the investor is prepared to assume the risk of a currency movement.

Interest rate parity theory is good at describing the here and now, but has limited application as a means of forecasting exchange rates, unless of course the investor has some reliable means of forecasting domestic and international interest rates.

It is often believed that exchange rates are driven by some long-term equilibrium, and that, despite frequently diverging from this, they will eventually converge to this 'natural' level. This is often known as mean reversion. Investors sometimes rely on this principle to justify adopting a 'passive', or currency neutral approach to currency management, buying enough foreign currency to fund asset purchases, then leaving the currency exposure to fluctuate according to currency movements on the assumption that, in the medium term, currency gains and losses will cancel each other out. The problem is, of course, that exchange rates often fail to mean revert, as Example 16.4 shows.

APPROACHES TO ACTIVE CURRENCY MANAGEMENT

Many investment managers devote considerable resources to analysing the health of whole economies in efforts to estimate the fair value of exchange rates. This is a sound approach, but it is very difficult to achieve meaningful results because of the complexity of the task. The advantages of building and applying models to forecast exchange rates is that they force investors and analysts to specify and quantify the factors that can influence exchange rate movements, and the relationships between them. This can help to ensure a consistent approach across all sector return forecasting efforts, which can in turn result in a strong and cohesive investment strategy. The danger of such models is that there is a temptation to place too much confidence in the output. The input to the models is usually diverse, complex and error prone; so few if any such models produce consistently reliable forecasts. The results need to be interpreted with appropriate caution.

Another approach is to abandon exchange rate forecasts altogether and focus on managing currency risk instead, buying enough foreign currency to support purchases of foreign assets, giving currency neutrality. The trick is then to closely monitor economic events, interest rates and derivatives markets to try to identify early signs of unusual currency volatility. When this occurs, the investment manager hedges all or part of the foreign currency exposure in the portfolio, usually using some kind of bought option position, so that the portfolio retains the possibility of positive currency returns. This approach is better than none at all, and can be effective if the investment manager is skilled at reading warning signs of impending currency volatility and he or she does not have access to an investment manager skilled in forecasting currency returns. Its weaknesses are that misinterpreting the vital early warning signs can result in the unnecessary purchase of options, with the consequent option premium imposing a drag on returns. Alternatively, failing to put in place the required hedge leaves the portfolio subject to volatility from its foreign currency exposure for which it is not earning any additional returns.

Because currency returns tend to have low correlations with other asset returns, effective currency management can add significantly to overall portfolio returns and reduce overall portfolio volatility at the same time. This low correlation with other asset classes can constitute a strong argument for treating foreign currency exposure as a separate asset class within the portfolio. Currencies are different from all other asset classes in two important respects:

- With other assets, the investor substitutes exposure in a risky asset for exposure in the riskless asset. In other words, cash is exchanged for some other, more risky asset. With currencies, one currency is exchanged for another, so buying one currency requires selling an equal amount of another.
- Currency markets are a zero sum game, meaning that the gains to one investor are equal to the losses to others. By contrast, other asset classes such as equity deliver net positive or negative gains over time.

For all other assets and derivatives, most portfolios limit the portfolio's exposure to some multiple of the funds invested in it. For example, most mutual fund, unit trust and pension portfolios are not allowed to invest more than 100% of investors' funds. Because every bought currency position is offset by an equal sold position, the net currency position is always zero. Therefore, in theory, potential gross currency exposure is unlimited. Of course, this would change very quickly, as currency volatility caused gains and losses to mount up, but it illustrates the importance of defining limits.

What limits to impose on active currency management depend on the overall appetite for risk in the portfolio, as well as how much and what kind of currency risk exists in other asset classes in the portfolio, and the correlations between currencies and the other assets.

Currency management can be undertaken as part of the management of another asset class, such as international equities or fixed interest, or it can be managed as a separate asset class with its own benchmark. For the latter, many investors seek the services of specialist currency overlay managers. This can incur slightly higher management fees, but can earn extra return for the portfolio.

DEFINING THE CURRENCY MANAGEMENT MANDATE

The first step is to define the benchmark. Theoretically, this can be a zero return, since overall currency markets are a zero sum game, but in practice most benchmarks are expressed as a positive rate of return, to cover management fees and other expenses. Which currencies can be traded should also be specified. This can be a very interesting question because, while currency returns tend to have low correlations with other asset classes, they can have quite high correlations with each other. At the same time, two currencies that are highly correlated with each other may be quite different in other respects, such as their **liquidity** and the availability of derivative instruments. For example, the Danish krone is very highly correlated with the euro, but the euro is much more liquid than the krone. Other things being equal, the investor benefits from as wide as possible a range of investment opportunities; but illiquidity can introduce risk to the portfolio for which there is no compensating return. Ideally, the range of currencies to be traded should take into account the foreign currency risk already in the portfolio through its holdings in other assets, allowing as much diversification as possible, subject to limits on liquidity. Target levels of risk and return need to be established, usually based on forecasts of return and risk. Risk forecasts are usually expressed as tracking error or probability-weighted ranges of expected return, and these are calculated using forecast returns and covariances for individual currency pairs.

IMPLEMENTATION

The foreign currency portfolio is implemented using a mixture of spot and forward currencies, possibly including options and futures contracts. If the investment mandate includes the management of physical assets, foreign currency cash is then invested in each currency zone, according to the mandate. Most specialist currency managers confine themselves to very low-risk instruments, although extra returns can be earned by assuming credit risk. Credit risk can be added to enhance returns by replacing short-term government or bank-backed instruments with bonds of slightly less credit quality. To exploit such opportunities, the investor should specify the permitted amount of credit risk for the portfolio.

Spot currencies (currency transactions to be settled within two business days), currency forwards (currency transactions to be settled more than two business days hence) and swaps are all traded by telephone, while currency futures and options are traded on futures exchanges in the same way as other futures contracts. The telephone market is augmented by a network of screens provided by Reuters, Bloomberg and other providers, where foreign exchange brokers can display indicative buy and sell prices for selected transactions. Large banks dominate the foreign currency market, trading both as principal (risking their shareholders' money) and brokers for other investors, importers, exporters and other buyers and sellers of foreign exchange. The volume of foreign currency traded each day sometimes astonishes because it is several times the value of traded goods and investment flows worldwide. This volume of transactions and the number of participants in the market usually means that the difference between a buy and a sell price is extremely small, particularly for large transactions. For example, a US dollar to euro rate might be quoted as selling at 1.0573 and buying at 1.0578, a difference of about 0.04% for a transaction of USD5 million.

To execute a foreign currency transaction by telephone, the investment manager first checks some market information system for indicative prices on transactions similar to the one to be implemented. He or she then rings a number of brokers and asks for indicative prices for the required transaction, specifying the currency to be bought, the currency to be sold, the settlement date and the approximate volume. The brokers quote prices that they may hold 'firm' for a specified period of time, usually two to three minutes, depending on the currencies, giving the investment manager time to compare prices and ring back to confirm the transaction. After the specified time interval, the same broker may quote a price that is quite different. The price quoted by the broker, while always consistent with prevailing market prices, is also influenced by what the bank is holding as principal. For example, if the bank holds more

Japanese yen than it wants, and someone rings up to buy yen, the bank will quote a keener price than if the request is to sell yen.

When the price has been agreed, the investment manager enters the information into some sort of deal register, either by filling in a slip of paper to be given to an administrative assistant, who then enters it into a computer system, or it might be entered directly by the investment manager into the firm's computer system. The broker sends the confirmation of the transaction to the investment manager and the custodian before the end of the day by either fax or email.

USE OF DERIVATIVES

Whether managed as an overlay or as part of another asset class, foreign currency portfolios nearly always make extensive use of derivatives. These may be simple forward transactions, or they may be more complex options and swaps. If managed as an overlay portfolio with a specified benchmark or target return, the investment manager may need also to use interest rate derivatives, such as futures and swaps based on short-term instruments, depending on the objectives set out in the mandate.

In addition to using a range of derivatives for day-to-day management of currency exposures, the investment manager may use futures and options to effect short-term changes to the overall position. This may be to participate in perceived short-term changes in forecast return trends, or simply to exploit some short-term price anomaly.

ONGOING MANAGEMENT

Nearly all foreign currency portfolios require close scrutiny of world economic events and trends in the currency markets to try to pick up early signs of significant price fluctuations, or events that may precipitate such fluctuations. When such events occur, the investor must decide if a rethink of the currency strategy is warranted or if some fine-tuning will do the trick.

Well-designed decision rules can be very helpful for managing foreign currency exposure. For example, the investment manager may forecast a 'band' within which a pair of currencies is expected to trade. A rule can then be set that a deviation of more than, say, 10% from either the upper or lower bound should trigger a review of tactics or some prescribed transaction, such as reversing half the position. Alternatively, regular reviews may be carried out to review tactics, or some combination can apply. When well thought out and applied with sufficient discipline, such rules can pre-empt the worst consequences of unforeseen exchange rate fluctuations.

The currency overlay manager is required to adjust the portfolio in response to changes in other portfolio holdings. For example, if there is a rebalancing of the underlying portfolio from one asset class to another, there will almost certainly be a concurrent rebalancing of the currency overlay. Similarly, the portfolio will need to be adjusted in response to external cash flows to and from the portfolio.

Currency forwards and other derivatives positions need to be rolled over from one delivery to the next. This is routine, and is usually delegated to trainee or junior dealers who keep a diary of impending rebalances, and in some cases implement them. Where short-term assets are held in foreign currencies, the currency manager may be responsible for ensuring that these funds are always invested appropriately.

ADMINISTRATION

Administration of currency portfolios starts with confirming the foreign exchange transaction. This is a document sent by the broker to the investment manager, usually with a copy sent to the custodian. The investment manager confirms the details of the transaction and it is entered in the firm's computer system for later reconciliation. The transaction exists only as a ledger entry with the bank/broker, the investment manager and the custodian. There are no share certificates or share registries to be transferred or amended, so administration is relatively simple.

Most foreign exchange settlements occur daily, using a system of net settlement. This means that, once the settlement date is given, the transaction will be finalized by a certain time, such as eleven o'clock in the morning, on that day. To ensure that this happens, nearly all 'spot' transactions are arranged for settlement in two days, also known as **t plus two**. This gives custodians, banks and other parties time to arrange the necessary funds transfers. Transfers between banks and other financial institutions are added up, with purchases and sales cancelling each other out, so that the amounts actually transferred are the net amounts owed by respective institutions. Daily settlement works nearly all the time, but glitches have been known to occur when a bank becomes insolvent in between settling one side of a transaction in one time zone and the other side in another time zone. This is called **Herstatt risk**, after the small German bank that demonstrated how it was done. To try to eliminate Herstatt risk, some countries are in the process of introducing the practice of real-time settlement. The argument is that most funds transfers are now arranged electronically, with very little paper to be prepared and transferred, so that the objective of settling foreign exchange transactions immediately is achievable. By reducing the time between transaction and settlement, a good deal of the risk of these transactions can be eliminated. In particular, it reduces the risk that an institution may fail to settle; an event that could, with a large enough sum involved, bring about a domino effect among banks. The shortcoming of real-time settlement is that all settlements need to be arranged in gross amounts, as the ability to net out transactions on a daily basis disappears.

Errors occur often enough in foreign exchange transactions, which is unsurprising in such fast-moving markets, but they tend to be detected quite soon, partly because individual transactions are usually large relative to the net amount traded, so the discrepancies generated during foreign exchange transactions become obvious at a relatively early stage.

VALUATION

The value of a foreign currency transaction is simply its profit and loss, usually expressed in terms of the base currency of the portfolio.

This sounds too simple, and it is. Foreign exchange markets are different from other financial markets in another important respect: they never close. While there is often talk in derivatives and stock markets about establishing global markets with continuous trading and settlement, foreign exchange markets have operated around the clock for years. In a market that never closes, there is no closing price. So the question becomes: What exchange rate should be used to value the transaction? The most popular convention is to value foreign exchange transactions using the exchange rates prevailing at **16.00 GMT**. A survey is conducted at that hour of buy and sell prices, which are then used to estimate some central reference price for each pair of currencies, which is then published widely.

There are a number to benefits of having one standard set of exchange rates for valuation purposes. The obvious one is that it is much less confusing to everybody, including the investor. Another is that, with many participants all valuing different positions, it is difficult for one group of participants to manipulate prices. By contrast, a **reference price** that is used only by a small group could be easily manipulated. Although the 16.00 GMT convention is widely used for portfolio and benchmark valuations, it is by no means universal, and investment managers may choose some other means to value foreign exchange transactions. Given the extreme volatility of foreign exchange markets, a small difference in time can translate into a significant difference in portfolio valuation.

PERFORMANCE MEASUREMENT AND ATTRIBUTION

With valuations consisting of profits and losses on foreign exchange transactions, return measurement for currency portfolios is not too difficult. If the currency component of the portfolio is managed as an overlay, then return measurement and attribution are carried out virtually automatically. If currency is managed as part of portfolio asset classes or as part of a balanced portfolio, then some sifting may be necessary to identify what component of portfolio return is due to currency effects and what is due to other assets.

In Example 16.5, the asset returned 5% in local currency, but because this currency declined by 4.55% against the portfolio's base currency, the net, unhedged benefit of holding the asset was 0.23%. To hedge the foreign currency exposure, the investor effectively sells forward currency at the same time as buying it, obtaining an exchange rate based on the interest rate differential. The forward rate was 1.1262, giving a return to the hedge of 2.38% (1.1262 ÷ 1.1000 – 1) and an overall portfolio hedged return of 2.61% (1.0023 × 1.0238 – 1). The cost of hedging, which is a function of the interest rate differential, is embedded in the forward exchange rate.

EXAMPLE 16.5 *Single period return in local and base currency: hedged*

	Start of period	End of period	Return in local currency %	Return in base currency %	Hedged return %
Asset Price	$100.00	$105.00	5.00	0.23	2.61
Exchange Rate	1.1000	1.0500	–4.55		
Interest Rate Local Currency	7.50%				
Interest Rate Base Currency	5.00%				
Forward Exchange Rate		1.1262	2.38		

PITFALLS

Probably the worst mistake to make with respect to foreign exchange exposure in an investment portfolio is to underestimate the potential impact of currency fluctuations on total portfolio outcome. This is easily done, especially where allocation to foreign assets is a minor component of the portfolio. Even for a portfolio carefully matched to its benchmark, there will be some foreign currency exposure in absolute terms, if not relative to the benchmark.

Any unrecognized or unintentional exposure can subject the portfolio to additional return volatility that is not compensated for by extra expected return.

The models developed to assist forecast currency returns tend to be extremely complex, requiring dozens if not hundreds of data items as input. With such impressive tools to work with, many investment managers are tempted to regard the results thus obtained as unimpeachable. This is a mistake. Complicated as the models are, they are invariably a simplification of the real world. Even if they were not, the real world has a habit of changing without telling the models or their creators. So even with impeccable input, the output from currency models needs to be treated with care. Add to this the probability that at least some of the data input to the model are inaccurate or fuzzy, and the results can require quite a bit of interpretation. This is not to say that currency modelling is a hopeless task. Models force analysts to refine and quantify their assumptions, ensure they are consistent with each other, and even to assign confidence estimates to them. Clearly articulated and quantified assumptions facilitate ongoing scrutiny, helping to ensure consistency of approach. In a notoriously complex sector, this discipline can yield enormous benefits.

The other main danger is lack of discipline. Currency markets defy analysis, and there is a temptation to take positions and to trade by instinct, following what appear to be market trends. This is akin to following a crowd without first asking where it is going. This can lead to disappointing results, and it can be particularly difficult to learn from the experience.

PITFALLS

[illegible] compatible graphical output [illegible] curves [illegible]

[illegible]

PART III

Peripherals

CHAPTER 17

Implementation of Equity Portfolios

THE TRADITIONAL APPROACH

Equity portfolios are implemented using the services of a stockbroker to seek the best price possible for each individual portfolio holding, subject to guidelines given by the investment manager. The objective is to effect the required purchases and/or sales as quickly as possible, while incurring the lowest possible cost.

Nearly all equity transactions are carried out on a stock market. There are a number of different trading systems, which can influence the type and amount of information available to the investment manager. Some stock markets still have trading floors, where stockbrokers send their representatives to deal personally with each other under the supervision of a representative of the stock market. Other markets have computerized trading, whereby stockbrokers remain in their offices, and access the market through a computer terminal. The former is definitely more theatrical than the latter, but evidence is emerging that the latter is more cost effective and it seems reasonable to suppose that it is more efficient at least for recording information about individual bids, offers and transactions, if not also for reducing transaction costs.

In addition to physical trading floor versus electronic exchanges, there is the distinction between **order-driven** and **quote-driven** exchanges. Both can operate in either the physical or electronic environment. Order-driven exchanges start with buy and sell orders initiated by investors. When a buyer and seller are willing to trade at the same price, a transaction occurs. As long as buyers are informed, either directly or through their broker, about the price at which sellers are prepared to sell, and vice versa, they will adjust their price as necessary to secure transactions. The role of the broker is to provide information to the investor about prices and quantities available, to help the investor to decide what price is achievable for a given quantity of stock. It sometimes happens, in order-driven systems, that some stocks have no buyers and sellers, in which case the broker may solicit other investors, or the investor may prefer to wait until a natural buyer or seller appears.

Quote-driven systems rely on market makers. **Market makers** are principal traders appointed by the exchange who use their own funds to buy and sell stock, usually specializing in a small number of stocks, with sometimes several market makers for a given stock. The obligation of a market maker is to ensure that there is always both a buy and a sell price for each of the stocks to which he or she is allocated. Most exchanges using this system stipulate that the difference between the market maker's buy and sell prices should not exceed a specified amount, and oblige market makers to deal a specified minimum quantity at both their buy and sell prices. Investors are not obliged to deal with market makers; if other buyers and sellers are available they are free to do business with them, and most do because other investors are usually prepared to deal in larger quantities, while market makers usually confine themselves to small parcels of stock.

With either system, the investor typically rings or emails a broker to instruct him or her to buy a certain quantity of stock at a given price. If the quantity is available at the specified price, the order can be quickly completed and reported to the investor. In volatile markets, the investment manager usually allows the broker some discretion to avoid the costs of failing to transact if prices move beyond the limits specified. If the investor is more concerned about completing the order quickly, then he or she will instruct the broker to 'buy at market'. It is up to the broker to achieve the best price possible within a short space of time.

When the transaction is completed, the broker reports it to the investor, either by telephone or email. A written confirmation is prepared at the end of the day and despatched by the broker to the investor and the stock exchange. Settlement takes place some time later. Most stock exchanges now insist on a fixed settlement period, which may be one, two, five or ten business days. This is when the seller of shares must deliver share certificates or other documentary evidence of ownership and the buyer must pay for them. Sometime later, if the shares are registered, the new owner of the shares receives from the company share registry share certificates or other documents proving ownership. If the shares are bearer instruments, the share certificates are transferred at the time of settlement.

The costs associated with a simple transaction can be itemized as follows:

- taxes
- commissions
- bid–ask spread

- market impact
- opportunity cost.

The first of these are usually known or can be accurately estimated in advance. Stockbrokers levy commissions usually as a percentage of the value of the transaction, but sometimes as a fixed price per share. For example, the commission might be 0.30% of the value of the trade, or $0.15 per share, for a stock trading at $50.00, which amounts to the same rate. The rate levied usually varies according to the value of the transaction, with large transactions attracting lower rates of commission. Some stock exchanges set a fixed scale of commissions, but the overall trend is towards deregulation, whereby the rate of commission is negotiated between the investor and the broker. This trend has encouraged growth in the market for discount brokers. **Discount brokers** offer a basic service, and often quote a fixed fee for a transaction, say $65, regardless of the number or value of the shares to be traded.

During the transition from regulated to deregulated commissions, informal arrangements may be agreed between investor and broker whereby the regulated commission is levied at the time of the transaction, with a subsequent, negotiated rebate.

The bid–ask spread is the difference in the prices quoted to buy and sell stock, either by market makers or by other investors. The amount of the bid–ask spread is affected by how liquid the shares are, with frequently traded shares having the smallest bid–ask spread. Liquidity is in turn largely determined by the number of shares on issue and available for regular sale and purchase, also known as the 'free float'. Free float excludes shares that are not traded because associate companies own them, or because they are otherwise controlled by a dominant shareholder.

Market impact can be thought of as the cost of transacting each additional share. For example, consider the buyer of one share; he or she will accept the offer price, which will probably remain unchanged after the transaction. If the same investor buys 1000 of the same shares the price may move slightly after the trade is complete, as each marginal seller in turn has completed his or her order, eliminating the most aggressive sellers and leaving only sellers at higher prices. A buyer of one million of the same shares may find that the sale price (and possibly the bid price) moves even before the trade is complete as other market participants read the signal that demand for the stock, and therefore perhaps its implicit value, has increased.

Opportunity cost applies to active investment managers who can alter the timing of their transactions. It is the cost incurred when an investor sets out to trade a stock at a certain price and fails to complete the trade because the stock price moves beyond the limit set. He or she is then obliged to increase the bid or lower the offer price. If the modification is not enough, which can easily happen in a volatile market, this process can be repeated several times before the transaction is completed, with the result that the average price transacted is less attractive than the initial price. Quite often the investor will decide to abandon the transaction, only to see the stock price continue in the same direction, further exaggerating the opportunity cost.

Simple transactions can therefore be both risky and costly. The problem becomes acute when the investment manager needs to conduct several dozen, or even hundreds of transactions, at the same time. To avoid such problems, many investment managers conduct basket trades.

BASKET TRADING

What it is

Execution cost and risk can be controlled by executing a basket or **block trade**, which is the practice of buying or selling a large number of stocks all at once. Typically, a 'basket' consists of many small parcels of stock. The benefit to the investor is that an entire portfolio can be implemented instantly, enabling it to start earning the anticipated returns straightaway. It effectively transfers the execution risk from the investor to the stockbroker implementing the transaction. It can also reduce the likelihood of dealing errors and can partially streamline the consequent paper trail. The attractiveness of this strategy depends, of course, on how much it costs. This will in turn depend on:

- which stocks are to be traded and in what proportions
- how liquid the market is at the time of the trade
- the willingness of brokers to execute the trade.

How it works

Basket trades rely on the broker using his or her own capital to buy the required basket of shares from the investor for subsequent resale on market. In principle, the price bid by the broker reflects both the price, including any taxes, at which he or she can buy or sell each stock, either in the market or against existing client orders, and some charge to compensate for the risk of taking principal positions in the stocks. How much the broker charges for this depends on how long the broker expects to hold the position, interest rates and other funding costs, and hedging costs. Other things being equal, a basket of stock that is easy to either trade or hedge will attract a smaller principal charge than one that is more difficult to trade or hedge. For example, if the basket of stock resembles a traded share price index futures contract, the broker's principal position is easy to hedge, and the holding charges should reflect this.

There are a number of ways of presenting a basket trade to brokers to solicit quotes. The most straightforward is to compile the basket to be traded and send this by fax or email to two or more competing brokers for quotes. Usually the investment manager demands a response at a particular time, say within 15 minutes, giving the brokers time to analyse the trade and prepare their bid. The problem with this is that, since only one broker will ultimately execute the trade, information about their principal position becomes known by one or more of their competitors. In a small market, with a strong etiquette in the market between brokers engaging in this specialist business, this is rarely a problem, as any misbehaviour by the unsuccessful bidder can carry high costs by way of foregone future business. If no such etiquette exists, or the market is large enough to camouflage misbehaviour, then the investment manager must seek other ways to present the trade.

One way is to describe the characteristics of the basket to competing brokers without disclosing its contents. The investment manager might describe the basket in terms of approximate value, beta and tracking error to a well-known share price index, number of stocks, how many of which are top 50 or top 100, any particular industry that is overrepresented relative to an index and so on. The broker then estimates some range of costs for possible baskets fitting the description, and comes up with a bid price. Not knowing the precise composition of the basket increases the risks to the broker and a further margin is generally added to compensate for this. There is also the risk that the investor's description of the portfolio is inaccurate, so the bid may include some extra margin for this.

There are plenty of variations on this arrangement, for example a guarantee from the broker that the transaction will be executed at the closing price of the day for each stock, or the average traded price. Which one is most appropriate depends on the particular objectives of the investment manager, and the conventions of the market in which the transaction is taking place.

Pitfalls

There are plenty of things that can go wrong with a basket trade, but most of these will affect the broker much more than the investment manager. From the investment manager's point of view, probably the worst thing that can happen is that one of the competing brokers fails to present a competitive bid on time. If there are only two brokers competing, this may oblige the investment manager to accept the price offered by the other broker, whether or not it is attractive.

Another potential problem arises for investment managers engaging in both traditional and quantitative investment management with centralized dealing. Dealers responsible for traditional implementation as well as basket trading may face a conflict of interest, whereby they can be tempted to buy, on behalf of a traditional portfolio, securities that they know must soon be purchased in quantity by a quantitative portfolio engaging in a basket trade. This directs a short-term trading profit to the traditional portfolio at an unknown cost to the quantitative portfolio. Insider trading and compliance rules have ruled out dealers deriving personal gain from this practice, known as 'front running', but a dealer or investment manager who is remunerated according to return targets might find front running on behalf of client portfolios lucrative too. The cost is borne by the quantitative investor whose impending share transaction stimulated the front running.

STOCK BORROWING AND LENDING

What it is

Most stock exchanges impose strict rules to ensure timely completion of transactions. Central to this process is the transfer from seller to buyer of share certificates or some equivalent proof of ownership. For investors wishing to sell short (sell shares they do not already own), for example as part of a long–short or market neutral strategy, or to offset a derivatives transaction, this can present a problem. The solution can be to borrow the share certificates from some long-term investor who has no immediate need for them. For the long-term investor, lending out share certificates can be a very attractive way of enhancing portfolio returns.

How it works

Stock lending is usually arranged through an intermediary, who draws up the contract, ensures availability of the share certificates, investigates the creditworthiness of the borrower and arranges appropriate margin calls. Often, the intermediary is also the custodian of the lender. This is logical, since the custodian has the best access to records of stock holdings and appropriate administrative resources, and so is in a position to make most stock available. Of course, this should always be done with the prior consent of the investor, who ultimately bears the risk of the share certificates not being available when they are required. For this reason, the investor should receive the bulk of the rental from the share certificates, with the intermediary receiving a commission for providing the service.

The borrower borrows stock from the lender at a notional value per share, usually the prevailing market price, later returning the shares to the lender at the same notional price. In the meantime, the borrower pays to the lender a rental for the shares, with the long-term investor retaining the risk of the share price rising or falling.

Details of loan contracts can vary. For example, the term may be fixed or flexible. The lender may require collateral at the beginning of the contract, or margin calls to match fluctuations in the stock's price during the term of the loan, or indeed both. The rental charged usually depends on prevailing interest rates, but also reflects the scarcity value of the stock in question as well as the credit quality of the borrower. The rental can be fixed or variable.

Entitlement to any dividends can either be transferred to the borrower or rest with the lender. The importance of this is that the objective of lending or borrowing the stock is sometimes to maximize dividend tax credits. For example, if the long-term investor is an offshore investor, with limited entitlement to the tax credits that go with dividends, he or she can, for a fee, pass the dividend entitlement to a local investor who can make full use of them, thus benefiting both investors. In this case, the loan contract stipulates that the borrower receives the dividends, and the price at which the shares are paid back is adjusted to reflect this, with the fee allowing the long-term investor to derive some of the dividend tax benefits that would otherwise be forfeited. The same objective can be achieved by means of an asset swap, as describe in Appendix 4.

Pitfalls

From the stock lender's point of view, the biggest risk is that the borrower is unable to return the share certificates. If this happens at the same time that the lender is, for some reason, obliged to sell the shares, then both parties could find themselves panic buying shares to cover the shortfall. This is unlikely because most loan agreements provide for enough collateral to cover the value of the shares at all times during the term of the loan. Therefore, the long-term investor would already have access to liquid assets to at least the value of the shares, and in any case the simplest solution would be to borrow the shares from someone else to fill the gap.

The borrower is often in a more risky position, because he or she often has borrowed the shares to sell them in the market, anticipating a decline in price, either in absolute terms, or relative to some other asset or derivative. If the analysis underlying the transaction is faulty, or if the share price rises sharply, the borrower may be forced to buy the shares back at a significant loss. At the same time, he or she may be obliged to meet margin payments against the borrowed stock. If unable to meet the margin calls, the borrower may be forced to liquidate the position, incurring further losses.

SOFT DOLLARS

What it is

Soft dollars are a sort of broker–investment manager loyalty scheme. Investment managers use many resources to help them to make investment decisions and for ongoing management, including online data and research services and software to analyse transactions and portfolios. To implement portfolios, there are computer screens showing current bid and ask prices for assets, derivatives and currencies all around the world. These services are very expensive.

At the same time as requiring many data and analysis tools, investment managers use the services of brokers to buy and sell equities, bonds, foreign exchange and derivatives. Brokers compete fiercely for the business of large institutional investors. This business is very valuable to them for a number of reasons. First, they deal in large quantities. Because most commissions are levied as a percentage of the value of the transaction, and the cost to the broker is the same for a large transaction as for a small one, large deals are more lucrative. Second, the prominence and profitability of brokers within a market are interactive. As a rule, a prominent broker attracts more business than a merely profitable one, so brokers are keen to increase their market share, particularly with the largest investment managers.

To attract business, brokers conduct research into share prices, which they offer to their investing clients as part of their overall service. This service is designed to encourage investment managers to use their broking services, but generally does not carry any obligation to do so. Similarly, many brokers offer to sponsor individual investment managers on seminars, conferences and research tours, sometimes in attractive locations, to further their understanding of securities and markets. This may persuade the investment manager to increase the amount by which he or she uses the services of that particular broker, but rarely carries any form of obligation to do so. In an attempt to ensure more business, many brokers offer to pay for some of the data and analytic services required by investment managers in return for a specified amount of business.

How it works

The arrangement itself is very simple. The investment manager asks the data or service provider to send invoices for a service period to the broker, who pays the invoice and advises the investment manager that this has been done. The investment manager agrees, over the service period, to transact a certain quantity of share purchases and sales with that broker. The quantity can be defined as a fixed value of transaction, say a thousand times the value of the service paid for, although more often it is defined as a fixed amount of commissions, say five times the value of the service paid for. Sometimes it is defined as a percentage of the total transactions for that investment manger, benefiting a broker who is keen to increase market share.

It is not too difficult to estimate the implied value of the arrangement to the broker. For example, if the amount of commission required is five times the value of the service paid for, then the average profit margin for the broker from that investment manager is probably at least 20%.

It rarely happens that the investment manager fails to deliver the required amount of transactions or commissions but, if this were to happen, the broker would either add the shortfall to the arrangement for the following service period or demand some kind of pro-rata reimbursement of the service paid for. The important difference between soft dollar agreements and other ancillary services rendered by brokers to investment managers is that, unlike the latter, the soft dollar agreement carries an obligation by the investment manager to transact with that broker.

Pitfalls

The most obvious pitfall is that, in order to comply with the terms of the soft dollar agreement, the investment manager may transact more than is in the interests of the investor, thus incurring unnecessary transaction costs on behalf of the investor. Alternatively, the investment manager may pay less attention to the competitiveness of the broking service provided by the broker, knowing that he or she is obliged to transact with them anyway. Concurrently, the broker, knowing that the investment manager is obliged to transact with him or her, may pay less attention to the quality of the execution of trades and other services it provides. Either way, there is a cost, albeit virtually impossible to quantify, that is ultimately borne by the investor.

Data and analytic services used by investment managers are a legitimate cost to the business of providing investment management services. Soft dollar agreements effectively transfer this cost from the investment manager's profit and loss account to that of the investor, often with little or no compensation.

DIRECTED COMMISSIONS

What it is

Nearly all brokerage houses are part of large organizations, such as banks and consultancies. Many of these organizations have business dealings with companies and investors who use the services of investment managers. Always looking for new ways to increase the amount of business enjoyed by their broking arms, these organizations sometimes enter into agreements with investors whereby the investor earns a discount on the fees for their services in exchange for an undertaking to direct transactions associated with their investments to nominated brokers.

How it works

The agreement between the investor and his or her service provider can provide for a discount or refund of the fees for its service, calculated as a percentage of commission directed to nominated brokers. The investor is not usually in a position to stipulate a minimum volume of transactions, an amount of commission or a percentage of total turnover, because the investment manager has direct control over these items. But the investor can influence these decisions by instructing the investment manager either to favour the nominated broker, or to direct a certain amount or percentage of total transactions to that broker. The investment manager may or may not be aware of the value of the discounts enjoyed by the investor for complying with the agreement.

Because directed commissions work as a discount or rebate after the transactions are completed, they do not represent a direct obligation on the part of the investment manager, who can still exercise discretion in choosing brokers. But few investment managers are prepared to blatantly refuse to comply with their client's instructions, except in the most extreme circumstances.

Pitfalls

If the nominated brokers happen to be those with whom the investment manager normally deals regularly, this arrangement can work quite well. If the investment manager does not usually deal with the nominated broker, for example because the services provided by the broker are not suitable to the investor's requirements, the investor suffers inappropriate service.

In either case, the broker, knowing that the investment manager is either obliged, or very likely, to transact with him or her, is likely to pay less attention to the quality of execution and other services. This will have a real, if unquantifiable, cost to the investor, which may well be greater than the discounts generated by the agreement.

CHAPTER 18

Performance Measurement and Attribution

Accurate measurement of portfolio return is very important to the overall investment management process. Apart from knowing how well or otherwise the portfolio is doing, it can help the investor and investment manager to decide whether or not the investment strategy is working. Sometimes, the portfolio's return is the basis on which the investment manager is remunerated. But possibly the most important function of measuring and analysing portfolio return is to help investors to compare investment managers and strategies.

SINGLE PERIOD RETURN MEASUREMENT

Measuring the return of a portfolio should be straightforward, and to an extent it is. For a simple, single period with no external cash flows, it is calculated as:

$$Rp = PV_t / PV_{t-1} - 1 \qquad (18.1)$$

Where:

Rp = portfolio return
PV_t = portfolio value at the end of the period
PV_{t-1} = portfolio value at the start of the period

The return of the benchmark, if there is one, is calculated in exactly the same way, and the return variation is usually given as the difference, also known as the arithmetic variation:

$$Va = Rp - Rb \qquad (18.2)$$

Where:

Va = arithmetic variation
Rb = benchmark return

Although it can sometimes be given as the geometric variation:

$$Vg = (1 + Rp)/(1 + Rb) - 1 \qquad (18.3)$$

Where:

Vg = geometric variation

In most cases the difference in results given by the two formulae are so small as to be immaterial.

With such a simple formula, there is little room for ambiguity in comparing investments over a single period. Ambiguity can arise with differences between investments regarding the investment period and valuation. For example:

- Investments can have different start and end dates. The most popular pricing policy is to use the last day in the period being measured, typically the last day of the month. Some investment managers choose to value their portfolios two or three days before month-end, giving a result that is not comparable with returns based on month-end valuations.
- Different pricing policies can be applied in valuations. Most valuations use official closing prices supplied by the exchange, although some portfolios are valued using the average price for the day.
- There are a number of different ways of pricing foreign currencies.

These apparently small differences in pricing policy can give surprisingly large differences in results, so it is a good idea, when comparing return data, to ensure that similar policies are employed.

Return calculations become potentially even fuzzier when complicated by external cash flows to the portfolio. For example, suppose a portfolio has a value of $10 000 000 at the start of the month. Sometime during the month, a further \$2 500 000 is invested in it. At the end of the month, the portfolio is valued at \$15 000 000. The benchmark returned 8% for the period. There are at least four ways of calculating the portfolio's return for the month (see Example 18.1).

The simplest approach is to pretend the cash arrived at the start of the period:

$$Rp = PV_t / (PV_{t-1} + cf) - 1 \tag{18.4}$$

Where:

cf = amount of cash flow

Giving the result:

$$\begin{aligned} Rp &= \$15\,000\,000 / (\$10\,000\,000 + \$2\,500\,000) - 1 \\ &= 20\% \end{aligned}$$

Alternatively, the investor can assume the cash flow arrived at the end of the period:

$$Rp = (PV_t - cf) / PV_{t-1} - 1 \tag{18.5}$$

Giving the result:

$$\begin{aligned} Rp &= (\$15\,000\,000 - \$2\,500\,000) / \$10\,000\,000 - 1 \\ &= 25\% \end{aligned}$$

The arbitrariness of these two is a bit annoying, so one could try allocating the cash flow half at the start and half at the end:

$$Rp = (PV_t - cf/2) / (PV_{t-1} + cf/2) - 1 \tag{18.6}$$

Giving the result:

$$\begin{aligned} Rp &= (\$15\,000\,000 - \$1\,250\,000) / (\$10\,000\,000 + \$1\,250\,000) - 1 \\ &= 22.22\% \end{aligned}$$

Knowing that the cash flow arrived on the tenth day of a 30-day month can lend further precision:

$$Rp = (PV_t - cf \times 20/30) / (PV_{t-1} + cf \times 10/30) - 1 \tag{18.7}$$

Giving the result:

$$Rp = (\$15\ 000\ 000 - \$1\ 666\ 667)/(\$10\ 000\ 000 + \$833\ 333) - 1 = 21.43\%$$

Dividing the return period into two, according to when the cash flow occurred, then compounding the two returns to give the overall return for the period, often referred to as money-weighted cash flows, achieves a more precise calculation still:

$$Rp = (PV_t/PV_{cf} + cf) \times (PV_{cf}/PV_{t-1}) - 1 \qquad (18.8)$$

Where:

PV_{cf} = portfolio value immediately prior to the cash flow

Giving the result:

$$Rp = (\$15\ 000\ 000/(\$12\ 000\ 000 + \$2\ 500\ 000)) \times (\$12\ 000\ 000/\$10\ 000\ 000) - 1 = 24.14\%$$

The methodology for calculating return must be agreed between the investor and the investment manager, usually to suit the investor's particular requirements, bearing in mind that the return calculations for a fund issuing units to the public need to facilitate comparisons with other funds.

EXAMPLE 18.1 *Single period portfolio return with cash flow*

Portfolio value at start of period	\$10 000 000
Portfolio value end of period	\$15 000 000
Days in period	30
Cash flow	\$2 500 000
Day of cash flow	10
Portfolio value on day of cash flow	\$12 000 000

Simple return calculation (compounding sub-periods)	20.00%
Simple return calculation (cash flow at end of period)	25.00%
Simple return calculation (cash flow at beginning and end of period)	22.22%
Money-weighted return calculation (cash flow 10/30 through period)	21.43%
Time-weighted return calculation (compounding sub-periods)	24.14%

Unsurprisingly, there is considerable pressure in the investment management industry to standardize the methods used to derive portfolio return data. This is proving more difficult to achieve than previously expected, and the process is not helped by the fact that there are two widely recognized standards for return calculations, and a number of less well-known ones. Investment managers in North America tend to comply with **AIMR** (Association for Investment Management and Research) standards, while European managers tend to comply with **GIPS** (Global Investment Performance Standard). The two are not significantly different, as it happens. A survey[1] in 2000 found that in both continents, more than 90% of investment managers responding to the survey said that they either complied, or intended to comply, with one or other of the standards. Further research by the same group found that, quite often, investment managers claiming to comply with reporting standards in fact failed to comply when put under closer scrutiny. This brings up the question of verification.

Verification is a type of audit, in the sense that it is intended as an independent report on the accuracy and reliability of the numbers being reported. Not all investment managers seek verification of the returns to the funds that they offer to investors, although investors are increasingly expecting to see that fund returns have been verified.

MULTIPLE PERIOD RETURN MEASUREMENT

Most investment managers report the returns of their portfolios and funds once a month. But they, and investors, are also very interested in what happens over longer time intervals, as this can help to decide whether the one month return is indicative of persistent skill on the part of the investor, whether it was just good (or bad) luck, or whether the portfolio and the investment manager perform better in some market conditions than in others.

Analysts of fund returns often publish the results of their research showing fund returns for one month, three months, six months, one, two, three and five years. Returns for multiple periods are obtained by compounding single month returns. For example, a portfolio that achieved a return of 12.5% in one month, followed by a return of 5% in the following month, has a return for the two months of:

$$(1 + 12.5\%) \times (1 + 5\%) - 1 = 18.1250\%$$

Returns for periods of more than one year are usually quoted as annualized figures. For example, a return for two years of 25% would be quoted as:

Square root of $(1 + 25\%) - 1 = 11.8034\%$ per annum

EXAMPLE 18.2 *Arithmetic and geometric linking*

	Portfolio Return %	Benchmark Return %	Arithmetic Difference %	Geometric Difference %
Period 1	21.00	10.00	11.00	10.00
Period 2	2.00	2.10	−0.10	−0.10
Two Periods	23.42	12.31	11.11	9.89

For most investments, return measurement is relevant only with respect to a benchmark, even if the benchmark is the return to cash, the rate of inflation or zero. For returns compounded over several periods, the difference between arithmetic and geometric variation, showing how the portfolio return differed from its benchmark, can be significant. Example 18.2 shows that a portfolio and benchmark return of 21% and 10% would give an **arithmetic link** of 11%, but a **geometric link** of 10% (1.21/1.10 – 1). If, in the ensuing period, the portfolio and benchmark returned 2.0% and 2.1% respectively, one expects to see the difference decline to reflect the poorer relative performance in the second period. Compounding portfolio and benchmark returns, and then linking them arithmetically, however, gives a two-month difference of 11.11%, while compounding them and then linking them geometrically gives a difference of 9.89%, which is what one would expect to see.[2]

THE LIMITATIONS OF RETURNS

For any given period, such as a month, quarter or a year, simple return comparisons are useful but limited. The apparent performance of the portfolio depends on the particular period being measured, with little or no indication of what occurred before or after. Consider the series of results for a domestic equity portfolio shown in Example 18.3.1.

Measured to 30 June 1996, the return of this portfolio and its benchmark looks like Example 18.3.2. The same return measurements taken one month earlier look like Example 18.3.3.

Neither set of results gives a good indication of the performance of the portfolio relative to the benchmark. In fact, it is not obvious that the two return summaries even refer to the same portfolio. Obviously, some form of continuous measurement is required to show how well the portfolio is performing

EXAMPLE 18.3.1 *Monthly portfolio returns*

Month	Portfolio %	Benchmark %	Difference %	Month	Portfolio %	Benchmark %	Difference %
31 05 94	1.00	1.15	−0.15	30 06 95	0.65	0.48	0.17
30 06 94	−3.95	−4.03	0.08	31 07 95	4.91	4.91	0.00
31 07 94	3.80	3.72	0.08	31 08 95	0.80	0.94	−0.14
31 08 94	3.00	3.04	−0.04	30 09 95	0.65	0.74	−0.09
30 09 94	−4.05	−3.88	−0.17	31 10 95	−2.27	−2.34	0.06
31 10 94	1.36	1.29	0.07	30 11 95	4.43	4.43	0.00
30 11 94	−7.06	−7.23	0.16	31 12 95	2.33	2.53	−0.20
31 12 94	1.80	1.65	0.15	31 01 96	3.85	3.93	−0.08
31 01 95	−4.16	−4.25	0.09	29 02 96	0.38	0.39	−0.01
28 02 95	5.00	5.07	−0.07	31 03 96	−2.18	−2.28	0.10
31 03 95	0.02	0.07	−0.05	30 04 96	4.20	4.38	−0.18
30 04 95	7.98	7.78	0.20	31 05 96	−1.89	−1.87	−0.02
31 05 95	−1.28	−1.19	−0.09	30 06 96	−0.30	−0.59	0.29

EXAMPLE 18.3.2 *Return summary to 30 June 1996*

Period	Portfolio %	Benchmark %	Arithmetic Difference %	Geometric Difference %
3 months	1.92	1.82	0.10	0.10
6 months	3.93	3.82	0.12	0.11
12 months	15.53	15.81	−0.28	−0.24
2 years	22.73	22.42	0.32	0.26

EXAMPLE 18.3.3 *Return summary to 31 May 1996*

Period	Portfolio %	Benchmark %	Arithmetic Difference %	Geometric Difference %
3 months	0.00	0.09	−0.09	−0.09
6 months	6.67	7.07	−0.40	−0.37
12 months	16.63	17.05	−0.42	−0.36
2 years	18.24	18.18	0.07	0.06

EXAMPLE 18.3.4 *Expected and observed beta and tracking error*

	Expected	Observed to 31 May 1996	Observed to 30 June 1996
Beta	1.0009	0.9946	0.9934
Tracking Error	0.4500%	0.3962%	0.4411%

relative to its benchmark. Because the CAPM tells us that asset returns fluctuate all the time but asset risk characteristics are steadier, some measure of the risk of the portfolio is required. This is given by the beta and the tracking error. The observed beta measures the sensitivity of the portfolio to its benchmark, while the tracking error gives a measure of random return variation from benchmark.

In addition to the observed or ex-post beta and tracking error, the investor is also usually interested in what the prospective or ex-ante beta and tracking error are of the portfolio. These are useful measures for new portfolios or where an old portfolio has been rebalanced, and allows comparison with results actually achieved. The ex-ante beta of the portfolio is simply the weighted average of the historical betas of the component securities in the portfolio. (Stock betas are calculated by conducting a regression analysis between the stock returns and benchmark returns.) The ex-ante tracking error takes into account the volatility of the securities in the portfolio and the covariances between them (Example 18.3.4).

A tracking error of 0.4416% per annum means that there is a 68% probability that the portfolio's performance will be within that range of the benchmark. In other words, if the benchmark index rises by 15% in a year, then there is a 68% chance that the portfolio will gain between 14.5984% and 15.4016% in that year.

The important thing to note here is that beta and tracking error do not change much over time, and so, unlike simple performance comparisons, they are less dependent on the period being measured. At the same time, it is also important to remember that the calculated tracking error is still only an estimate: although calculated from actual returns it gives an estimate of the portfolio's risk based on the period being measured. It represents only one outcome out of all possible outcomes.

Knowing something about the return and risk of a portfolio, fund or investment, the manager can give the investor some basis for comparison, and can help to distinguish between investments. But it can be useful to put this information into perspective.

First of all, it must be remembered that past return is, by itself, no guide to future return, either in absolute terms or relative to a benchmark. Investment management companies change tactics for various reasons, such as:

- If the chosen investment strategy is not working, and it appears that it may not do so in the foreseeable future, then it is natural to expect the strategy to be revised or replaced, impacting future returns.
- Many investment managers experience very high staff turnover, so even with the strongest intention to follow consistent investment policies and strategies, the investment management company's skill base and balance of strengths and weaknesses changes constantly.
- What worked before may not work in future. Even with consistent strategies and stable investment staff, the range of available investment opportunities fluctuates over time, so the scope for higher returns can wax and wane.

Second, return and risk figures say little about how the results were achieved. For example, was the return variation achieved evenly across asset classes and securities, or due mainly to one or two large imbalances or mismatches relative to benchmark? Knowing where the return came from, and what sorts of risks the portfolio is exposed to can help investors to decide whether the investment return variation was the result of luck or skill, whether it is likely to do well in the future, and how well it will mix with other investments. The process of probing the sources of return variation is known as attribution analysis.

SINGLE PERIOD ATTRIBUTION ANALYSIS

There are various approaches to attribution analyses, all of which try to break the portfolio down into manageable chunks and then see how each contributed to return variation. For diversified portfolios, the logical unit of disaggregation is asset classes. Within asset classes, disaggregation is according to the components of the asset class, such as industry groups or factors within domestic equity portfolios. For international equity portfolios, countries, industry groups or factors can be used. If necessary, the attribution analysis can be carried out at the level of individual securities.

To illustrate how an attribution analysis might look, the return over one month of a simple domestic equity portfolio is analysed. This portfolio was compiled simply by selecting the 100 largest of the 300 odd stocks in the benchmark index. It is measurably overweight in three industry groups: diversified resources, media and banks because these groups claim a disproportionate number of large stocks within the benchmark index.

During the period in question, the portfolio returned –2.46% while the benchmark returned –2.35% as shown in Example 18.4.1. This analysis seeks to identify how much of the return variation is due to the portfolio's being over- or

EXAMPLE 18.4.1 *Summary attribution analysis by industry group*

Attribution Summary	%
Portfolio Return	−2.46
Benchmark Return	−2.35
Difference	−0.10
Industry Group Allocation Effect	−0.25
Stock Selection Within Industries Effect	−0.31
Residual	−0.05

underweight in each industry group, and how much can be explained by stock selection within each industry group.

The first of these, the allocation mismatch effect can be calculated as follows:

$$AAa = (Wip - Wib) \times (Rip - Rb) \tag{18.9}$$

Where:

AAa= the arithmetic asset allocation effect

Wip = the weight of industry i in the portfolio

Wib = the weight of industry i in the benchmark

Rib = the benchmark return to industry i

Rb = the return to the benchmark

In other words, for each industry group, the difference between the portfolio and benchmark allocation is multiplied by the difference between the benchmark return to the industry group and the overall benchmark return.

The stock selection effect measures the impact on return variation of the differential composition of each industry group. For each industry group it is calculated as:

$$SSa = Wib \times (Rip - Rib) \tag{18.10}$$

Where:

SSa = the arithmetic stock selection effect

Rip = the portfolio return to industry i.

EXAMPLE 18.4.2 *Attribution analysis by industry group*

	Average Portfolio Allocation %	Average Benchmark Allocation %	Industry Group Allocation Effect %	Portfolio Industry Group Return %	Benchmark Industry Group Return %	Stock Selection Within Industries Effect %
Gold	3.62	5.01	0.15	−13.97	−13.00	−0.05
Other Metals	6.17	6.16	0.00	1.80	1.43	0.02
Diversified Resources	16.57	14.18	−0.02	−3.14	−3.04	−0.01
Energy	4.23	4.23	0.00	−2.00	0.61	−0.11
Infrastructure & Utilities	0.92	0.99	0.00	−9.43	−9.32	0.00
Developers	2.94	2.93	0.00	−11.25	−11.13	0.00
Building Materials	4.57	4.23	−0.01	−4.53	−3.96	−0.02
Alcohol & Tobacco	2.26	2.17	0.01	13.69	11.57	0.05
Food	3.39	3.21	−0.01	−6.94	−6.81	0.00
Chemicals	1.50	1.60	0.02	−16.78	−16.39	−0.01
Engineering	0.32	1.81	−0.11	−1.60	5.30	−0.12
Paper & Packaging	2.37	2.24	0.00	−1.25	−1.19	0.00
Retail	3.41	3.33	0.00	−2.34	−3.13	0.03
Transport	3.31	1.56	−0.26	−17.26	−17.08	0.00
Media	9.41	8.83	0.06	7.49	7.33	0.01
Banks	21.94	18.84	0.38	9.89	9.94	−0.01
Insurance	2.33	2.33	0.00	−5.50	−4.55	−0.02
Telecommunications	0.00	0.55	0.00	0.00	−2.84	0.02
Investment Services	1.11	1.77	−0.03	6.67	2.41	0.08
Property Trust	2.66	4.49	−0.05	−1.66	0.22	−0.08
Misc Services	0.26	1.25	0.03	−17.77	−4.99	−0.16
Misc Industrials	0.58	1.44	0.08	−9.85	−12.15	0.03
Diversified Industrials	3.82	4.03	−0.01	4.40	2.47	0.08
Tourism	2.32	2.83	0.01	−3.93	−3.87	0.00
Total	100.00	100.00	0.25	−2.46	−2.35	−0.31

The results of the analysis are set out in Example 18.4.2, which shows that the portfolio benefited from being overweight in banks because this sector delivered a higher return than the benchmark. Applying equation 18.9:

$$\text{Arithmetic asset allocation effect} = (21.94\% - 18.84\%) \times (9.94\% + 2.35\%)$$
$$= 0.38\%$$

Within this sector, the portfolio's selection of banks did slightly worse than the benchmark (9.89 versus 9.94%) giving a stock selection effect of –0.01%. On the other hand, while the portfolio benefited significantly from being underweight in gold stocks, it did less well if it held more small gold stocks rather than only large ones. The portfolio's overweight position in media also contributed significantly to return variation. Overall, the portfolio benefited from industry allocation, adding a total of 0.25% to overall return, but this was more than offset by poor security selection within industry groups, which reduced return by 0.31%. Together they explain –0.06% of return variation, leaving an interaction effect of 0.05%.

It should be noted that this attribution analysis is unusually simple because the portfolio did not trade during the period. To accommodate transactions or cash flows, the investment period is broken down into sub-periods according to the day on which the transaction or cash flow occurred. The return is calculated for each industry group and sub-period and these compounded to give the return for the period. This gives an extra column in the attribution analysis, usually headed **market timing** or 'trading activity', which tries to capture value added or subtracted from stock purchases and sales.

Attribution analysis by asset class, country, sector, industry or factor groups can enhance significantly understanding of the sources of return variation from the benchmark. The investment manager should find the results at least as interesting as the investor because he or she should want to see that excess return was derived from deliberate investment policy, rather than secondary or unintended portfolio risks, or worse, completely at random. If the investment underperformed its benchmark, then the investment manager should be curious to see if this was the result of investment policy and therefore likely to correct in coming periods, or whether the portfolio is subject to unwanted risk.

ANALYSIS OF DEADWEIGHT AND ACTIVE HOLDINGS

Another approach to attribution analysis is to view the portfolio as being made up of an indexed portfolio plus an actively managed long–short portfolio. Simply subtracting benchmark security allocations from the portfolio alloc-

EXAMPLE 18.5 *Portfolio equals benchmark plus long–short*

Single Period Return	%
Portfolio	9.11
Benchmark	5.58
Difference	3.53

	Change in Value	Percentage of Portfolio %	Return %	Contribution to Return %
Benchmark	2 789 371	87.99	5.58	61.22
Long–Short	1 766 898	12.01	3.53	38.78
Total	4 556 269	100.00	9.11	100.00

ations does this. It recognizes the fact that a significant proportion of nearly all actively managed portfolios are simply the benchmark. Securities held by the benchmark but not by the portfolio are effectively short in the active component of the portfolio. As benchmark holdings do not contribute to active return, they are a **deadweight**, and it is logical to exclude them from the attribution analysis, concentrating on the differences between the portfolio and the benchmark. Allocations to the active component sum to zero, and the return they deliver is compared with cash, as for a long–short portfolio that one might encounter in an alternative investment fund. Since no reasonable investor would pay active management fees for an indexed portfolio, it is the active component of the portfolio for which active management fees are paid.

In Example 18.5, 39% of the overall return is generated by the active, long–short component, while 61% is simply the market return. The absolute value of the active component, measured as the total value of the long or the short positions, represents about 12% of the value of the portfolio. The investor may wish to increase this proportion of the portfolio to earn even higher returns. Alternatively he or she may propose to pay indexed management fees for 88% of the portfolio and active fees for 12%.

MULTIPLE PERIOD ATTRIBUTION ANALYSIS

Having carried out the attribution analysis, the investor would like to know whether the patterns of portfolio variation identified in a single period are in fact characteristic of this fund or investment manager, or whether it was an isolated event, unlikely to be repeated. To find out, the single period attribution analysis can be extended to cover consecutive return periods.

When calculating returns over multiple periods, single period returns are compounded. Within return periods, by contrast, return variation is usually the simple arithmetic difference between portfolio and benchmark. Although the two approaches are not entirely compatible, generally this does not cause too much of a problem, until one approaches the task of multiple period return attribution.

Linking return periods for attribution analysis is conceptually easy but in practice achieving meaningful results is not straightforward. Neither arithmetic nor geometric linking of returns gives an ideal outcome, in which all asset or industry group returns for each return period add or compound to give exactly the portfolio return for the linked periods.

Example 18.6 shows that arithmetic and geometric linking can give quite different results.

The arithmetic variation is simply the portfolio return minus the benchmark return.

$$Va = Rp - Rb \tag{18.2}$$

For the S&P500 in 1998, this is

$$\begin{aligned} Va &= 30.49\% - 26.67\% \\ &= 3.83\% \end{aligned}$$

The geometric variation applies a compounding formula:

$$Vg = (1 + Rp)/(1 + Rb) - 1 \tag{18.3}$$

For the S&P500 in 1998, this is

$$\begin{aligned} Vg &= (1 + 30.49\%)/(1 + 26.67\%) - 1 \\ &= 3.02\% \end{aligned}$$

The contribution to portfolio variation from stock selection is the arithmetic and geometric variations times the benchmark allocation to the asset class.

$$SSa = Wib \times (Rip - Rib) \tag{18.10}$$
$$SSg = Wib \times ((1 + Rip)/(1 + Rib) -) \tag{18.11}$$

Where:

SSg = geometric shock selection effect

EXAMPLE 18.6 *Attribution analysis: three assets, three periods, arithmetic and geometric linking*

	Return		*Difference*		*Stock Selection Effect*		*Allocation Effect*
Year	**Portfolio** %	**Benchmark** %	**Arithmetic** %	**Geometric** %	**Arithmetic** %	**Geometric** %	
1998							
S&P500	30.49	26.67	3.83	3.02	1.53	1.21	−0.93
NASDAQ100	80.52	85.31	−4.78	−2.58	−0.96	−0.52	5.24
10YR TREASURIES	13.81	12.88	0.92	0.82	0.37	0.33	5.00
Total	43.00	32.88	10.12	7.61	0.94	1.02	9.31
1999							
S&P500	18.93	19.53	−0.60	−0.50	−0.24	−0.20	−0.80
NASDAQ100	95.90	101.95	−6.05	−3.00	−1.21	−0.60	7.71
10YR TREASURIES	−8.44	−8.41	−0.03	−0.03	−0.01	−0.01	8.31
Total	37.91	24.84	13.08	10.47	−1.46	−0.81	15.23
2000							
S&P500	−7.61	−10.14	2.53	2.82	1.01	1.13	−0.67
NASDAQ100	−37.35	−36.84	−0.50	−0.80	−0.10	−0.16	−3.12
10YR TREASURIES	14.94	14.45	0.48	0.42	0.19	0.17	−5.02
Total	−13.15	−5.64	−7.51	−7.95	1.10	1.14	−8.82
1998–2000							
S&P500	43.38	36.05	7.33	5.39	2.93	2.16	−3.07
NASDAQ100	121.56	136.34	−14.79	−6.26	−2.96	−1.25	7.98
10YR TREASURIES	19.76	18.33	1.43	1.21	0.57	0.48	9.55
Total	71.28	56.52	14.76	9.43	0.55	1.39	14.46
Summary							
1998	43.00	32.88	10.12	7.61	0.94	1.02	9.31
1999	37.91	24.84	13.08	10.47	−1.46	−0.81	15.23
2000	−13.15	−5.64	−7.51	−7.95	1.10	1.14	−8.82
1998–2000	71.28	56.52	14.76	9.43	0.55	1.39	14.46

For the S&P500 in 1998 using arithmetic variation, this is:

$$
\begin{aligned}
SSa &= 40\% \times 3.83\% \\
&= 1.53\% \\
SSg &= 40\% \times 3.02\% \\
&= 1.21\%
\end{aligned}
$$

The allocation effect is the difference between portfolio and benchmark allocation to the asset times the difference between benchmark return to the asset and overall benchmark return.

$$AAa = (Wip - Wib) \times (Rip - Rb) \tag{18.9}$$

For the S&P500 in 1998 using arithmetic variation, this is:

$$
\begin{aligned}
AAa &= (55\% - 40\%) \times (26.67\% - 32.88\%) \\
&= 15\% \times -6.21\% \\
&= -0.93\%
\end{aligned}
$$

Add in trading activity and external cash flows – with the different ways of incorporating them into the result – and the picture becomes very complex indeed.

There are a number of mathematical procedures to smooth out the wrinkles in the analysis, each with advantages and disadvantages, but so far, no standard approach has been identified. For this reason, any comparisons between portfolios should be interpreted with great care, as a small change in methodology can result in significantly different apparent results.

Comparison of return periods for one portfolio, fund or investment manager can have limited validity because the investment strategy, skills base and investment opportunity set change over time. Even comparing consecutive investment periods may be like comparing apples with pears.

Therefore, when making comparisons, it is essential to look beyond mere numbers to establish that returns analyses really do have a common basis for comparison.

Notes

1. The Spaulding Group, Performance Presentation Standards Surveys. 2000
2. Menchero, Jose G., A Fully Geometric Approach to Performance Attribution. Vestek Pre-Publication Article. 2000

CHAPTER 19

The Use of Software in Investment Management

Investment managers, both quantitative and traditional, rely increasingly on computer systems at virtually all stages of the investment management process. Unsurprisingly, the software industry has risen to the challenge, providing computer programs and databases to serve most functions. Accelerating improvements in computer hardware and communication capabilities is resulting in software, the sophistication of which now seems to be limited only by the imagination of its users. Even as recently as the mid-1980s, most advanced finance and portfolio theory could not be routinely applied for want of processing capacity at a reasonable price, and because the necessary data to support it was not available in an easy to use format. Investment management techniques remained low-tech, relying on traditional methods for security analysis, portfolio construction and management. That is no longer the case. It is probably true to say that no major investment theory has now been produced that does not have some user-friendly application to put it into practice.

The danger of getting bogged down in the complexity and overlapping functions of products and services on offer is probably worse than the danger of oversimplifying, so this chapter errs towards the latter. It describes the types of tools available for each stage of the investment management process, following as far as possible a chronological sequence, from discovering what is going on in the world and its markets to explaining to the investor what his or her investment did last quarter and why. Finally it discusses some issues common to all or most software functions, including choices often faced by investment management companies, and some of the advantages and disadvantages of different approaches.

MARKET INFORMATION

Investment managers are paid to be very interested in what is happening in the markets in which they invest, and in outside events that might influence asset prices in those markets, including conditions in related markets. Managers of portfolios of equities, bonds, short-term interest rates, foreign exchange, derivatives and asset allocation managers need immediate and continuous information about market prices to evaluate investment strategies, spot asset mispricing and facilitate portfolio implementation. Depending on the particular investment strategy being pursued, even quite small price movements can trigger significant portfolio adjustments, so timely and accurate market information is often indispensable.

Therefore, nearly all investment managers subscribe to one or more online market data services, which send market information, such as bid, ask and last sale prices and volumes traded via telephone or dedicated cables to computers located in the offices of investment managers. The information can be transmitted either in **real time**, that is, as it happens, or at very short time intervals, say every five to ten minutes.

There are several large suppliers of online market information, some bundling market data service with news services, others providing the various services separately, with cost reflecting the amount and timeliness of the information supplied. The most comprehensive services provide real-time price information for markets around the world, with wide news coverage, including politics, sport and entertainment. Many suppliers also provide a wide range of online analytics, performing simple price comparisons, calculation of theoretical prices and analysis of price differentials between related instruments. Investment managers can also access research reports on individual securities and economic events from selected stockbrokers. This information comes in a variety of formats, including detailed descriptions of companies through to return forecasts of a wide range of security returns and economic variables, presented in standardized format, often tabulated for easy comparison and analysis.

Data can be transmitted either to dedicated screens located in the investment manager's office or directly to the investment manager's computer network. The former usually requires the investment manager to use the analytic software of the data supplier, while the latter allows information to be fed into other programs for storage and analysis, enabling a great deal more flexibility, and can encourage more innovation by investment managers than simple data feeds.

Live market data feeds are available on a subscription basis, usually with some base fee, depending on the extent and timeliness of the data required, with additional fees per user.

Investment managers managing portfolios benchmarked to a standard benchmark index, such as a stock price index or bond index, are interested to know what the constituents of those indices are at any point of time and when the index provider proposes changes the constituents. Most index providers are stock exchanges, but banks and independent companies also provide indices that are used as benchmarks. Subscription services are available from most index providers, allowing the investment manager to obtain this information in time to conduct the necessary analysis and portfolio adjustments, although some index providers supply constituent data without charge.

In addition to current market and benchmark information, a surprising range of historical information can be purchased, such as online price and return histories for securities, currencies and commodity prices, and macroeconomic variables, including such items as agricultural production through to weather statistics and industry-specific data, such as sales of umbrellas in Madrid.

RETURN FORECASTING FOR ASSET CLASSES AND INDIVIDUAL SECURITIES

Forecasting returns for asset classes and individual securities is how many investment managers distinguish themselves from their competitors. Applying complex return forecasting models helps to achieve this, and these models typically rely on current and historical data, so software and data services are important. Many investment managers claim to employ an unique approach to the task, necessitating the creation of their own return forecasting programs.

Some investment management companies subscribe to or buy macroeconomic models to help to forecast things such as interest rates and currencies. These are then usually customized and combined with programs developed in-house to reflect their interpretation of how events affect the economy, and to make use of their own particular insights into what drives returns to those assets and markets.

RISK MODELLING, PORTFOLIO ANALYSIS AND CONSTRUCTION

Once asset class and security return forecasts have been prepared, nearly all quantitative managers use some kind of analysis tool to help to construct a portfolio with the risk and diversification characteristics required to meet the investment objective. Risk analysis usually relies on some kind of optimization program, and several are available, each with particular strengths and weaknesses.

Optimizers, risk models and programs for portfolio analysis and construction deal specifically with the asset allocation decision or at the level of individual securities, usually equities. **Asset allocation** optimizers work at the level of market proxies, such as share price indices, bond indices, commodity indices, currencies and so on, and these form the primary input to the programs. The investment manager enters:

- The base currency of the portfolio.
- The universe of permitted investments.
- Benchmark allocations.
- Current portfolio allocations.
- A forecast return for each asset class in the investment universe.
- Guidelines or constraints on the composition of the portfolio.

The program combines this information with a covariance matrix computed from historical returns, which may be supplied with the optimization program or estimated by the investment manager, and identifies a series of optimal or efficient portfolios. It also computes some summary statistics for the existing and each optimal portfolio, including:

- Expected return, absolute and relative to the benchmark.
- Expected beta of the portfolio to the benchmark.
- Expected volatility and tracking error.
- Estimates of the sources of volatility and tracking error.
- The Sharpe ratio, a measure of the relationship of expected return to expected risk.
- A summary of the transactions required to transform the current portfolio to each optimal portfolio.

Optimizer and portfolio analysis programs are available for both asset allocation and **security selection**, the latter working at the level of individual equities. These may be concerned simply with a single market, such as the US or UK, although the creeping globalization of equities markets is causing this approach to become anachronistic. Investment managers are increasingly cognizant of the international nature of equity portfolios, and are seeking portfolio analytics that apply a truly global approach, so programs for security selection across markets are increasingly used.

As with asset allocation optimizers, equity optimizers use as their primary input:

- The base currency of the portfolio.
- The universe of permitted securities.
- Benchmark security allocations.
- Current portfolio allocations.
- A forecast return for each security in the investment universe.
- Guidelines, limitations and constraints on the composition of the portfolio.

The program then computes a covariance matrix using historical returns to produce a risk and return analysis of the existing portfolio and an array of efficient portfolios, together with summary statistics and proposed transactions required to transform the existing portfolio into an efficient one.

Most optimizers come with a range of added features, such as the ability to conduct some kind of historical analysis on the optimal portfolio and benchmark, scenario analyses, and the ability to analyse the portfolio and benchmark according to a range of selected portfolio characteristics, such as country or industry exposures, dividend yield, average market capitalization of the component stocks, price to book ratio and so on. They also usually support quite appealing graphics that can be copied to word-processing software for incorporation into investment reports. Some optimizers incorporate a reverse optimization. This tells the investment manager what individual asset returns are implied by specified current portfolio allocations, allowing the investment manager to check for consistency between return forecasts and portfolio construction.

Portfolio optimizers and risk analysis packages are usually sold by subscription because they rely on large quantities of historical asset price returns. To keep this return data up to date, most optimizer providers send data updates regularly, usually once a month, to the investment manager. Some providers make data available more frequently, which can be useful for obtaining reasonably accurate mid-month estimates of portfolio exposures. Mid-month data for optimizers should be handled with care, however, as it may not be consistent with the covariance matrix, which is usually designed to incorporate monthly returns.

Sometimes investment managers prefer to build their own optimizers. The advantage of this approach is that the program can be designed around the particular strengths, in terms of return forecasting and portfolio construction, of the investment manager and can accommodate the objectives of individual portfolios. For example, if the manager is particularly good at managing portfolios of equities in emerging markets, the optimizer can be structured to exploit this ability, thereby forming an important part of the manager's marketing arsenal. The disadvantages are mainly cost and reliability. Because optimizers are very data-hungry, the manager would need to bear the entire cost of supporting an extensive database required to feed the optimizer. This usually necessitates subscribing to several, if not dozens, of separate data suppliers, then, each month, checking and cleaning the data and preparing it in the format accepted by the program. Checking and verifying optimizer models and output is a labour-intensive operation, for which in-house models may receive less attention than off-the-shelf varieties, which enable this cost to be defrayed across many users.

A number of analysis packages are available specifically to analyse **bonds and bond portfolios**, but many asset managers find that these need significant modification to enhance their relevance to particular bonds and bond market segments. Most work by applying the principles of scenario analysis, whereby the investment manager defines a number of scenarios corresponding to possible future economic environments. Returns are forecast for each bond in each scenario, and the model computes portfolio characteristics for each portfolio. The investment manager can make small changes to each scenario to see what effects these have and to test the chosen portfolio allocation for robustness. These programs are sometimes available for outright purchase, although many are sold by subscription, which entitles the buyer to any subsequent program improvements and upgrades. Many investment managers prefer to build their own bond models to exploit their special insights and reflect their particular approach to investment in this sector.

ANALYSIS OF DERIVATIVES

Simple derivatives, such as forwards, futures and standard swaps and options, are usually priced and analysed using standard spreadsheets, most often written on the spot by individual investment managers or analysts. More complex derivatives, such as complex options, swaps and hybrid instruments, often need something more powerful, usually supported by specialist data. Most can be bought either as an outright package or, if ongoing data support is required, as a subscription service. Many investment managers choose to develop pricing and analysis programs for complex derivatives in-house, as this can afford greater flexibility, and allows the manager to claim some exceptional expertize with the instruments in question.

RECORDING AND RECONCILING TRANSACTIONS

Having constructed the portfolio, and defined the transactions required to put it in place, the next step is to implement and record transactions. In the days of manual transaction processing, the investment manager executing, say, a share purchase, would fill out a deal slip with information pertinent to the transaction, such as:

- Whether buying or selling – usually indicated by a blue or pink slip respectively.
- The date and time of the transaction.
- The portfolio on behalf of which the transaction is executed.
- The name of the stock.
- The number of shares.
- The price.
- The name of the broker.
- The rate of commission payable.
- Any comments, such as if the shares are ex- or cum-dividend, or any settlement peculiarities.
- The signature and identity of the dealer or investment manager.
- The signature and identity of another manager confirming the transaction.

These slips were collected several times a day from each dealer or investment manager and entered into a ledger for later reconciliation with contract notes from brokers confirming the same details for each transaction.

For a bond transaction, the information is similar:

- Whether buying or selling – usually indicated by a blue or pink slip respectively.
- The date and time of the transaction.
- The portfolio on behalf of which the transaction is executed.
- The name of the bond issuer.
- The face value of the bonds.
- The yield to maturity or price.

- The name of the broker.
- The rate of commission payable.
- Any comments, such as if the bonds are ex- or cum-coupon, or any settlement peculiarities.
- The signature and identity of the dealer or investment manager.
- The signature and identity of another manager confirming the transaction.

Transactions were recorded throughout the day by a clerk called a penciller, who entered the information into a ledger, with the overall portfolio position monitored by the head dealer or investment manager.

Many investment managers supplemented this recording system with a personal diary of the transactions they effected, helping to settle any disputes.

Automating this process offered the obvious benefit of eliminating all the pink and blue slips, reducing the opportunities for error and enabling records of portfolio holdings to be updated instantly instead of at the end of each day. Most investment management firms have systems that allow dealers and investment managers to enter details of each transaction directly into a computer terminal on their desk, theoretically doing away entirely with small pieces of paper. It is less colourful, but more efficient. It also limits the ability of individual investment managers to subjectively allocate transactions to portfolios, a practice that allows allocation of the most attractive prices to those portfolios against the return of which the investment manager is evaluated and remunerated.

Most of these systems now accommodate a wide range of assets, including most derivatives, although complex derivatives may still cause problems. Combining all types of securities and derivatives in a single system is a powerful capability, as it enables constant monitoring of portfolio holdings. This in turn allows the investment manager to program the computer system to generate a warning if specified exposure or risk limits are breached, helping to ensure that investor guidelines and mandate limitations are strictly observed.

One of the most difficult tasks is to ensure that common investment strategies, reflecting the investment manager's 'house view', are applied as consistently as possible across portfolios with different exposure limits and risk tolerances. This is usually addressed with a mixture of **off-the-shelf** software and in-house modifications.

Systems for recording transactions are often called **front office** or **front end** systems because that is where information about portfolio holdings originates. These systems are either purchased outright, with supplements for later program improvements and enhancements, or developed in-house if the investment manager estimates that none of the 'off-the-shelf' solutions meets the requirements of the mandates under management.

MAINTAINING PORTFOLIO RECORDS

Usually the computer system used to record transactions is linked to or even part of a much larger system maintaining records of portfolio holdings. This is logical because many changes in portfolio holdings result not from on market transactions but from regular asset price changes and routine events such as receipt of dividends and coupon income, stock splits, bonus issues, mergers, capital restructures, bond maturities and other corporate activity, as well as derivatives expiring, margin requirements, swap settlements and so on.

The system installed to keep track of all these events, for each holding in each portfolio, is at the core of the investment manager's software requirements. The same system records aggregate portfolio holdings, deposits and withdrawals from each investor's account, and maintains records for any unit trusts or mutual funds managed by the investment manager. This administration is simple enough in concept, but can use enormous amounts of processing capacity and memory, particularly if there are a large number of portfolios under management, or if they tend to be transacted frequently.

These systems can be bought outright, with supplements and enhancements available at additional cost. Large investment managers tend either to develop their own or, more frequently, to engage a specialist software provider to modify an off-the-shelf program or develop a fully customized system.

TAX

Many regimes require the investment manager to maintain records of taxable income and gains, so the investment manager is sometimes obliged to purchase a system or supplement to perform this function. Obviously the system needs to conform to local conditions, possibly accommodating both domestic and international investors as well as domestic and international investments. Suitable products may not be available off-the-shelf, obliging the manager to either develop one in-house or contract to have one built by a specialist provider.

PORTFOLIO VALUATION

This is a logical extension of the system that maintains records of portfolio holdings and is probably the simplest of the functions provided by the main portfolio management system, since portfolio valuation for most assets is simply the quantity held times the market price. The main difference between the portfolio valuation functions of various portfolio management systems is in their flexibility in presenting portfolio holdings for inspection and analysis, and how accurately they represent the exposure of derivatives in the portfolio.

Most systems allow the manager to generate the following standard reports for segregated accounts and funds:

- Portfolio holdings by portfolio or client account, usually organized by asset class, country and/or industry group.
- Aggregate investments for all clients and funds ordered by holding, showing, for each security, the quantity held on behalf of each account.
- Individual transactions executed, accruals and cash flows in any period on behalf of any client or fund.
- Transactions in any period for any security, showing, for each security, the quantity executed on behalf of each account.
- Transactions by broker or counter-party.
- Commissions paid by portfolio, broker and time period.
- Income accrued and earned for each asset and portfolio.

Many valuation programs now allow individual investment managers to design the layout of portfolio valuation and activity reports to meet precise information requirements, and to insert these into regular reports prepared using a word processor.

One of the most frequent shortcomings of portfolio valuation programs is that they often present derivatives holdings in terms of cash flows rather than economic exposure. This can seriously misrepresent the portfolio, giving the appearance that the portfolio is underinvested, and even in breach of its mandate. Equally as dangerous, it can fail to alert the manager if the portfolio breaches its mandate by being overinvested. The problem pertains to any derivatives or other investment where the cash paid for the investment is not exactly equal to the economic value of the investment at the time of purchase.

Example 19.1 shows how the apparent exposure of a portfolio can differ according to how the cash collateral underlying derivatives is treated. It shows that the portfolio is holding $115 000 000 in liquids, but that this cash is largely

EXAMPLE 19.1 *Futures exposure*

	Economic Exposure Based on Physical Equity Index		Economic Exposure Based on Equity Futures Price		Cash Exposure Based on Equity Futures Price	
	$	%	$	%	$	%
Physical Holdings						
Physical Equities	50 000 000	25.64	50 000 000	25.64	50 000 000	25.64
Physical Bonds	30 000 000	15.38	30 000 000	15.38	30 000 000	15.38
Liquids	115 000 000	58.97	115 000 000	58.97	115 000 000	58.97
Total Portfolio	195 000 000	100.00	195 000 000	100.00	195 000 000	100.00
Exposure						
Futures Initial Margins	15 000 000	7.69	15 000 000	7.69	15 000 000	7.69
Futures Variation Margins	0	0.00	0	0.00	0	0.00
Futures Collateral	60 000 000	30.77	78 750 000	40.38	0	0.00
Total Equity Futures	75 000 000	38.46	93 750 000	48.08	15 000 000	7.69
Total Equities	125 000 000	64.10	143 750 000	73.72	65 000 000	33.33
Total Bonds	30 000 000	15.38	30 000 000	15.38	30 000 000	15.38
Liquids Exposure	40 000 000	20.51	21 250 000	10.90	100 000 000	51.28
Total Portfolio	195 000 000	100.00	195 000 000	100.00	195 000 000	100.00
Exposure Summary						
Equities	125 000 000	64.10	143 750 000	73.72	65 000 000	33.33
Bonds	30 000 000	15.38	30 000 000	15.38	30 000 000	15.38
Liquids	40 000 000	20.51	21 250 000	10.90	100 000 000	51.28
Total Portfolio	195 000 000	100.00	195 000 000	100.00	195 000 000	100.00

collateral for equity futures contracts. How this collateral is assigned affects the apparent exposure of the portfolio to equities. The economic exposure based on the physical equity index calculates the effective futures **face value** as the number of contracts held times the point value of the futures contract times the current value of the physical index. The middle columns show the effect of using the futures price instead of the physical, and the right-hand column shows a pure cash-based calculation, which assumes that the face value of the futures contract is the same as the value of initial and variation margins paid. The amount apparently exposed to equities varies from 73% to 33%. The left-hand columns reflect the economic allocations of the portfolio. Applying the futures price instead of the physical, as in the middle columns, introduces bias due to any mispricing in the futures premium. It also leads to an apparent change in portfolio asset allocation as futures contracts are rolled to the next expiry month.

While the cash-based report is necessary to show where all physical assets, including cash holdings, are held, it should be clearly distinguished from the portfolio valuation report, showing the economic asset class allocations of the portfolio.

Flexibility and accuracy of representation are probably the two most valuable attributes of a portfolio valuation and reporting program. It is this part of the program that forms the basis of all information presented to the client.

RETURN MEASUREMENT, ATTRIBUTION AND REPORTING

Basic return measurement can be carried out using simple programs developed in-house, often using spreadsheets, while return attribution requires more sophisticated resources. Because both functions draw on the same data, programs developed for the latter usually calculate returns as well. There are a number of off-the-shelf attribution analysis packages on offer, varying widely in quality, accuracy and comprehensiveness.

Some systems offer a very simple algorithm to disaggregate portfolio returns by asset class and sector, with the possibility of estimating the contribution to portfolio return of individual securities. Simple algorithms can offer only an approximate attribution. For more reliable answers, more sophisticated packages are required. More advanced systems allow return to be attributed not just by simple asset categories such as countries and industry groups, but also by risk factor, allowing direct links between forecast portfolio factor exposures and their contribution to actual return. This leads to the problem of data management. Complex algorithms, designed to give accurate answers to portfolio attribution questions, must be fed with accurate information about portfolio holdings, usually daily, including accurate information about transactions occurring during the period of analysis.

For portfolios with frequent trading or cash flows, the data management problem dominates the computational problem. For this reason, many managers have sought to develop sophisticated attribution analysis systems in-house that can read portfolio holdings and transactions data directly from the main portfolio management and valuation system. This can give very accurate results, depending on the quality of the underlying mathematics and the ability to build in advanced attribution functions, such as factor attribution, but development and maintenance can be very expensive in terms of programming and management time.

BUY VERSUS BUILD

Many stages of the investment management process offer the manager the choice of buying off-the-shelf systems, building them in-house or customizing an off-the-shelf system. Each application offers its own costs and benefits, but some generalizations are valid. The two obvious benefits of building systems in-house are that:

- They can be tailored precisely to the needs of the investment manager, with built-in flexibility to meet perceived future needs.
- Where the application rests on some sophisticated analysis, as in the case of return forecasting, portfolio optimizers, complex derivatives and attribution analysis programs, the investment manager can claim to be incorporating some special insight or expertize into the program, making it better than those used by his or her competitors. The program thus doubles as a marketing tool.

The disadvantages of building software rather than buying it are:

- It nearly always costs more to build than buy because the investment manager bears all the cost of development and maintenance for in-house solutions, while this cost is spread across many users in the case of off-the-shelf solutions. If the application needs to be supported by regular data updates, the relative cost of in-house development rises steeply.
- It can lead to heavy dependence on the individual programmers who developed the program. Sooner or later the program usually develops a bug, or

some new or altered functions are required of it. Regardless of how well the program is documented (sometimes meticulously, often hardly at all), if the original programmers no longer work for the company, the problem tends to prove very difficult and occasionally impossible to solve. If the program is the main portfolio management system, this can leave the investment management company quite vulnerable.

Contracting a specialist software house to develop a customized solution or customize an off-the-shelf product is usually a workable compromise, because the software house probably has produced similar products for other investment managers, and so can reduce costs and development time by adapting parts of other successful applications.

INTEGRATED VERSUS CHERRY-PICKING WITH MIDDLEWARE

Unsurprisingly, with such an array of software performing quite different functions for people in all parts of the company, and with potentially thousands of links to organizations outside the company, the different systems are difficult to link successfully. Even systems built in-house can be quite incompatible if they were built at different times when different programming and hardware resources were available. Yet the functions performed by each system are all linked in some logical way within the investment management process, so each function somehow needs to share data with each other function.

The ideal is a fully integrated system that shares data across all functions, and several such systems exist, affording considerable convenience. The problem is that individual components of integrated systems can be of variable quality and competence, and rarely present the best solution for each manager. A system that is very strong on portfolio administration and record keeping might have a very weak analytics component. If the manager needs high quality analytics, a separate system is required for this function, defeating the purpose of the integrated system.

One compromise is to buy or build the individual components required, and then build or contract to build a system to link these systems together. Such projects are often called 'middleware' solutions. The task is still enormous and error prone, and the investment manager cannot be quite sure that it will work until it is in place and someone turns it on. So the ideal solution remains elusive, at least for the moment.

CHAPTER 20

Trends in Investment Management

OWNERSHIP AND STRUCTURE OF INVESTMENT MANAGEMENT FIRMS

Twenty years ago, the largest and best-known investment managers were in fact the investment divisions of large life insurers. These institutions managed enormous quantities of savings on behalf of a great many savers, whose long-term investments were often tied to life insurance policies. Wealthier private investors, by contrast, invested directly using the services of stockbrokers, private banks or financial advisors. In most countries, the life offices were quite heavily regulated, with limits on how much of their portfolios could be held in equities, and how much could be held in offshore assets. This limited the rate of return that could be earned, and discouraged innovation. Because each insurer managed a large proportion of the savings of its clients, and all were constrained by the same rules, they all tended to offer their clients the same range of services with about the same rates of return and implied fees. With little competitive pressure, profits were assured and comfortable.

As financial markets were deregulated during the 1980s, and individual savings and investment products became unbundled from insurance policies, the attractiveness of investment management as a profit centre became evident to other companies and institutions. This was highlighted by predictions of vastly increased savings rates among individuals due to retire in two to three decades, and who were becoming increasingly aware that they could not rely on state pensions to fund their golden years. Important among these were the banks. With the introduction of the Basle accords in the late 1980s, which specified the ratio of assets to be held against loans, and potentially limiting the profitability of lending, banks were keen to increase the proportion of the revenue they earned from fee income, as opposed to loan margins. Investment management was an obvious diversification.

Competition entered the investment management industry as investors sought ever-more attractive returns, and became increasingly sophisticated in their approaches to managing their savings. By the end of the 1980s, specialist investment management companies were taking business away from the banks and insurance companies, offering investors real choice in investment management services. In response to the challenge, life insurers began to define their investments division as a source of business growth in its own right rather than simply as an adjunct of the insurance business. They began to market their services to attract non-insurance investment management business.

BOUTIQUES VERSUS FULL SERVICE MANAGERS

Although still growing fast, by the late 1980s the investment management industry began to exhibit some of the signs of a maturing industry. One of the more interesting developments was its segmentation, as investment managers sought to differentiate their services from each other and market niches developed. This sequence would be predicted by almost any marketing professional, but the investment management industry exhibited, and continues to exhibit, some peculiarities not evident in most other industries.

The emergence of specialist, independent, investment management companies is not surprising. Often referred to as 'boutique managers', free of much of the baggage of the traditional, institutional managers and often concentrating on one asset class, some of these managers were able to adopt truly innovative investment strategies, allowing them to generate very attractive investment returns compared with traditional investment houses. They therefore enjoyed enviable success and consequent growth.

With growth came decisions about business strategy. Highly successful boutique managers often recognize that there is a natural limit to their potential growth. Specializing in one or two asset classes, or in a particular investment style, often imposes a limit to the growth of an investment management company. This may be because the appetite for that particular type of investment has a limit or, more frequently, because the opportunities for outstanding returns are available only for limited sums under management. It is much easier to achieve very high returns from relatively small sums invested than from large funds. As shareholders become accustomed to rapid growth in profitability, there may be strong pressure on the boutique manager to keep growing. Sometimes this can only be achieved by diversifying into other asset classes and strategies.

Soon, the boutique investment manager starts to look and behave more like traditional competitors, complete with increasingly unspectacular returns, as the manager moves into areas of investment management where he or she has little or no special skills to offer. At the same time the demands of managing a medium to large organization start to take over, consuming more and more business management as opposed to investment management skills. This can lead to deteriorating investment performance even in the original area of speciality.

One of two things often then happens to make the sequel interesting. The first is a new boutique manager appearing, offering expertise quite similar to that previously offered by the first boutique manager, filling the gap apparently left vacant by the first boutique and sometimes stealing client business along the way. Alternatively, the people who started the first boutique may recognize that they are unlikely to enjoy continued success in a large, less focused organization, so they leave to start a new boutique management company, specializing in the area in which they are known to excel, and so presenting formidable competition to their erstwhile employer. And so on, in Wagnerian style.

FEE STRUCTURES

Sooner or later, competition in investment management was bound to put downward pressure on investment management fees. Investment management companies still tend to levy management fees as a percentage of funds under management, even though their costs are identical for large and small accounts with the same investment objectives and guidelines. Realizing this, large, wholesale investors, such as company pension plans, have started to insist that management fees be modified to reflect more closely the costs of providing the service.

Also, the appearance and stunning success of indexed funds exerted noticeable pressure on fees. This occurred mainly by presenting a point of comparison, highlighting the extra costs of active management versus likely extra returns. Many investors responded by voting with their feet, while others have stayed substantially with active management, demanding that fees be lowered or levied differently.

Investors increasingly regard investment management as a commodity service, like day-to-day banking or general insurance, with the result that investment management companies' ability to justify active fees levied simply according to funds under management depends more and more on their ability to differentiate themselves from the competition as providers of specialist services.

The most visible result is the emergence and growth of very specialized investment managers, such as alternative investment managers. These companies do not pretend to provide mainstream investment management services, but are targeting investors seeking to complement mainstream investments with high-risk, high-return, high fee-paying investments.

The growing success of indexed portfolios and the emergence of alternative investment portfolios has encouraged investors to take a different view of the fees paid for traditional portfolio construction. Recognizing that most portfolios do not differ very much from, and in fact hold large elements of, the benchmark, investors are right to ask why they pay active fees for that part of the active portfolio that is essentially an indexed portfolio. Would it not be better to overtly invest the bulk of the portfolio in an indexed portfolio, and reserve a small portion for an aggressively active long–short mandate? This presents the possibility of improving overall performance and reducing fees. The indexed portfolio provides a buffer, while the long–short manager, whose benchmark is the cash return, has less incentive to follow the herd than managers benchmarked to an equity return. It reduces overall fees, because the investor is paying active fees only for that part of the portfolio that is in fact actively managed.

The next logical step for active investment management is performance-based fees. Many managers already offer this alternative, the principle of which is that the investment management service attracts a base fee similar to that levied by an indexed portfolio of similar size in the same asset class. This is designed to cover the administrative and other fixed costs to the investment manager, but not by itself to deliver a significant profit. The manager's profit derives instead from delivering returns above those achievable by an indexed portfolio. To the extent that the investment does outperform its benchmark, the investment manager is rewarded with a percentage of the amount of the outperformance. If the investment underperforms, the underperformance must be recovered by subsequent outperformance before the investment manager again enjoys a share of the spoils.

This arrangement presents a number of benefits. The most obvious is, of course, that the interests of the investment management company are much more closely aligned with those of the investor than under a conventional fee structure. The other is that, because the profitability of the investment management company is determined by the returns it achieves for its clients, it now has an interest in rewarding its investment staff on the basis of their performance. By contrast, conventional fee structures make this difficult. Because conventional fee income is unrelated to investment return relative to benchmark, rewarding investment staff according to this criterion means that, in the immediate term, the company's costs increase with superior investment return, while revenues remain constant, with the result that its profitability declines with the success of its clients' investments. Of course, in the longer term, better investment performance should be rewarded with more client business, but this relationship is indirect and uncertain.

THE CUSTODIAN AS INVESTMENT MANAGER

The traditional role of the custodian is to take physical charge of the assets being managed. The custodian finds a place to store all the pieces of paper and a means of keeping track of what they all are and to whom they really belong. With increasing competition between investment managers, and the associated requirement for independently prepared reports of investment returns, custodians stepped in to provide the functions of portfolio valuation and reporting.

Because the costs of managing indexed portfolios are made up largely of administrative costs, custodians, who already provide most of the administration, have often been in a special position to offer indexed fund management at little marginal cost.

With growth in demand for borrowed share certificates, and the profitability of meeting the demand by lending certificates from long-term portfolio holdings, many custodians recognized that they were the natural providers of this lucrative service. After all, they know better than anyone else where all the certificates and other titles to ownership of the assets are, and they have computer systems built specifically to keep track of movements of the paper and changes of ownership.

In some circumstances, stock lending can be more profitable than providing custodian services, and can compare favourably the fee income from investment management. Some custodians offer to provide global custodian services combined with basic indexed portfolio management, often at little more than the fees for custodian services, provided this includes a stock lending agreement. Under these agreements, the custodian-manager has the right to lend stock and often to receive all the rent from doing so. Naturally, this can appear very attractive to investors, but there are some potential shortcomings. If the investor accepts this arrangement, he or she needs to be sure that the custodian discloses stock lending revenue and assumes all the risk, including that of the stock not being returned.

The second potential shortcoming is that there may be a conflict of interest between the roles of custodian and manager. One of the objectives of the investment manager, particularly the indexed fund manager, is to minimize transactions and administrative costs associated with the portfolio. On the other hand, the custodian has no such objective, and may in fact derive extra profit from more transactions. Moreover, an important role of the custodian is to separate investment decisions from settlements flowing from those decisions. The investment manager decides what to buy, from whom and for how much, while the custodian writes the cheque. Having the two functions taking place in the same organization, while by no means necessarily inviting unintended consequences, nevertheless removes the biggest safeguard against them.

THE ROLE OF THE CONSULTANT

With the increasing importance of corporate pension schemes, industry-based schemes and other funds that are overseen by a board of trustees, consultants have seen their role in the investment management process expanded.

The role of many consultants has its origins in advising fund trustees and managers on how to manage the liabilities of the fund. Their actuarial background equipped them to project the timing and magnitude of future calls on the fund's assets. These projections, combined with forecasts of investment returns, enabled the consultant to advise on the rate of member contributions necessary to keep the fund healthy.

With the expansion of choice of investment managers, and the associated choice of investment strategies, fund trustees and managers sought advice on how to choose between investment strategies and products. The consultant, being familiar with the fund's liabilities, and therefore its tolerance for risk and its long-term investment requirements, was often in a unique position to give advice on investment strategy as well.

Although many consultants prefer to limit their role to advising on liability management and asset-liability matching, others have expanded the resources at their disposal to meet the growing need of fund trustees and managers for help in implementing the most suitable investment strategy and seeing that it meets expectations. Often this role extends to articulating the best long-term strategic asset allocation for the fund, if the managers of the fund feel ill-equipped to do this for themselves. By providing independent expert advice on investment strategy, the consultant can help fund trustees to protect themselves against the consequences of disappointing investment outcomes.

The independence and numeracy of investment consultants can also equip them for evaluating investment managers, so many firms of consultants conduct research into and maintain databases of investment managers, the range of products they offer, their strengths and weaknesses and, of course, the returns they achieve. This constitutes an intensive research effort on their part, and can be a very valuable resource for pension fund managers when trying to choose between investment managers. Some consultants are very thorough, to the extent of getting to know individual investment managers in order to understand their contribution to the investment management process. This can be important because some investment management companies become dependent on individual staff members, with the consequence that the quality of service they offer, and the reliability of the investment returns they achieve, can be seriously affected by the departure of key investment staff.

Once the consultant has established a role in determining investment strategy and choosing investment managers, the same consultant usually continues to contribute by monitoring and evaluating the ongoing performance of the investment strategy against expectations and benchmarks. The consultant is thus very important in deciding if the strategy is working, and at what point revisions are warranted.

Given the potential importance of the consultant to the fund's success, it is useful to know whether or not his or her objectives are being met. Certainly, if the fund is earning acceptable or above expected returns, one could say that they are. But this could be due to exceptional performance on the part of investment managers, higher than expected returns in the markets in which the fund happens to be invested or because the fund is assuming more risk than appropriate

Unfortunately, the role of the consultant is very difficult to evaluate objectively and definitively. Some funds try, by engaging the services of independent investment analysts. This can give interesting results, but it is impractical to go through this exercise very often.

Most funds find it very difficult to change consultants, even if they are unhappy with the quality of service or advice they are receiving. This is hardly surprising in view of the importance of the consultant's contribution. A change of consultant can lead to a change of investment strategy, and almost certainly leads to changes in investment managers, which can be a very costly process, with no guarantee that the results will be worth it.

Many consultants levy fees according to the time spent working for each client. This can have some unintended consequences. For example, manager and strategy research are not directly chargeable to any client, so they may not get much attention; or they may be delegated to junior consultants. Consultants who are reluctant to spend valuable time coming to grips with new developments in investment technology and the potential benefits and risks of new investment instruments cannot be fully equipped to evaluate investment managers using those instruments and technology, or advise investors on the most suitable investments to meet particular return and risk requirements.

Other consultants levy a fixed fee, according to the required consulting services. This certainly frees the consultant from the strictures of maximizing charged hours, but the knowledge that the fee is to be earned regardless of service quality may deny the consultant the incentive to explore innovative investment solutions, and to stick with what is familiar, even if it is not entirely satisfactory.

CORPORATE GOVERNANCE

Corporate governance is making sure that companies really are working in the interests of those investors who have invested in their shares. The movement to promote corporate governance in listed companies gained momentum during the 1990s, led by, among others, **CALPERS** (California Public Employees Retirement Service).

The movement started in response to what was perceived by the late 1980s as a divergence between the interests of senior managers in listed companies and those of their owners, the shareholders. At the top of the list of concerns was the scale of bosses' remuneration, which was sometimes very high even when the firm in their charge was losing its owners' money. This was closely followed by measures to protect the rights of minority shareholders. It also focused on efforts by senior managers to make the company invulnerable to takeover, thereby ensuring continuation of their own lucrative positions, while denying shareholders the opportunity to gain by selling the company at above market prices. The corporate governance movement has notched up some impressive achievements. For example, many firms now disclose the earnings, including those paid in the form of shares and options, of directors and senior managers, even if this disclosure is not mandated in the market in which they are listed. By the end of the 1990s, a much greater proportion of directors were likely to be independent and non-executive than had been the case before corporate governance became a force.

In practice, the corporate governance movement works by encouraging shareholders, however passively their investment is managed, to use the voting rights accorded them by their shareholding to help to align the interests of senior management with those of the firm's shareholders. Institutions such as pension funds, mutual funds and unit trust funds together own the majority of listed assets in many developed markets, and, because nearly all the shares they own carry voting rights, they have the ability to affect a wide range of actions by managers and directors of listed companies. By ensuring that major decisions are taken in shareholders' interests, the theory goes, the value of the company must improve, so benefiting all shareholders.

Actually exercising voting rights is not always as straightforward as it may seem. From the point of view of the investment manager, it is necessary first to check with the owner of the shares whether or not he or she intends to vote, and if so, whether this should be done by the investment manager. If the investor wants the investment manager to do the voting, is there a preference regarding which specific issues to vote for and against? To exercise voting rights responsibly requires a good understanding of the workings of the company. Of course, it is expected that the investment manager knows the companies in which the portfolios are invested, but this is hardly ever the case with indexed portfolios and other forms of passive management; an important point in view of the amount of investment now held in passive portfolios.

Recognizing this, and the limits to which even active equity managers can monitor all the activities of the companies in which they hold shares, a number of independent services have been set up specifically to research the corporate governance aspects of listed companies. Investors and investment managers can subscribe to these services to obtain an independent view on the likely effects of proposed activity and vote accordingly.

Altogether, the impact of the corporate governance movement has been impressive, and mostly to the overall benefit of investors, but there are some potential dangers. Having succeeded so far, the temptation is to seek other ways of enhancing shareholder value by improving management practices in general. By intruding into areas of corporate strategy, grey areas can appear. For example, a decision to use a cash pile to take over another company may be simply implementing corporate strategy, clearly the preserve of the company's management. If the share price subsequently slumps, which it often does following an acquisition, management might be accused of having carried out the purchase as a means of making the company less attractive to potential predators, which is a corporate governance issue. Or shareholders who are disappointed with recent stock returns may insist on a change in leadership of the company, whether or not this would unambiguously improve matters, possibly leading to uncertainty, further reducing the market value of the firm.

Measures intended to keep management honest can easily develop mission-creep, usurping roles that may be best left to the firm's management.

THE ROLE OF THE COMPLIANCE OFFICER

With the increasing complexity and number of participants in investment management and the increasing use of ever more complex investment strategies and instruments, the room for things to go wrong is perceived to be growing. Fund managers, trustees and investment managers are acutely aware of their legal obligations, both with respect to investors' wealth, and in a wider context. The 1990s saw a growing emphasis on ensuring that the letter, as well as the spirit of all laws, regulations and contractual obligations are met at all times.

The sophistication and flexibility of modern computing is a big help in ensuring that investment portfolios comply with all relevant laws, regulations and mandate specifications. Most investment managers augment this with human oversight in the form of a compliance officer. This person's job is to ensure that computer systems are programmed correctly to warn of any potential breaches of mandates and guidelines, and to ensure that appropriate back-up measures are in place should the primary checks fail. If a breach does occur, the compliance officer needs to be equipped to limit the consequent damage.

In order to do this effectively, the compliance officer needs some formidable training. To begin with, a good understanding of the legal environment is essential, and should be combined with both familiarity with the investment processes applied to all mandates and a qualification in economics and, preferably, finance at an advanced level to ensure an understanding of the relationship between risk and return for various investment vehicles. Common sense is indispensable. Since the compliance officer may need to establish house rules to help to reduce the risk of compliance breaches, he or she needs the authority to ensure that these are respected.

Therefore the compliance officer is usually a senior member of staff. The importance of the position within the organization, and the calibre of the person, reflect the company's commitment to abide by the rules.

Naturally, the way the compliance officer does the job is largely a matter of personal style, ranging from very formal to informal but close, and frequent communication with investment staff. One approach, for example, is to commission regular reports from investment staff detailing specific aspects of portfolio management, which can then be compared with some kind of checklist for possible discrepancies. Such an approach depends heavily on the reports being well designed and presented, but has the advantage of ensuring a permanent record of all items covered in the reports. Another approach is to engage the cooperation of investment staff and encourage them to highlight potential weak spots in investment management processes and compliance systems. This approach foregoes the permanent record, an important shortcoming if something does go wrong, but can encourage the assistance of the very people most able to prevent things going wrong in the first place.

Another approach is to compile all the house rules into a document, usually called a compliance manual, and tell everybody that they must read it. This is fine as far as it goes, but it does not ensure compliance unless somebody checks that the document is read and understood, and that the rules are being adhered to. The assumption that merely having a set of rules constitutes compliance can itself be a compliance risk. Frequent changes to the rules may give the impression that the compliance officer is busy and therefore doing a good job, but in fact it merely compounds the problem by reducing the likelihood that the rules are read and understood by investment management staff, and introduces confusion.

Sadly, some investment managers mouth support for a strong compliance function, but betray their intentions either by hiring someone who is underqualified for this demanding role, or by failing to accord them the necessary authority to fulfil it effectively. Another sign of how serious the company is about compliance can be indicated by who bears responsibility for compliance breaches. Obviously, the member of investment staff responsible for the function where the breach took place needs to be accountable. For the compliance officer to take the role seriously, and to be taken seriously, he or she needs also to be held accountable if the safety nets prove to be ineffective.

PEOPLE VERSUS PROCESSES: ATOMIZATION OF INVESTMENT MANAGEMENT FUNCTIONS

Individual investment managers often used to be asked what their track record was; their success rate for identifying investments that subsequently delivered above average rates of return. Investment managers with good track records were rewarded with highly paid positions and promoted to senior management. Companies employing these managers often found it easier to attract new clients than those without such stars.

The problem was that the stars were quick to cotton on. Realizing how valuable they were enabled them to demand increased rewards, and to threaten to leave and work for a competitor if their demands were not met. Companies frequently found themselves vulnerable to the actions of individuals or small groups of staff members. Consultants carrying out research into the strengths and weaknesses of investment management companies would note that the company's investment performance was predicated on keeping certain individuals on the payroll.

One way that investment management companies have tried to deal with this problem is to subordinate individual investment managers to the investment management process. Rather than rely on the insights of a very gifted equity analyst to decide what stocks to include in a portfolio, the chief investment manager charges a team with devising a set of decision rules for screening stocks for inclusion in the portfolio. The set of decision rules becomes a process, and individual investment staff members are each allocated a part to play in the process. If one or two people leave the company, others with similar capabilities can easily fill their roles, and the investment management process continues without interruption. With the possible exception of the chief investment manager, no individual is allowed to become so important in the investment management process that they can disrupt it.

Most large investment management companies have found that this arrangement works well, and consultants often regard it favourably because it can ensure both discipline at each stage of the investment management process and a consistency of performance and standard of service.

Subordinating people to processes first appeared in the context of quantitative investment management, where discipline and consistency of approach are all-important. Many traditional managers, seeking similar consistency and discipline in their approaches, have also established formal processes for portfolio construction and management, with people playing a minor role.

While in theory this approach appears to promote stability and consistency, it can be disrupted by staff changes at senior levels. When this happens, the disruption can be complete. It can also stifle creativity and innovation at all levels of the organization. Most companies that favour processes would deny this on the grounds that most jobs demand advanced skills of one sort or another, but most of the jobs defined by the process are too limited to keep really gifted investment management professionals interested. Unless tempted by either promotion, more money or both, they leave for more challenging and creative roles elsewhere, leaving their posts filled by individuals who are competent but unlikely to add extra value to the overall process.

Atomizing investment management functions also has the unfortunate consequence that general management skills become impossible to develop, with the result that senior managers often have a very narrow skill base, which excludes managing people. This can make for very incohesive investment teams, high staff turnover and, paradoxically, internal instability.

Possibly the worst danger is that the process becomes ossified and unresponsive to the changing investment environment. True discipline in investment processes becomes reduced to plain, old-fashioned rigidity, often with the consequence that the risk control that was a central aim of the structure becomes subordinate to, and eventually a casualty of, the structure.

The alternative approach involves collecting a group of very gifted people and encouraging innovation and individualism. This might be thought of as a type of constructive anarchy, which very few organizations succeed in managing. When it does work, it does so spectacularly; and although such organizations have been known to work over periods of a decade or more, the structure, because it depends heavily on an unusual mix of talent and how it is managed, is inherently unstable.

The trend towards increased discipline and consistency in investment management has already advanced too far for a reversion to the old star-led regime, but there is a case for recognizing the advantages and applying the best aspects of both approaches.

Because investment management is a complex business, and the investment environment inherently anarchic, it makes sense to allow room for some creativity in the investment management process. If well managed, this serves to reinforce the spirit of risk control and discipline rather than merely the letter. It makes sense to engage people who can understand the mechanisms of the investment management process and therefore help to adapt it to the changing opportunities of markets and the changing demands of investors.

Students of management are sometimes bemused by the application of atomized production processes in investment management because it contradicts wisdom developed long ago in industries such as manufacturing. What is happening in many investment management companies looks strangely like scientific management, the segmenting of a process into its smallest components, each to be performed repetitively by a different individual. Not only did this turn out, for most functions, to be horribly inefficient, inhumane and error-prone, it also made any progression to a position of wider responsibility all but impossible for the individuals concerned.

If this is true of manufacturing, it is even more so for investment management, where the assets of the company are not dyes, casts and pulleys, but the people who work there. Too much segmenting of investment management can make it impossible for companies to develop general management skills in their staff. And if the people in the company are not well managed, nothing at all will work.

CHAPTER 21

Conclusions: Traditional versus Quantitative

Quantitative investment techniques have become increasingly popular since the mid-1980s. Their growth reflects other trends, such as:

- The availability of hardware, software and data to put into practice the breakthroughs in finance theory that took place in the 1950s, 60s and 70s.
- The availability of liquid derivatives markets, facilitating the creation of synthetic assets and short positions.
- More widespread investment in managed investment products, resulting in increased choice of investment products and much more sophistication on the part of investors.
- The increasing perception that traditional investment techniques are not delivering adequate returns for risk and value for money.
- The perception that financial markets are becoming increasingly volatile, increasing the importance of risk control.

Quantitative investments are seen to introduce discipline and rigour into the investment management process, with predefined decision rules applied consistently to give tailored investment outcomes, such as minimum and maximum variation from benchmark, protection against losses and even guaranteed minimum rates of return.

Passive investments, such as indexation, also enable investors to reduce significantly the costs and uncertainty of investing in risky assets.

An important distinction of quantitative investment management is that it encourages the incorporation of risk management in both portfolio construction and ongoing management. It also requires a consistency of assumptions throughout the portfolio construction and analysis processes.

Quantitative techniques can be applied to most parts of diversified portfolios, starting with asset allocation, where asset class models generate return forecasts that are used in conjunction with mean-variance optimization, either to construct the portfolio, analyse its likely risk and return profile, or both. Option pricing technology may be used in conjunction with this to construct portfolio strategies designed to deliver minimum returns tailored to specific investment requirements.

While quantitative models are most widely applied to domestic and global equity markets, they are also widely used to construct and analyse fixed interest portfolios and currencies. Probably their biggest limitation is that they are difficult to apply to assets that are not frequently traded, such as direct property, direct equity and venture capital. Quantitative techniques are ideally suited to most commodity and derivative markets.

Because investment managers often seek to differentiate themselves from their competitors by means of superior return forecasting techniques, there are many different approaches to this task, all with legitimate claims to being quantitative. Most are based on some modelling technique.

Nearly all quantitative investment models are based on either the capital asset pricing model (CAPM), Black–Scholes option pricing theory or the principle of the present value equivalent of future income. CAPM describes the relationship between the risk and return of individual assets, and their contribution to portfolio risk and return. It allows the diversification of a portfolio's holdings relative to a benchmark portfolio. Black–Scholes option pricing theory facilitates the estimation of the value of options and instruments comprising option-like return patterns. Both technologies demand relatively sophisticated computational capabilities. This is especially true of CAPM, which uses large quantities of historical data to compute covariance matrices. The fact that, as recently as 1980, neither technology was seen outside universities while both are ubiquitous in investment today, is an indication of the increased sophistication in investment management. By contrast, present value computation has been used for many decades, requiring fairly simple calculations.

MODELS FOR INVESTMENT MANAGEMENT

Much of the increased sophistication in investment management is associated with the use of models to help to design and analyse investment portfolios. A model is an attempt to represent quantitatively the real-life behaviour of a portfolio, with the trick for investment management models being to identify and quantify the important influences on portfolio risk and return. A model railway is a simplified imitation of a real one. It is designed to behave recognizably like the real thing, with some simplifying assumptions. For example, it does not require tons of coal to be shovelled into it, and it doesn't fill your living room with soot. It doesn't go on strike, although it can be derailed and have other accidents. A model portfolio is designed to exhibit most of the characteristics of a real portfolio – enough to be recognizable, but necessarily omitting some real world details that are not practical to incorporate in the scaled-down version. Most financial models include a random error term to accommodate these imponderables.

The benefits of models in investment management are that they can:

- encourage a consistency of approach throughout the investment management process
- contribute to robust portfolio construction by facilitating sensitivity analyses
- encourage discipline by prescribing contingencies and appropriate actions
- facilitate risk control by quantifying relationships between asset returns and economic events.

The risks associated with models are that they:

- can be prone to data errors
- may be subject to the limitations of relying on historical data
- may be vulnerable to computational errors
- may be vulnerable to incorrect assumptions
- can be prone to oversimplification
- are subject to model error, the mistake of choosing the wrong model
- produce results that may be hard to check if the model is applied as a black box
- may generate results that are difficult to interpret.

While the biggest risk in portfolio modelling is choosing the wrong model, even if the model selected is the most appropriate one available, there are other risks. For example, it is recognized that all models oversimplify the problem they are modelling. Therefore it is often what is left out of the model that can cause problems. The people who create the models often assume that the effects of items left out of the model will cancel each other out, at least when all assets are aggregated into a portfolio. Often this is true, but sometimes all the omitted effects work in the same direction, so that the model systematically misestimates some important aspect of the portfolio, such as its risk.

The other danger of models for investment management is that they attempt too much detail, so that too much data is needed to make them work. The more data needed, the greater the chance there is for errors in the data, and the harder it is to spot the errors.

Investment management models are at least as susceptible to GIGO (garbage in, garbage out) as any other model or computer program.

For equity portfolios, most quantitative techniques incorporate some kind of mean-variance optimization technology, based on some kind of risk model describing the factors that are most likely to explain portfolio variance, and the relationship of individual assets to each of the factors. There are many different approaches to equity risk modelling, each with its own strengths and weaknesses, and suited to different kinds of portfolio.

Most market neutral and long–short investment strategies are based on some application of quantitative investment techniques, with extensive use of derivative instruments, delivering potentially very attractive investment returns. Being high risk, they are usually intended as a complement to traditional investments, but can be made available to small investors by means of funds of funds.

Both mean-variance optimization and many forecasting models rely on historical return data. For return forecasting, this can be perilous because asset returns tend to vary enormously over different time periods. When developing return forecasting models, researchers routinely test the model on past data before trying it out in the real world. The idea is that if it worked in the past, it will work again. This can lead into the trap known as 'data-mining', whereby the model works on selected data sets, from which it is assumed to work in general.

TRADITIONAL VERSUS QUANTITATIVE INVESTMENT MANAGEMENT

A common misunderstanding is to assume that traditional and quantitative investment management techniques are incompatible within a portfolio, so the investor must decide to adopt one or the other. Some of the shrewdest investment strategies combine the best of both worlds. For example, combining a core, indexed portfolio with an aggressively active, traditionally managed portfolio has been shown to yield impressive results for large investors otherwise limited by the size of their portfolios to modest return. Traditionally managed equity and bond portfolios are often successfully combined with quantitative currency overlay portfolios. Similarly, traditional portfolios can be combined successfully with quantitative risk management and control, including overlays designed to deliver guaranteed minimum rates of return.

By contrast, combining traditional and quantitative investment management within the same investment management company can be difficult to manage. It is hard for an investment management company to find and retain talented staff in both sides of the discipline, partly because there are nearly always enormous cultural differences. Traditional managers usually have qualifications that are not intensely mathematical, focusing more on applied security analysis and microeconomics. Meanwhile, quantitative managers are, on average, younger, typically with tertiary qualifications in mathematics, physics and finance. The difference in age and backgrounds, combined with a different approach to portfolio management, usually contributes to a marked difference in workplace culture. Traditional managers have more meetings, both formal and informal. Because they have more say over how much and when they buy and sell assets, they tend to develop much closer relationships with brokers. Quantitative managers make heavier use of models and require more sophisticated computer resources. Because their buy and sell decisions are generated by modelling or decision rule systems, quantitative managers tend not to discuss their decision processes with brokers, merely communicating orders when required.

Traditional mangers tend to focus on the current price of a stock and its prospects for high returns. Single events, such as company announcements, can stimulate a lot of activity. Quantitative managers tend to be more concerned with asset prices relative to fair price or the price of another asset, while single events are important only in the portfolio context.

Probably the most difficult combination in one house is traditional active and (quantitative) indexed management. This is particularly tricky if the traditional manager is delivering disappointing returns. Although all active managers are bound to have periods when they fail to achieve return objectives, being in the same camp as the indexed portfolio when it is delivering higher returns can be discouraging.

Many investment management companies that try to combine traditional and quantitative investment processes under one roof find that the two teams' cultural differences sometimes develop into rivalry that can hinder cooperation and even communication between them. Some companies try to resolve this by getting the two teams to work closely together, and to share as many common resources as possible. Often this does not work, usually because the people who must work with both teams, such as client services, performance measurement and administration, often find the two approaches so different as to be thoroughly confusing. The different applications of derivative instruments, for example, can place conflicting demands on administrative and reporting systems; return and attribution analysis calculations must accommodate different approaches, and client services must try to communicate quite different, sometimes contradictory, results to the clients. Worse, the rival teams may try to impose their own way of doing things on each other.

One of the worst traps the company can fall into is to expect both traditional and quantitative managers to share the same dealing resource. Apart from confusing the dealers and the brokers with whom they deal, combining dealing for both teams can create enormous inefficiencies and even lead to conflicts of interest such as front-running. This is where a dealer applies knowledge of a significant transaction that is about to take place by taking positions in advance of the transaction in order to benefit from the consequent price movement. Insider trading and compliance rules have ruled out dealers deriving personal gain from front-running, but a dealer or investment manager who is rewarded according to specific return targets might find front-running on behalf of client portfolios lucrative too. The cost is borne by the investor whose impending share transaction stimulated the front-running. Since dealing for traditional portfolios is usually discretionary, while for quantitative portfolios it usually is not, quantitative portfolios are more likely to suffer.

THE GREY AREAS

Despite the culture clashes and the sometimes very different feel of traditional and quantitative investment management teams, there are plenty of overlapping areas, and opportunities for quantitative and traditional managers to learn from each other.

Many of the techniques described in this book can be legitimately claimed as their own by both traditional and quantitative investment managers.

Some traditional managers complement their return forecasting capabilities with reverse optimization. While not affecting the forecasting process itself, this can enhance the consistency and robustness of the portfolio construction process.

Value-at-risk is an example where a quantitative approach can be applied to traditional portfolio construction, providing forward estimates of portfolio risk.

Quantitative investment management, while seeking to apply as many objective decision criteria as possible to the investment management process, nevertheless requires judgement at many stages. For example:

- Selecting the best models for return and risk forecasting.
- Determining the most reliable data to apply.
- Determining what is the best method of covariance calculations.
- Interpreting the results.
- Deciding when a model needs to be upgraded or retired.
- Determining the best approach to risk management.
- Determining the most suitable approach to currency management.
- Deciding how to design and implement decision rules.

Performance measurement and attribution analysis are examples of quantitative aspects of traditional portfolio management. How performance is to be measured and how the portfolio should be disaggregated for attribution analysis requires judgement. Once this had been decided, however, the processes are purely quantitative. As for quantitative investment management, where portfolios are constructed and analysed according to the output of return forecasting and portfolio risk and return models, it is important to note that the choice of the models and how they are used is based purely on judgement.

PART IV

Appendices

APPENDIX 1

Pricing Interest Rate Securities

Interest rate securities come in two broad forms, known as discount securities and bonds. The difference between the two is that bonds pay coupons periodically, whereas discount securities pay interest in one payment at maturity. Interest rate securities are nearly always quoted in terms of an interest rate, sometimes referred to as the yield to maturity. The yield to maturity of a discount security is often quoted as 100 minus the interest rate, so a 5% yield is quoted as 95.00.

To work out the settlement value of the security from the interest rate, it is necessary also to know the maturity of the instrument and, in the case of bonds, the amount of the coupon and when and how often it is paid. Once these details are at hand, it is a matter of applying the appropriate pricing formula.

THE SETTLEMENT VALUE OF A DISCOUNT SECURITY

To work out the settlement value of a discount interest-bearing instrument, one applies the following formula:

$$P = FV/(1 + i \times d/365) \tag{A1.1}$$

Where:

P = the settlement value
FV = the face value
i = the interest rate
d = the maturity in days of the instrument

Some discount securities are priced using a 360-day year instead of 365. This simplifies the calculation but, before applying the formula, it is necessary to check which pricing convention is used.

EXAMPLE A1.1.1 *The settlement value of a discount security*

The face value of a discount security is $1 000 000, the period is 90 days, with a 360-day calendar year. The security has recently traded at 94.95 – an interest rate of 5.05% (100 – 94.95). The settlement price of the security is thus:

$$\text{Settlement value} = \$1\ 000\ 000/(1 + ((100 - 94.95)/100) \times 90/360)$$
$$= \$987\ 532$$

Thus an investor paying $987 532 now and receiving $1 000 000 in 90 days' time will earn an annualized return of 5.05%.

THE POINT VALUE OF A DISCOUNT SECURITY

Knowing the settlement value is a big help, but usually investors are also interested to know how the settlement value changes with a given change in the interest rate. This value, often referred to as the **point value**, is usually derived by calculating the settlement value for interest rates slightly higher and slightly lower than the current rate, then halving the difference to get an average. The point value depends on both the maturity of the security and the current interest rate.

To calculate the point value, the price formula is applied using an interest rate 0.01% higher and lower than the current market. The difference between the settlement values thus obtained is halved to give the point value. The formula can be expressed as:

$$\text{Point value} = (P_1 - P_2)/2 \qquad \text{(A1.2)}$$

Where:

P_1 = settlement value with interest rate less 0.01%
P_2 = settlement value with interest rate plus 0.01%

EXAMPLE A1.1.2 *The point value of a discount security*

In this case it is:

$$\text{Settlement value} = \$1\,000\,000/(1 + ((100 - 94.96)/100) \times 90/360) = \$987\,557$$
$$\text{Settlement value} = \$1\,000\,000/(1 + ((100 - 94.94)/100) \times 90/360) = \$987\,508$$
$$\text{Point value} = (\$987\,557 - \$987\,508)/2$$
$$= \$24.38$$

The point value will change slightly for short-term instruments, such as this 90-day example, as interest rates go up and down. In general, the longer the maturity of the interest rate security underlying the futures contract, the greater will be the change in point value as absolute interest rates rise and fall.

THE SETTLEMENT VALUE OF A BOND

The coupons paid during its life complicate the calculation of the bond price. In addition to discounting the face value of the bond, as in the discount security, each coupon payment needs also to be discounted in the same way. The formula that achieves this is as follows:

$$P = c \times (1 + a) + 100 \times v^n \qquad \text{(A1.3)}$$

Where:

v = 1/(1 + interest rate)
a = $(1 - v^n)$/interest rate
n = years to maturity times the number of coupons per year
c = annual coupon income divided by the number of coupons per year

EXAMPLE A1.2.1 *The settlement value of a bond*

A bond has a face value of \$1 000 000, a maturity of ten years, a coupon rate of 5% per annum, with two coupon payments per year. The settlement price of the bond, with an interest rate of 5.85% is calculated as follows:

$$\text{Price} = \$\,50\,000/2 \times (1 + (1 - 1/(1 + 2.925\%)^{20})) + 100 \times 1/(1 + 2.925\%)^{20}$$
$$= \$\,961\,330$$

THE POINT VALUE OF A BOND

As with discount securities, the point value of the bond changes with the interest rate. Estimating the point value is done in exactly the same way for the bond, that is, the bond settlement value is calculated for an interest rate slightly higher and slightly lower, and the difference is halved to give an average. This value is also known as the dollar value of one point and the portfolio value per basis point.

EXAMPLE A1.2.2 *The point value of a bond*

Thus the settlement value for this bond with an interest rate of 5.84% is \$962 050, and the settlement value with an interest rate of 5.86% is \$960 611. The difference is \$1439, so the point value is \$720.

$$\begin{aligned}\text{Point value} &= (\$962\ 050 - \$960\ 611)/2 \\ &= \$720\end{aligned}$$

APPENDIX 2

Forward Contracts

THEORY

Forward contracts are the simplest of all derivative instruments, and can be used in nearly all types of commercial transactions. A forward contract is simply an agreement to buy or sell something at an agreed price at some point in the future. Many goods are bought and sold uniquely by means of forward contracts. For example, if you order a new suit from your tailor, you will expect to pay a fixed sum of money for the suit on the day that it is finished. Most home purchases link an agreed price to a settlement date. These are examples of forward contracts.

Forward contracts are frequently used by agricultural producers, mining companies and many manufacturers as a means of ensuring that they will receive enough sale proceeds to cover their cost of production for the coming season or production or accounting period. Their customers might wish to buy their products forward to ensure that they have continuity of supply to meet critical secondary production or distribution requirements. Thus a producer of raw iron ore might sell production forward to cover extraction costs, while the customer, who is a steel maker, will buy enough iron ore forward to ensure that all blast furnaces are kept busy and there is enough steel to meet expected, or contracted, demand.

This activity can also be thought of as hedging, because it eliminates the uncertainty that revenues will not cover the costs of production (for the primary producer), or that the price of raw materials rises so much that the end product cannot be sold at a profit (for the secondary and subsequent producers).

An important feature of forward contracts is that you can sell forward something you do not currently own, otherwise known as selling short, or shorting. Of course, this can be risky: the iron ore producer selling forward his or her production runs the risk that the quantity sold forward will not be produced on time. Such an event would necessitate buying the shortfall from another producer, perhaps a competitor. Despite such risks, the ability to sell short can be very useful.

If physical goods can be bought and sold in this way, then why not financial assets? After all, both primary and secondary producers can also lose if interest rates go up so much that they can no longer comfortably service their debts. Similarly, if their customers or suppliers are in a different country, they can lose if the exchange rate moves against them.

This widespread appeal explains why forward contracts, and their descendants, futures, swaps and options, have been used for centuries in everyday commerce – and why they are used so extensively nowadays.

In the context of investment management, forward contracts are nearly always used to hedge some kind of investment risk. The most frequent application is to hedge foreign currency exposure. Forwards may also be used to gain immediate exposure to risky assets in anticipation of new investment to the portfolio, hedging against the risk that the price of that asset rises in the meantime.

PRICING

When the settlement date is some distance in the future, the settlement price takes into account the fact that it is not an immediate or 'spot' transaction. The difference between the spot price and the forward price reflects the cost to the seller of not having the use of the proceeds of the sale until the settlement date. It also includes the cost of storage and insurance of physical goods, and is adjusted for any pecuniary benefit of still having possession of the goods, such as rent received. If the goods in question are shares, for example, the buyer expects to be compensated for any dividends paid before he or she actually takes possession.

The difference between today's price, otherwise known as the spot price, and the price actually paid (the settlement price) is known as the forward premium. The formula for the settlement price is:

$$P = s \times (1 + i + h - cf) \tag{A2.1}$$

Where:

P = the settlement value
s = the spot price
h = storage, insurance and other holding costs
cf = cash flows to the asset
i = the interest rate

The interest cost plus other holding costs less income received from holding the physical asset are collectively known as the **cost of carry**.

EXAMPLE A2.1.1 *The settlement value of a forward contract*

A farmer is expecting to harvest 100 000 bushels of wheat at the end of August. It is now late February and he has just finished sowing his fields. He notes that, at the current price of $50 per bushel, he will make a respectable profit, as the direct cost of producing the wheat is expected to be only $40 per bushel. If the wheat price goes to $55, he will make an even greater profit, but if it drops to $40, his end of year celebrations will be more meagre. Note that the farmer's cost of production is the same whether he produces the wheat for sale now or in six months' time. Interest rates are now 5% per annum, so the price he can expect to receive for wheat in six months' time is calculated as:

$$\begin{aligned} P &= \$50 \times (1 + 5\% \times 6/12) \\ &= \$51.25 \end{aligned}$$

Another way of looking at this is to say that the farmer is receiving $51.25 in six months' time instead of $50.00 now. This equates to an interest rate of 2.50% (51.25/50.00) or 5.00% annualized.

EXAMPLE A2.1.2 *The settlement value of a forward contract*

A couple nearing retirement want to buy an apartment at the beach. They have found the one they want and have set their heart on it. The problem is that they won't retire for another year and a half and, until they do, they cannot move away from their present home in the city. The current owner of the beachside apartment is not in a hurry for the cash, but wants to take advantage of this opportunity to sell because he thinks property prices might go down. They agree a current price of $200 000. Interest rates are currently 6% per annum. The apartment is currently rented out for \$17 000 (8.5%) per year, and regular maintenance is about \$2000 (1%) per year. The forward price can be calculated as:

$$P = \$200\,000 \times (1 + (6\% - 8.5\% + 1\%) \times 18/12)$$
$$= \$195\,500$$

The vendor thus receives the current price of the apartment, adjusted for related income and expenses, plus an annual rate of interest of 6.0%.

Note that the forward price is less than the current price. This is because the cost of holding the asset, comprising the interest cost plus maintenance, is less than the amount received in rent by the holder of the asset.

An important feature of forward pricing is that it does not take into account any estimation of whether the price of the goods will rise or fall. The forward price is often referred to as the fair price because it is the price at which an investor is indifferent between holding the forward contract or the asset itself.

FOREIGN EXCHANGE FORWARDS

Pricing forward foreign exchange contracts follows the same principle, that is, that the forward premium equates holding the forward and holding the spot. Interest is thus received on the physical currency held, analogous to the cash held in the earlier examples, and it is paid on the currency to be purchased forward, analogous to dividends or rent foregone in the earlier examples. When applied to currencies, these two interest rates are compounded, which means that they are divided rather than subtracted. This gives a more exact price, as follows:

$$P = s \times (1 + i_1 \times d/365)/(1 + i_2 \times d/365) \qquad \text{(A2.2)}$$

Where:

s = current or spot exchange rate
i_1 = interest rate in numerator country
i_2 = interest rate in denominator country

If the current spot exchange rate is £0.65, UK interest rates are 6.5% while US interest rates are 5% per annum. The price of a 90-day forward contract can thus be calculated as follows:

$$P = £0.65 \times (1 + 6.5\% \times 90/365)/(1 + 5\% \times 90/365)$$
$$= £0.6524$$

EXAMPLE A2.2 *The value of a foreign exchange forward contract*

Hold US$ Asset		**Create Synthetic US$ Asset**	**Buy/Sell £**	**Asset £**
	US$		**US$**	**£**
Buy 3-month Treasuries	−100	Buy Spot Sterling @ £0.65	−100	+65.00
		Buy 3-month Gilts		−65.00
		Sell 3-month Gilts		+ 66.04
Value of 3-month Instrument	+101.23	Sell 3-month Sterling @ £0.6524	+101.23	−66.04

Thus the four inputs to the foreign exchange forward price calculation are the spot exchange rate, the expiry of the forward contract and the interest rates in the two currencies for the length of the forward contract. In this case, the forward exchange rate implies that sterling is worth more in terms of US dollars three months hence than it is now. The slightly higher interest rate in the UK is responsible for this.

The pricing of forward exchange rates is based on interest rate parity theory. This theory says that an investor will be indifferent between holding assets in, say the UK or the USA, providing it is possible to hedge the exchange rate risk for the expected duration of the transaction. Thus, holding a three-month US dollar treasury bond will deliver the same result to a US dollar investor as would buying sterling, investing it in three-month UK gilts and selling sterling three months forward, as described in Example A2.2.

INTEREST RATE FORWARDS

Interest-bearing securities, including fixed interest assets such as bonds, represent an important application of forward agreements. The price at which forward interest rates are agreed is determined by how much it would cost to create the forward synthetically. In other words, at what price would the investor be indifferent between holding the forward and some equivalent physical asset? For example, the price of a forward three-month security – starting in two months' time – is based on the difference between the current yield for two- and five-month securities. The two-month security can be thought of as the spot, analogous to the physical security in the previous exam-

EXAMPLE A2.3 *Interest rate forward: physical 2-month investment plus 3-month forward versus 5-month physical investment*

Physical 2-month plus 3-month Forward	**Annual Rate %**	**Days**	**Settlement Amount**
Invest 2 Months	4.50	61	9 744 702
Redeem 2 Months			−9 817 988
Invest 3 Months	7.36	92	9 817 988
Redeem 3 Months			−10 000 000
5-month Interest			2.62%
Annualized			6.25%
5-month Physical			
Invest 5 Months	6.25	153	9 744 702
Redeem 5 Months			−10 000 000
5-month Interest			2.62%
Annualized			6.25%

ples, while the five-month security is analogous to the forward. The three-month forward that connects them is analogous to the forward premium. In other words, the investor should have exactly the same outcome from investing for two months compounded with a three-month forward agreement as for a simple five-month investment.

Obviously, both the short- and long-term instruments should have the same credit quality. In practice, these agreements are usually based on securities guaranteed by a government or major bank. Example A2.3 provides an illustration.

This example uses discount securities. Thus, an annualized interest rate of 7.36% for the three-month forward contract fills the gap between the end of the two-month physical security with an annualized interest rate of 4.50% and the five-month security with an annualized interest rate of 6.25%. The formula is given as:

$$i_2 = [(1 + i_3 \times d_3/365)/(1 + i_1 \times d_1/365) - 1] \times 365/(d_3 - d_1) \qquad \text{(A2.3)}$$

Where:

i_2 = interest on the intermediate security
i_3 = interest on the distant security
d_3 = number of days to maturity of the distant security
i_1 = interest on the near security
d_1 = number of days to maturity of the near security

Applying this formula, we have:

$$\begin{aligned} P &= [(1 + 6.25\% \times 153/365)/(1 + 4.50\% \times 61/365) - 1] \times 365/(153 - 61) \\ &= (1.0261/1.0075 - 1) \times 365/92 \\ &= 7.36\% \end{aligned}$$

Working backwards, the near month and intermediate month interest rates compound to give the distant month interest rate:

$$\begin{aligned} i_3 &= [(1 + i_1 \times d_1/365) \times (1 + i_2 \times d_1/365) - 1] \times 365/(d_1 + d_2) \qquad \text{(A2.4)} \\ &= (1 + 4.50\% \times 61/365) \times (1 + 7.36\% \times 92/365)] \times 365/(61 + 92) \\ &= (1.0075 \times 1.0185 - 1) \times 365/153 \\ &= 6.25\% \end{aligned}$$

The same principle holds for forward bond contracts. The short dated bond compounded with the forward agreement should deliver the same outcome as the long dated bond. The difference is that the formula for pricing bonds takes into consideration the amount and timing of coupon payments as well as the interest rate yielded by the investment. A bond forward is an agreement to deliver a specific bond at an agreed price and date. This means that each agreement must specify such details as the issuer, maturity date, coupon and yield of the bond. The requirement for such details, together with the more complex bond price formula, mean that bond forward agreements are usually more complex than forward agreements for discount securities.

IMPLEMENTATION

Forward contracts are most often used in investment management for buying and selling foreign exchange and some bond and swap instruments. The time to expiry can be as little as a few days, or it can be several months, but it is not often very much longer than that.

Entering into a forward foreign exchange contract, for example, is not very different from entering a spot foreign exchange contract. When placing the order with the broker, the investor nominates the amount to be either bought or sold, the currency, or currencies required and the required settlement date. Foreign exchange dealers nearly always have computer systems that give the exact settlement amount within a few seconds.

When dealing in well-established forward markets, such as foreign exchange, contracts have become standardized by the financial institutions and brokers that deal frequently in these instruments. This means there is usually little legal ambiguity in these transactions, although the documentation may vary slightly depending on which broker or institution the trade is with.

One important aspect of the forward contract that is usually standardized by the broker or institution, if not by the nature of the underlying asset and current practice pertaining to its relevant forward market, is whether it is a **delivery** or **cash settled contract**. This can be important. The couple buying the apartment at the agreed price on the agreed date have a delivery contract. A bank buying foreign exchange for forward delivery is quite happy to be paid (or to pay) in cash the difference between the agreed forward rate and the spot exchange rate prevailing at the expiry of the contract.

If the contract is for a cash settlement, the contract must stipulate how the market price for the underlying asset is to be determined. For financial instruments that are not traded on an exchange, a panel often determines this price. A panel usually consists of five or six professional dealers or investors in the market. Each is asked to quote a price to buy and/or sell the agreed amount of the underlying instrument, usually within a fixed time interval, such as a half-hour. The settlement price is then derived as some kind of average of the prices thus obtained. Another way is to nominate a reference price. This is a price quoted by some independent organization, such as a data service or news provider. An example reference price might be the exchange rate quoted by the *Financial Times* at a given hour and day.

Complications can arise when dealing in forward contracts for thinly traded or exotic currencies or instruments. The unfortunate outcome is that sometimes a reasonable price cannot be obtained, and sometimes, no price at all – although this is unusual. The reason for the difficulty is that the banks that deal in such currencies usually buy and sell them as principal, meaning that they use their own money. This means they bear all gains and losses associated with that currency until they can find another trader to sell it to, or buy it from. The longer the bank thinks it will take to balance the position, the higher will be the 'spread' – the difference between buying and selling prices required to compensate for the risk of holding an illiquid investment. If there is a large gap between the buy and sell prices, it is difficult to know what the 'fair' price is for the investment.

Complicating the problems posed by thinly traded currencies and instruments is the fact that forward contracts, once set in place, are generally destined to stay there until the expiry or settlement date. This can pose a problem if the investor wishes to terminate, or **unwind** the position. The solution is usually to enter into an equal, opposite transaction with the same expiry or settlement date. Thus, two forward agreements can be in place concurrently. These will cancel each other out at the time of their mutual expiry.

Forward transactions do not usually attract visible commissions and other transaction costs. The cost is in the difference between the price at which the broker buys and sells the same contract, that is, the spread. The spread reflects the ease with which the broker will find another party to take the other side of the transaction, and the number and competitiveness of other brokers and intermediaries dealing in similar instruments. Transaction costs for forwards are therefore difficult to quantify, but, on average, they are less than those of dealing in the underlying physical asset, although this generalization should be read with caution, as spreads can vary enormously, particularly in volatile markets and illiquid assets.

ONGOING MANAGEMENT

Once in place, the forward contract is usually very easy to maintain. Naturally, as the settlement date approaches, the investor must be ready to either pay or receive the required funds. Most custodians and intermediaries provide the necessary reminders as part of their service. Investment managers usually have administration systems in place to perform the same function, so there is usually at least one fail-safe mechanism in place. The penalties for failing to meet a settlement can be very high, usually taking the form of punitive interest and administration charges by the other party and the custodian. If the investor is unable or unwilling to settle his or her part of the transaction, the other party can institute legal proceedings to recover the sum involved.

Thus, one of the most important aspects of forward contracts is that they can carry significant counterparty risk. This is the risk that the investor taking the other side of the forward contract will be unable to meet his or her obligations when the settlement date arrives.

To deal with this risk, investors employ systems, formal or informal, of ensuring that they avoid having too much exposure to any one counterparty. Usually these systems rely on the notion of credit limits, which are fixed amounts that can be exposed to each bank or other financial institution with whom forward agreements are struck. The amounts nominated take into account the total credit exposure of the investor and the credit quality, usually indicated by some rating given by a recognized credit rating agency, such as Moody's or Standard & Poor's. Investment managers generally establish credit limits against each counterparty on behalf of each of their client funds and a collective one for all the funds they manage. The former is, of course, to protect each of their clients against the consequences of default on the part of a counterparty. The latter is to protect the investment management company: even though their own equity is not at risk, their business would suffer enormously if the default of a financial institution were to affect a large number of their clients.

Unlike transactions in physical assets, forward transactions require no initial payment. Settlement occurs at the end of the agreement – the settlement date. This means that the portfolio needs to hold enough short-term, liquid instruments (cash), at least equal to the face value of the futures contract. If this sum is not maintained, then the portfolio is in danger of being overinvested, or 'geared'. Economically, this is the same as being in debt, so the portfolio could conceivably lose more money than it owns. If the portfolio has entered into a contract to buy US$1 000 000 at £0.6524 in three months' time, then the portfolio should have at least £652 400 in cash at all times throughout the life of the contract. This sum is often referred to as the 'collateral'.

ADMINISTRATION

The three administrative issues posed by forward contracts within investment portfolios are maintaining sufficient cash collateral, the danger of missing a settlement date and revaluation. Most investment managers have some kind of capture system to ensure that there is enough collateral to ensure that the portfolio is never overinvested. These are not complicated systems, involving only very simple arithmetic. Managing settlement dates is achieved by streamlining, as far as possible, the procedures surrounding cash flows. Usually this means ensuring that the people nominated as authorized signatories are competent, with adequate understanding of the instruments being used and the strategy they form part of. They need to be generally available to sign relevant documents at short notice. And the number of different signatures required for each transaction type needs to be sufficient to protect against mistakes, while not so numerous that transactions take hours to authorize.

The question of valuation can be tricky, especially if there is not an active market in the forward contract. With major currencies, this is not usually a problem, as the relevant forward markets are very liquid. Minor currencies and some bond contracts may be less liquid. In such cases, the value of the forward contract needs to be estimated from the current spot price of similar instruments. Obviously, if these are known with certainty, setting up pricing systems is relatively easy. Where the inputs to the forward price calculation need to be estimated, such as maintenance costs on real property, the basis for estimating these should be formalized. If the pricing system fails to make clear exactly how the price is estimated, then the forward valuation can be manipulated, with the possible consequence of inaccurate portfolio valuation and return calculations.

Some accounting systems also have a problem with forward contracts. They get confused because there is no cash transaction at the outset. Thus it can appear that there is no 'asset' to revalue. These systems need to be modified so that they are able to allocate collateral correctly to reflect the economic exposure of the forward.

The distinction between cash-settled and delivery contracts matters for administrative purposes as well. If the forward contract is for physical delivery, then it is a good idea to ensure that the asset to be received (for a purchase contract) or to be delivered (for a sale contract) can actually be received or delivered on the delivery date. If it is not, then the investor faces the cost of either a forced purchase or sale of the asset, or compensating the other party to the transaction. There is also the risk of legal action. Similarly, for cash-settled contracts, the fund must have enough cash to settle any unrealized losses on the contract or face having to liquidate other assets quickly to meet the shortfall. Urgent cash demands like this can be quite costly, not to mention embarrassing!

APPENDIX 3

Futures Contracts

THEORY

The difference between futures contracts and forwards is that forward contracts are usually traded party to party (over-the-counter), while futures contracts are traded on exchanges (exchange traded), where the exchange is a legal party to each contract traded. The advantage of exchange-traded instruments is that the exchange brings together many buyers and sellers, allowing competition to ensure the best prices for both buyers and sellers. The exchange also acts as a kind of central counterparty, ensuring that the obligations under all contracts are met. Exchange-traded instruments must be standardized, so they are less flexible than forwards. The theoretical economic implications are identical for the two instruments, but the practical differences are significant, relating to trading and administrative procedures, costs, ongoing management and risk management, and performance attribution and analysis.

PRICING

The theoretical premium, or discount to the spot, physical asset price is identical for futures and forward contracts. That is, it is the current price of the underlying security, adjusted for holding costs and cash flows that occur during the life of the contract. As with forwards, futures contracts can be cash settlement or delivery.

APPLICATIONS

Futures contracts are used by investment managers mainly in conjunction with equities, bonds and short-term interest-bearing investments. The most frequent application is to manage liquidity and to effect short-term asset allocation decisions. They can also be used to create much more complex investment structures such as synthetic swaps, market neutral funds and commodity funds.

As with forward contracts, the main attractions of futures contracts are the ability to sell short at little or no cost and the ability to defer settlement.

The denomination and other characteristics of a futures contract are determined by the exchange on which it is traded. For example, a contract could be on a kilo of gold, in which case the exchange will nominate the precise grade of gold, the source of the reference price for valuing the contract at its expiry, the expiry dates (and the time of day at which expiry takes place), and whether the contract is cash settlement or delivery. When the futures contract expires, delivery contracts will mandate that the buyer receives and the seller delivers the specified quantity of the underlying goods or securities. For cash-settled contracts, the buyer will receive and the seller must pay a sum of money equal to the difference between the price of the underlying asset and the price at which the futures contract was transacted (if the price has gone down the buyer must pay).

The next most important defining feature of a futures contract is its face value. Also determined by the exchange, this is the measure of the size of the contract: the amount of the underlying asset that is represented by each futures contract. The face value indicates how many contracts are required for a specific investment objective. It is usually expressed as a multiple of the futures price, indicating how much money is gained or lost with a given change in the futures price.

EXAMPLE A3.1 *Futures on share price indices*

The face value of an S&P500 futures contract is 500 times the traded price of the contract. So an S&P500 price of 850 indicates a face value per contract of $425 000 ($500 × 850). This means that, for each contract purchased, a rise of one point in the price of the S&P500 brings an unrealized profit of $500. Thus US$500 is known as the point value of the contract. If one were seeking to gain exposure to $4 000 000 of US equities, one could buy 10 contracts and get $4 250 000 worth, or 9 contracts and get $3 825 000 worth. The formula is given as:

$$\text{Number of contracts} = \text{FV}/(\text{pv} \times \text{pf}) \qquad \text{(A3.1)}$$

Where:

FV = face value of investment
pv = point value of futures contract
pf = price of futures contract

Which gives:

Number of contracts = $4 000 000/($500 × 850)
= 9.41

When the investor is ready to invest physical cash, the futures contract is sold and physical shares are bought. If the market has appreciated in the meantime, the 'opportunity costs' of having delayed purchase of shares is offset by gains in the futures position.

Conversely, if the investment manager needs to divest shares, futures can be used to effectively reduce exposure. While leaving in place the physical shares, futures contracts are sold. To the extent that the sold futures position offsets the holding of physical shares it is said to be a position in **synthetic cash**. Economically, this is the same as holding short-term interest-bearing instruments.

FUTURES ON DISCOUNT INTEREST-BEARING SECURITIES

Futures contracts on discount securities and bonds follow the same principle as share price index futures, but the actual calculation is slightly different. This is because, in these markets, it is interest rates that are being traded. Interest rates have the annoying characteristic that when they rise the economic benefit to the investor who has bought them goes down, and vice versa. To accommodate this, futures contracts on bonds and discount securities are quoted as 100 minus the interest rate. So an interest rate of 8% is quoted as 92, while 6.5% becomes 93.5, and so on.

The exchange tells you that the face value of the futures contract on a discount security is $1 000 000, the period is 90 days, with a 360-day calendar year. You learn that the contract has recently traded at 94.95 – an interest rate of 5.05% (100 – 94.95). The settlement price of the futures contract is calculated using the formula for a discount security:

P = $1 000 000/(1 + ((100 – 94.95)/100) × 90/360)
= $987 532

EXAMPLE A3.2 *Interest rate future: physical 2-month investment plus 3-month forward versus 5-month physical investment*

Physical 2-month plus 3-month Forward	Annual Rate %	Days	Settlement Amount
Invest 2 Months	4.50	61	9 744 702
Redeem 2 Months			−9 817 988
Invest 3 Months	7.36	92	9 817 988
Redeem 3 Months			−10 000 000
5-month Interest			2.62%
Annualized			6.25%
5-month Physical			
Invest 5 Months	6.25	153	9 744 702
Redeem 5 Months			−10 000 000
5-month Interest			2.62%
Annualized			6.25%

Thus an investor paying $987 532 now and receiving $1 000 000 in 90 days' time will earn an annualized return of 5.05%.

There is no cost of carry for a future on a discount security. Instead, the interest rate implied by the future should be consistent, when compounded with a security maturing on the day of the future's expiry, with the interest rate for a security maturing on the same day as the security for which the future is exchangeable. For example, a future on a 92-day security, expiring in 61 days, should compound with a 61-day security to give exactly the same outcome as a security maturing in 153 (92 + 61) days.

Example A3.2 shows that an annualized interest rate of 7.36% for the three-month future contract fills the gap between the end of the two-month physical security with an annualized interest rate of 4.50% and the five-month security with an annualized interest rate of 6.25% is 7.36%.

FUTURES ON BONDS

The principle of compounding also applies to bond futures, with the difference that the price must take into account coupons paid on the bonds. Thus a three-year bond future expiring in two months' time must compound with a two-

EXAMPLE A3.3 *Pricing a bond future*

Physical 2-month plus 3-month Forward	Annual Rate	Days	Settlement Amount
Bond Coupon Rate	5%		
Coupons Per Year	2		
Invest 2 Months	4.50%	61	–9 826 800
Redeem 2 Months			–9 900 703
Invest 3 Years	6.30%	1095	9 900 703
Redeem 3 Years			10 000 000
5-month Physical			
Bond Coupon Rate	5%		
Coupons Per Year	2		
Invest 3 Years & 2 Months	6.50%	1156	9 826 802
Redeem 3 Years & 2 Months			–10 000 000

month security to give a yield equal to a bond maturing in three years and two months (see Example A3.3).

PRICING A BOND FUTURE

The fair price for the bond future is the interest rate that equates the initial investment and the redemption value for a two-month investment compounded with a three-year bond and a bond with a maturity of three years and two months.

IMPLEMENTATION

Because they are traded on exchanges, futures contracts are standardized. Thus the contract is defined by the underlying asset and the date on which the futures contract expires. The investor entering into such a contract has no knowledge of who takes the other side of the contract, as every contract is purchased from, or sold to, the futures exchange in question.

Unlike forward contracts, where no money is exchanged between parties at the outset, futures exchanges require an initial margin, usually on the day of the transaction, or by the start of the next business day. The size of the initial margin is determined by the relevant futures exchange, and usually takes into account the face value of the contract, and the volatility of the underlying asset or security. The amount can range from about 10% of the face value of the contract to over 50%. Some exchanges pay interest on the initial margin, while some do not. Some exchanges allow the broker to collect and manage the initial margin, in which case the payment of interest is a matter of negotiation between broker and client (the investor). If interest is paid on margins, it is usually at below market rates.

Once a futures contract has been bought or sold, the investor is liable for **variation margins**, whereby an adverse price move must be matched by a 'top-up' to the initial margin, equal to the value of the adverse price fluctuation. A drop in price of two points for a bought contract with a point value of $500 requires a 'top-up' of $1000. This money is refunded if the price subsequently moves in the investor's favour. The purpose of variation margins is to ensure that all transactions are honoured.

Trading futures contracts is not usually a complicated business. Because most futures markets are a good deal more liquid than markets for physical assets, execution usually takes place quickly. The investment manager is normally advised within a few moments at what price the contract has been struck. The worst danger in dealing futures contracts is that the order, which is usually conveyed by telephone from investor to broker, might be misunderstood. Because many prices are quoted as the last one or two digits of the price, rather than the whole figure, there is a danger that an incorrect assumption is made about the 'big number'. Thus, it can happen that someone pays 2753.4 instead of 2743.4 in a volatile market where the price was indicated simply as '3.4'. If the point value of the contract is, say $100 per point, and the order is for 200 contracts, the cost would be $20 000. Occasionally, a buy order is confused for a sell order and vice versa. For this reason, nearly all futures brokers and many investment managers have installed call monitoring and recording systems, which typically use audiotapes to record all telephone conversations. When a mistake occurs, the tapes can be retrieved, the fault, if any, assigned, and compensation for losses effected.

The cost of transacting futures contracts is usually both very small and visible. The exchange attracts a fee per transaction, usually no more than a few dollars per contract. Since contracts can have face values in the hundreds of thousands of dollars, this fee as a percentage of face value is negligible. The broker will generally take a commission, also usually a few dollars per contract.

The real cost of dealing in futures comes from interest income foregone on sums paid as initial and variation margins.

When buying or selling a futures contract, the investor is wise to stipulate whether it is an **opening** or a **closing** transaction, as this has the potential to reduce the cost of variation margins. An open bought position can be offset by an open sold position in the same contract in which case the two will simply cancel each other out at the expiry of the contract. But, while they are both open, the investor must pay variation margins on them both, unless arrangements have been made with the broker and the exchange to calculate margins on the net open position.

Most investment managers do this by executing **closing trades** with the same broker with whom the trade was opened. In this way the broker can see immediately where bought and sold positions can be offset.

Once in place, it is usually the job of the investment manager to ensure that futures positions that are due to expire are **rolled** to the next expiry month at an opportune moment. Rolling the position is a fairly simple exercise, involving closing the existing position and replacing it with another one in a later expiry month. Because the number of futures held has been calculated using the price of the underlying physical, not the futures price, the number of contracts sold and bought (or bought and sold) is identical from one futures expiry month to the next, and the order is placed as a **spread** (the price differential between the two expiry months). This leaves only the job of working out what is a good spread. Like the difference in price between the physical and the future, so the price between two futures expiry months depends on the cost of carry. In practice, this means treating the near month as a spot, physical instrument.

EXAMPLE A3.4 *Pricing a futures roll*

Underlying physical market	2 725.0
Days to near month expiry	53
Near month interest rate	4.50%
Near month dividend yield	1.20%
Days to distant month expiry	143
Near distant interest rate	4.75%
Near distant dividend yield	1.50%
Near month futures price	2738.1
Distant month futures price	2759.7
The fair price of roll	= 2759.7 – 2738.1
	= 21.6

If the position to be rolled is long (bought) then the trade is to sell the near month and buy the next month (a short roll). In this case, the investor will be willing to trade the spread for less than 21.64. The opposite is true for a short position (long roll). In practice, the spread rarely trades at exactly the fair premium, but usually it is within a band of plus or minus 1% or 2%, reflecting the cost of transacting the basket of physical stock that makes up the index. After all, it is the ability to substitute futures for physical and vice versa that drives the relative prices of the two instruments, so the spread reflects the cost of transacting the underlying physical securities.

In practice, most investment managers take various other things into consideration when planning their roll tactics. Most avoid trading too close to the expiry of the contract, especially if it is a delivery contract. It is unfortunate but true that, despite the best efforts of exchanges and regulators, many markets (futures and physical) can be subject to manipulation by large traders during the last days of the contract. This short-term volatility makes trading very hazardous for the investor taking care of long-term investment positions. If the investor has information leading him or her to believe there are some large positions to be closed by a certain date that might push the spread in one direction or another, then it might be worth the risk to wait and profit from these. But, in general, the direction of last-minute volatility is hard to predict, and the costs of getting it wrong can be high.

ONGOING MANAGEMENT

The main issue here is paying variation margins. Some margining systems are more complicated than others, but all are intended to ensure that all parties to futures contracts are able to meet their obligations at the end of the contract. Margins can be payable for both delivery and cash settlement futures contracts. Having placed the initial margin, which covers some adverse movements in the futures price, the investor may see the price move even further against him or her. Each day, at the close of trading, the exchange calculates the amount of unrealized profit and loss for each and every open contract, and aggregates this for each account. If the amount of unrealized loss is greater than the deposit already held, the investor is asked to put more money in.

EXAMPLE A3.5 *Calculation of simple variation margins*

Two hundred share price index futures contracts are purchased at an index level of 2743.4. The contract has a point value of $100, so the face value is $54 868 000. The initial margin is $3000 per contract, so the investor deposits $600 000. On the first day of closing, the contract closes at 2 802.0, giving an unrealized profit of $1 172 000 (2802.0 – 2743.4) × 100 × 200. The following day, the contract closes lower, at 2725.5. The unrealized loss on the position is now –$358 000 (2725.5 – 2743.4) × 100 × 200. No variation margin need be callėd at this point because the loss is still covered by the initial margin. (Some exchanges require that the variation margin is always held in addition to the initial margin.) On the third day, the contract falls to 2705.0, and the investor is called for the appropriate margin. In practice, the investor would probably have paid a larger sum to begin with, say $1 000 000, because this is obviously a very volatile contract and it is intended to hold the position for some weeks or months. Paying more than the minimum required margin avoids frequent top-ups, which can be costly in management time. This cost must be weighed up against the interest forgone on the excess margins paid.

If, on the fourth day, the contract rises again to 2750.0, the investor has surplus funds deposited with the exchange or the broker of $132 000, the amount already paid in variation margins. Because the position is now showing a paper profit (unrealized gain), the investor has the right to withdraw these, leaving just the $600 000 initial margin.

Profits realized from closing, or terminating, a position could be held by the broker to meet future variation margins, or withdrawn by the investor.

If the investor fails to meet the demand for variation margins by the stipulated time (usually mid-morning the following business day), the exchange will close out the position without delay. Closing out the position means that bought contracts are sold 'at market' (whatever price is bid, no matter how low), and sold contracts are bought back at market. The exchange then demands any losses to be made good. If they are not, the exchange is entitled to treat them as a bad debt, seeking appropriate legal redress. The investor taking the other side of the transaction will, unless the futures exchange is particularly inept, remain blissfully unaware of all this: the exchange, as party to both sides of the transaction, will have ensured that this side of the transaction is honoured.

ADMINISTRATION

The two administrative issues are managing margins and ensuring that suitable assets are available for delivery if required.[1] Theoretically, managing margins is quite straightforward, but in practice can be quite tricky.

The need to manage margins carefully stems from the fact that not all margins attract interest income, and those that do often attract rates of interest that are substantially less than the going market rate. This is how most futures brokers remain profitable, since commissions are very low. Therefore the job of the investment manager is to negotiate the best terms possible for earning interest on initial and variation margins, and then to ensure that the balance of margins left with brokers is minimized.

In practice, it is almost impossible to maintain a zero or near zero variation margin. To do so would require frequent transfers of small sums, with attendant administrative headaches.

If the exchange rather than the broker levies variation margins, the investor can often arrange for net payments of variation margins. This means that offsetting positions dealt with different brokers do not each attract their own variation margins, but that the investor's overall position is evaluated at the end of each closing day and margins levied accordingly. This is known as **net margining**. Net margining can simplify administration enormously, especially if the investor is dealing frequently with several different brokers, and in several different instruments.

Net margining becomes more interesting when several currencies are involved. Most large futures brokers are able to meet the foreign currency demands for initial and variation margins, as long as the investor is able to maintain a sufficient balance in the base currency account. The broker may require consideration for this service in the form of a buy–sell spread on the foreign currency involved. For the investor, the saving in administrative effort and the consequent reduction in the risk of falling short of the right currency to meet each margin call can be well worth the extra cost.

Nearly all futures exchanges insist that separate accounts be maintained for each client. This ensures that the interests of clients cannot be confounded. Nor can they be confused with positions taken on the broker's own account. Brokers, in other words, cannot net settle with the exchange by aggregating their clients' accounts. Most investment managers apply the same principle to their clients' investments, maintaining separate accounts with each broker for each client mandate and investment type. In general, this is accepted as the soundest way of administering large numbers of potentially complex transactions. Sometimes this safety precaution occurs at the expense of confidentiality, when the investment manager needs to tell the broker to which account the transaction must be attributed.[2] Some managers get around this problem by ascribing code names to their clients. This generally works well for investment managers with a small number of clients, but errors can creep in, and worse, remain undetected, if code names get confused and trades attributed to the wrong client.

PERFORMANCE MEASUREMENT AND ATTRIBUTION

Performance measurement and attribution issues are almost identical for futures as for forward contracts. The primary difference is that, for futures, some cash, in the form of initial and variation margins, does change hands before the settlement or expiry date of the contract. Therefore portfolio valuation and performance attribution systems must be capable of recognizing the difference between the payment of an initial margin and settlement for a physical asset. Similarly, the distinction should be clear between variation margins and dividend income, or capital calls on physical assets.

Many systems treat the initial margin as settlement for the future, thus implying that this reflect the portfolio's exposure to the instrument.

Another frequent mistake is to use the futures price in this valuation instead of the price of the underlying physical. For the purpose of calculating the economic exposure of the portfolio to the physical asset underlying the futures contract, one multiplies the price of the underlying physical by the point value and the number of contracts.

Some managers use the futures price for simplicity, since it can be derived from the same documents as other margin information. But this choice can have unfortunate consequences, for several reasons. The first is that the price of the futures contract does not always trade at or near its fair price relative to the underlying physical. So, if the futures price is too low, the portfolio will appear to be underinvested, and geared if the futures trades above its fair value relative to the physical. This is no trivial difference. Futures markets and their underlying physical market can often respond quite differently to similar events, with the result that the futures price can move significantly even though the physical market is stable, with the consequence that the portfolio will show an apparent change in asset allocation with no corresponding investment decision or underlying asset price movement. The other anomally of using the futures price is that the apparent exposure to the asset class will change as the position is rolled from one futures expiry to the next.

Example A3.6 shows three ways of valuing a portfolio containing the share price index futures position set out earlier in this appendix. It also illustrates some of the implications of each method on performance attribution. Method 1 allocates cash collateral according to the current physical share price index. Method 2 uses the futures price instead, while method 3 does not allocate collateral at all, but treats the margin payments as full settlement of the contracts. Note that the three methods give quite different impressions of how the portfolio is invested.

EXAMPLE A3.6 *Valuation and attribution analysis for a bought futures contract*

Point Value of Contract	$100
Initial Margin per Contract	$3 000
Number of Contracts Bought	200
Number of Contracts Sold	0
Price at which Futures Traded	2 743.4
Current Futures Price	2 750.0
Current Physical Index	2 693.9
Interest Rate for Cash	4.50%
Current Portfolio Value	$100 000 000

The Valuation Statement	**The Right Way 1 ($)**	**The Wrong Way 2 ($)**	**The Wrong Way 3 ($)**
Initial Margin	600 000	600 000	600 000
Variation Margin	132 000	132 000	132 000
Interest Accrued on Collateral	2 288 584	2 336 900	0
Cash Collateral	53 146 000	54 268 000	0
Equities	53 878 000	55 000 000	732 000
Interest Accrued	1 986 115	1 937 799	4 274 699
Cash	46 122 000	45 000 000	99 268 000
Total	100 000 000	100 000 000	100 000 000

Attribution Analysis Using Method 1	**Profit/Loss** $	**Sum Employed** $	**Return on Transaction** %	**Contribution to Portfolio Return** %
Profit/Loss on Futures	132 000			
Interest on Collateral	2 288 584			
Return on Equities	2 420 584	53 878 000	4.4927	2.4206
Return on Cash	1 986 115	46 122 000	4.5000	1.9861
Total Return	4 406 699	100 000 000	4.4067	4.4067

Summary Attribution Analysis for Three Methods	**1** %	**2** %	**3** %
Return on Equities	2.4206	2.4689	0.1320
Return on Cash	1.9861	1.9378	4.2747
Total Return	4.4067	4.4067	4.4067

Notes

1. The story is frequently told of a speculator who bought a contract of live beef on the Sydney Futures Exchange in the 1960s. Having congratulated himself on a comfortable profit at the expiry of the contract, he was perturbed when, the following day, 10 000 cows were herded into the street in front of his office in the financial district of Sydney.
2. Preferably at the time the order is placed, not after execution is complete.

APPENDIX 4

Swaps

THEORY

Swaps are, economically speaking, no different from a forward or a futures contract. They are agreements to pay the change in value of a security or good, and receive the change in value of some other good or security. Thus two investors holding two different assets, but desiring the return on the other, agree to swap the change in value and possibly the income streams of their respective assets. Forward agreements and futures contracts are essentially special cases of swap agreements: the investor receives the change in value of the security underlying the forward or futures contract, and gives up the change in value of the cash collateral.

Swaps are transacted over-the-counter, as are forwards. Nearly all swaps are arranged by intermediaries who draw up the agreements, help to negotiate prices and arrange settlements.

The main benefit of swaps is that they are almost infinitely flexible, allowing any number of risky assets to be transacted in any combination. Investors entering into swap contracts often swap the returns to quite exotic baskets of securities which might be very expensive and risky to transact in physical form, and for which no viable futures markets exist. Unsurprisingly, the more complicated the swap, the more expensive it is to implement, while swaps that are not much more complicated than futures cost about the same to put in place.

Most swaps take place for liabilities, currency exposures, or both at once. A borrower, who can borrow cheaply in USD, but needs to borrow in GBP, might initiate a typical swap, agreeing to exchange interest rate liabilities with a GBP borrower who needs to borrow in USD, but cannot do so cheaply. Both parties can reduce their borrowing costs and hedge their currency exposures in one go by arranging a swap.

Asset swaps are virtually custom-made for investment portfolios and are becoming widely used, especially in emerging markets portfolios. Example A4.1 illustrates how.

EXAMPLE A4.1 *Asset swap*

	Investor A	Investor B
Earned on index portfolio of physical assets held	+ Return on Market A	+ Return on Market B
Swapped asset returns	– Return to Market A	– Return to Market B
Swapped asset returns	+ Return to Market B	+ Return to Market A
Earned on index portfolio of physical assets held	+ Imputation tax credits A – Margin	+ Imputation tax credits A – Margin
Net Outcome	+ Return to Market B	+ Return to Market A
	+ Imputation tax credits A – Margin	+ Imputation tax credits B – Margin

	USD Investor	JPY Investor
Physical Asset Held	S&P500	TOPIX
Asset Start Price	1229.23	1086.99
Asset End Price	1388.91	1641.53
Currency Start Price	1.00	112.80
Currency End Price	1.00	102.19
Asset Return	12.99%	51.02%
Dividend Yield	2.50%	0.25%
Tax Credit	30.00%	35.00%
Total Return in Local Currency	15.49%	51.27%
Return in USD to Physical Assets	15.49%	37.04%
Amount Paid	–15.49%	–37.04%
Amount Paid or Received	37.04%	15.49%
Tax Credit	0.75%	0.09%
Net Outcome	37.79%	15.58%

Imagine a US dollar investment fund, with normal US tax liabilities. The fund would benefit from holding a portfolio of Japanese yen-denominated stocks benchmarked to the TOPIX index. At the same time, a Japanese investment fund seeks exposure to the US equity market. The two investors agree to swap the total returns in US dollars to their respective portfolios. The outcome is shown at the bottom of Example A4.1.

The USD investor has the best nominal outcome because the TOPIX performed so well over the period, especially in USD terms. He or she also did well out of the dividend tax credit, whereas the JPY investor's tax credit is low because the dividend yield to Japanese assets was very low during the period. A swap like this one usually occurs in the context of a much larger portfolio, in which case the overall outcome for the Japanese investor, who would have other, significant, fairly high yielding (at least in JPY terms) investments, was probably higher than for the USD investor.

In this example, the investors have agreed to swap **total return indices.** This means that they will swap not only the change in the price of the two equity holdings, but also the dividends accrued to them during the period. Many asset swaps differ from this example in that they are designed to swap only the change in the **price index**, leaving the dividends to the holder of the physical asset. This can greatly simplify administration and revaluation.

Bond index swaps work in much the same way. Bond indices ignore coupon payments, so they are a much simpler way to swap bond exposures than by swapping returns to physical bonds, where coupon payments are usually included.

The main limitation of swaps is that they can be cumbersome to implement and administer. Because the cost and time taken by both the investor and the intermediary can be significant, and the intermediary's remuneration is normally a fixed percentage of the face value of the swap, small swaps are rarely worth the cost. This often excludes small funds from benefiting from swaps (although standardization of documentation has gone some way to minimizing this problem).

PRICING

Swaps are priced according to how much it costs to construct a hedge, or a replicating portfolio. For a simple asset swap, the intermediary would use the closest futures contract available. If this is trading close to its fair price relative to the underlying physical contract, then it provides an obvious solution, as set out in Example A4.2. In other cases, there may be no price quotes, or the futures

EXAMPLE A4.2 *Pricing an asset swap*

Asset	Investor A S&P500	Investor B TOPIX
Date Now	31 December 1998	31 December 1998
End Date of Swap	30 November 1999	30 November 1999
Asset Price Now	1229.23	1086.99
Interest Rate	4.50%	1.50%
Dividend Yield	2.50%	0.25%
Tax Credits	30.00%	35.00%
Spot Exchange Rate	1.00	112.80
Forward Exchange Rate	1.00	109.83
Futures Price	1251.73	1099.42
Return in Local Currency	1.83%	1.14%
Return in USD	1.83%	−1.52%
Value of Tax Credit	0.75%	0.09%
Swap Price (+ve = receive, −ve = pay)	3.35%	−3.35%

contract does not provide a close enough proxy. This can occur when the required end date of the swap is in the distant future, beyond the date of actively traded futures contracts. A suitable proxy may also be lacking when the swap does not expire near a futures expiry date, or if the asset to be swapped does not resemble an existing, actively traded futures contract. In such cases, the intermediary might estimate the forward price for each side of the swap directly from the physical, taking into account the value of the dividend tax credit available to each party when estimating the swap spread.

IMPLEMENTATION

From the investor's point of view, the main considerations are how well the swap agreement fits the investment strategy and price. Swaps are usually customized to meet investors' precise needs, but sometimes a small amount of flexibility on the part of the investor can lead to a big saving. For example, if both investors were happy with S&P500 and Nikkei 225 instead of needing, say, MSCI USA and Japan for their foreign exposure, the basis risk to the intermediary would be elim-

EXAMPLE A4.3 *Revaluation and reset of an asset swap*

Revaluation Date	15 December 1999		
Last Reset Date	30 November 1999		
Face Value of Swap	$100 000 000		
Investor Pays	S&P500	Total Return in USD	
Investor Receives	FT100	Total Return in USD	
Return on	S&P500	Total Return in USD	1.8132%
Return on	FT100	Total Return in USD	−0.2305%
Investor Pays	$1 813 213		
Investor Receives	−$230 479		
Investor Pays	$2 043 692		
Swap Reset Value	$97 956 308		

inated (because futures contracts can be used to hedge it). This would allow the intermediary to significantly reduce the fee required for arranging the swap.

Like forward contracts, investors engaging in swaps need to bear in mind that swaps carry counterparty risk that needs to be managed.

The documentation of swap agreements has become much simpler in the last decade or so with the widespread acceptance of **ISDA** (International Swap Dealers' Agreement) documents. This sets out a standard wording for swap agreements, with room for additions to accommodate any unusual features. For most swaps, ISDA has cut weeks off the negotiation and implementation time, increasing the potential benefit to investors of this very useful instrument.

Currency management is fairly simple for most asset swaps. If the investor requires foreign currency to be hedged, this can be incorporated into the swap agreement, such that the reference prices are based on hedged rather than unhedged returns. Example A4.3 is an example of a hedged asset swap.

ADMINISTRATION

Because of counterparty risk, and because swap agreements tend to last at least a year, swaps usually have several settlement dates within their lifetime. The most popular arrangement is for quarterly settlement dates and **swap resets**. Thus, all unrealized profits and losses are paid after three months, leaving no amounts outstanding, helping to guard against counterparty risk becoming unmanageable.

Normally, the intermediary calculates the amount of the settlement and sends the draft calculation to the investor who checks it. The custodian and trustees are then informed of the impending cash flow. The investor then pays or receives payment, depending on the relative changes in the prices of the assets swapped.

At the same time the face value of the swap is reset to reflect the changes in the values of the assets underlying the swaps.

Revaluation of swaps between resets can be a headache, especially if the assets and liabilities being swapped are not traded on recognized markets. Example A4.3 shows how to revalue a simple equity swap.

PERFORMANCE ATTRIBUTION

Once the revaluation problem has been solved, performance attribution should fall into place. The return to the swap is the end value, including settlements, divided by the start value minus one. In short, the impact on the fund's performance of an asset swap will be no different from that of holding the underlying assets minus fees paid for arranging it.

SYNTHETIC SWAPS

Sometimes it is not necessary to arrange a swap through an intermediary because all the required components of the swap exist in the form of traded markets. A strategy that uses exclusively exchange-traded instruments, but whose composition resembles a swap, is often called a 'synthetic swap', as in Example A4.4.1.

As with a standard asset swap, the physical assets are held in domestic securities where the investor has some comparative advantage, in this case the right to domestic dividend tax credits. The essential components of the swap are effected by selling short futures on domestic stocks (the assets physically held) and buying futures in the required foreign market, in this case the UK market. The physical share portfolio will nearly always be indexed to the share price index with the most liquid futures contract, for example, S&P500 in the USA.

The synthetic swap is structured and managed slightly differently from a regular swap because of the need to allocate cash to initial and variation

EXAMPLE A4.4.1 *Synthetic swap structure*

Swap Details	Revaluation Date	15 December 1999	
	Last Reset Date	30 November 1999	
Face Value of Swap	$100 000 000		
Investor Pays	S&P500	Price Only in USD	
Investor Receives	FT100	Price Only in USD	

	30 11 1999			*15 12 1999*		
Portfolio Structure	**Face Value $**	**Percentage of Portfolio**	**Number of Contracts**	**Face Value $**	**Percentage of Portfolio**	**Number of Contracts**
Physical Shares Indexed to S&P500	90 000 000	90.00		91 631 891	91.87	
Short S&P500 Futures	−90 502 767	−90.50	−130	−92 084 876	−92.33	−130
Long FT100 Futures	100 376 103	100.38	381	100 095 439	100.36	381
Short-term Securities	5 742 146	5.74		5 752 765	5.77	
Initial Margins S&P500	2 437 500	2.44		2 437 500	2.44	
Initial Margins FT100	1 820 354	1.82		1 776 224	1.78	
Variation Margins S&P500				−1 582 109	−1.59	
Variation Margins FT100				−280 665	−0.28	
Total Cash	10 000 000	10.00		8 103 715	8.13	
Total	100 000 000	100.00		99 735, 607	100.00	

margins relating to the futures positions. The starting proportion will usually be about 90% shares and 10% liquids, although if one share market is a lot more volatile than the other, a higher proportion in cash might be necessary. Liquidity management is fairly straightforward most of the time, at least while equity markets move in the same direction from day to day. As long as this is the case, variation margins on the short domestic futures position will largely offset those on long offshore futures positions. If the futures broker is happy to call variation margins on a net basis for the whole portfolio, the problem is greatly simplified (Example A4.4.2).

This simple asset swap structure approximates a hedged international portfolio because all physical assets are held in domestic currency. This is fine if the investor wants the risk and return of the foreign stock markets, but not the associated currency risk and return. For a fully hedged return, the investment manager must ensure that futures profits on offshore markets are repatriated at regular intervals to minimize unwanted currency exposure. If the investor

EXAMPLE A4.4.2 *Synthetic swap outcome*

	$	%
Physical Shares Indexed to S&P500	1 631 891	1.63
Short S&P500 Futures	−1 582 109	−1.58
Long FT100 Futures	−280 665	−0.28
Short-term Securities	10 619	0.01
Variation Margins S&P500	−1 582 109	−1.58
Variation Margins FT100	−280 665	−0.28
Total Cash	−1 896 285	−1.90
Total Portfolio	−264 393	−0.26

requires an unhedged return, then the manager must unhedge the face value of the foreign futures contracts by buying forward foreign exchange to give the appropriate currency exposure on the face value of assets held in each country.

Example A4.4.2 illustrates the effect of currency risk on the unrealized profit on the FT100 position. It is this currency effect that accounts for the difference in outcome between the synthetic swap (which is implicitly currency-hedged) and its standard counterpart (which is usually not currency-hedged). Had the investor unhedged the synthetic swap position by selling forward contracts in pounds equivalent to the face value of the FT100 position, the return to the swap would have been 2.48% less because the investor would have bought pounds at a forward rate of £0.6279 on 30 November, rather than at £0.6435 on 15 December.

The main benefit of the synthetic swap is that, because physical assets are invested in the domestic equity market, it can entitle the investor to dividend tax credits on 90% of the international portfolio, which can amount to about 25% of the dividend yield. Because it comprises only exchange-traded instruments, the synthetic swap is easy to revalue, with no fee payable to an intermediary, making it quite cost efficient. Of course, there are drawbacks. Implementation and ongoing management can be tricky.

Liquidity management is critical. The manager needs to ensure that there is always enough ready cash to meet variation margins. At the same time, too much available cash means that the physical portfolio will be underinvested, foregoing some of the benefits of the dividend tax credit. Most of the time, liquidity of about 10% is sufficient, as equity markets tend to move up and down together, and the net short and long futures positions approximately offset each other. Occasionally, though, the domestic market might move sharply up while most other markets move sharply down, or vice versa, straining the 10% cash allowance.

ADVANTAGES AND DISADVANTAGES OF SWAPS OVER FUTURES AND FORWARDS

The overwhelming advantage of swaps is their flexibility. Investors can construct any combination of assets and liabilities to fine-tune their exposure to return and risk to exactly match their requirements. Swaps enable investors to venture beyond the limitations of recognized markets, while largely avoiding the risk of illiquidity and settlement headaches that usually deter investors from such exotic investment destinations. Moreover, this can be achieved within virtually any time frame imaginable. Settlement and reset dates need not coincide with traditional quarter-ends or month-ends, but can comply with the exact time horizon of the investor.

Currency hedging can be automated by stipulating the currency in the swap agreement, largely obviating the need to establish and manage forward foreign exchange positions.

Asset swaps provide a very effective way of maximizing the benefit of dividend tax credits by allowing the investor to hold physical assets in domestic equities, while still enjoying the superior return and risk combinations afforded by holding international assets.

The main disadvantage is that the cost of setting up can be prohibitively expensive, if the face value of the swap is small or the nature of the swap complex. Similarly, for complex swaps, finding enough suitable intermediaries to ensure competitive bids can be hard, and ongoing valuation can be troublesome, particularly for some 'total return' (as opposed to price only) equity swaps.

Both swaps and forward agreements, being the over-the-counter transactions, are subject to counterparty risk. Because they are exchange-traded, futures contracts are not subject to counterparty risk as the exchange guarantees the performance of each transaction.

Counterparty risk needs to be managed. While swaps rarely constitute such a large proportion of an investment portfolio to pose a serious threat to the quality of the overall investment, swap counterparty risk needs to be incorporated at the portfolio level with bond, money market and foreign exchange counterparty risks.

APPENDIX 5

Options

Forwards, futures and swaps oblige buyers and sellers to trade at fixed prices, regardless of how unattractive the prices are at expiry relative to the going market rate. Options, on the other hand, allow the investor to walk away from the deal if the contracted price does not compare favourably with what is currently offered by the market at the time of the contract's expiry. This is the essential feature that sets options apart from forwards, futures and swaps.

Options come in two flavours: call options and put options. The buyer of a call option benefits if the underlying asset appreciates, while the call seller loses. A put buyer benefits from price decreases, while the seller of puts loses.

To obtain the benefit of the right to walk away from a deal that has become unattractive, the option buyer must pay a premium. This can be thought of an insurance premium.

Think of an individual who has learned that he is about to receive a significant sum of money in about three months' time. He is keen to invest this money in the stock market, where he intends to leave it to appreciate for several years. He would like to effect this investment as soon as possible, but has reservations about the market's likely behaviour between now and when the cash is actually available. He could do nothing and wait until the cash materializes. If the market appreciates in the meantime, he will have missed this opportunity. Alternatively, he could buy futures. This covers the danger of the market going up, but what if it falls sharply? He would lose money. The other solution would be to buy options on the stock market. That way, if the market goes up, he can exercise his option to buy shares at a preagreed price (the exercise price). If the market falls, as he fears it might, instead he buys shares at the lower market price, abandoning his option. In this case, he will have forfeited the premium paid at the outset, but, nevertheless, has insured himself against the market appreciating too much before he can get his investment in place.

PRICING

The primary determinant of the how much an option is worth is the underlying asset. The option cannot be worth more than this asset. The second element is the price at which it is exercisable, the exercise price. The call option cannot be worth less than the difference between the current price of the underlying asset and the exercise price of the option, which is also known as the **intrinsic value** of the option. The asset price and the intrinsic value serve as the upper and lower bounds for calculating the option price. To narrow it down further, we need to know:

- The time to expiry of the option.
- The interest rate.
- The volatility of the underlying asset.

These elements determine the time value of the option, which, together with the intrinsic value, make up the option price. The most frequently used method of estimating option prices is known as the Black–Scholes option pricing formula. For a call option on a physical asset, this is:

$$pc = s \times N(d1) - pe \times N(d2)/e^{iy} \qquad \text{(A5.1.1)}$$

Where:

pc = the price of the call option
s = the current price of the asset
pe = the exercise price of the option
i = the risk-free interest rate
vol = the volatility of the underlying asset
y = the time to expiry in years
e^{iy} = the interest rate continuously compounded

N(d1) and N(d2) are terms describing the probability of the share price being sufficiently volatile that the option expires in-the-money. They are calculated as:

$$N(d1) = [\ln (pa/pe) + (i + vol^2/2) \times y]/vol \times y^{0.5} \qquad \text{(A5.1.2)}$$
$$N(d2) = N(d1) - vol \times y^{0.5} \qquad \text{(A5.1.3)}$$

The option premium reflects the likelihood that the option will expire in-the-money. An option is in-the-money if the asset price is greater than the exercise price for a call option, and less than the exercise price for a put option. An option on a volatile asset is more likely to expire in-the-money than a fairly stable one, so other things being equal, a volatile asset will have a higher option premium. Similarly, the more time to expiry the option has, the more time there is for it to move into the money. The interest rate serves a similar purpose in options prices as in forward and futures prices: it adjusts for the fact that most of the settlement occurs at the expiry of the option, even though the holder has gained exposure to movements in the price of the underlying asset.

Increase in	*Call Price*	*Put Price*
Value of underlying investment	up	down
Exercise price	down	up
Time to expiry	up	up
Risk-free interest rate	up	up
Volatility of underlying investment	up	up

Some options can be exercised at any time up to the exercise or expiry date, while others can only be exercised on the last day. **American options** can be exercised before the exercise, while **European options** cannot. In practice, there is little distinction: most options traded on recognized markets are American, but early exercise does not happen often, for reasons that are explained below. So, although American, most options are priced as European.

By exercising an option early, the holder is forfeiting the remaining **time value** of the option. This is rarely a rational thing to do. If the option holder wishes to cash in the gains made on the option, it makes more sense to sell it, by which action the remaining time value is received as part of the sale price of the option. Sometimes options are exercised early; most often when the option is on a physical share that is close to its ex-dividend date. As the option holder is not entitled to receive dividends and the owner of the share is, it is entirely possible that the value to the investor of the dividend (including tax credits) is greater than the remaining time value, in which case the investor happily forfeits the time value of the option in exchange for entitlement to the dividend.

OPTIONS ON FUTURES

Many futures contracts have options traded on them, and these instruments offer an important source of flexibility for implementing short-term asset allocation shifts. Conceptually, options on futures are no different from options on physical assets, but they are priced slightly differently, as the delayed settlement aspect is already taken into account in the futures premium. The formula for pricing a call option on a futures contract is:

$$pc \quad = [s \times N(d1) - pe \times N(d2)]/eiy \qquad (A5.2.1)$$

Where:

$$N(d1) = [\ln (s/pe) + vol^2/2 \times y]/vol \times t^{0.5} \qquad (A5.2.2)$$
$$N(d2) = N(d1) - vol \times y^{0.5} \qquad (A5.2.3)$$

Example A5.1.1 shows the structure of a call option price. The value of the underlying asset is shown as the diagonal line starting at zero. Note that a fully paid share can be thought of as an option with an exercise price of zero. (The share price cannot go below zero, so the buyer cannot lose more than what he paid for it.) The other diagonal line shows the intrinsic value of the option. This represents the relationship between the price of the option and the underlying asset at the option's expiry. It is zero at the exercise price, then appreciates one-for-one with the underlying asset. The curved line between the asset price and the intrinsic value is the value of the call option. An option with a very long time to expiry behaves very much like the underlying asset. As the option approaches its expiry date, the time value decays, and the price of the option converges to its intrinsic value. Note that the option time value is always

EXAMPLE A5.1.1 *The call option*

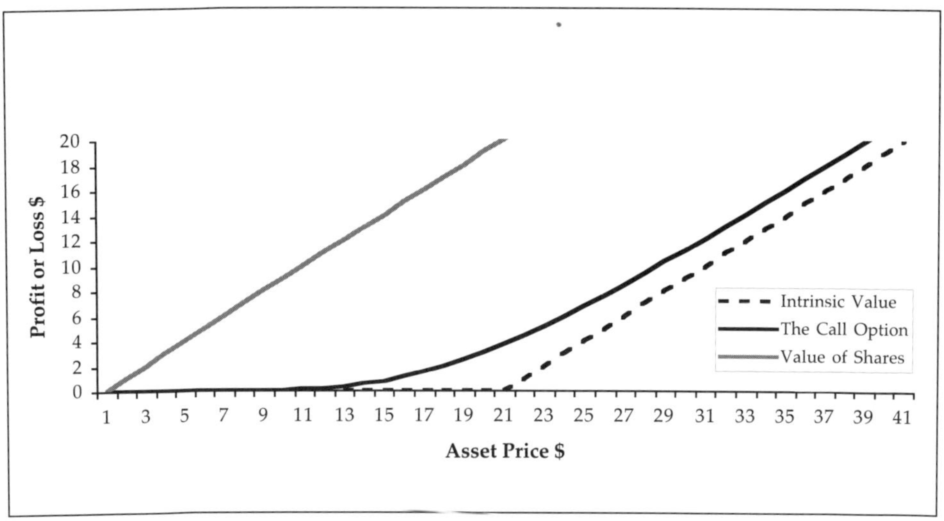

EXAMPLE A5.1.2 *The option premium*

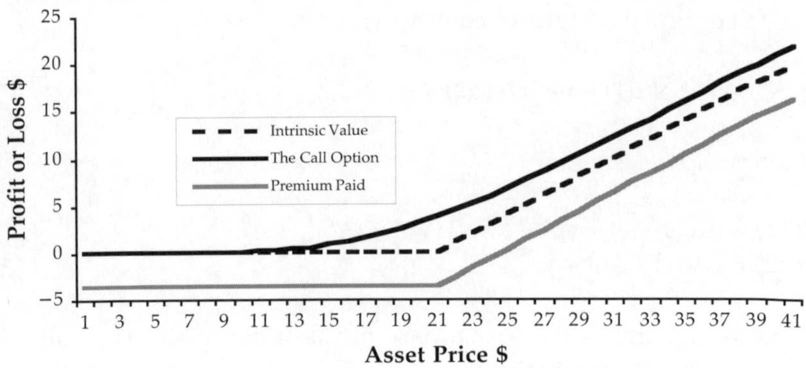

greatest when the option is at-the-money, that is, when the asset price is about the same as the exercise price, reflecting the fact that this is the price where uncertainty about the option's final value is greatest.

The potential gains to the buyer of an actual option are theoretically unlimited, at least for a call option, while losses are limited to the premium paid for the option. For the seller of an option, the outcome is the reverse: a predefined maximum gain and potentially unlimited losses, especially for call options.

Example A5.1.2 shows the payoff to the holder of a call option when it expires. If the price of the underlying asset goes up, potential profit is unlimited. If it goes down, the option buyer loses no more than the premium paid. The point of indifference of the option holder in this case is when the asset price is equal to the exercise price less the premium paid. In this case \$16.29 (\$20.00 – \$3.71).

The call option buyer will generally be happy if the underlying asset appreciates, as his or her gains will be those of the asset less the option premium paid. If the asset price goes down, the call option holder will lose the premium paid, but avoid potentially larger losses from holding physical assets. But what happens if the asset price stays at the same level? The option buyer has lost the option premium, seemingly for nothing. All options suffer time decay (**Option Time Decay**) because the time value of the option dwindles to nothing as the option nears expiry. Time decay is most obvious when the asset price is stable.

As with forward, futures and swap prices, option prices take no account of the likely direction of the price of the underlying security.

ASSUMPTIONS

The formula for pricing an option relies on a number of simplifying assumptions about the behaviour of the price of the underlying asset. The most important of these is that the asset returns are approximately normally distributed (lognormally to be precise, the difference is that lognormal prices cannot go below zero, while normal prices can, meaning that positive and negative price fluctuations are equally likely); and that the price moves incrementally, not in large jumps.

Other assumptions implicit in option price theory are that the interest rate and the volatility of the underlying asset remain stable for the life of the option, that markets are perfectly liquid and that there are no transaction costs. Of these, the most troublesome is the assumption of stable volatility. Volatility is a measure of how quickly and how far the price of the asset moves about, regardless of direction, in a given time frame. Asset price volatility often remains stable for extended periods, and then changes significantly without warning. The effect on the option price of changing volatility is most acute for at-the-money options with plenty of time left to expiry.

PUT–CALL PARITY

Put–call parity is one of the most endearing features of options. It says that call options can be constructed using put options and vice versa.

Example A5.2.1 shows that combining a short put and a long call option with the same exercise price gives the same outcome as a forward or futures contract on the underlying asset. The relationship is expressed arithmetically as:

$$pc - pp = pf - pe \qquad \text{(A5.3)}$$

Similarly, combining a short call with a long put gives the same result as a short forward or futures. (But minus call equals exercise minus future.)

The implication is that an investor holding a risky asset might believe that the asset is going to depreciate in the short term, although its long-term prospects are bright. Rather than incurring the costs of selling the asset and buying a call option, the exact same outcome can be achieved by buying a put option and continuing to hold the physical asset.

In Example A5.2.2, the investor wishes to temporarily reduce his exposure to one particular asset in his portfolio. The stock is currently trading at $11.50. He can either sell the shares and buy call options or he can hold the stock and buy put options. Both option series have an exercise price of $10.00 and time to expiry of 90 days. The calls are trading at $1.66 and the puts are trading at $0.04.

EXAMPLE A5.2.1 *Put–call parity*

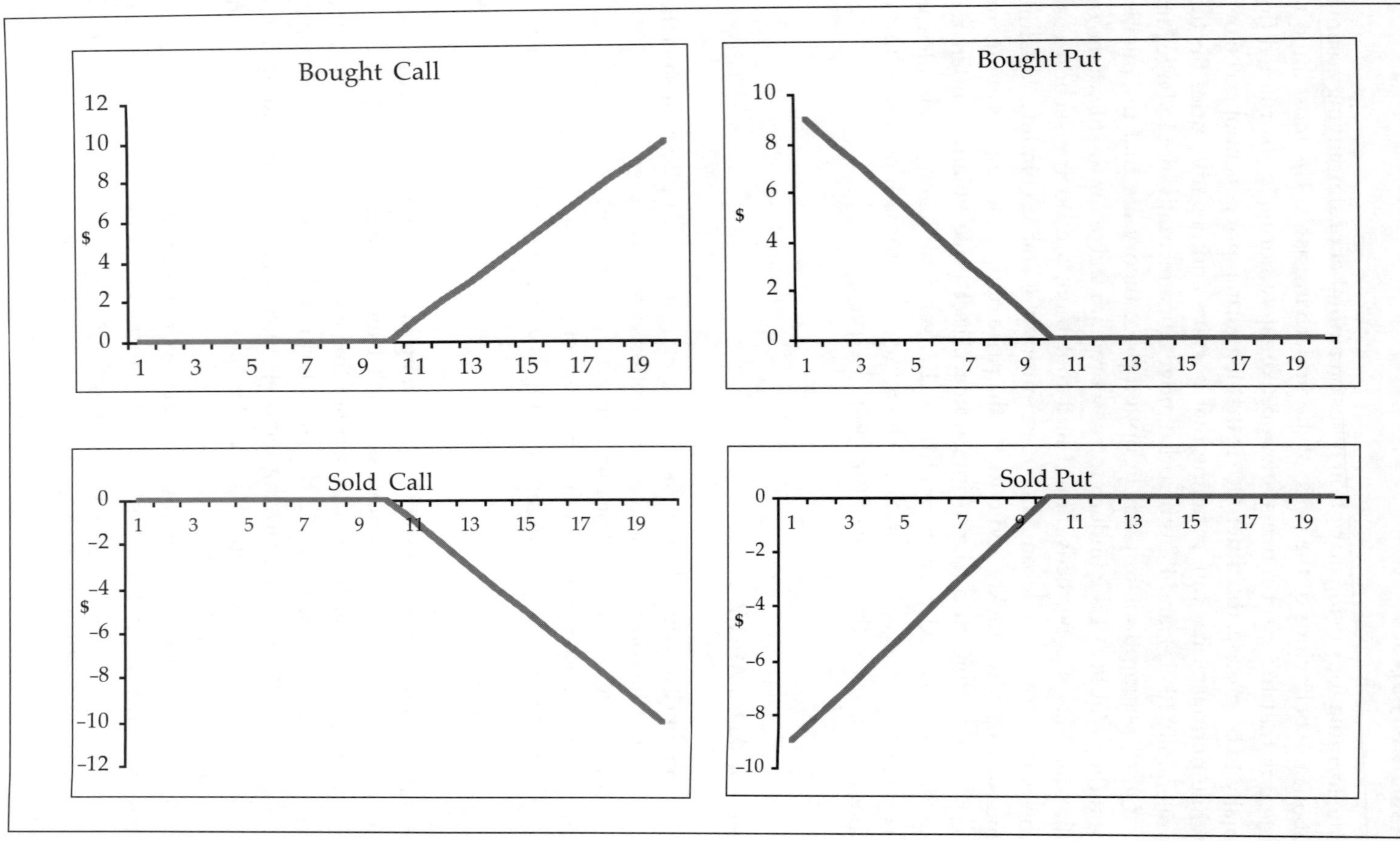

EXAMPLE A5.2.2 *Sell stock and buy call versus hold stock and buy put*

Share Price	$11.50	x	1000
Exercise Price	$10.00	x	1000
Call Premium	$1.66	x	1000
Put Premium	$0.04	x	1000
Interest Rate	5%		
Volatility	22%		
Time to Expiry	90 days		
Transactions Costs	0.50%		

	Strategy 1 Sell Stock, Buy Call $	**Strategy 2 Hold Stock, Buy Put $**
Sell 1000 Shares	11 500.00	
Buy 1000 Calls	−1 660.00	
Buy 1000 Puts		−40.00
Interest on Proceeds of Share Sale	121.32	
Transaction Costs	−65.80	−0.20
Outcome A: Share Price =	15.00	
Profit/Loss on Shares	−3 500.00	
Exercise Options	5 000.00	0.00
Option Premium	−1 660.00	−40.00
Interest Income	121.32	
Transaction Costs	−65.80	−0.20
Net Outcome	−104.48	−40.20
Outcome B: Share Price =	8.00	
Profit/Loss on Shares	3 500.00	
Exercise Options	0.00	2 000.00
Option Premium	−1 660.00	−40.00
Interest Income	121.32	
Transaction Costs	−65.80	−0.20
Net Outcome	1 895.52	1 959.80

In strategy 1, the investor benefits from share price appreciation by exercising the options. The put buyer is protected against the fall in the share price because by exercising the puts he is able to effectively sell shares at $10.00, so he only suffers the loss of $1.50 from the starting position. The difference in outcome for the two strategies is always $64.28, which is mostly made up of the difference in their transaction costs. The remainder is due to the call and put prices diverging very slightly from fair price.

Combining call options and the underlying asset to create a put is often referred to as creating a synthetic put option. The limitation of **synthetic options** is that bought options can only be replicated using other bought options and vice versa.

Options can also be created by combining cash and the underlying asset. This is known as a replicated option. Example A5.3 illustrates this, showing the relationship between the change in the price of the option and that of the underlying asset. The x-axis shows the underlying asset and the curved line shows the price of a call option. The change in direction of the intrinsic value of the option shows where the exercise price is. When the asset price is equal to the exercise price, a movement in the price of the asset of 1 causes the call option to move by 0.5 in the same direction. Thus the option is said to have a delta of 0.5. When the asset price is very low, the call option is very unresponsive to movements in the asset price, so the delta is close to zero. On the other hand, when the asset price is much greater than the exercise price, the delta of the option converges to 1, and the option behaves like the underlying asset. Mathematically speaking, the delta is the slope of the tangent to the curved line describing the price of the option.

This relationship can be used to construct a replicated option. To do this, the investor simply holds a portfolio of cash and the underlying risky asset such that the percentage of the risky asset held corresponds to the delta of the option to be replicated. To replicate a long call position, the investor then progressively buys the asset as its price increases and sells it as it goes down.

If all the assumptions applied in option pricing hold true, the outcome would be identical for the replicating and the actual option. Unfortunately, prices move

EXAMPLE A5.3 *Replicating options*

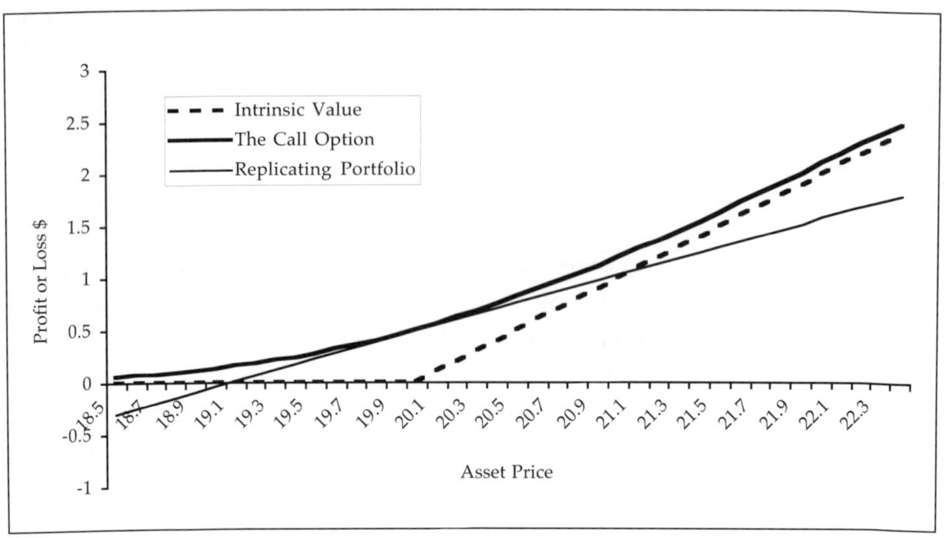

EXAMPLE A5.4 *Replicated call options*

Initial Asset Price	$20.00
Exercise Price	$20.00
Time to Expiry	1 month
Interest Rate	5%
Implied Volatility	20%
Option Delta	0.5395

		Constant Hedge			Dynamic Hedge				
Day	Share Price $	Value of Call $	Value of Replicating Call $	Difference $	Option Delta	Change in Option Delta (Shares Bought & Sold)	Cumulative Cost of Shares Bought & Sold $	Market Value of Portfolio $	Cumulative Cost of Dynamic Hedge $
Col	1	2	3	4	5	6	7	8	9
1	20.00	0.50	0.50	0.00	0.5395	0.5395	10.79	10.79	0.00
2	22.30	2.39	1.74	−0.65	0.9780	0.4385	20.57	21.81	1.24
3	21.50	1.62	1.31	−0.31	0.9180	−0.0600	19.28	19.74	0.46
4	19.00	0.11	−0.04	−0.15	0.2000	−0.7180	5.64	3.80	−1.84
5	23.40	3.47	2.34	−1.14	0.9987	0.7987	24.33	23.37	−0.96
6	25.60	5.67	3.52	−2.15	1.0000	0.0013	24.36	25.60	1.24
7	22.00	2.08	1.58	−0.50	0.9733	−0.0267	23.77	21.41	−2.36
8	18.00	0.01	−0.58	−0.59	0.0231	−0.9501	6.67	0.42	−6.25
9	19.50	0.21	0.23	0.02	0.3352	0.3121	12.75	6.54	−6.22
10	21.50	1.58	1.31	−0.27	0.9425	0.6073	25.81	20.26	−5.55
11	23.00	3.05	2.12	−0.93	0.9988	0.0563	27.11	22.97	−4.13
12	22.00	2.06	1.58	−0.48	0.9840	−0.0148	26.78	21.65	−5.13

in erratic ways, jumping this way and that. Because the replicated option is always following price movements, it will be buying too high and selling too low. (The replicating portfolio moves along the straight tangent, while the actual option moves along the curved option price line.) This shortcoming is compounded when the underlying asset price zigzags, causing losses to the replicating position to accumulate. Similarly, if the asset turns out to be more volatile than originally estimated, the outcome to the replicating option will deteriorate further. This effect is exacerbated by transaction costs incurred along the way by the replicating option, resulting in a further difference between the outcomes of the replicating and actual options.

Example A5.4 illustrates this effect. If the replicating portfolio is left unchanged, then as the share price moves, the value of the actual option diverges from the value of the replicating option. This is seen in column 4 of the table. On the other hand, the cost of adjusting the hedge can be punitive when the price of the underlying asset is very volatile. This is demonstrated in columns 7, 8 and 9 of the table. Column 7 tracks the cumulative cost of shares bought and sold to replicate the option. Column 8 is the market value of those shares and Column 9 is the difference between the two, which is the effective cost of replicating the option.

Just as replicating bought options using dynamic hedging can be costly if markets are volatile, the same volatility can work to the advantage of the investor who has bought options and hedges them dynamically using the underlying asset.

The practice of constructing a replicating portfolio is also known as 'delta hedging'. The risk of the replicating portfolio underperforming the actual option because of large, discrete price movements in the underlying asset is known as 'jump risk'.

OPTION VOLATILITY – GAMMA

The risks associated with decay of time value and of losses due to underestimating the volatility of the underlying asset are indicated by the option's **gamma**. Gamma is the rate of change in the option delta for a small change in the price of the asset underlying the option.

Gamma is positive for all bought options, call or put, and is negative for all sold options. A high absolute option gamma says that time decay is happening quite fast, and that the delta of the option is likely to move about very quickly. A positive gamma means that the portfolio can do quite well in a volatile market, but will suffer in a static one. A negative gamma indicates the opposite.

The options in Example A5.5 are all on a single underlying asset, with a share price of $20.00 and an estimated volatility of 25%. The delta is 0.3194 and the

EXAMPLE A5.5 *Delta and gamma of an option portfolio*

Date Now	01 01 2000
Share Price	$20.00
Interest Rate	5%
Volatility	25%

Number Bought & Sold	Exercise Price $	Exercise Date	Call/Put	Option Price $	Option Delta	Option Gamma	Option Price $	Option Delta	Option Gamma	Option Price $	Option Delta	Option Gamma
				Share Price $20.00			Share Price $22.00			Share Price $24.00		
310 000	20.00	31 03 00	Call	1.73	0.5632	0.0557	2.96	0.8230	0.0243	4.50	0.9482	0.0084
–40 000	25.00	31 03 00	Call	0.05	0.0507	0.1760	0.77	0.1919	0.1180	1.65	0.4326	0.0733
200 000	22.50	31 03 00	Call	0.29	0.2148	0.1124	1.69	0.4912	0.0651	2.83	0.7514	0.0329
–150 000	27.50	31 03 00	Call	0.01	0.0081	0.2417	0.25	0.0507	0.1760	0.78	0.1742	0.1227
180 000	21.50	30 06 00	Call	1.00	0.4265	0.0522	2.53	0.6391	0.0328	3.89	0.8024	0.0191
500 000	27.50	30 06 00	Call	0.08	0.0567	0.1188	0.57	0.1487	0.0907	1.18	0.2919	0.0675
1 000 000.00					0.3194	0.0652		0.5275	0.0407		0.6912	0.0250

gamma of this portfolio is 0.0652. A 10% increase in the price of the underlying asset brings the delta to 0.5275, making the option considerably more sensitive to changes in the price of the underlying asset.

When the share price goes up to $24, the aggregate delta increases to 0.6912, but the gamma reduces to 0.0250. This is because the large position in March $20 call has moved further in-the-money, with a consequent reduction in its gamma which, because of the size of the holding relative to the overall portfolio, has a strong impact on the portfolio's aggregate delta and gamma. The effect is even more dramatic with a further 25% shift in the price of the underlying asset, after which the aggregate delta is 0.9089 and the gamma 0.0076.

When analysing the gamma of a portfolio, most managers generally do not try to aggregate options on different assets, although they may look at collective gamma measures in assets that are highly correlated.

IMPLIED VOLATILITY

Accurate or effective estimations of option prices, volatilities and gammas depend on correctly forecasting the volatility of the underlying asset. This can be difficult, as asset volatilities can shift quite suddenly, changing the risk profile of the entire options portfolio. Investors with negative gamma (having sold more options than they have bought) can lose from an upward shift in volatility, while a downward shift will hurt investors who have bought options, in the expectation of plenty of volatility in the underlying asset.

Of all the things that determine the price of an option, only the volatility cannot be determined in advance. This means that, given the price of an option, the volatility of the underlying asset implied by that option price can be deduced easily and precisely. So, when comparing the prices of options and the physical asset, or those of different options series, many investment managers calculate the volatility that is implied by the option price. Computing the implied volatility of an option is a matter of trying different volatility estimates in the option price formula until the calculated price matches the one quoted.

IMPLEMENTATION

Buying and selling options follow much the same principles as for other derivatives. Exchange-traded options are transacted in the same way as futures contracts, while over-the-counter options resemble forwards or swaps.

Exchange-traded options are available on most major share price index futures, futures on interest rate instruments such as bonds and bills, currency and commodities futures as well as on individual stocks. Option premia are normally quoted in the same units as the underlying asset or derivative contract, with exercise dates corresponding to the futures expiry dates. Exercise prices for exchange-traded options are usually set so that there is at least one option series that is in-the-money and one that is **out-of-the-money**. As the futures price moves up and down, new exercise price series are added to ensure enough choices. Not all are always liquid enough to trade; as most trading takes place in those series that are near the money.

Like futures contracts, options can be traded as spreads, in which case the order is given as the difference between the prices of the two option series. In addition to the spread between two expiry months, investors can also trade the spread between two exercise prices within the same expiry month.

OPTIONS ON PHYSICAL SECURITIES

Trading options on physical stock is not very different from options on futures, with the main difference that most markets for options on physical stocks are not as liquid as options on futures contracts, particularly for put options. This is because hedging put options requires the ability to sell short the underlying asset, which for physical securities is expensive on some markets, and impossible on others.

OVER-THE-COUNTER

Implementing over-the-counter options is similar to implementing swap contracts, with similar limitations: they can be expensive to document and implement, especially for small face values, and, once set in place, they can be expensive to reverse. Most over-the-counter option agreements are for at least one year, often using ISDA standardized contracts for swaps.

The premium applying to over-the-counter options is theoretically identical to the exchange-traded kind. Because the option price is driven by the cost of hedging, for an option agreement is relatively standard, the price quoted will be close to that for comparable exchange-traded options. If the option has some unusual features, the price quoted will be higher.

Other things being equal, standard features that will keep the price of the over-the-counter option down include:

- an easily traded underlying asset
- an exercise date that is near the expiry date of a futures contract on a similar asset
- denomination in a major currency
- reasonably standard exercise provisions.

As a rule, any option that is difficult to hedge is likely to be expensive.

Like swaps, the main advantage of over-the-counter options is flexibility. The investor can implement the precise asset exposure required to meet the particular investment objective, perhaps applying exotic options. Exotic options are options with non-standard exercise provisions, such as an exercise price that is specified at the option expiry rather than at the outset. Alternatively, the exotic exercise price might be specified as the average price of the underlying asset over a given period (which may or may not be the period of the option itself) or it might be exercisable against the maximum, or the minimum, price of a given asset within a given time interval.

The main disadvantages of exotic and other over-the-counter options are that, once in place, the option agreement can be difficult to terminate, and as the price of the option is not transparent, it is hard to be sure that the price quoted is fair. This problem is much worse for highly customized options agreements because fewer intermediaries have the resources to quote prices for difficult to hedge options and exotic options.

ONGOING MANAGEMENT

Once in place, the requirements for managing options vary enormously according to whether the options are exchange-traded or over-the-counter and whether they are bought or sold. Exchange-traded options have the same administrative requirements as futures contracts with the exception that variation margins for bought options are limited to the amount of the option premium. Some exchanges demand that this amount is paid when the option is purchased; others apply margining procedures until the full premium is paid.

Most brokers remind their clients about in-the-money options nearing expiry, to avoid forfeiting a valuable asset, but ultimately it is the responsibility of the investor to notify the exchange or the seller of the option that he or she intends to exercise.

Over-the-counter options are managed in very much the same way as swaps, again with the exception that, once the option premium has been paid, quarterly settlements, if they are due, are only paid by the seller to the buyer of the option.

ADMINISTRATION

Administration of options need not be too complicated, for exchange-traded options at least. Premiums are usually paid at the time of the purchase, although some exchanges have introduced systems of margined premiums, by which the premium is applied in the same way as variation margins. Sellers of options on futures contracts usually pay variation margins, as for a futures position. Sellers of options on physical shares may be required to pledge or deposit the shares with the exchange to ensure delivery.

Over-the-counter options are more complex, mainly because they are much more difficult to value. Valuation is achieved by applying some estimate of the implied volatility of the option, which in turn can be derived from some asset or basket of exchange-traded assets that resemble the underlying asset.

Once the valuation problem has been solved, administration follows the same principles as for swap agreements.

PERFORMANCE MEASUREMENT AND ATTRIBUTION

Effective attribution depends on the correct treatment of cash collateral. The issues are similar to those for futures, with the extra consideration of the option delta, as set out in Example A5.6.

The correct allocation to equities takes into account, as with futures, the value of the underlying physical – not the futures price. This is then adjusted by the current delta of the option to reflect the extent to which the option is behaving like the underlying asset class.

The error with method 2 is that the futures price is used instead of the underlying physical to estimate the equivalent equities exposure. Method 3 makes the mistake of only allocating the amount of the premium to equities. Method 4 goes to the other extreme, neglecting the adjustment for the delta, and so treating the option as if it were a futures position.

Performance attribution is shown in Example A5.6.

If the purpose of the option transaction is to modify the risk of an investment in physical assets, then the option can be evaluated by comparing its outcome with that of the physical assets. If, on the other hand, the objective of the options trade is simply to enhance the return to the investment portfolio, independent of the portfolio's exposure to other asset classes, then the best approach is to compare the total outcome of the options activity with a position invested only in short-term liquid assets.

EXAMPLE A5.6 *Valuation and attribution analysis for a bought call option on a futures contract*

Point Value	$100
Initial Margin per Futures Contract	$3 000
Number of Contracts Bought	200
Number of Contracts Sold	0
Option Premium Traded	311.0
Current Option Premium	302.5
Exercise Price of Option	2 500.0
Option Delta at Purchase	0.74
Current Option Delta	0.77
Futures Price at Option Purchase	2 743.4
Current Futures Price	2 750.0
Current Physical Index	2 693.9
Interest Rate for Cash	4.50%
Current Portfolio Value	$100 000 000

The Valuation Statement	**The Right Way 1 $**	**The Wrong Way 2 $**	**The Wrong Way 3 $**	**The Wrong Way 4 $**
Option Premium	6 220 000	6 220 000	6 220 000	6 220 000
Variation Margin (sold options only)	0	0	0	0
Interest Accrued on Collateral	1 518 634	1 555 837	0	2 052 258
Cash Collateral	35 266 060	36 130 000	0	47 658 000
Equities	41 486 060	42 350 000	6 220 000	53 878 000
Interest Accrued on Cash	2 519 739	2 482 536	4 038 373	1 986 115
Cash	58 513 940	57 650 000	93 780 000	46 122 000
Total	100 000 000	100 000 000	100 000 000	100 000 000

Attribution Analysis using Method 1	**Profit/Loss $**	**Sum Employed $**	**Return on Transaction %**	**Contribution to Portfolio Return %**
Profit/Loss on Futures	–170 000			
Interest on Collateral	1 518 634			
Return on Equities	1 348 634	41 486 060	3.2508	1.3486
Return on Cash	2 519 739	58 513 940	4.5000	2.5197
Total Return	3 868 373	100 000 000	3.8684	3.8684

Summary	**1 %**	**2 %**	**3 %**	**4 %**
Return on Equities	1.3486	1.3858	–0.1700	1.8823
Return on Cash	2.5197	2.4825	4.0384	1.9861
Total Return	3.8684	3.8684	3.8684	3.8684

The results of applying the same analysis using all four methods are given in the last three rows of Example A5.6 .

APPENDIX 6

Convertible and Converting Notes

Also known as **hybrids**, convertible and converting notes are usually issued by listed companies, and comprise a bond and one or more options. The simplest kind of convertible note is a bond with the right to convert the bond, at specified dates, to common equity in the issuing company.

They are called hybrids because they do not fit neatly into the categories of either bonds or equity. Companies issue them when the equity market is trading at a low price to earnings ratio. In such conditions, issuing common equity can be expensive, and the market may be demanding too high a yield on the company's bonds to make a simple bond issue attractive. Convertible notes can seem to do the trick of bridging these discrepancies .

THEORY

In theory, a convertible note is a bond with some option agreement added on. The simplest is a European call option exercisable at or near the maturity date of the bond at an exercise price similar to the redemption value of the bond. If, at the maturity of the bond or the expiry of the option, the price of the company's common equity is greater than the face value of the bond, then the investor will exercise the option and either hold the equity in the portfolio, or sell it at market to realize the profit. If the equity is trading below the face value of the bond, then the investor will simply redeem the bond for cash.

Many convertible notes have more complicating modifications. The most common is substitution of a forward agreement for the option. In such cases, the investor is obliged to take equity at the maturity of the bond, whether or not this is an attractive proposition. These securities are more accurately called converting bonds.

PRICING

As the pricing of any hybrid depends on the precise terms of the security, only simple convertible notes and converting bonds will be dealt with in detail here. For more complex securities, estimating the fair price depends on correctly identifying all the components of the instrument. Sometimes this is more easily said than done, and careful scrutiny of the issue documentation is required. It is not uncommon to find, or worse, to overlook, some embedded short put provision secreted away on page 119. The good news here is that sometimes these securities with obscure provisions that are not clearly documented can trade above or below their fair price and so represent opportunities for risk-free profits for the investor patient enough to conduct the required research and scrutiny. If there is an embedded short put position, then the laws of put–call parity mean that the right to convert the debt instrument to equity becomes an obligation, with quite different implications for asset allocation and risk management.

CONVERTIBLE NOTES

A convertible note is a bond plus an option. The bond component is priced using the standard bond price formula:

$$P = c \times (1 + a) + 100 \times v^n \qquad \text{(A6.1)}$$

Where:

$v = 1/(1 + \text{interest rate})$
$a = (1 - v^n)/\text{interest rate}$
n = years to maturity times the number of coupons per year
c = annual coupon income divided by the number of coupons per year

The option component is priced using the formula for a call option on physical shares with one or two modifications:

$$\text{Call} = s \times N(d1) - pe \times N(d2)/e^{iy} \qquad \text{(A6.2.1)}$$

Where:

s = the current price of the asset
pe = the exercise price of the option
i = the risk-free interest rate
vol = the volatility of the underlying asset
y = the time to expiry in years
e^{iy} = the interest rate continuously compounded

N(d1) and N(d2) are terms describing the probability of the share price being sufficiently volatile that the option expires in-the-money. They are calculated as:

$$N(d1) = [\ln(s/pe) + (i + vol^2/2) \times y)/vol \times y^{0.5} \qquad \text{(A6.2.2)}$$
$$N(d2) = N(d1) - vol \times y^{0.5} \qquad \text{(A6.2.3)}$$

The modifications stem from the fact that it is the company issuing the options. This is important because it means that when and if the options are exercised, some of the company's debt will be replaced with equity, thus diluting the interests of the existing equity holders and altering the debt to equity ratio, and therefore the value of the company itself and its shares.

In Example A6.1.1, the bond is valued as a normal bond with maturity and coupon patterns the same as for the note itself. The yield input to the bond valuation is the current risk-free interest rate for a similar maturity plus the margin over the risk-free rate at which the firm's bonds would normally trade.

The most straightforward way of pricing the option is to use the Black–Scholes formula with some adjustments. The first adjustment to be made is to discount the current share price for dividends to which holders of common stock, but not convertible note holders, are entitled. To do this, the present value of the dividend stream is calculated and deducted from the current share price, as follows:

Adjusted share price = current share price – present value of dividends
= \$35.00 – \$7.02
= \$27.98

This is then adjusted for the **dilution factor**. The dilution factor reflects the amount of new equity issued when the options are exercised. It is estimated as follows:

$$\text{Dilution factor} = \frac{\text{face value of the convertible notes at maturity}}{\text{face value of the convertible notes + current value of equity}} \quad \text{(A6.3)}$$

$$= 50\,000 \times \$1000/(50\,000 \times \$1000 + 500\,000\,000 \times \$35)$$
$$= 0.2849\%$$

The share price applied to the option pricing formula is the share price adjusted for dividends divided by one plus the dilution factor:

$$\text{Share price} = \text{adjusted share price}/(1 + \text{dilution factor})$$
$$= \$27.98/(1 + 0.2849\%)$$
$$= \$27.90$$

EXAMPLE A6.1.1 *A simple convertible note*

Date Now	1 January 2000
Interest Rate	5.00%
Convertible Bond Details	
Face Value of Each Note	$1 000.00
Conversion Rate: 1 Bond =	20 Shares
Maturity Date of Bond	31 December 2009
Annual Coupon Rate of Bond	8.50%
Coupons per Year	2
Next Coupon Date	1 March 2000
Number of Notes on Issue	50 000
Conversion Periods	One month prior to each coupon date plus one month prior to bond maturity
Equity Details	
Current Share Price	$55.00
Annual Dividend Yield	2.50%
Dividends per Year	2
Next Dividend Date	1 February 2000
Bond Rating: LIBOR plus:	3.75%
Share Price Volatility	28%
Number of Shares on Issue	500 000 000

EXAMPLE A6.1.2 *A simple convertible note*

Value of Bond	\$1 011.68
Present Value of Equity Dividends	\$11.04
Dilution Factor	0.1818%
Value of Call Option	\$20.30
Value of Convertible Note	\$1 031.98

The exercise price of the option is the value of each note converted into equity at the maturity of the note. This is the face value of each note (\$1000) divided by the number of shares to which it is convertible (20), giving an exercise price of \$50.00.

Unless otherwise specified in the documentation accompanying the notes' issue, the expiry date of the option is the maturity date of the note. Early conversion is usually possible at prespecified dates, but converting before maturity effectively forfeits the remaining time value of the option.

To give a price for the convertible note that is comparable with its face value, the option value is adjusted to reflect the number of shares received on exercise.

The convertible note price calculation is summarized as Example A6.1.2.

CONVERTING NOTES

A converting note is a bond plus a forward contract. Sometimes the forward contract is explicit, but more often it comes in the form of a sold put option combined with a bought call. (See the section on put–call parity in Appendix 5.) To complicate things further, the put option sometimes has an effective exercise price and/or date different from the call. This can make pricing and risk analysis very labour intensive and prone to error.

Example A6.2 is an example of a simple converting bond. The bond details are identical to those in the previous example but conversion in this case is mandatory, whereas in Example A6.1.1 it was optional. As the implied short put option is very much in-the-money, it is quite valuable, so its inclusion significantly changes the value of the instrument.

EXAMPLE A6.2 *A simple converting note*

Value of Bond	$1 011.68
Present Value of Equity Dividends	$11.04
Dilution Factor	0.1818%
Value of Forward	$25.92
Value of Converting Note	$1037.80

In this case the value of the equity forward is calculated as:

the current share price adjusted for the dilution factor
less the present value of the conversion price
less the present value of common stock dividends.

The value of the converting bond is the sum of the value of the bond and the value of all forwards, taking into account the number of shares for which the bonds are redeemed.

As with convertible notes, converting notes can be converted before the maturity of the bond. The note documentation usually specifies dates on which conversion can occur. These dates are called conversion periods.

APPLICATIONS

Convertible and converting instruments are usually issued by firms wishing to issue debt without borrowing from banks. By incorporating an equity component in the bond, they hope to reduce their cost of borrowing by offering a slightly lower coupon than would otherwise be necessary. The only problem with this approach is that markets frequently undervalue the equity component, so while the firm is reducing its apparent cost of borrowing, it is doing so at the cost of giving away equity cheaply. Investors buy hybrid instruments for a number of reasons:

- They find the yield on the instrument attractive, and are not averse to converting it to equity in due course.
- They find the yield on the instrument attractive, and will sell the security when the yield drops sufficiently.

- They see the instrument as a way of buying the equity cheaply.
- They intend to strip the bond from the equity component, selling both separately for a short-term gain.

Typically, the last group transact during or near a conversion period. This activity can be very lucrative if the required trades can be effected at low cost. One error frequently committed is to buy the convertible note and sell short an exchange-traded option with a similar exercise price. In effect this amounts to selling on market a short dated option against a long dated call option embedded in the hybrid. This strategy runs the risk that the short option is exercised, forcing the investor to either convert the hybrid to meet the option obligation, or purchase the common stock in the market. Either way, the investor forfeits some time value of the option embedded in the note. The cost of doing the latter can eat into the profits expected from the hybrid strategy. Selling longer dated options can reduce this risk and allow the investor to benefit from a greater amount of time decay.

IMPLEMENTATION

Hybrids are traded on most stock markets alongside common equity issues, and so follow the same trading rules that apply to equities.

The limitation with nearly all hybrid instruments is liquidity. Trading activity in hybrids is often patchy, except when an interest payment or conversion period is imminent. Along with patchy trading activity, hybrids frequently suffer from wide bid–ask spreads. This can pose a number of problems, mainly for valuation.

ONGOING MANAGEMENT

For the investment fund holding hybrids as a long-term investment, ongoing management is not much different from holding shares. The most important issue is valuation of the instruments, and assessing their contribution to the riskiness of the portfolio.

Long-term holders of hybrids usually have the choice once or twice each year of converting their fixed interest investment to equity. Few do so, except at the final conversion date because early conversion is the same as early exercise of an option: it forfeits the remaining time value of the option and so fails to derive the full economic benefit of the instrument.

ADMINISTRATION

Along with over-the-counter derivatives such as forwards, swaps and over-the-counter option agreements, valuation is a significant administrative hurdle because the lack of liquidity in these instruments often means that the price quoted by the exchange is quite different from either its economic value or the price at which it actually could be sold.

Once the valuation is solved, or at least recognized, the administration of hybrid instruments follows very much the same procedures as common equity holdings; except that, if and when the bond is converted into equity, there will be a change in asset allocation for the fund, which will occur without an apparent decision prompting it. The holding will disappear from the equity part of the portfolio report and miraculously reappear as a bond. It will not appear in the related transaction report, save perhaps as a miscellaneous entry.

PERFORMANCE MEASUREMENT AND ATTRIBUTION

Hybrids pose some interesting questions for performance measurement and attribution analysis because they straddle the divide between fixed interest and equities. The most common approach is to treat them as pure equity. After all, they are traded on equity exchanges. This approach is sensible enough for converting instruments (bond plus forward). But the economic value represented by convertible (bond plus option) is primarily a bond, especially if the option is out-of-the-money.

Identifying and separating the value of the bond and the equity component of hybrids is important not just for attribution analysis. It also makes asset allocation easier by quantifying the changing value of both with changes in equity prices, credit ratings and interest rates. Thus, if the price of the underlying equity goes into serious decline, the equity component will converge to zero, while the bond component will decline to reflect the company's altered credit rating. When the final conversion period arrives, the instrument will already be recognized as virtually all bond, so no noticeable adjustment needs to take place. Alternately, if the instrument has always been treated as an equity, and conversion does not take place, then a sudden shift will occur for no reason that is apparent to the asset allocation committee or the fund's trustees.

One solution to the asset allocation problem is to put hybrids in an asset class of their own. This idea has the appeal of simplicity, but clouds over some fairly important considerations. Treating them as a separate asset class implies that they are essentially different from other asset classes. The problem is that they are not: they are combinations of bonds and equities, and form part of both these asset classes. Measuring their real impact on portfolio performance and risk means assessing the contribution to portfolio bond and equity performance of each component of the instrument. This includes treating coupons received as interest received, and when the fixed interest is converted to equity, dividends are equity dividends.

In practice, this can be tiresome. Because the separate components of the instrument do not have traded prices, they must be valued as if they were over-the-counter instruments. To carry out a thorough revaluation and performance appraisal, therefore, means finding an objective measure of the volatility of the underlying equity and applying it to the option components of the instrument.

In method 1, the exposure to equities resulting from a holding in convertible notes is calculated as:

> The number of convertible notes held times the conversion rate times the current share price times the current option delta:
>
> $8000 \times 20 \times \$35 \times 0.63 = \$1388\,900$

The exposure to bonds is

> The number of convertible notes held times the current bond value:
>
> $8000 \times \$1011.68 = \$8\,093\,440.00$

Method 3 makes the mistake of only allocating the amount of the premium to equities. Method 2 goes to the other extreme, neglecting the adjustment for the delta, and so treating the option as if it were a futures position. These methods are shown in Example A6.3.

EXAMPLE A6.3 *Valuation and attribution analysis for a simple convertible note*

Date Now	1 January 2000
Interest Rate	5.00%
Portfolio Value	$100 000 000
Convertible Bond Details	
Number of Notes Held	8,000
Conversion Rate	20
Current Price	$1 168.48
Purchase Price	$1 084.22
Purchase Date	1 July 1999

continued on next page

Bond Details	
Current Price	$1 011.68
Purchase Price	$968.82
Option Details	
Current Share Price	$35.00
Purchase Share Price	$28.00
Current Price	$7.84
Purchase Price	$5.77
Current Option Delta	0.61

The Valuation Statement	**The Right Way 1 $**	**The Wrong Way 2 $**	**The Wrong Way 3 $**
Option Premium	1 254 400	1 254 400	1 254 400
Interest Accrued on Collateral	54,484	109 533	0
Cash Collateral	2 161 600	4 345 600	0
Equities	3 470 484	5 709 533	1 254 400
Bonds	9 347 840	9 347 840	9 347 840
Cash	87 181 676	84 942 627	89 397 760
Total	100 000 000	100 000 000	100 000 000

Attribution Analysis for Method 1	**Profit/Loss $**	**Sum Employed $**	**Return on Transaction %**	**Contribution to Portfolio Return %**
Profit/Loss on Options	331 200			
Interest Accrued on Collateral	54 484			
Return on Equities	385 684	3 470 484	11.1133	0.3857
Return on Bonds	342 880	9 347 840	3.6680	0.3429
Return on Convertible Notes	728 564	12 818 324	5.6838	0.7286
Return on Cash	2 143 430	87 181 676	2.4586	2.1434
Total Return	2 871 994	100 000 000	2.8720	2.8720

Summary	**1 %**	**2 %**	**3 %**
Return on Equities	0.3857	0.4407	0.3312
Return on Bonds	0.3429	0.3429	0.3429
Return on Convertible Notes	0.7286	0.7836	0.6741
Return on Cash	2.1434	2.0884	2.1979
Total Return	2.8720	2.8720	2.8720

Glossary of Terms

16.00 GMT (Greenwich Mean Time)	Widely used time of day to revalue foreign currencies.
Accrual	An accounting entry to recognize an impending transaction settlement.
Accumulation Index	A share price index contract that incorporates reinvested dividends. *See also* Price Index, Total Return Index.
Active Weight	The portfolio weight less the benchmark weight for a security.
ADR	American Depository Receipt – an instrument listed on a US exchange, backed by shares listed on a non-US exchange. *See also* SDR.
Agency Trading	The practice of purchase and sale of securities on behalf of another party.
Aggressive Portfolio	A portfolio that differs greatly from its benchmark. *See also* Conservative Portfolio.
AIMR	Association for Investment Management and Research.
Alpha	The component of the return to an asset or portfolio that is due to mispricing of the asset. True alpha represents riskless returns.

Alternative Investments Assets or asset classes with unusual return characteristics or investment structures.

American Option An option that can be exercised before the exercise date. *See also* European Option.

Arbitrage The simultaneous purchase and sale of two economically identical instruments or assets to yield a risk-free profit.

Arbitrage Pricing Theory (APT) Stock valuation theory equating the value of an asset with the sum of the market valuations of its subsidiaries.

Arithmetic Link Adding returns for consecutive investment periods. *See also* Geometric Link.

Asset Swap Transaction whereby two investors exchange the change in value of nominated asset held by each.

At-the-money Asset price equals exercise price. An option with zero intrinsic value.

Attribution Analysis The analysis of investment returns over single or consecutive investment periods to determine where and by how much investment returns varied from benchmark returns.

Balanced Portfolios A portfolio that invests in several asset classes simultaneously. Balanced portfolios combine asset allocation and security selection within asset classes.

Basis Risk The risk that a derivative position will not exactly offset the physical asset that it is intended to hedge.

Basket (or Block) Trades The aggregation of a number of individual purchases or sales to a single transaction.

Benchmark A reference portfolio for the purpose of comparing actual portfolios.

Benchmark-hugging An active portfolio with insufficient active risk to meet return objectives.

Beta The correlation of an asset or a portfolio to another asset or benchmark portfolio. A beta of one indicates a direct relationship.

Bid–ask Spread The concurrent difference in the buy and sell price of a security or contract.

Black Box A quantitative asset allocation or stock selection model which does not permit the user to check intermediate calculations or carry out reasonableness checks.

Black–Scholes Fisher Black and Myron Scholes are the authors of the widely used eponymous technique of pricing options on assets and portfolios.

Block Trades *See* Basket Trades.

Bond Volatility The change in settlement value of a bond that corresponds to a change in interest rate of 0.01%. *See also* Dollar Value of One Point, Volatility of Bonds.

Bonus Issue The practice of replacing existing shares with a larger number of new ones. *See also* Stock Split.

Bottom-up Management Stock picking based on detailed knowledge of individual companies, regardless of sector exposures.

Boutique Managers Investment management companies specializing in a particular asset class or investment strategy.

Call Option The right, but not the obligation, to buy an asset or futures contract at an agreed price at an agreed time. *See also* Put Option.

CALPERS California Public Employees Retirement Service.

Capital Guarantee An assurance by an investment manager that the return to the portfolio will not be below zero in nominal terms in a given period.

Capitalization-weighted Index Index of share or other asset prices the composition of which is determined by the market value of component assets. *See also* Price-weighted Index

Cash Short-term low yield liquid instruments, usually guaranteed by a major bank. *See also* Liquid Assets, Risk-free Asset.

Cash Settled Contract A derivative contract which ends with a cash payment of the difference between the traded price and the final price of the contract.

Charting The practice of scrutinizing charts of historical prices to identify visible, repeating patterns in price movements. *See also* Technical Analysis.

CIO Chief Investment Officer.

Clearer A bank or other financial institution, or a consortium, that stands between parties trading assets or other instruments on an exchange. By taking part in exchange transactions, the clearer ensures performance of transactions taking place on the exchange. Also known as a Clearing House.

Clearing House A company that guarantees performance of transactions by participating in each. *See also* Clearer.

Close Trade The transaction to sell (buy) a bought (sold) derivative contract.

Closed Funds Closed Pooled Funds are subscribed at the outset with no new units issued subsequently. Investors wishing to exit the fund must seek a buyer for their units. Closed Funds are often traded on stock exchanges, and may or may not have a preset termination date. *See also* Open Funds.

Closet Index The sum of the various portfolios within a fund add up effectively to form an index fund because the risks in each component portfolio are offset by other portfolios in the fund.

Collateral An asset held or pledged to support performance of a transaction.

Comingled A portfolio with multiple owners. Each investor purchases a share of the portfolio. Each share or unit participates in capital gains and losses and income to the portfolio. *See also* Unitized, Pooled.

Compound Interest Interest calculated for each period on interest accrued in previous periods. *See also* Compounding, Continuously Compounded Interest, Simple Interest.

Compounding The arithmetic procedure of calculating interest payable on interest. *See also* Compound Interest, Continuously Compounded Interest, Simple Interest.

Conservative Portfolio A portfolio that resembles the benchmark. A low-risk portfolio. *See also* Aggressive Portfolio.

Constraints Limitations on the allowable allocations characteristics or transactions in a portfolio.

Consultant Person or company providing independent advice to investors on investment type, structure and management.

Continuously Compounded Interest Interest calculated continuously on interest accrued in previous periods. *See also* Compounding, Compound Interest, Simple Interest.

Contribution Holiday A period during which members pay lower contributions than normal, or even none at all.

Convertible Hedge An investment strategy combining convertible instruments and derivatives or other instruments, designed to eliminate unwanted risk.

Convertible Notes Instruments combining a bond and a call option on an equity. *See also* Converting Bonds, Hybrids.

Converting Bonds Instruments combining a bond, a call option and a put option on an equity. Sometimes combines a bond and a forward agreement. *See also* Convertible Notes, Hybrids.

Convexity The change in duration of a bond or portfolio of bonds for a given change in interest rate.

Core Portfolio A low-risk portfolio complemented within a fund by high-risk satellite portfolios.

Core–satellite Portfolio structure comprising low-risk core portfolios and high-risk, specialist satellite portfolios. *See also* Indexation.

Corporate Action An activity by a listed company that changes its capital base or structure in some way.

Corporate Governance Exercising shareholder rights, such as casting votes at general meetings and voicing opinions on management policies of companies in which the fund has a significant holding.

Correlation The degree to which the returns to assets or portfolios resemble each other. Correlations range from –1 (perfectly offsetting returns) through zero (no relationship at all) to + 1 (perfectly similar returns). *See also* Covariance.

Cost of Carry Ancillary costs associated with holding an investment, including interest cost, insurance, income foregone.

Counter-cyclical Stocks Stocks that outperform other stocks in a period of economic slowdown or recession. Usually includes basic foods, tobacco and discount retailers.

Counterparty Risk The risk that a person or entity participating in a transaction will be unable to perform his, her or its obligations under the terms of the transaction.

Coupon Regular payments to holders of bonds.

Covariance The degree to which the returns to assets or portfolios resemble each other. Covariances can be negative (offsetting returns), zero (no relationship at all) or positive (similar returns). *See also* Correlation.

CPPI Constant Proportions Portfolio Insurance. An alternative technique to Black–Scholes for constructing portfolio protection programs.

Credit Risk The risk that a borrower will be unable to honour all the terms of a loan.

Credit Spread The difference in return between interest rate securities with different risks of default.

Cum-dividend After the dividend has been declared but before the date of entitlement. *See also* Ex-dividend.

Cum-interest A bond that is about to make an interest or coupon payment. *See also* Ex-interest.

Currency Hedge Derivative contracts designed to modify or cancel the risk of holding physical assets in a foreign currency.

Currency Neutral An asset or portfolio where the foreign currency held exactly equals the value of the asset or portfolio.

Data-mining The practice of using the same series of historical data both to test and to validate investment models.

Deadweight The benchmark weight equivalent of a portfolio holding.

Deal Arbitrage An investment strategy designed to exploit price changes associated with corporate activity.

Debentures Bonds issued by companies.

Debt to Equity The ratio of total debt to the market value of total equity. It can be expressed as D/E.

Defined Benefit Funds Contributors pay in an amount determined by the administrator, and receive a preset amount or annuity, usually a multiple of final salary at a given date, usually retirement.

Defined Contribution Funds Contributors pay into the fund, and receive the sum of what they have paid in plus investment returns, less administration and other costs.

Delivery Contract A derivative contract which ends with delivery of physical assets from the seller to the buyer.

Delta The change in the value of an option relative to the change in the market value of the underlying asset or portfolio.

Delta Hedging Ongoing management of replicating options. Continuous readjustment of portfolio weightings according to estimated delta of replicated option. *See also* Dynamic Hedging, Replicating Options.

Dilution Factor The amount by which the share price is affected by a new share issue.

Directed Brokerage A fund manager or sponsor stipulates to an investment manager that a given proportion of

	the portfolio trades must be assigned to brokers nominated by the fund manager. *See also* Directed Commissions.
Directed Commissions	A fund manager or sponsor stipulates to an investment manager that a given proportion of the portfolio trades must be assigned to brokers nominated by the fund manager. *See also* Directed Brokerage.
Discount Brokers	Brokers offering execution-only services.
Discount Security	A debt instrument paying no coupons, where interest is subtracted (discounted) from the purchase price and the face value is paid at maturity.
Discounted Cash Flow	A procedure designed to adjust the value of future cash flows to reflect their timing. *See also* Dividend Discounting and Net Present Value.
Discounting	The arithmetic procedure for imputing interest payable in the price of a fixed interest security.
Dividend	Sum paid by a company to its shareholders as part of the return on investment.
Dividend Discounting	A procedure designed to adjust the value of future cash flows to reflect their timing. *See also* Discounted Cash Flow and Net Present Value.
Dividend Yield	The ratio of dividends paid annually to the market price of the share.
Dollar Value of One Point (DV01)	The change in settlement value of a bond that corresponds to a change in interest rate of 0.01%. *See also* Volatility of Bonds.
Duration	A measure of the maturity and timing of cash flows of a fixed interest instrument. *See also* Macauley Duration, Modified Duration.
Dynamic Hedge	The technique of constantly adjusting the hedge ratio of an asset or portfolio. Most often used in replicating option positions and portfolio protection programs.
Dynamic Hedging	Ongoing management of replicating options. Continuous readjustment of portfolio weightings

according to estimated delta of replicated option. *See also* Delta Hedging, Replicating Options.

Earnings Yield — The ratio of annual earnings per share to the market price of the share.

EBIT — Earnings Before Interest and Taxes.

Efficient Frontier — The line described by all assets or portfolios that have the best possible mix of expected returns and risk.

Efficient Portfolio — A portfolio with the lowest possible risk for a given expected return, or the highest possible expected return for a given level of risk.

Employee Stock Options — Options granted to employees of the company, usually to help align the interests of the employees with those of the company's shareholders.

Equilibrium — The point at which supply and demand are matched. *See also* Fair Price.

Equitize — Convert exposure of a non-equity asset to an equity exposure, usually using share price index futures contracts.

Equity Dilution — Change in share value resulting from new issue of shares.

Equity Risk Premium — The difference in return between equities and long-term bonds that reflects the difference in risk.

European Option — An option that cannot be exercised before the exercise date. *See also* American Option.

Event Driven — An investment strategy designed to exploit changes in strategy and structure of selected companies, or the markets in which they are traded.

Ex-ante — Predicted or forecast.

Ex-dividend — After the entitlement date of the dividend, but before the dividend is paid. *See also* Cum-dividend.

Ex-interest — A bond that has just made an interest or coupon payment. *See also* Cum-interest.

Ex Post	Observed.
Exchange-traded	Transactions taking place within recognized stock or futures exchanges. *See also* Over-the-Counter.
Exchange-traded Fund	A portfolio of investments listed on a stock exchange.
Exercise Date	The date on which an option is exercisable, and after which it lapses.
Exercise Price	The amount payable (receivable) by a call (put) option holder to purchase (sell) the underlying asset on the exercise date.
Exponential Weighting	Incremental weighting historical returns where increments increase exponentially. *See also* Linear Weighting.
Face Value	The value at which a security is issued. *See also* Par Value.
Factor Models	Programs to assist in portfolio construction and risk analysis of equity portfolios using predefined factors to create covariance matrices.
Factors	Influences on the price of an asset or portfolio.
Fair Price	The price at which the expected return to an asset exactly reflects its expected riskiness. *See also* Equilibrium.
Fitted Curve	A diagram applying a smoothed line to show the change in interest rate corresponding to changes in maturity.
Fixed Interest	Instruments that earn a fixed interest rate until they mature.
Floor	The exercise price as applied in Constant Proportions Portfolio Insurance.
Forward Contract	An agreement to buy or sell a fixed asset or security at a fixed date in the future.
Forward Foreign Exchange	A foreign exchange transaction with a settlement date more than two days after the date on which the transaction was struck.

Frictional Liquidity	Cash held in a portfolio as a result of income received, awaiting investment or required to meet small redemptions and other requirements for cash, such as rights issues.
Front Office/Front End	The transactions and implementation function of an investment management company.
FTA	Financial Times Actuaries – a provider of international equity indices.
Fund of Funds	An investment fund that buys units in other investment funds. *See also* Manager of Managers.
Fund Manager	A person or company charged with overseeing the investments of a pension fund, mutual fund or other jointly owned investment.
Gamma	A measure of the change in an option delta relative to a change in the value of the underlying asset or portfolio.
Gapping	A significant discrete change in the market value of an asset or portfolio.
Gearing	The sum of the face value of all assets and derivatives contracts exceeds the value of the physical assets in the fund. Alternately, where the company or fund has borrowed. *See also* Leverage.
Gearing Ratio	The ratio of total debt to the market value of the company (measured as total debt plus market value of total equity). It can be expressed as D/(D+E).
General Level of Interest Rates	The average risk-free interest rate over all maturities. *See also* Yield Curve.
Geometric Link	Compounding the returns for consecutive investment periods. *See also* Arithmetic Link.
GIGO	Garbage in, garbage out.
GIPS	Global Investment Performance Standards.
Growth Stocks	Stocks with a high price to book ratio.
Herstatt Risk	The risk, associated with time zone disparities, that a bank will fail after having settled one side of a foreign exchange transaction but before settling the other.

Hybrids — Instruments combining a bond and a call option, a bond, a call and a put option, or a bond and a forward agreement on an equity. *See also* Convertible Notes, Converting Bonds.

Implied Volatility — The standard deviation of the movement of the price of an asset that is indicated by the price of an option on that asset.

Information Ratio — Return variation from benchmark divided by tracking error. *See also* Sharpe Ratio.

In Specie — Transferring assets from one investment manager to another without effecting any change of ownership.

Initial Margin — A sum paid on opening a derivative position to provide collateral for adverse price movements in the contract.

Interest Cover — The ratio of total earnings (usually EBIT) to interest payable over the same period.

Interest Rate Parity — Theory of exchange rate equilibrium that says that exchange rates are determined by the difference between interest rates in the two currency zones.

In-the-money — An option with positive intrinsic value.

Intentional Risk — Active risk, for which return is forecast.

Intrinsic Value — Asset price less exercise price for a call option. Exercise price less asset price for a put option. Total option price less time value.

Investment Manager — The company engaged by the fund manager to conduct day-to-day management of the investments.

Investment Universe — The set of assets from which portfolios and benchmarks are selected.

Investor — The owner of the money invested.

ISDA — International Swap and Derivatives Association.

Jump Risk — The risk of significant, discrete changes in the market value of an asset or portfolio.

Lambda | A measure of the relationship of portfolio risk and expected return.

Leverage | The value of a company's total debt divided by the value of its total equity. *See also* Gearing.

LIBOR | London Inter-Bank Overnight Rate. A frequently used reference interest rate.

Linear Weighting | Incremental weighting historical returns where increments are equal. *See also* Exponential Weighting.

Liquid Assets | Short-term low yield instruments, usually guaranteed by a major bank. *See also* Risk-free Asset, Cash.

Liquidity | A description of the volume of transactions in an asset or market. Very liquid indicates many or frequent transactions, illiquid indicates few transactions.

Long | Net bought. *See also* Short.

Long-term Benchmark | Asset mix designed to deliver required return over the life of a fund. Used as a comparison for short-term and tactical asset mixes. *See also* Strategic Benchmark.

Macaulay Duration | A measure of the maturity and timing of cash flows of a fixed interest instrument. *See also* Duration, Modified Duration.

Manager of Managers | An investment management company that specializes in investment strategies that engage other investment managers. *See also* Fund of Funds.

Manager Risk | The risk to an investor that an investment manager fails to meet expected performance criteria.

Margin Trading | The practice of borrowing money to invest, whereby the investments form the collateral for the loan.

Market Efficiency | Asset prices that reflect all information available about the asset.

Market Impact	The change in share price due to reaction to a transaction.
Market Makers	Individuals or companies designated by stock and derivatives exchanges to provide liquidity in nominated instruments by quoting buy and sell prices.
Market Neutral	An investment strategy where overweight and underweight holdings exactly cancel out, leaving the overall portfolio with zero risk relative to a specified market index.
Market Timing	The practice of timing purchases and sales to exploit very short-term fluctuations in asset prices.
Mean	Average.
Mean Reversion	The tendency of values in series of data to move towards their long-term average.
Mean-variance Efficiency	The optimal combination of expected return and risk. Lying on the efficient frontier.
Mean-variance Optimization	The technique of using expected returns and covariances to choose portfolio weightings giving the highest portfolio return for a given level of risk; or the lowest risk for a given portfolio expected return. *See also* Optimization.
Modified Duration	A measure of the maturity and timing of cash flows of a fixed interest instrument. *See also* Macaulay Duration, Duration.
Money-weighted Cash Flow	Treatment of mid-period cash flows whereby the period is divided into sub-periods and the returns compounded.
Moody's	A company that publishes ratings of debt quality. *See also* Standard & Poor's.
Moving Average	The average share price over a rolling period of a given length, such as the most recent 3, 30 or 90 days.
MSCI	Morgan Stanley Capital International – a provider of international equity indices.

Net Margins — The practice of calculating margins for derivatives positions on the basis of overall holdings instead of on individual holdings.

Net Present Value — A procedure designed to adjust the value of future cash flows to reflect their timing. *See also* Dividend Discounting and Discounted Cash Flow.

Nominal Returns — The increase or decrease in the face value of an asset or portfolio over of an investment period divided by the face value of the asset or portfolio at the start of the investment period. *See also* Real Returns.

Off-the-shelf — Products developed commercially. Usually refers to software products.

Open Funds — Open Pooled Funds allow new funds to be invested, and withdrawals at any time. Open Funds do not generally have a termination date. *See also* Closed Funds.

Open Outcry — System for transacting securities and derivatives on an exchange whereby traders deal face to face with each other.

Open Trade — The starting or initial transaction to buy or sell a derivative contract.

Opportunity Cost — The return foregone.

Optimal Portfolio — The portfolio weightings giving the highest portfolio return for a given level of risk; or the lowest risk for a given portfolio expected return.

Optimization — The technique of using expected returns and covariances to choose portfolio weightings giving the highest portfolio return for a given level of risk; or the lowest risk for a given portfolio expected return. *See also* Mean-variance Optimization.

Option Delta — The ratio of the movement in the price of an option to a corresponding move in the price of the underlying asset or contract. *See also* Option Volatility, Option Gamma.

Option Gamma The ratio of the movement in the delta of an option to a corresponding move in the price of the option. *See also* Option Volatility, Option Delta.

Option Time Decay The attrition of the time value of an option as the expiry date approaches. Sometimes referred to as 'theta'.

Option Volatility The movement in the price of the option corresponding to a movement in the price of the underlying asset or contract. *See also* Option Delta, Option Gamma.

Order-driven An exchange trading system that relies on prices from intending buys and sellers of securities. *See also* Quote-driven.

Orthogonal Correlations equal to zero. Changes in asset prices that are unconnected with each other. *See also* Statistical Independence.

Out-of-sample Historical data covering a different period.

Out-of-the-money An option with zero intrinsic value.

Over-the-counter Transactions taking place outside recognized stock or futures exchanges. *See also* Exchange-traded.

Par Value The value at which a security is issued. *See also* Face Value.

Participation Rate The ratio, in the context of portfolio protection, of option face value to risky assets in the underlying portfolio.

Passive Investment An investment strategy which uses no judgement at all, but relies solely on predefined decision rules for all ongoing investment decisions.

Path Dependency The relationship, for an asset or portfolio, between future returns and past returns.

Payout Ratio The ratio of the dividend paid per share and the earnings per share for the same period.

Performance Analysis The analysis of compound periods of attribution analysis to identify patterns of strengths and weaknesses in an investment strategy.

Point Value The local currency value of a one point move in the price of a futures contract.

Pooled A portfolio with multiple owners. Each investor purchases a share of the portfolio. Each share, or unit participates in capital gains and losses and income to the portfolio. *See also* Unitized, Comingled.

Portfolio Manager The person employed by the investment manager to manage specific components or aspects of the investment portfolio.

Portfolio Optimization The technique of using expected returns and covariances to choose portfolio weightings giving the highest portfolio return for a given level of risk; or the lowest risk for a given portfolio expected return. *See also* Mean-variance Optimization.

Premium The price payable for an option.

Price Index A share price index contract that does not incorporate reinvested dividends. *See also* Accumulation Index.

Price Momentum A measure of recent return history of an asset.

Price to Book The ratio of the market price of the share to its book value (usually the price at which it was issued, adjusted for stock splits and other relevant corporate actions).

Price-weighted Index Index of share or other asset prices, the composition of which is the market price of each component asset. *See also* Capitalization-weighted Index.

Principal Components The technique of applying regression analysis to quantify factors relating to historical returns to an asset or portfolio. The factors are identified subsequently by inspection.

Principal Trading The practice of purchase and sale of securities for the benefit of the person or entity carrying out the trade.

Protection Strategies Investments that are designed to limit the extent of adverse outcomes in a given investment period.

Pull to Par Convergence to par or face value of fixed interest security prices as the instrument approaches maturity.

Purchasing Power Parity (PPP) Theory of exchange rates that says that equilibrium exchange rates equate the real price of goods in different currencies after adjusting for transport costs, taxes and regulations.

Pure Alpha An investment strategy with non-zero relative returns but zero market risk.

Put Option The right, but not the obligation, to sell an asset or futures contract at an agreed price at an agreed time. *See also* Call Option.

Quote-driven An exchange trading system that relies on prices quoted by designated market makers. *See also* Order-driven.

Real Returns The return to an asset or portfolio over an investment period, minus inflation. *See also* Nominal Returns.

Real Time Continuously. Usually refers to transmission of market information.

Recovery Rate The percentage of the value of a loan that can be repaid following default by the borrower.

Reference Price An asset or commodity price quoted by an independent, official or semi-official source.

Reinvestment Risk The risk of interest rates changing between bond coupon payments.

Relative Value The market or fair value of a security relative to the market or fair value of another security.

Replicated Options Options created using a combination of liquid securities and the underlying asset or contract. *See also* Delta Hedging.

Reserve A sum of money held as a 'cushion' to allow a fund to meet its liabilities during periods of lower than expected investment returns or higher than expected liquidity demands on the fund.

Residual Risk A measure of the risk of an asset or portfolio that is not 'explained' by factor analysis or market exposure. The square root of Residual Variance.

Residual Variance A measure of the risk of an asset or portfolio that is not 'explained' by factor analysis or market exposure. The square of Residual Risk.

Return to Equity A company's total profits divided by the total value of its equity.

Return Variation Portfolio return minus benchmark return.

Reverse Optimization The technique of computing the expected returns to individual assets implied by a particular portfolio allocation.

Rights Issue Sale of rights by a company, usually in lieu of new share issue.

Risk-adjusted Return Portfolio return minus benchmark return times portfolio beta.

Risk Model A program to simulate the risk and return of a portfolio.

Risk Preference Appetite for risk, or tolerance of losses.

Risk-free Asset Short-term low yield liquid instruments, usually guaranteed by a major bank. *See also* Liquid Assets, Cash.

Risky Assets Assets more risky than short-term low yield liquid instruments. *See also* Risk-free Assets.

Roll A special case of a spread trade, where a derivatives position in a near settlement month is exchanged for an identical position in a more distant month.

Satellite Portfolio A high risk portfolio that complements a low risk, 'core' portfolio.

Scenario Analysis Calculations of portfolio returns resulting from different sets of asset returns. *See also* Stress Test.

Scrip Lending Lending share certificates, or access to the entitlements of share certificates by long-term investors to other investors for short periods in

	return for rent paid on the face value of the shares in question. *See also* Stock Lending.
SDR	Statutory Depository Receipt – an instrument listed on a US exchange, backed by shares listed on a non-US exchange. *See also* ADR.
Settlement Date	The date on which payment is made for the purchase of an asset or security.
Settlement Price	The price actually paid for an asset or security.
Share Buy-backs	The practice of a company buying its own shares in the marketplace.
Sharpe Ratio	Forecast active return divided by forecast tracking error. *See also* Information Ratio.
Short	Net sold. *See also* Long.
Short Selling	Selling securities or derivatives that are not currently owned.
Short Squeeze	The requirement to quickly repurchase, in an appreciating market, securities sold short.
Short-term Asset Allocation	Asset allocation that exploits the investor's insights into near term macroeconomic conditions. *See also* Tactical Asset Allocation.
Simple Interest	Interest payable as for a single period. *See also* Compound Interest, Compounding, Continuously Compounded Interest.
Soft Dollar	A broker 'pays' for a service, such as online security prices or security research, to be delivered to an investment manager in return for a predefined amount of the investment manager's share purchase and sale business in a given period.
Spot Foreign Exchange	A foreign exchange transaction that is settled within two days of it being struck.
Spot Price	The current price for a physical asset or security.
Spread Trade	A transaction comprising the simultaneous buying and selling of very similar instruments, such as futures which vary only in their settlement month.

Standard & Poor's	A company that publishes ratings of debt quality. *See also* Moody's.
Standard Deviation	The distance from average describing 32% probability. One standard deviation either side of the mean captures 68% of all eventualities. Two standard deviations either side captures 95%.
Statistical Independence	Correlations equal to zero. Changes in asset prices that are unconnected with each other. *See also* Orthogonal.
Stock Lending	Lending share certificates, or access to the entitlements of share certificates by long-term investors to other investors for short periods in return for rent paid on the face value of the shares in question. *See also* Scrip Lending.
Stock Split	The practice of replacing existing shares with a larger number of new ones. *See also* Bonus Issue.
Strategic Benchmark	Asset mix designed to deliver required return over the life of a fund. Used as a comparison for short-term and tactical asset mixes. *See also* Long-term Benchmark.
Stress Test	Calculations of portfolio returns resulting from a set of negative asset returns. *See also* Scenario Analysis.
Strike Price	The price at which an option is exercised. *See also* Exercise Price.
Style Managers	Investment managers who manage to a style index, such as growth or value.
Swap Reset	Redesignation of the face value of a swap contract, usually coinciding with periodical settlement of amounts due on the swap.
Synthetic Cash	The economic position resulting from simultaneously buying a physical asset and selling its exact face value in futures, forward contracts or swaps.
Synthetic Options	Options created using a combination of options and the underlying asset or contract.
T Plus Two	Two days after the date on which a transaction is struck.

Tactical Asset Allocation Short-term asset allocation that exploits the investor's insights into near term macroeconomic conditions. *See also* Short-term Asset Allocation.

Takeover Premium The amount by which the price paid for a dominant shareholding exceeds the traded price for normal parcels of the same shares.

Technical Analysis The practice of scrutinizing charts of historical prices to identify visible, repeating patterns in price movements. *See also* Charting.

Thin Market A very illiquid market.

Time Value That part of the option price that is a function of the asset volatility, time to maturity and interest rate. Total option price less intrinsic value.

Time-weighted Cash Flow Treatment of mid-period cash flows whereby the cash flow is allocated according to how far into the period it occurred.

Top-down Management Portfolio construction in the context of overall sector management.

Total Return Index A share price index contract that incorporates reinvested dividends. *See also* Price Index, Accumulation Index.

Tracking Error A measure of the amount by which a portfolio's performance is likely to differ from some known benchmark portfolio. The standard deviation of the sum of differences between portfolio and benchmark returns. Also the square root of the Variance.

Trend Analysis The analysis of the direction of asset price movements to assist forecasting future prices.

Unintentional Risk Risk for which no return is expected.

Unitized A portfolio with multiple owners. Each investor purchases a share of the portfolio. Each share or unit participates in capital gains and losses and income to the portfolio. *See also* Pooled, Comingled.

Unwind To reverse or close a position, especially one comprising multiple transactions.

Value Stocks Stocks with a low Price to Book ratio.

Variance A measure of the amount by which a portfolio's performance is likely to differ from some known benchmark portfolio. The sum of differences between portfolio and benchmark returns over a defined period. Also the square of the Standard Deviation.

Variation Margin A sum paid subsequent to opening a derivative position to cover existing unrealized losses and to provide collateral for adverse price movements in the contract.

Volatility The standard deviation of squared absolute returns. The range within which returns are expected to fall 68% of the time.

Volatility of Bonds The change in settlement value of a bond that corresponds to a change in interest rate of 0.01%. *See also* Dollar Value of One Point, Bond Volatility.

Whipsawing Losses incurred by a delta hedge in a zigzagging market.

Yield Curve The shape of a line describing the relationship between interest rate and time to maturity for fixed interest instruments. *See also* General Level of Interest Rates.

Yield to Maturity The interest rate implied by the settlement price of a bond.

Zero Coupon Curve A theoretical yield curve describing pure interest rates for various maturities, excluding the effects of risk and coupon payments.

Bibliography

Bodie, Z., Kane, A. and Marcus A.J. *Investments* (Burr Ridge: Irwin, 1993).

Braudel, F. *Capitalism and Material Life 1400–1800* (London: Collins, 1981).

Chiang, A.C. *Fundamental Methods of Mathematical Economics* (New York: McGraw-Hill, 1974).

Clarke, R. and Tullis, M. How Much International Exposure is Advantageous in a Domestic Portfolio? *Journal of Portfolio Management*, **25**(2) 1999.

Das, S. *Swap Financing* (Sydney: The Law Book Company, 1989).

Das, S. *Risk Management and Financial Derivatives, A Guide to the Mathematics* (Sydney: The Law Book Company, 1997).

Kritzman, M. *The Portable Financial Analyst* (Chicago, IL: Probus, 1995).

Lakonishok, J., Schleifer, A. and Vishny, R.W. *Study of the US Equity Money Manager Performance*, Brookings Institute Study, 1992.

Mackay, C. *Extraordinary Popular Delusions and the Madness of Crowds* (New York: John Wiley & Sons, 1996).

Manchero, J.G. *A Fully Geometric Approach to Performance Attribution*, Vestek Pre-Publication Article, 2000.

Markowitz, H.M. *Portfolio Selection: Efficient Diversification of Investment*, Cowles Foundation Monograph 16 (New Haven, CT: Yale University Press, 1959).

Rosenberg, B. Extra Market Components of Covariance in Security Returns, *Journal of Financial and Quantitative Analysis*, March 1974, pp. 263–74.

Rudd, A. Optimal Selection of Passive Portfolios, *Financial Management*, Spring 1980, pp. 57–65.

Rudd, A. and Clasing, H.K. Jr *Modern Portfolio Theory*, 2nd edn (Orinda, CA: Andrew Rudd 1988).

Sharpe, W.F. Capital Asset Prices: A Theory of Market Equilibrium Under Conditions of Risk, *Journal of Finance*, **19**(3) 1970, pp. 425–42.

Sharpe, W.F. *Portfolio Theory and Capital Markets* (New York: McGraw-Hill, 1970).

Schneeweis, T. The Myths of Traditional and Alternative Investment. Paper delivered to ICBI Fund Forum (Juan-les-Pins: June 2000).
The Spaulding Group *Performance Presentation Standards Surveys Detail Results* (Somerset, NJ: September 2000).
Taylor, M.P. *Technical Analysis*, Warwick Business School and Centre for Economic Policy Research (Warwick: October 2000).
Van Tuyll, H.-W. Fund of Funds and Hedge Funds: Alternative Investments in Italy. Paper delivered to IIR Conference Fund Management Opportunities in Italy (Milan, March 2000).

Index

D

P

Q

R